written by: *Chuck Dixon*

illustrated by: *Esteve Polls*

colored by: *Marc Rueda*

lettered by: *Simon Bowland*
and *Bill Tortolini*

cover by: *Dennis Calero*

dedicated to: *Sergio Leone*

Dynamite
ENTERTAINMENT®

NICK BARRUCCI • PRESIDENT
JUAN COLLADO • CHIEF OPERATING OFFICER
JOSEPH RYBANDT • EDITOR
JOSH JOHNSON • CREATIVE DIRECTOR
RICH YOUNG • DIR. OF BUSINESS DEVELOPMENT
JASON ULLMEYER • GRAPHIC DESIGNER

WWW.DYNAMITEENTERTAINMENT.COM

For media rights, foreign rights, promotions, licensing, and advertising: marketing@dynamiteentertainment.com

First Printing
ISBN-10: 1-60690-124-9   ISBN-13: 978-1-60690-124-3
10 9 8 7 6 5 4 3 2 1

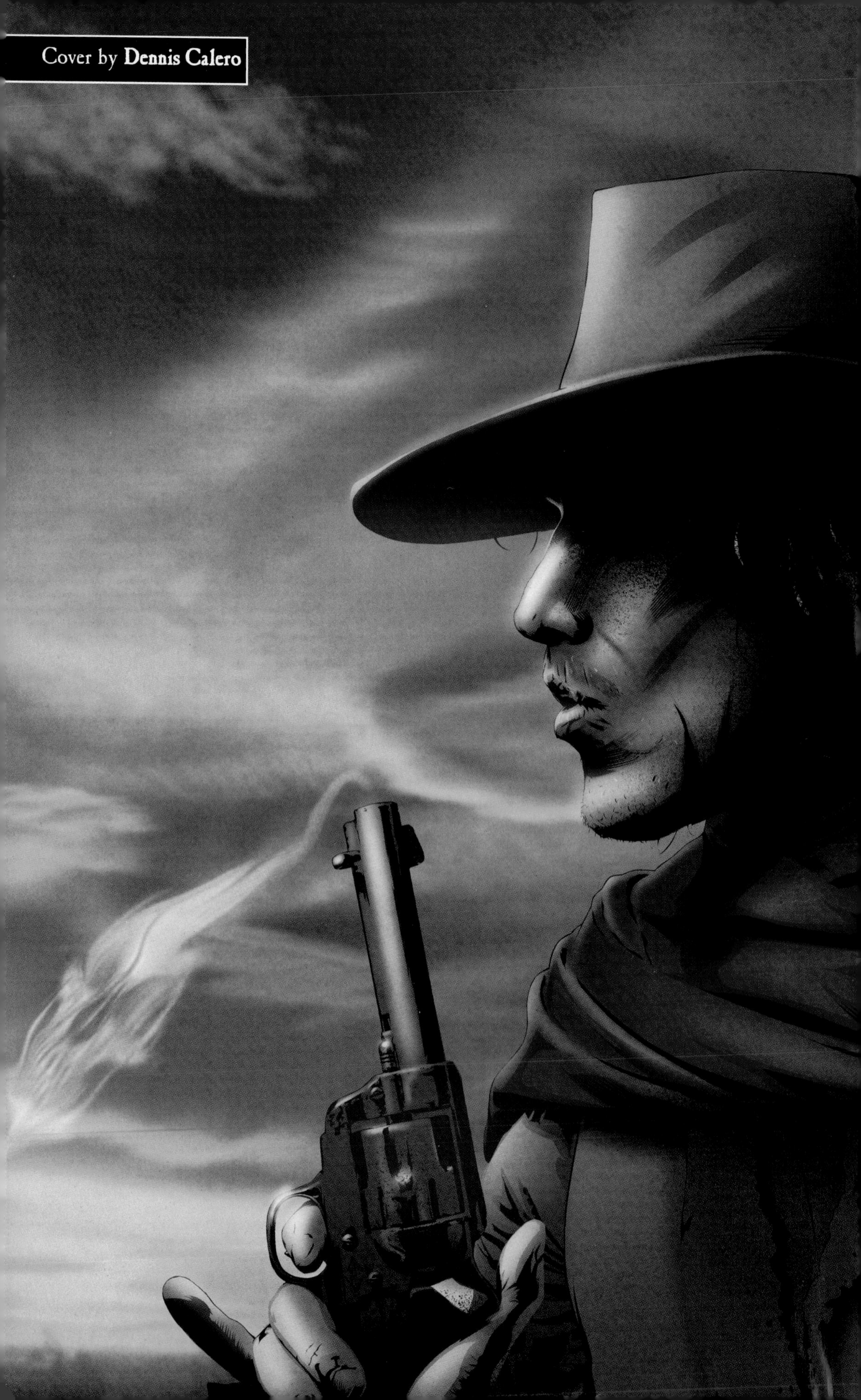

Cover by **Dennis Calero**

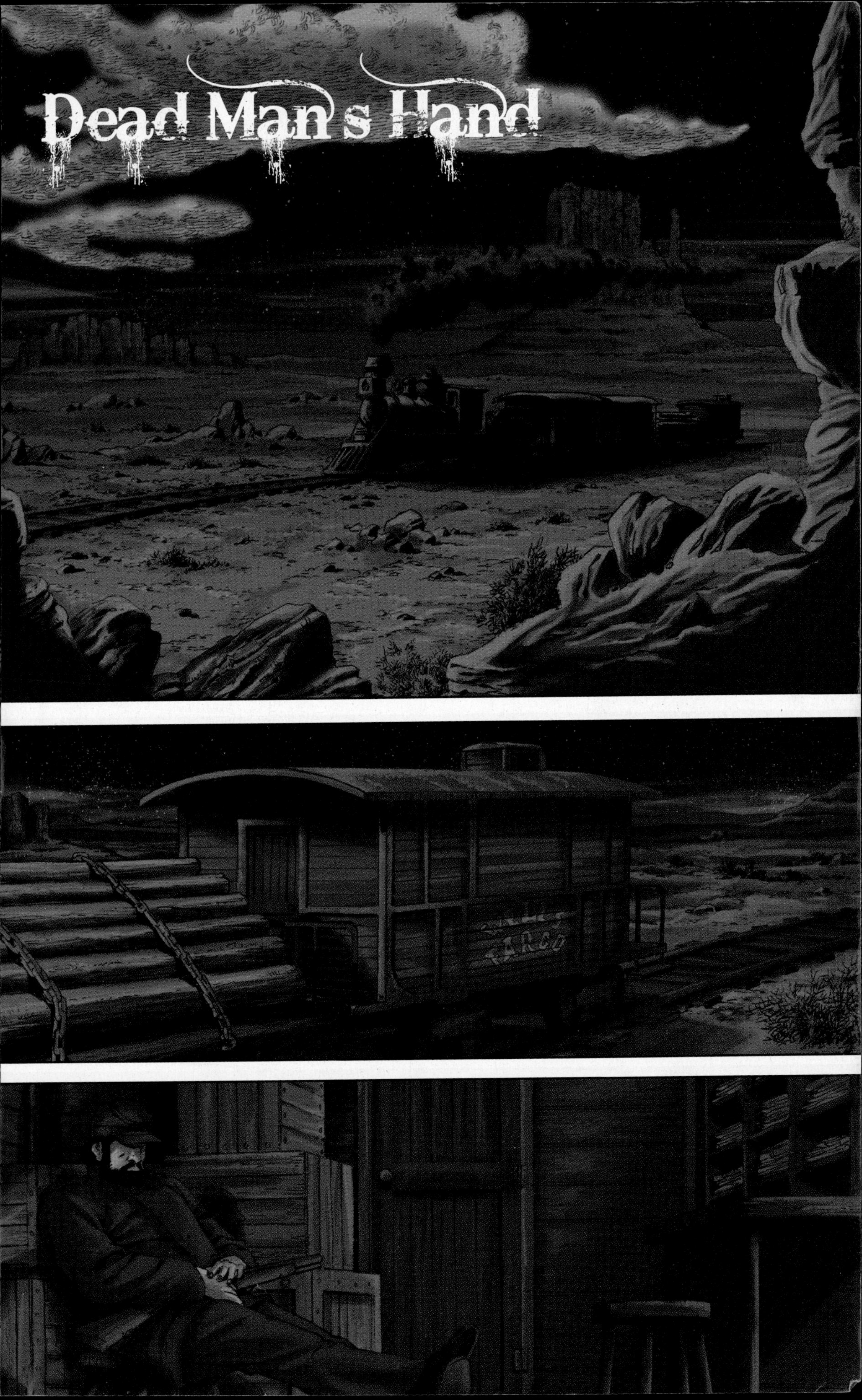
Dead Man's Hand

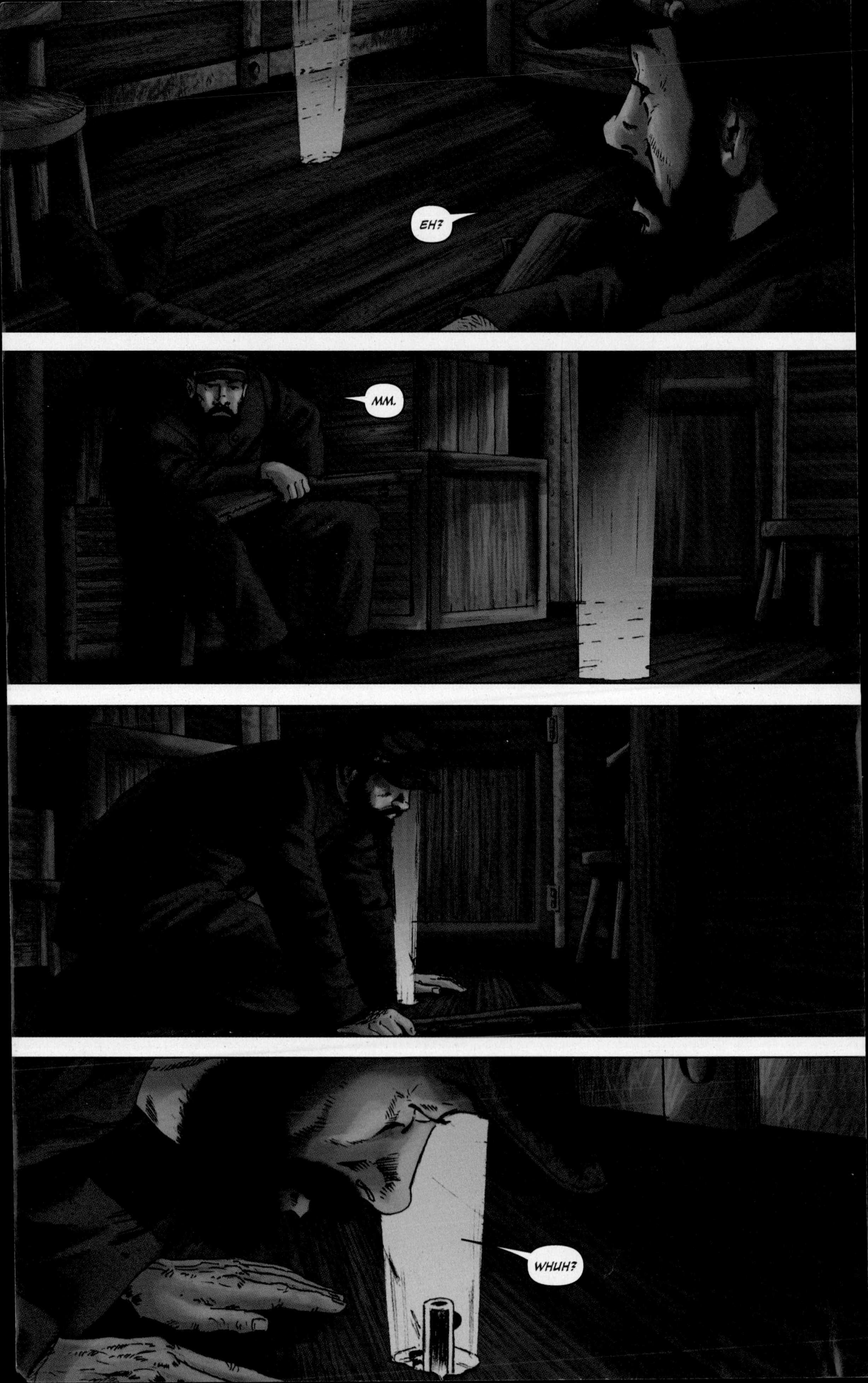
EH?
MM.
WHUH?

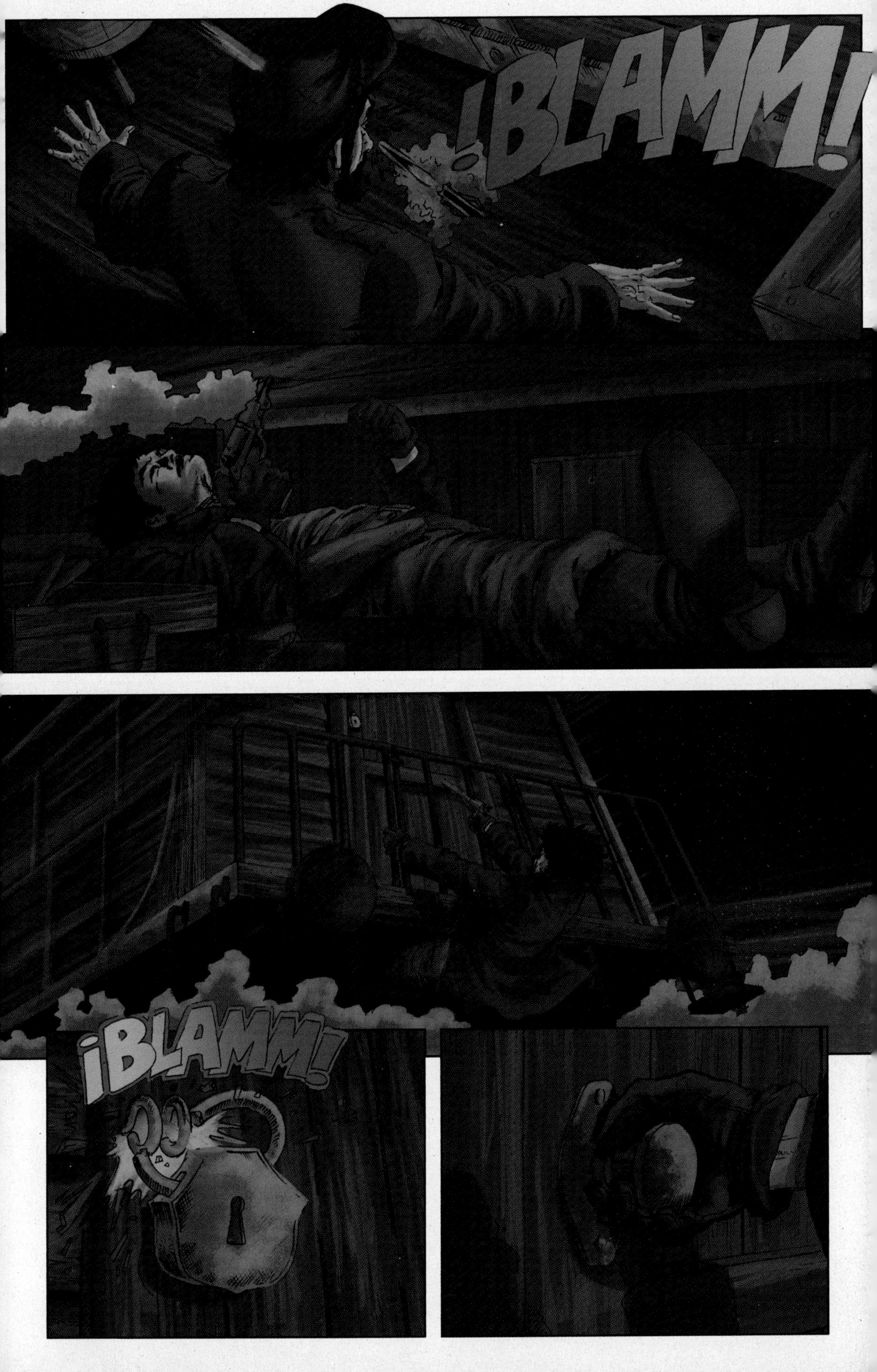
¡BLAMM!
¡BLAMM!

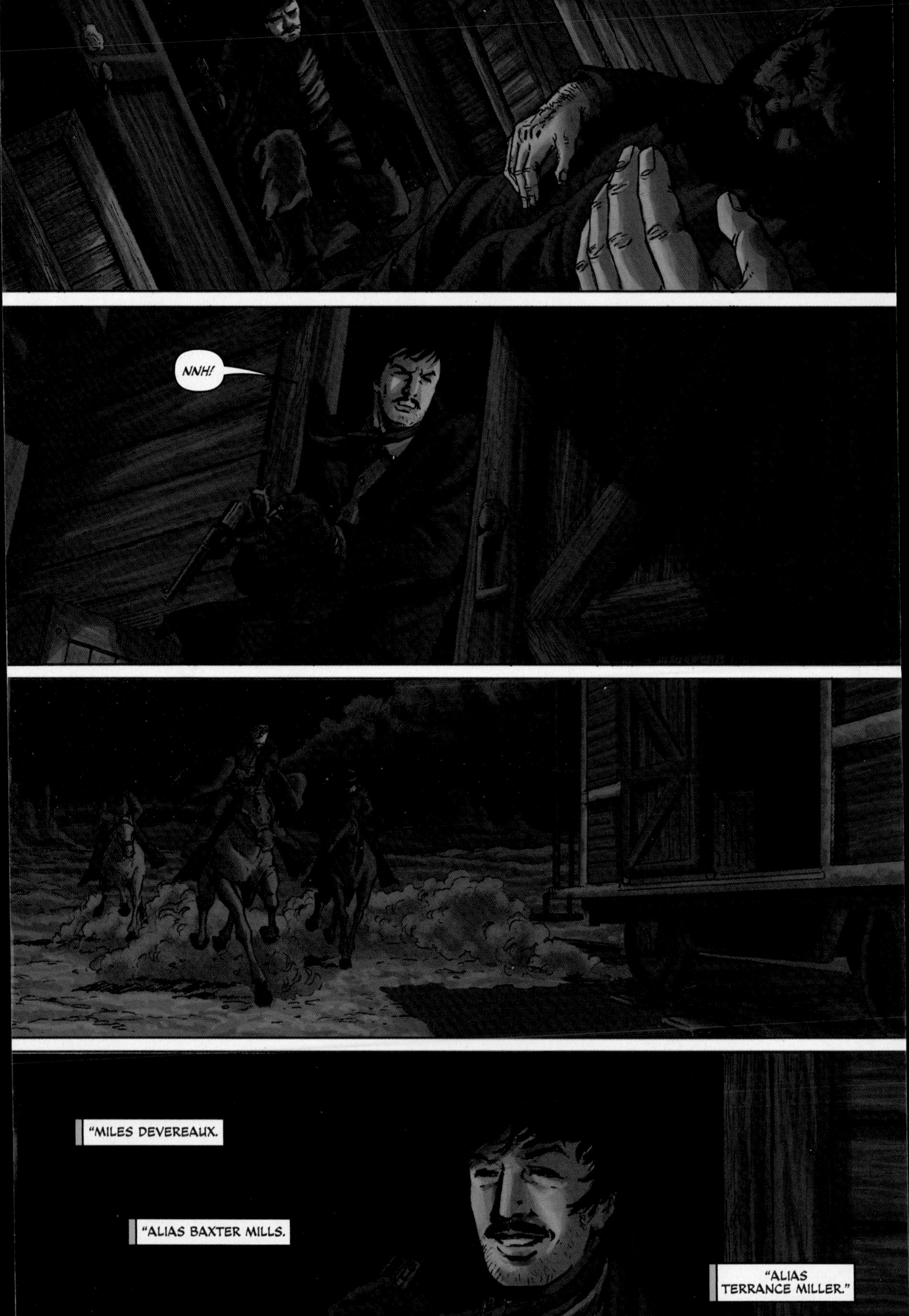
NNH!
"MILES DEVEREAUX.
"ALIAS BAXTER MILLS.
"ALIAS TERRANCE MILLER."

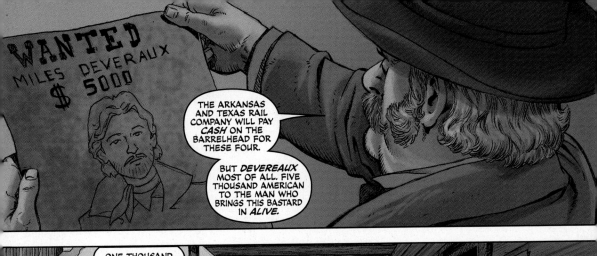

WANTED
MILES DEVERAUX
$ 5000

THE ARKANSAS AND TEXAS RAIL COMPANY WILL PAY *CASH* ON THE BARRELHEAD FOR THESE FOUR.

BUT *DEVEREAUX* MOST OF ALL. FIVE THOUSAND AMERICAN TO THE MAN WHO BRINGS THIS BASTARD IN *ALIVE*.

ONE THOUSAND FOR HIS *CADAVER*.

SEE, WE WANT TO SEE HIM *HANG* AS AN *EXAMPLE* TO THE *REST* OF THE THIEVING TRASH.

FSSHT

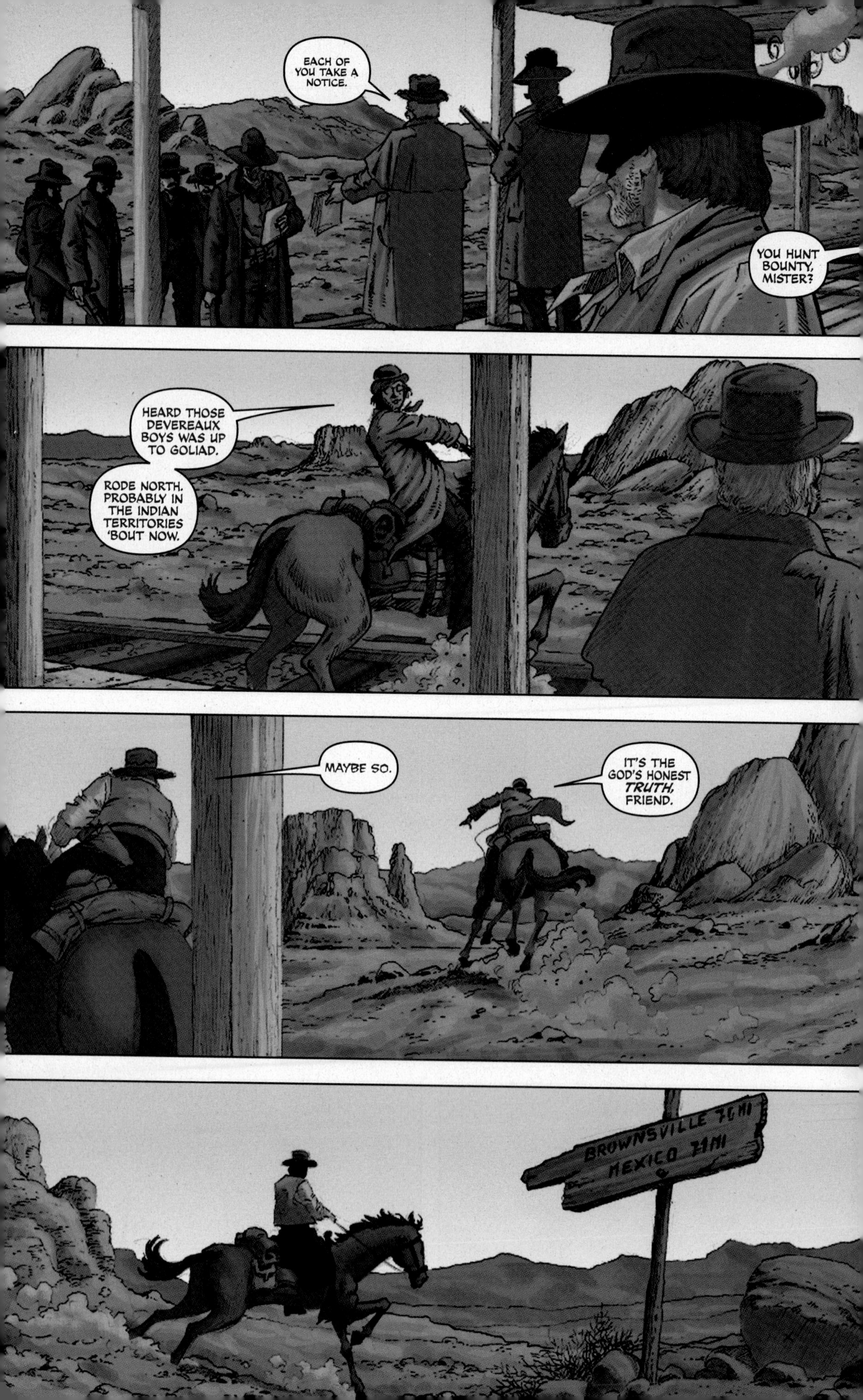
EACH OF YOU TAKE A NOTICE.
YOU HUNT BOUNTY, MISTER?
HEARD THOSE DEVEREAUX BOYS WAS UP TO GOLIAD.
RODE NORTH. PROBABLY IN THE INDIAN TERRITORIES 'BOUT NOW.
MAYBE SO.
IT'S THE GOD'S HONEST *TRUTH*, FRIEND.
BROWNSVILLE 70 MI
MEXICO 21 MI

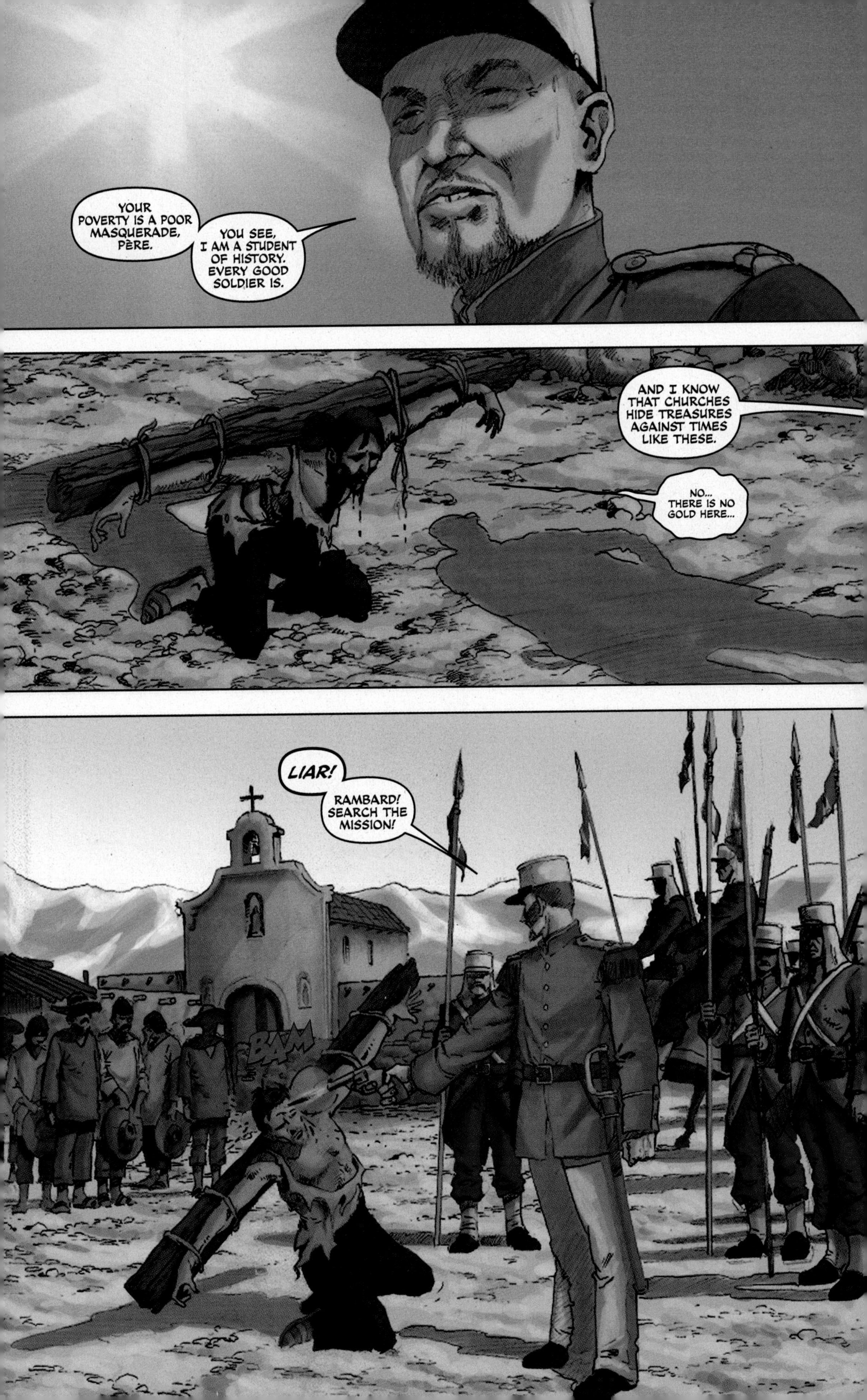

YOUR POVERTY IS A POOR MASQUERADE, PÈRE.
YOU SEE, I AM A STUDENT OF HISTORY. EVERY GOOD SOLDIER IS.
AND I KNOW THAT CHURCHES HIDE TREASURES AGAINST TIMES LIKE THESE.
NO... THERE IS NO GOLD HERE...
LIAR!
RAMBARD! SEARCH THE MISSION!
BAM

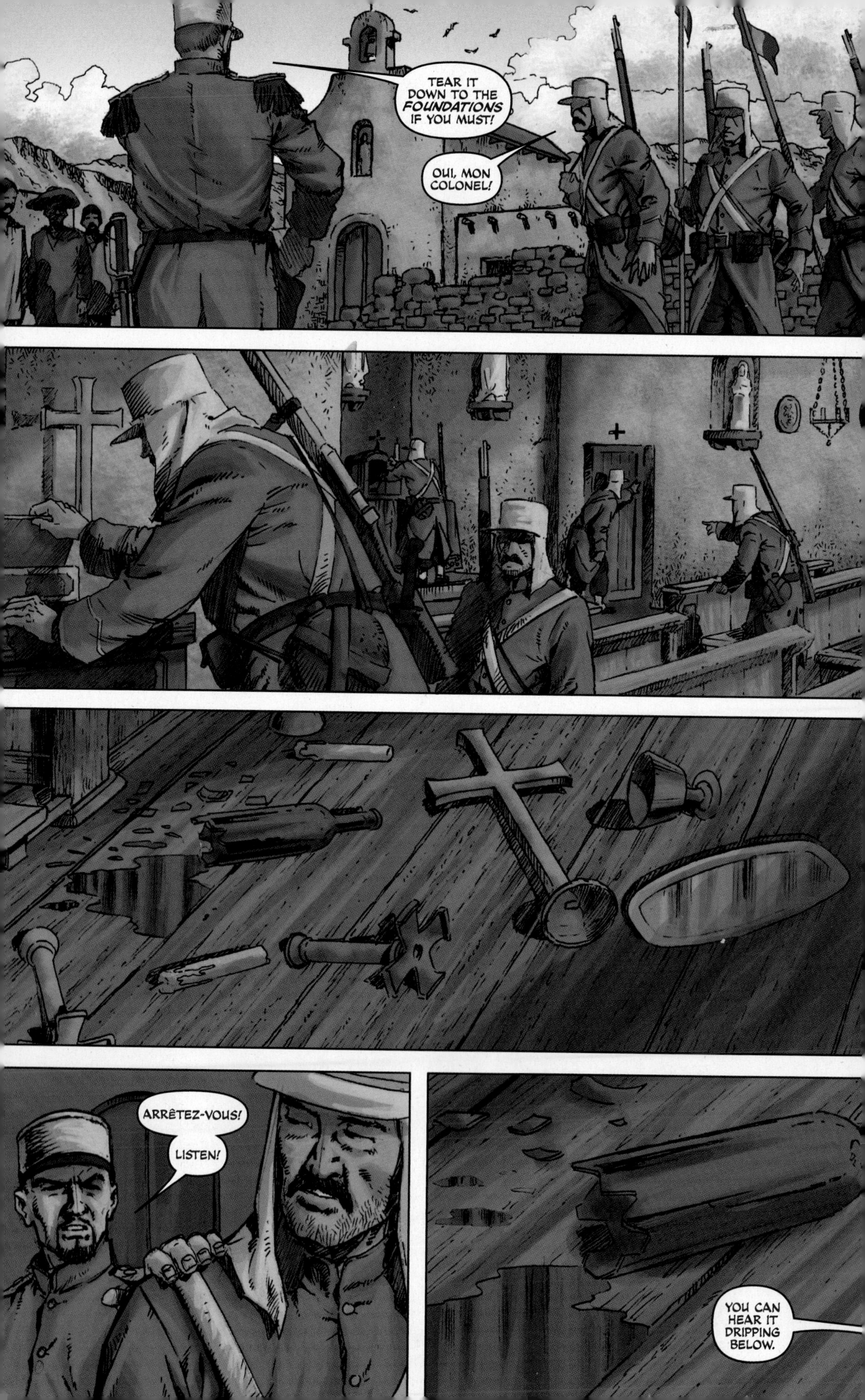
TEAR IT DOWN TO THE *FOUNDATIONS* IF YOU MUST!
OUI, MON COLONEL!
ARRÊTEZ-VOUS!
LISTEN!
YOU CAN HEAR IT DRIPPING BELOW.

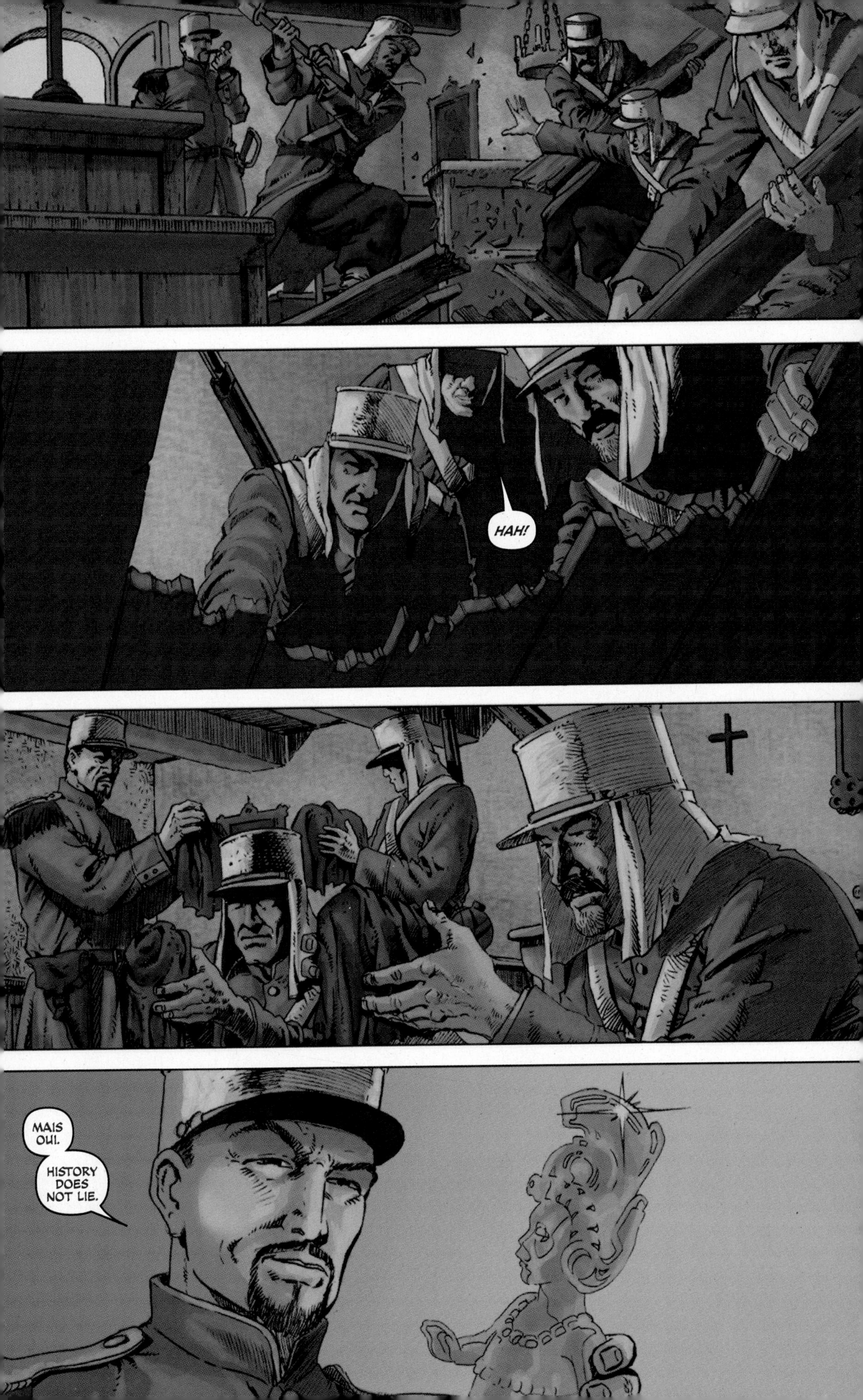
HAH!
MAIS OUI.
HISTORY DOES NOT LIE.

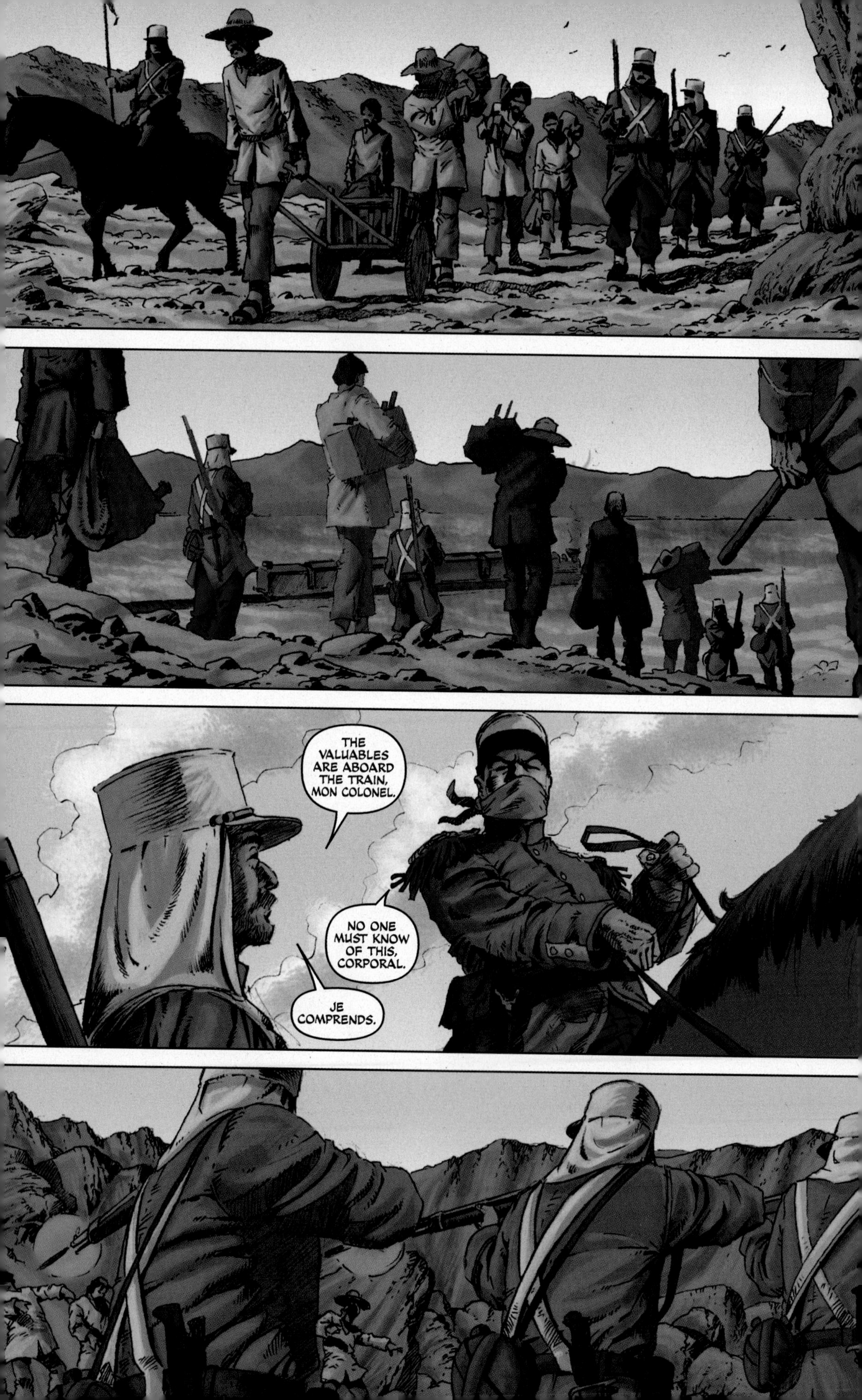
THE VALUABLES ARE ABOARD THE TRAIN, MON COLONEL.
NO ONE MUST KNOW OF THIS, CORPORAL.
JE COMPRENDS.

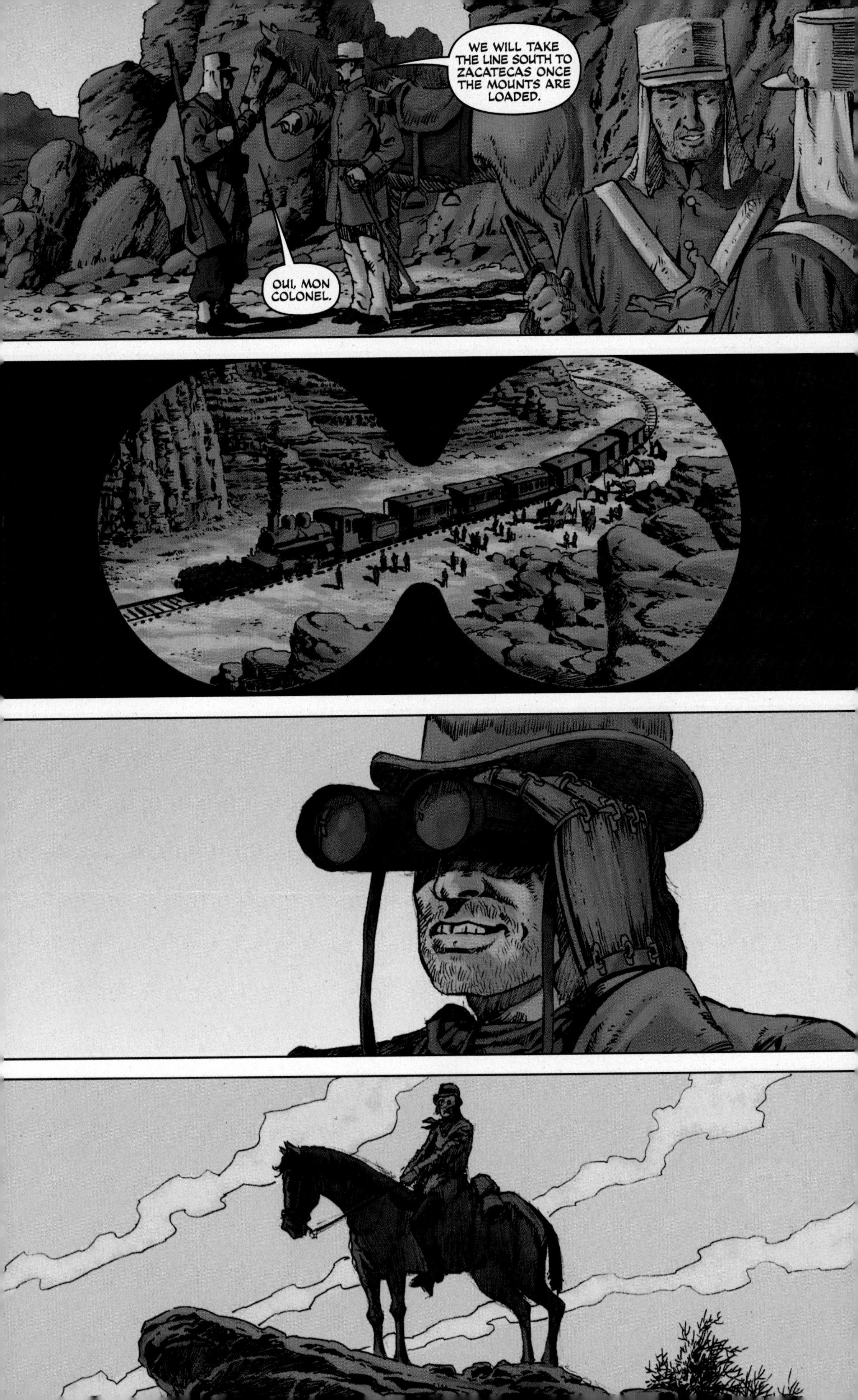
WE WILL TAKE THE LINE SOUTH TO ZACATECAS ONCE THE MOUNTS ARE LOADED.
OUI, MON COLONEL.

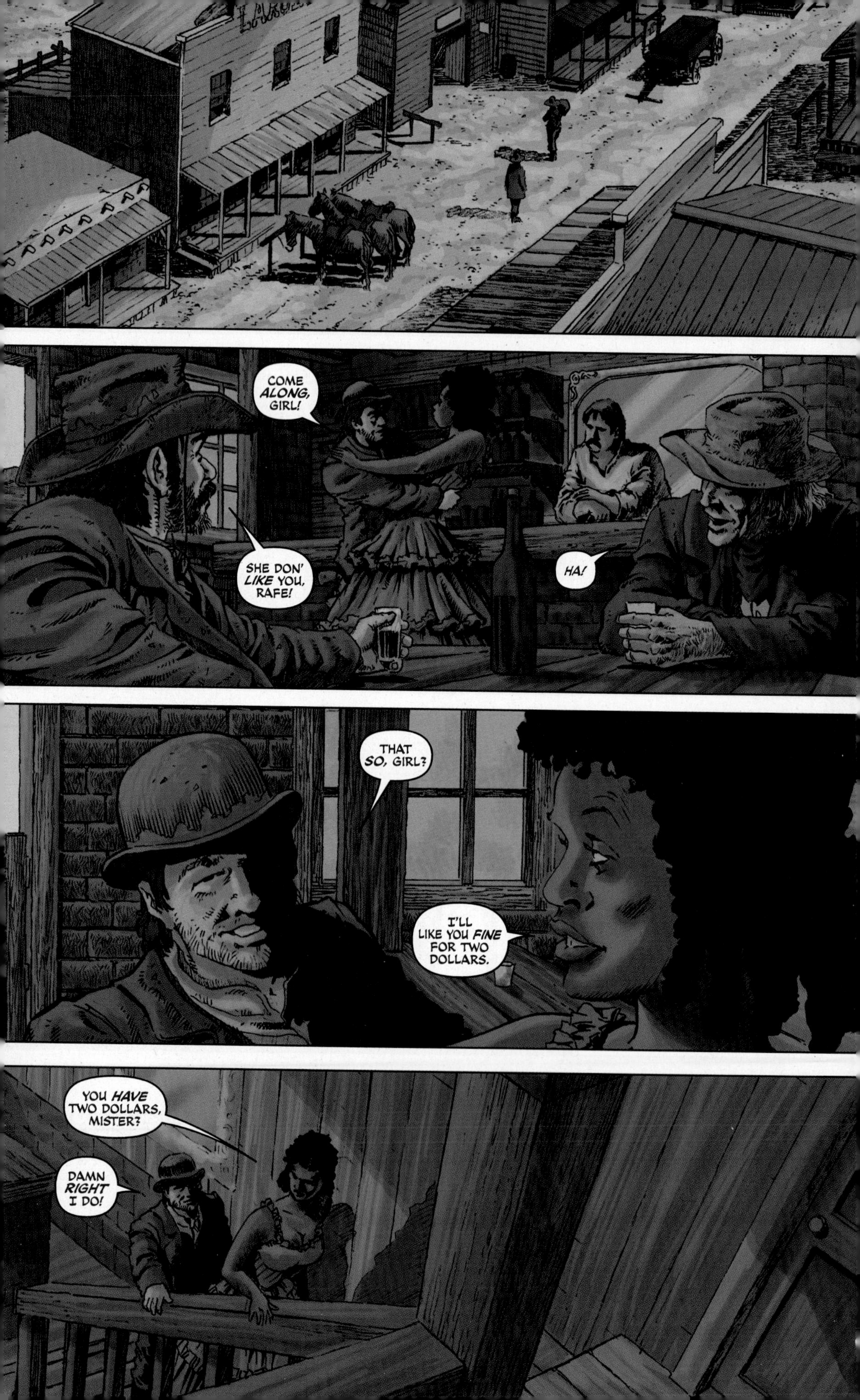
COME ALONG, GIRL!
SHE DON' LIKE YOU, RAFE!
HA!
THAT SO, GIRL?
I'LL LIKE YOU FINE FOR TWO DOLLARS.
YOU HAVE TWO DOLLARS, MISTER?
DAMN RIGHT I DO!

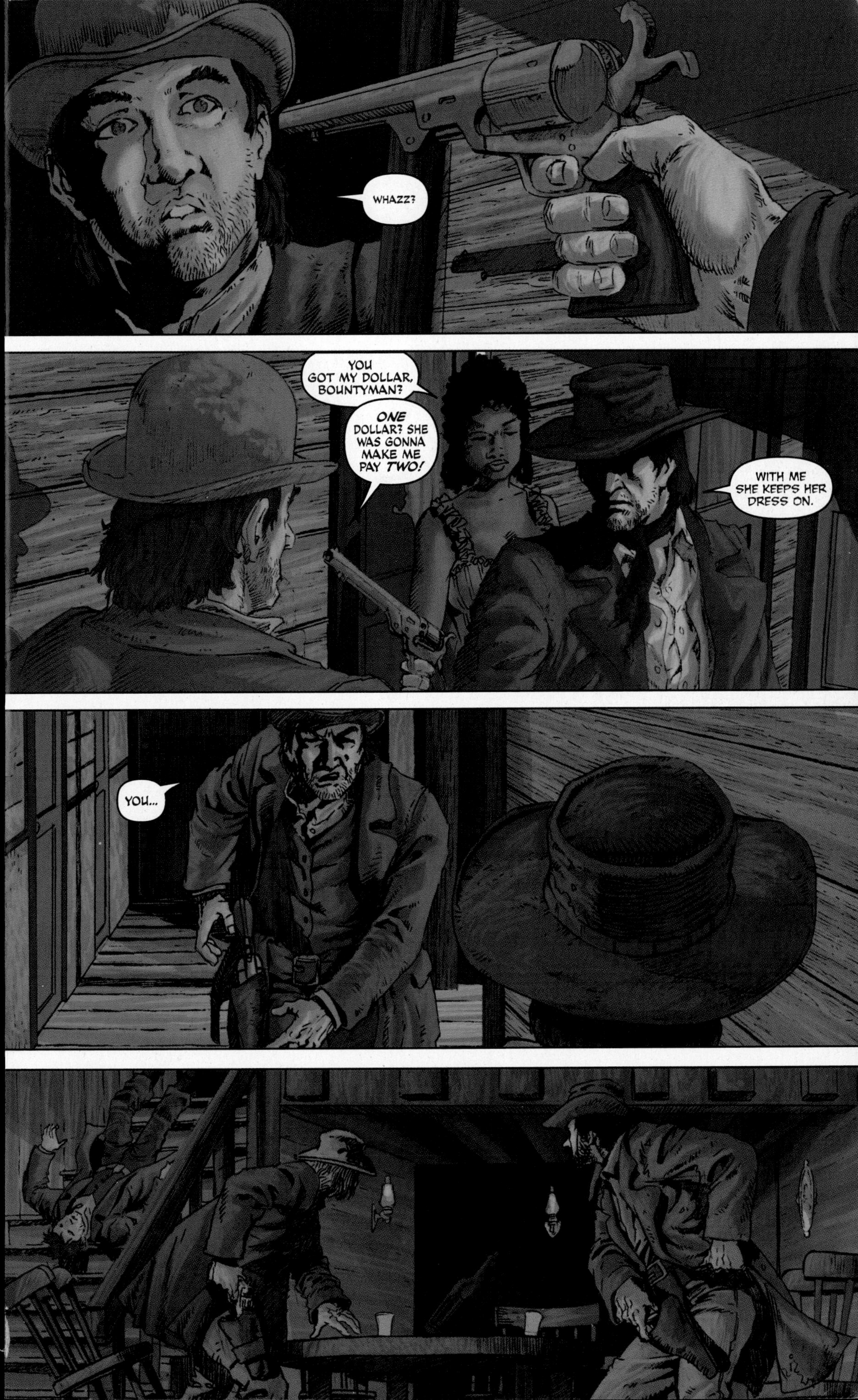
WHAZZ?
YOU GOT MY DOLLAR, BOUNTYMAN?
ONE DOLLAR? SHE WAS GONNA MAKE ME PAY *TWO!*
WITH ME SHE KEEPS HER DRESS ON.
YOU...

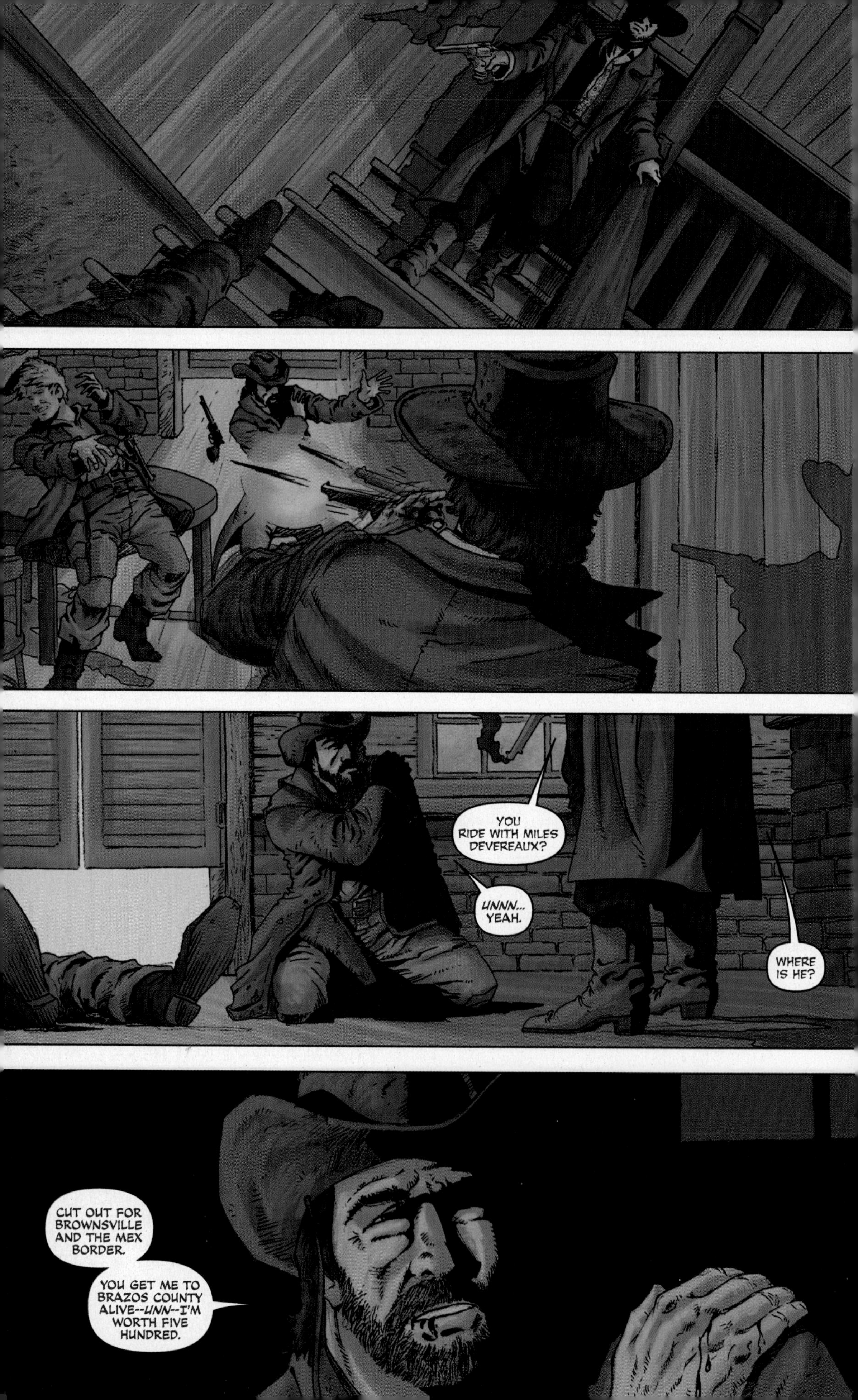
YOU RIDE WITH MILES DEVEREAUX?
UNNN... YEAH.
WHERE IS HE?
CUT OUT FOR BROWNSVILLE AND THE MEX BORDER.
YOU GET ME TO BRAZOS COUNTY ALIVE--UNN--I'M WORTH FIVE HUNDRED.

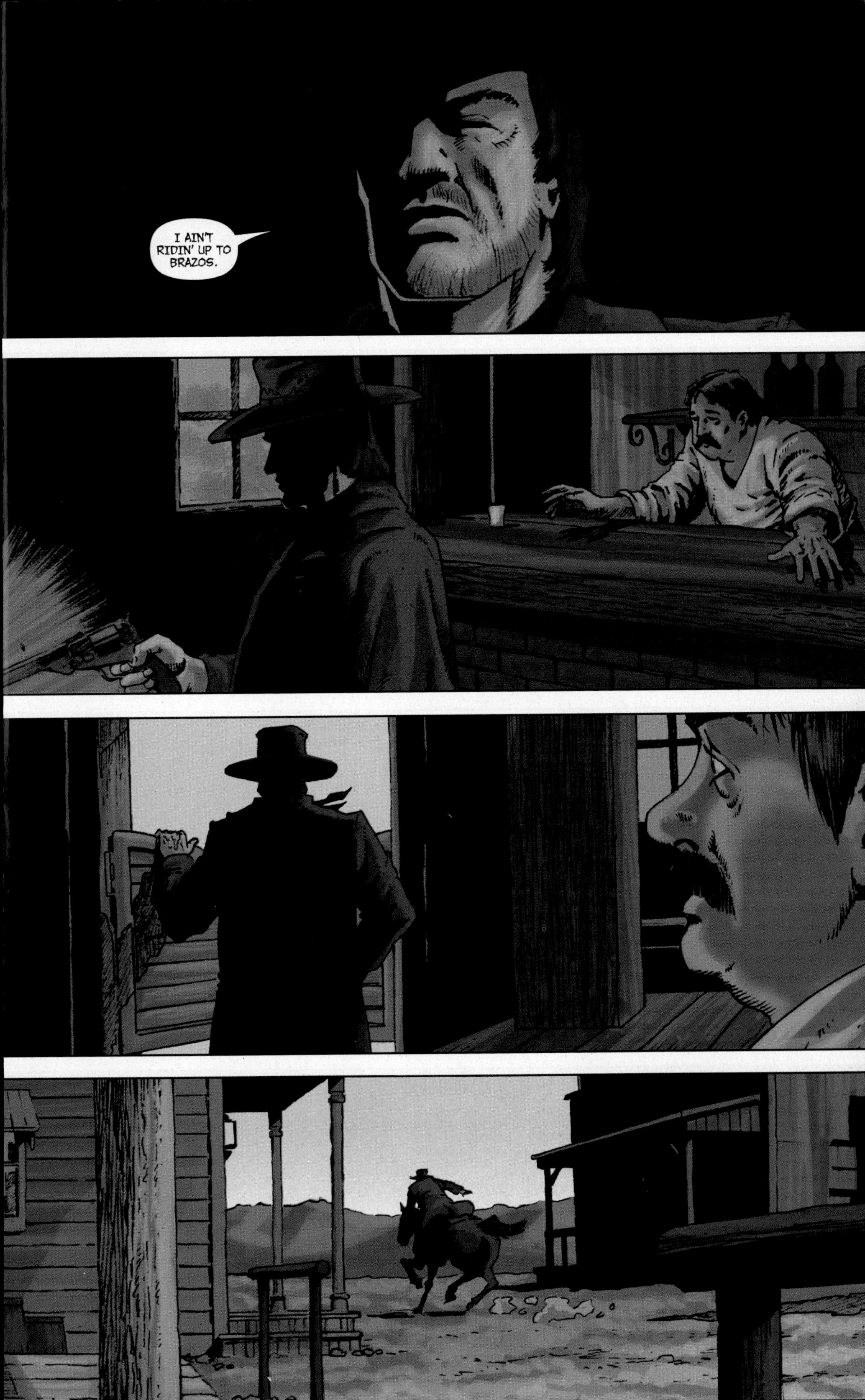
I AIN'T RIDIN' UP TO BRAZOS.

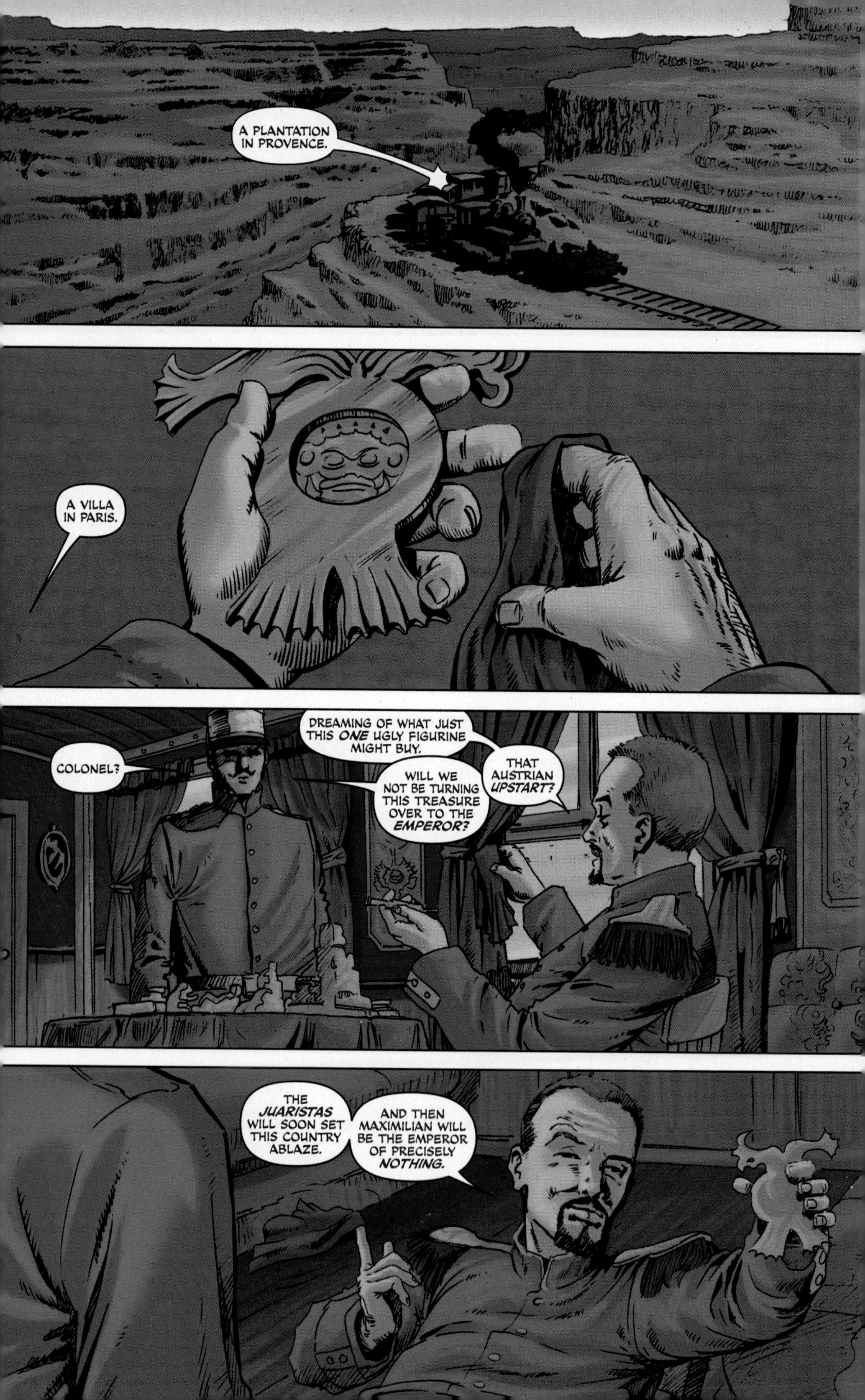
A PLANTATION IN PROVENCE.
A VILLA IN PARIS.
DREAMING OF WHAT JUST THIS ONE UGLY FIGURINE MIGHT BUY.
COLONEL?
WILL WE NOT BE TURNING THIS TREASURE OVER TO THE EMPEROR?
THAT AUSTRIAN UPSTART?
THE JUARISTAS WILL SOON SET THIS COUNTRY ABLAZE.
AND THEN MAXIMILIAN WILL BE THE EMPEROR OF PRECISELY NOTHING.

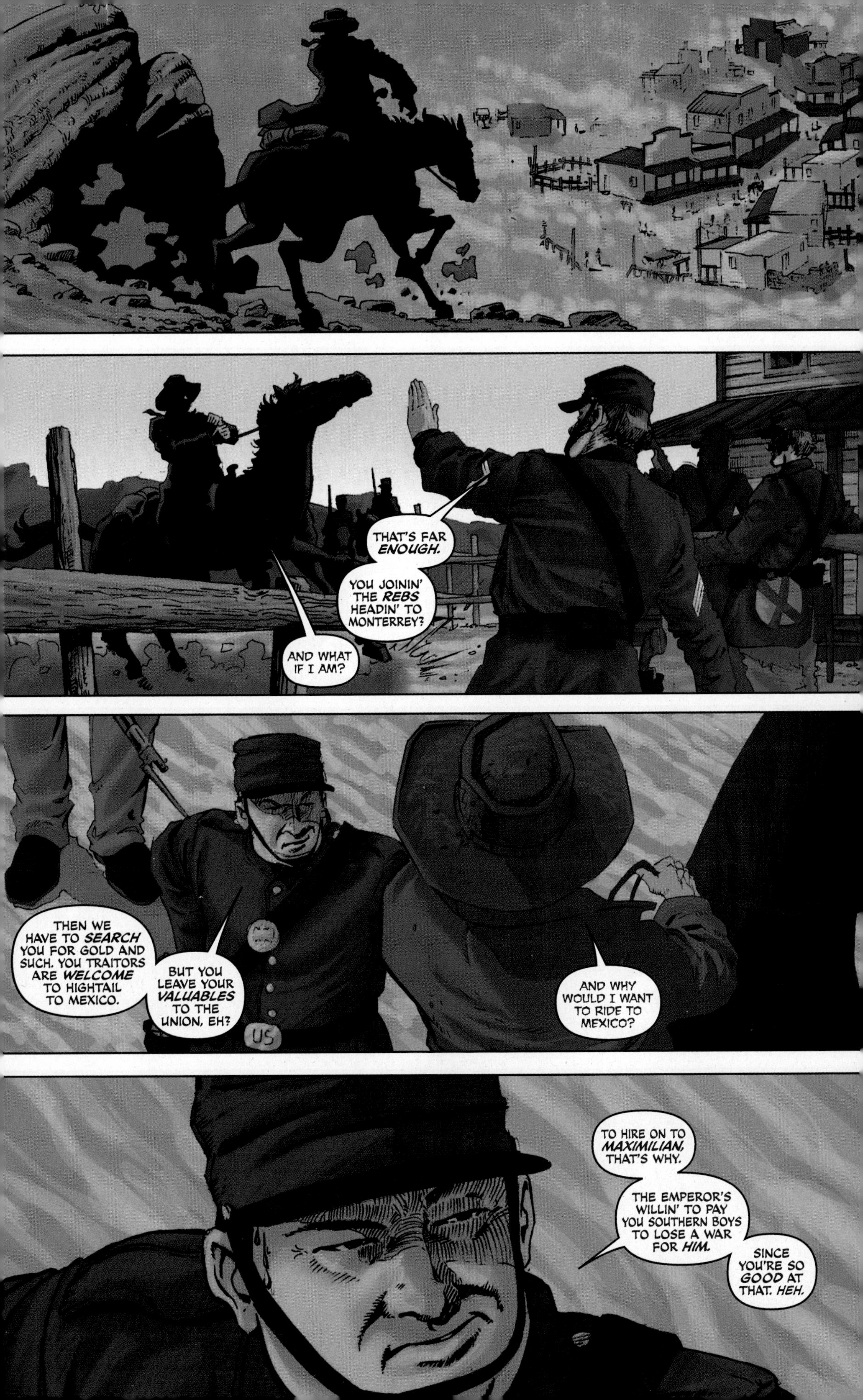

THAT'S FAR ENOUGH.
YOU JOININ' THE REBS HEADIN' TO MONTERREY?
AND WHAT IF I AM?
THEN WE HAVE TO SEARCH YOU FOR GOLD AND SUCH. YOU TRAITORS ARE WELCOME TO HIGHTAIL TO MEXICO.
BUT YOU LEAVE YOUR VALUABLES TO THE UNION, EH?
AND WHY WOULD I WANT TO RIDE TO MEXICO?
US
TO HIRE ON TO MAXIMILIAN, THAT'S WHY.
THE EMPEROR'S WILLIN' TO PAY YOU SOUTHERN BOYS TO LOSE A WAR FOR HIM.
SINCE YOU'RE SO GOOD AT THAT. HEH.

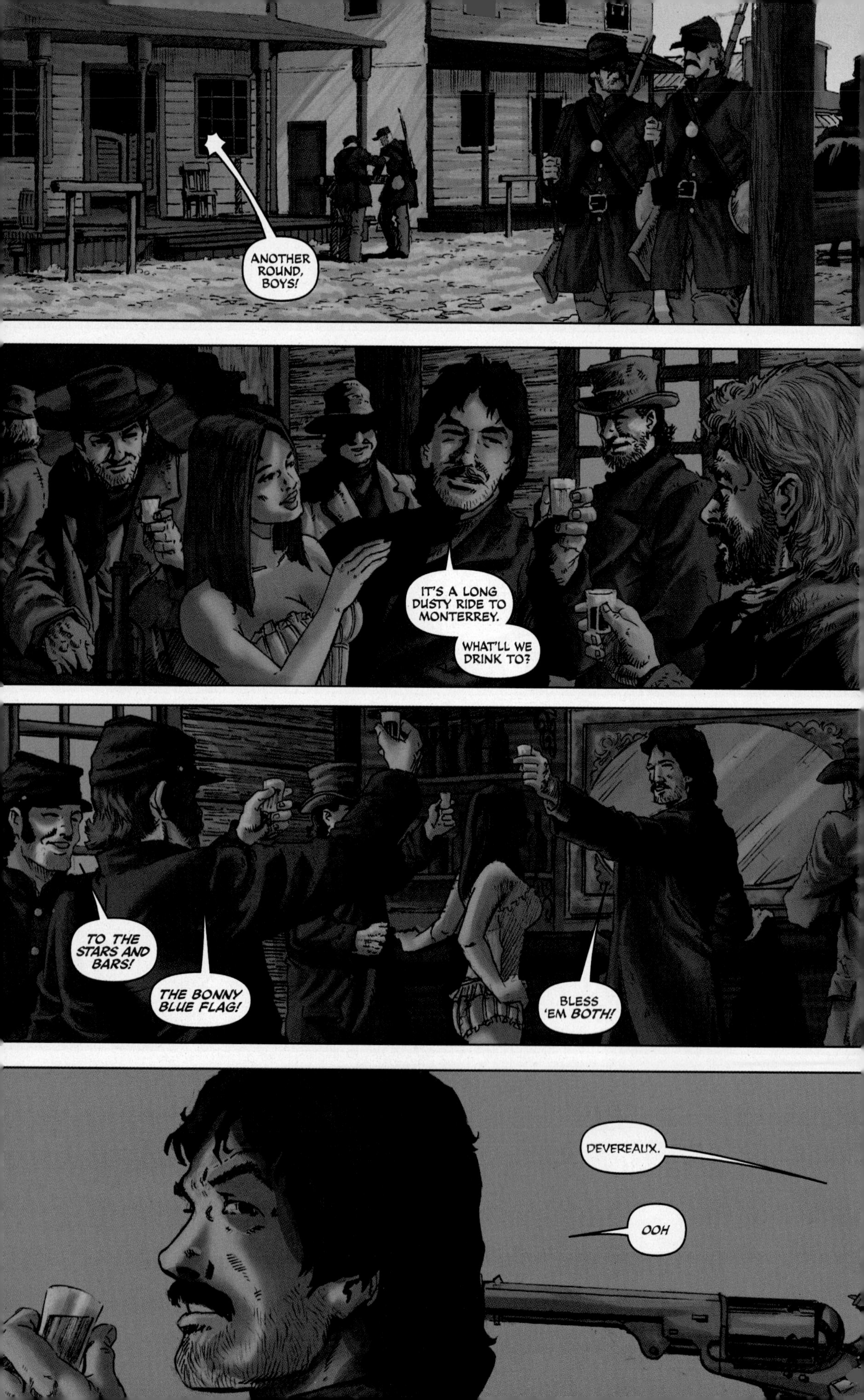
ANOTHER ROUND, BOYS!
IT'S A LONG DUSTY RIDE TO MONTERREY.
WHAT'LL WE DRINK TO?
TO THE STARS AND BARS!
THE BONNY BLUE FLAG!
BLESS 'EM BOTH!
DEVEREAUX.
OOH

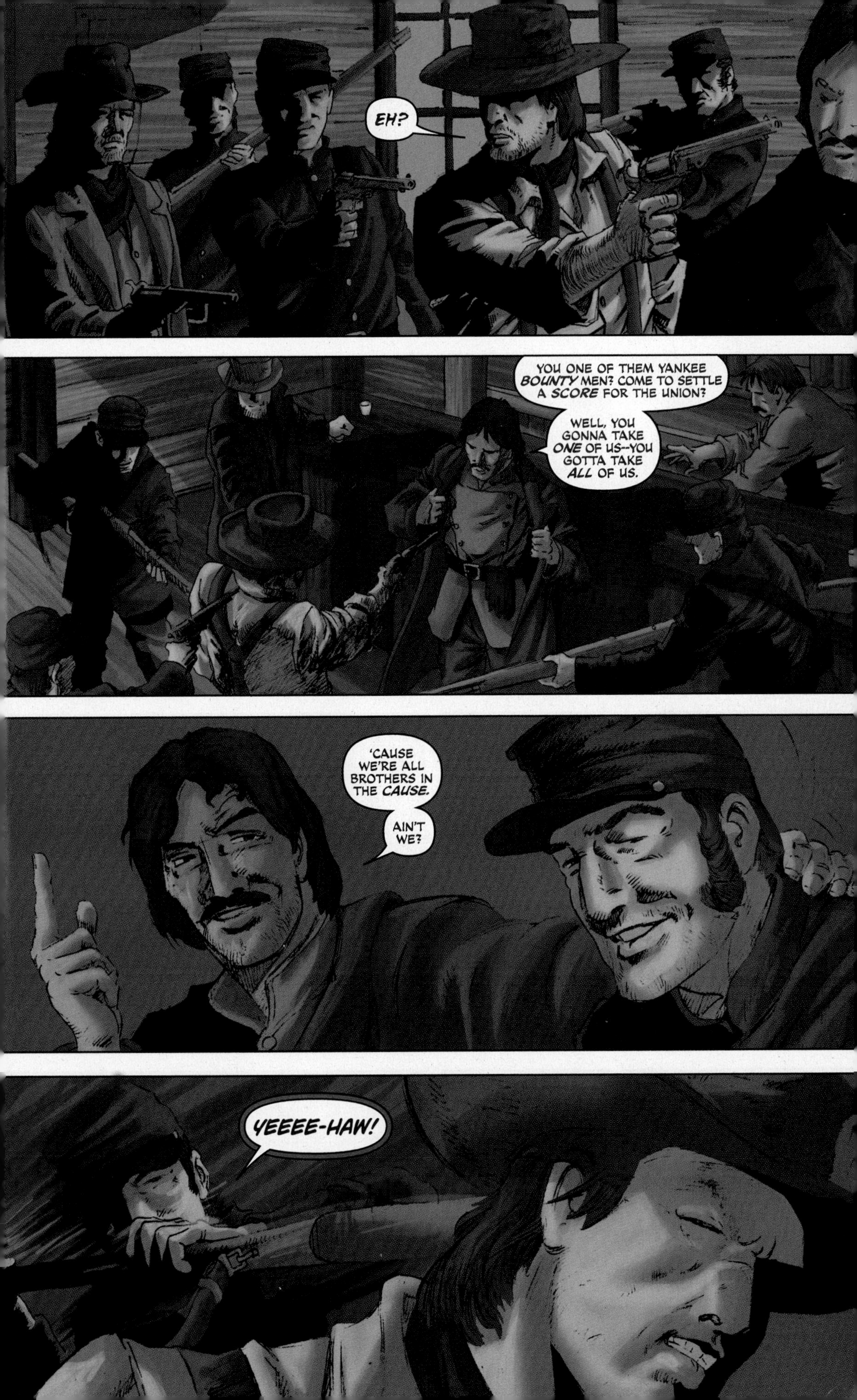
EH?
YOU ONE OF THEM YANKEE BOUNTY MEN? COME TO SETTLE A SCORE FOR THE UNION?
WELL, YOU GONNA TAKE ONE OF US--YOU GOTTA TAKE ALL OF US.
'CAUSE WE'RE ALL BROTHERS IN THE CAUSE.
AIN'T WE?
YEEEE-HAW!

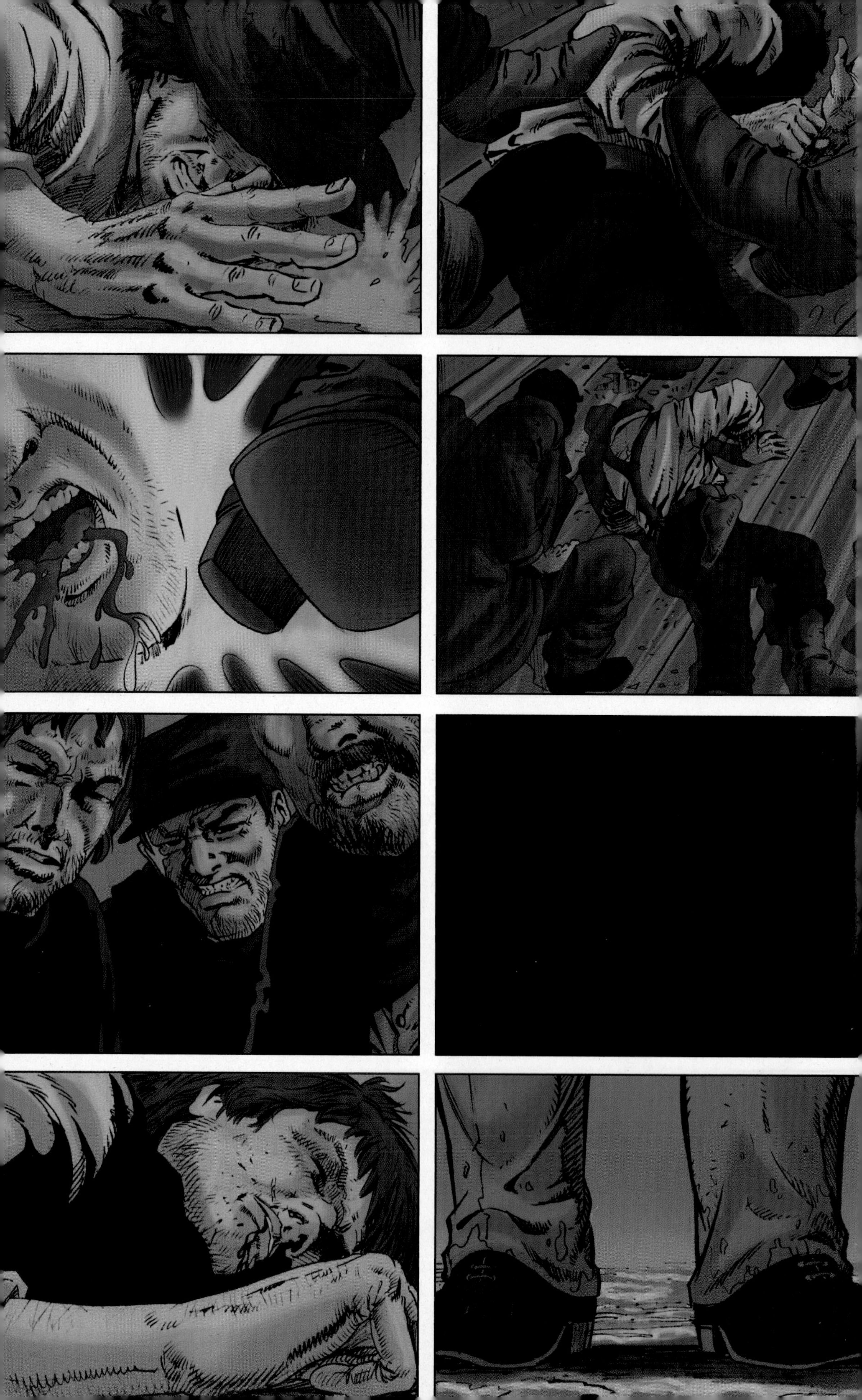

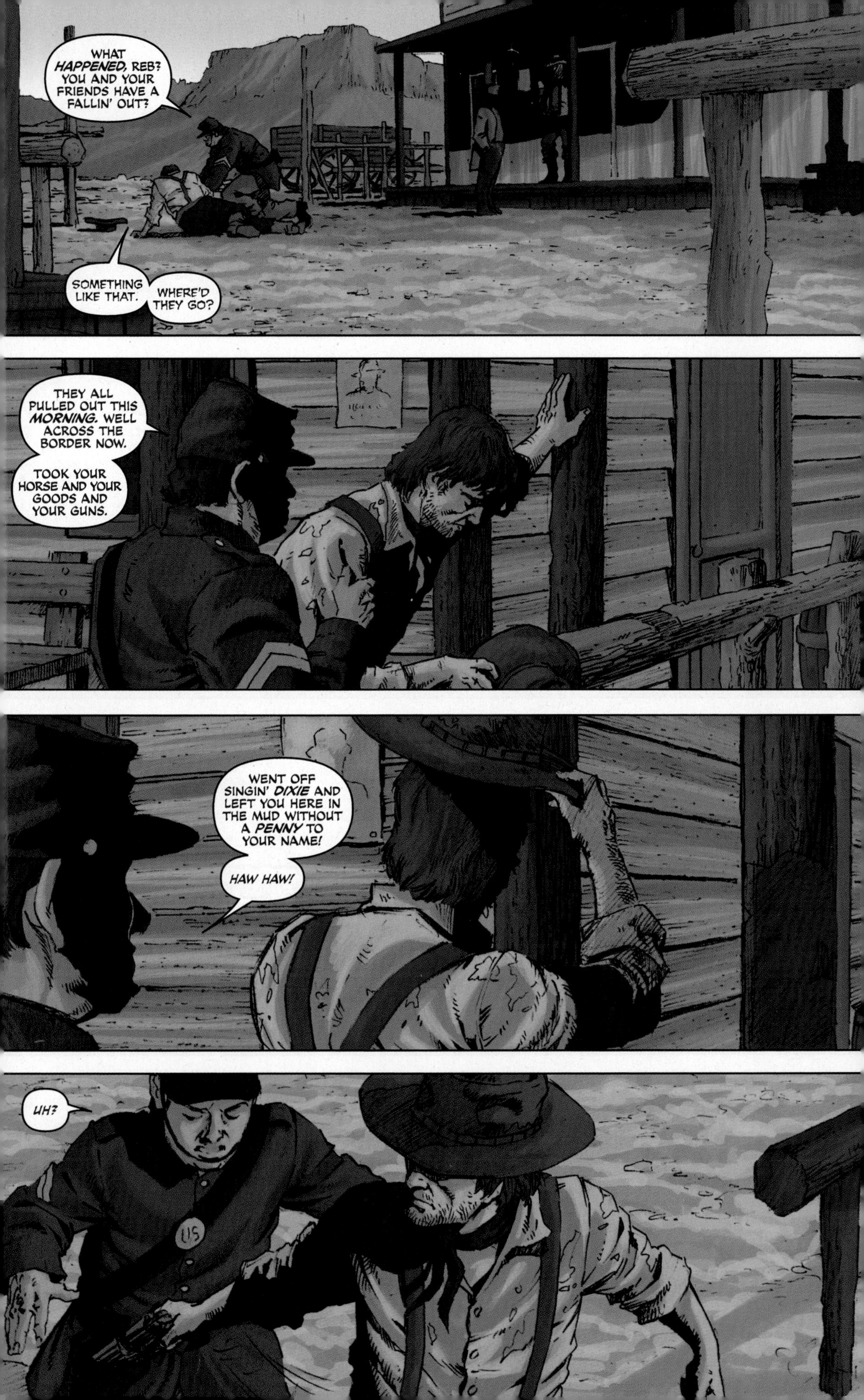
WHAT *HAPPENED,* REB? YOU AND YOUR FRIENDS HAVE A FALLIN' OUT?
SOMETHING LIKE THAT.
WHERE'D THEY GO?
THEY ALL PULLED OUT THIS *MORNING.* WELL ACROSS THE BORDER NOW.
TOOK YOUR HORSE AND YOUR GOODS AND YOUR GUNS.
WENT OFF SINGIN' *DIXIE* AND LEFT YOU HERE IN THE MUD WITHOUT A *PENNY* TO YOUR NAME!
HAW HAW!
UH?
US

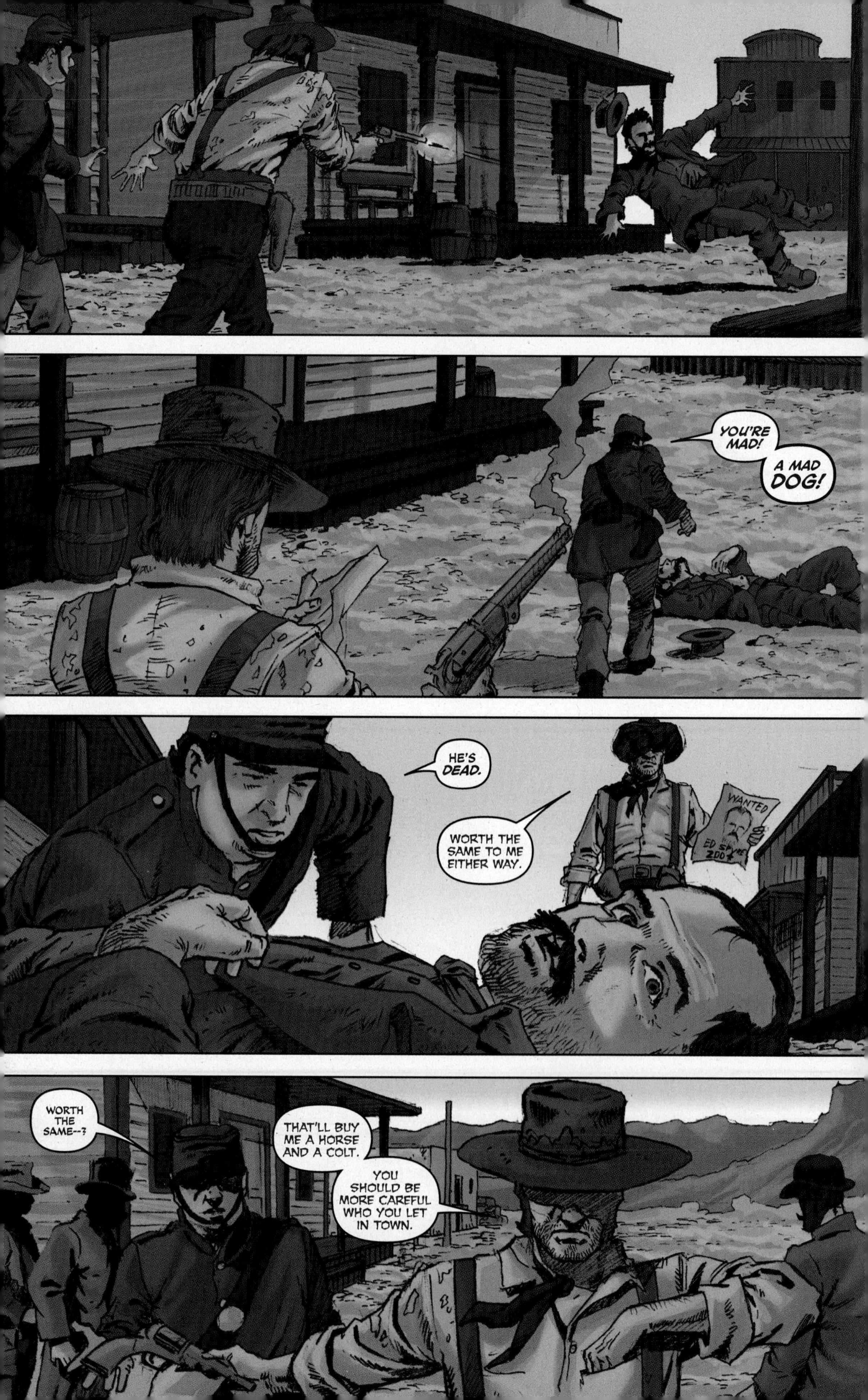
YOU'RE MAD!
A MAD DOG!
HE'S DEAD.
WORTH THE SAME TO ME EITHER WAY.
WANTED
ED SPYKE
2004
WORTH THE SAME--?
THAT'LL BUY ME A HORSE AND A COLT.
YOU SHOULD BE MORE CAREFUL WHO YOU LET IN TOWN.

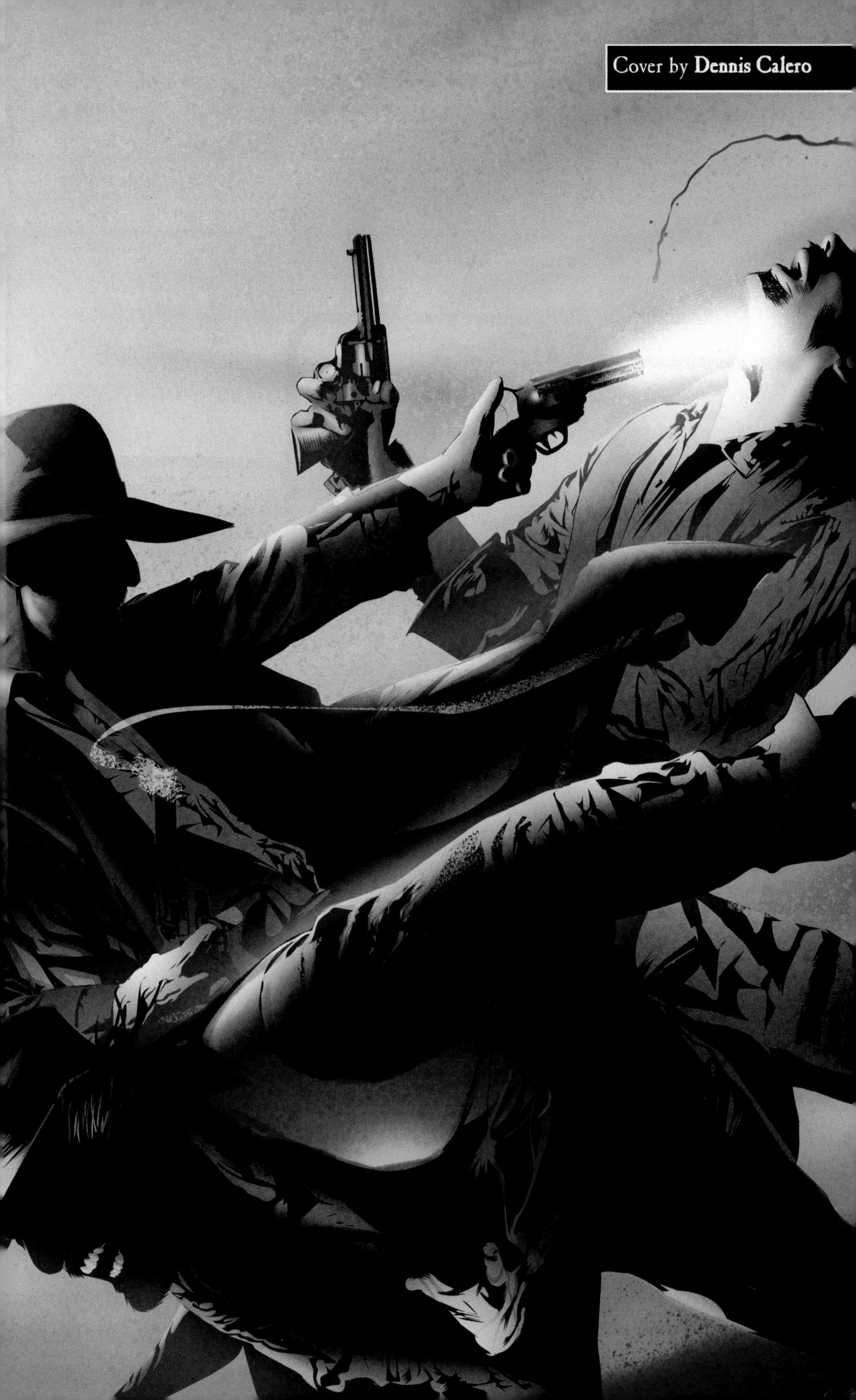

Cover by **Dennis Calero**

Cover by **Sergio Cariello**

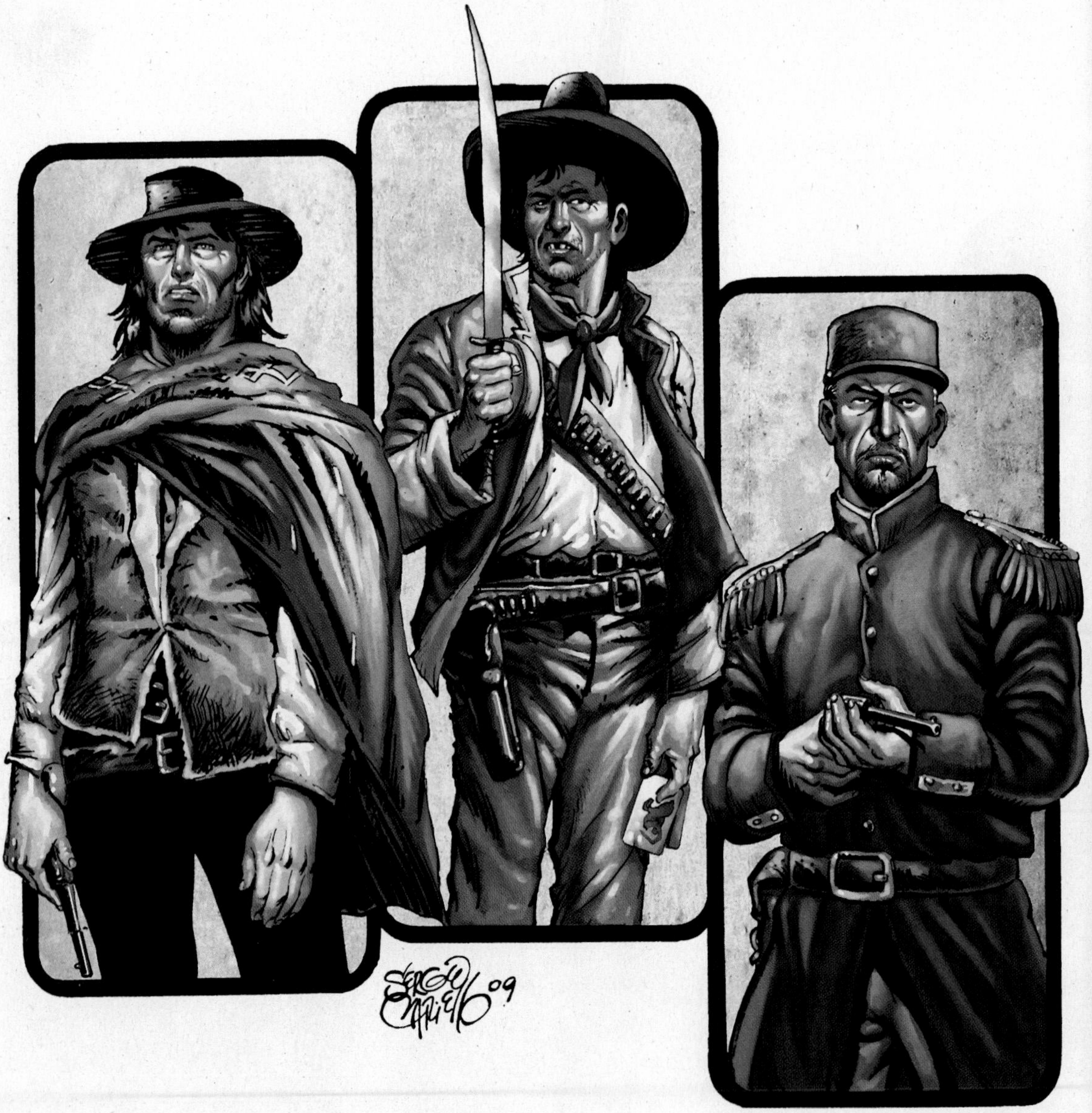

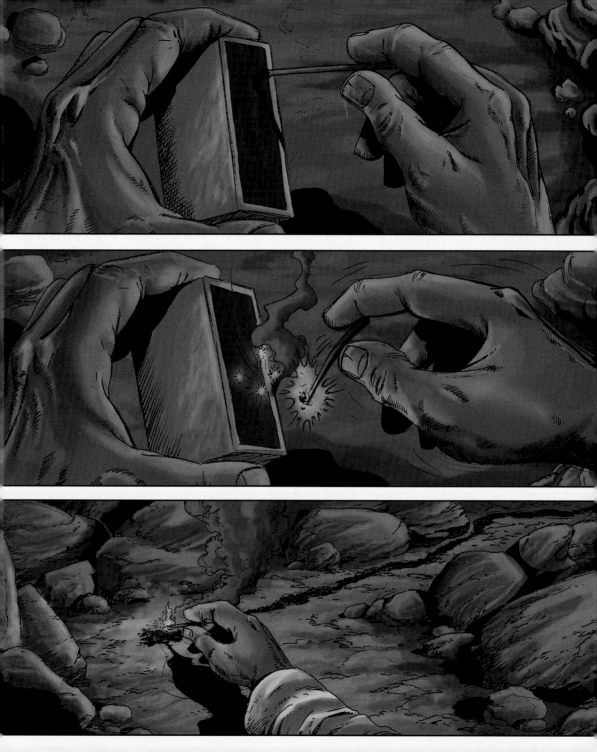

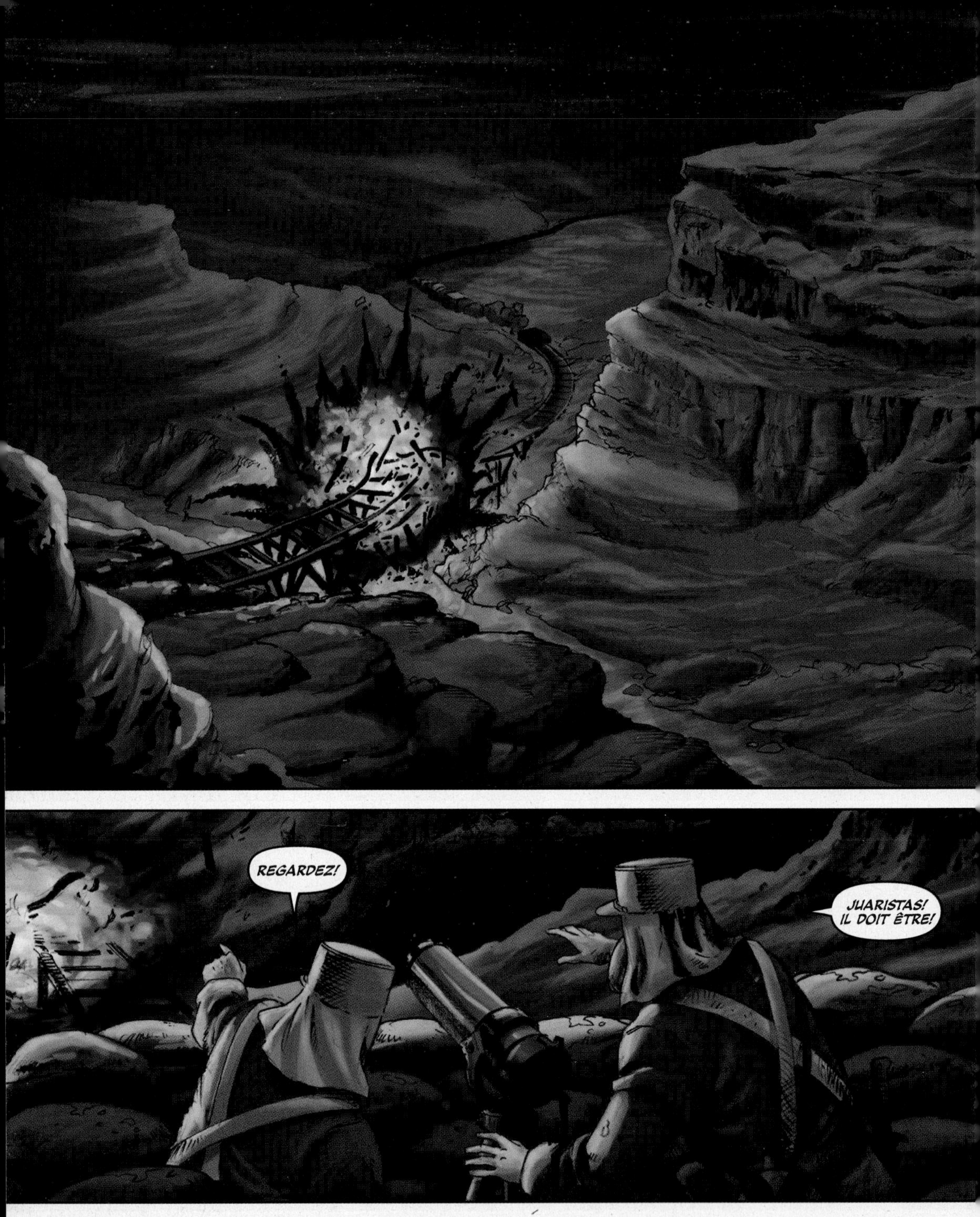
REGARDEZ!
JUARISTAS! IL DOIT ÊTRE!

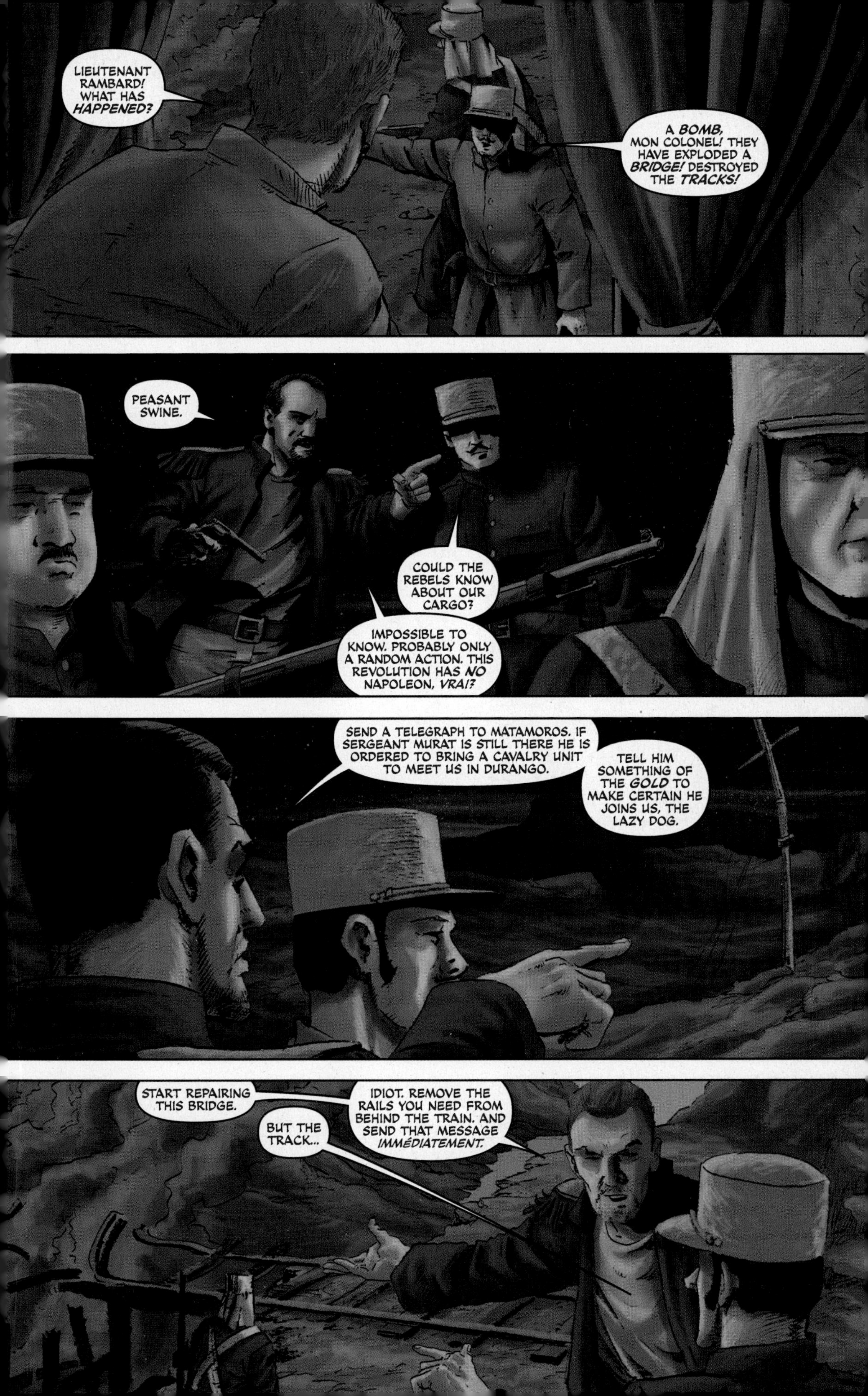
LIEUTENANT RAMBARD! WHAT HAS HAPPENED?
A BOMB, MON COLONEL! THEY HAVE EXPLODED A BRIDGE! DESTROYED THE TRACKS!
PEASANT SWINE.
COULD THE REBELS KNOW ABOUT OUR CARGO?
IMPOSSIBLE TO KNOW. PROBABLY ONLY A RANDOM ACTION. THIS REVOLUTION HAS NO NAPOLEON, VRAI?
SEND A TELEGRAPH TO MATAMOROS. IF SERGEANT MURAT IS STILL THERE HE IS ORDERED TO BRING A CAVALRY UNIT TO MEET US IN DURANGO.
TELL HIM SOMETHING OF THE GOLD TO MAKE CERTAIN HE JOINS US, THE LAZY DOG.
START REPAIRING THIS BRIDGE.
BUT THE TRACK...
IDIOT. REMOVE THE RAILS YOU NEED FROM BEHIND THE TRAIN. AND SEND THAT MESSAGE IMMÉDIATEMENT.

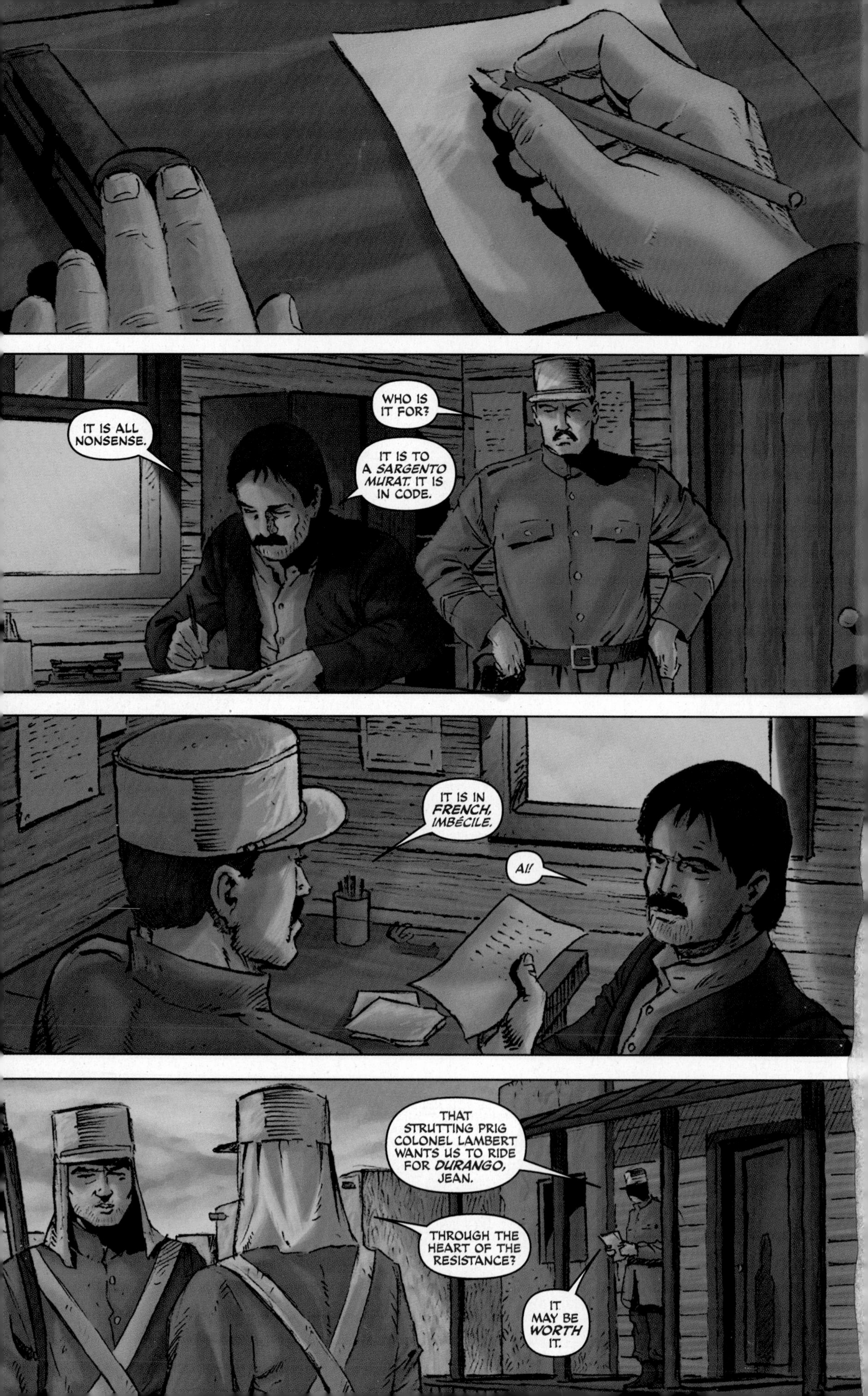
IT IS ALL NONSENSE.
WHO IS IT FOR?
IT IS TO A *SARGENTO MURAT.* IT IS IN CODE.
IT IS IN *FRENCH, IMBÉCILE.*
AI!
THAT STRUTTING PRIG COLONEL LAMBERT WANTS US TO RIDE FOR *DURANGO,* JEAN.
THROUGH THE HEART OF THE RESISTANCE?
IT MAY BE *WORTH* IT.

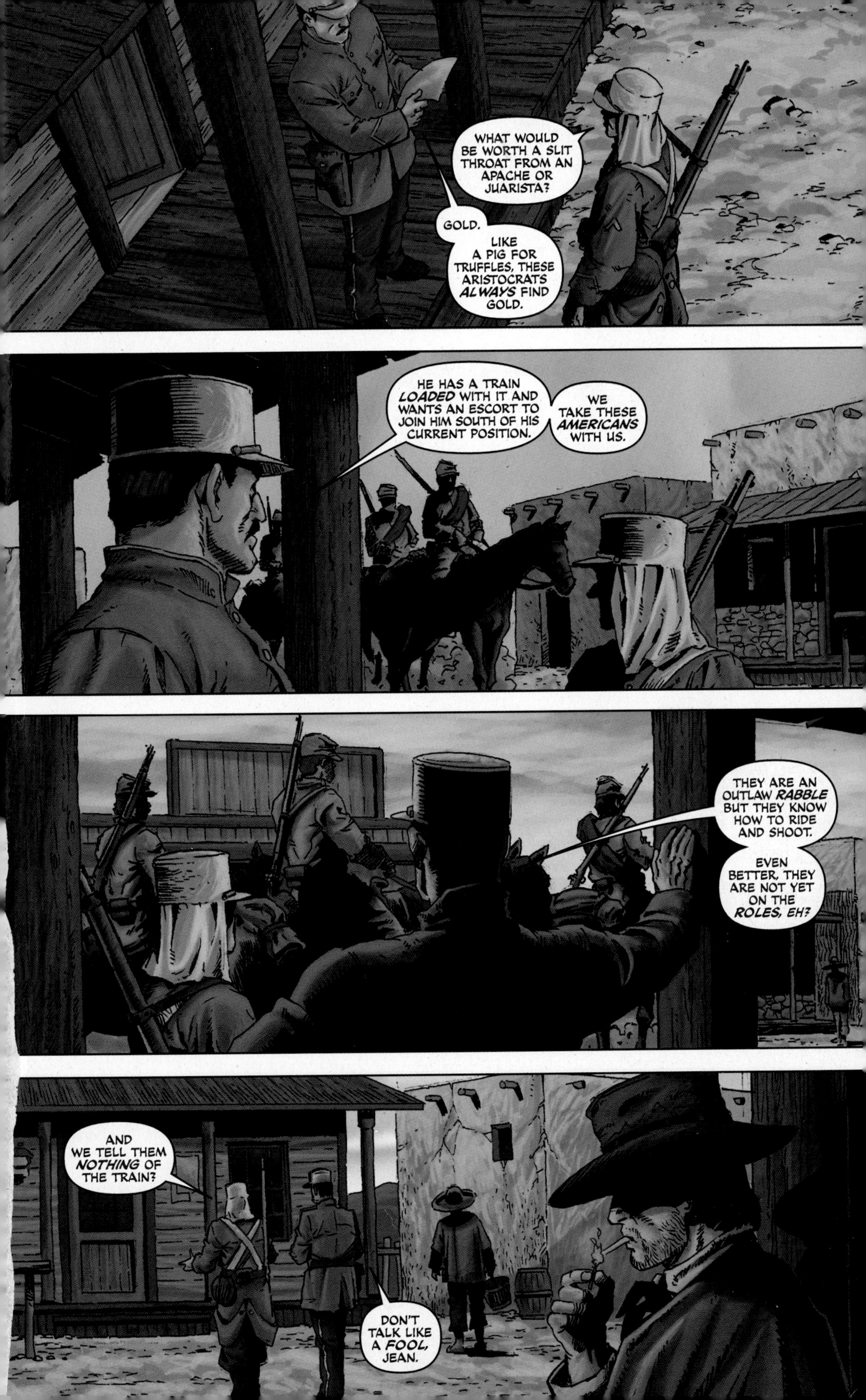
WHAT WOULD BE WORTH A SLIT THROAT FROM AN APACHE OR JUARISTA?
GOLD.
LIKE A PIG FOR TRUFFLES, THESE ARISTOCRATS ALWAYS FIND GOLD.
HE HAS A TRAIN LOADED WITH IT AND WANTS AN ESCORT TO JOIN HIM SOUTH OF HIS CURRENT POSITION.
WE TAKE THESE AMERICANS WITH US.
THEY ARE AN OUTLAW RABBLE BUT THEY KNOW HOW TO RIDE AND SHOOT.
EVEN BETTER, THEY ARE NOT YET ON THE ROLES, EH?
AND WE TELL THEM NOTHING OF THE TRAIN?
DON'T TALK LIKE A FOOL, JEAN.

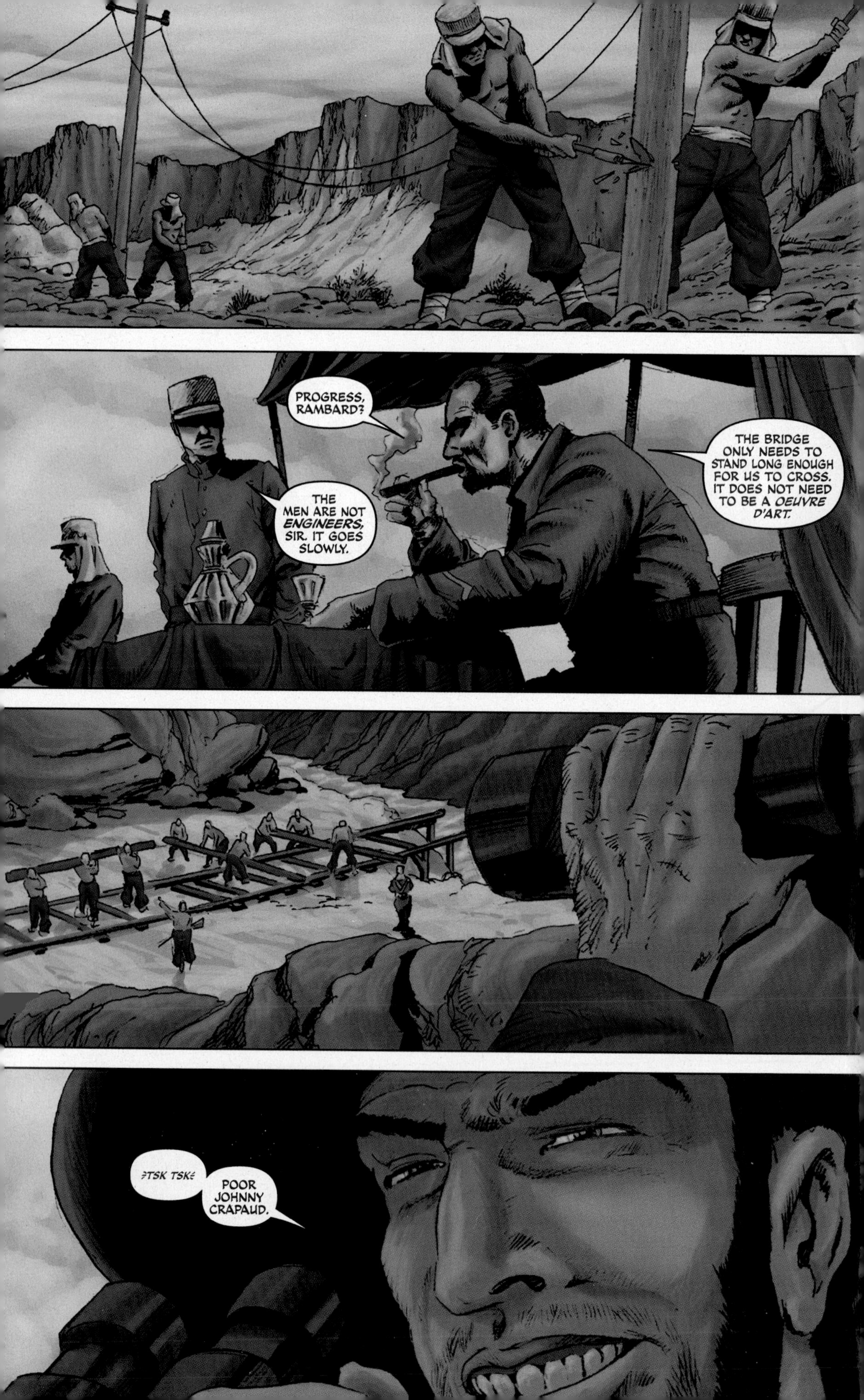
PROGRESS, RAMBARD?
THE MEN ARE NOT ENGINEERS, SIR. IT GOES SLOWLY.
THE BRIDGE ONLY NEEDS TO STAND LONG ENOUGH FOR US TO CROSS. IT DOES NOT NEED TO BE A OEUVRE D'ART.
TSK TSK
POOR JOHNNY CRAPAUD.

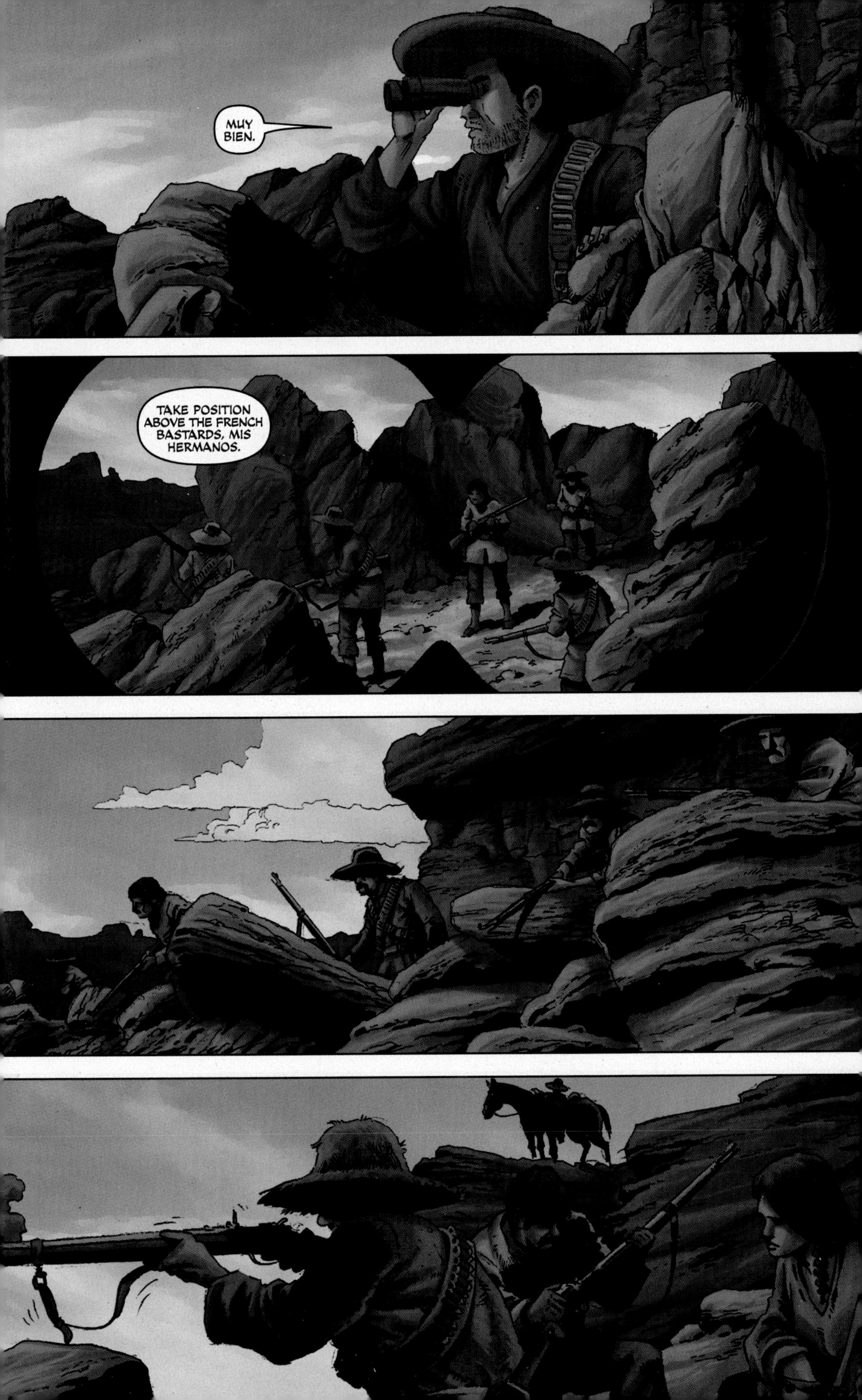
MUY BIEN.
TAKE POSITION ABOVE THE FRENCH BASTARDS, MIS HERMANOS.

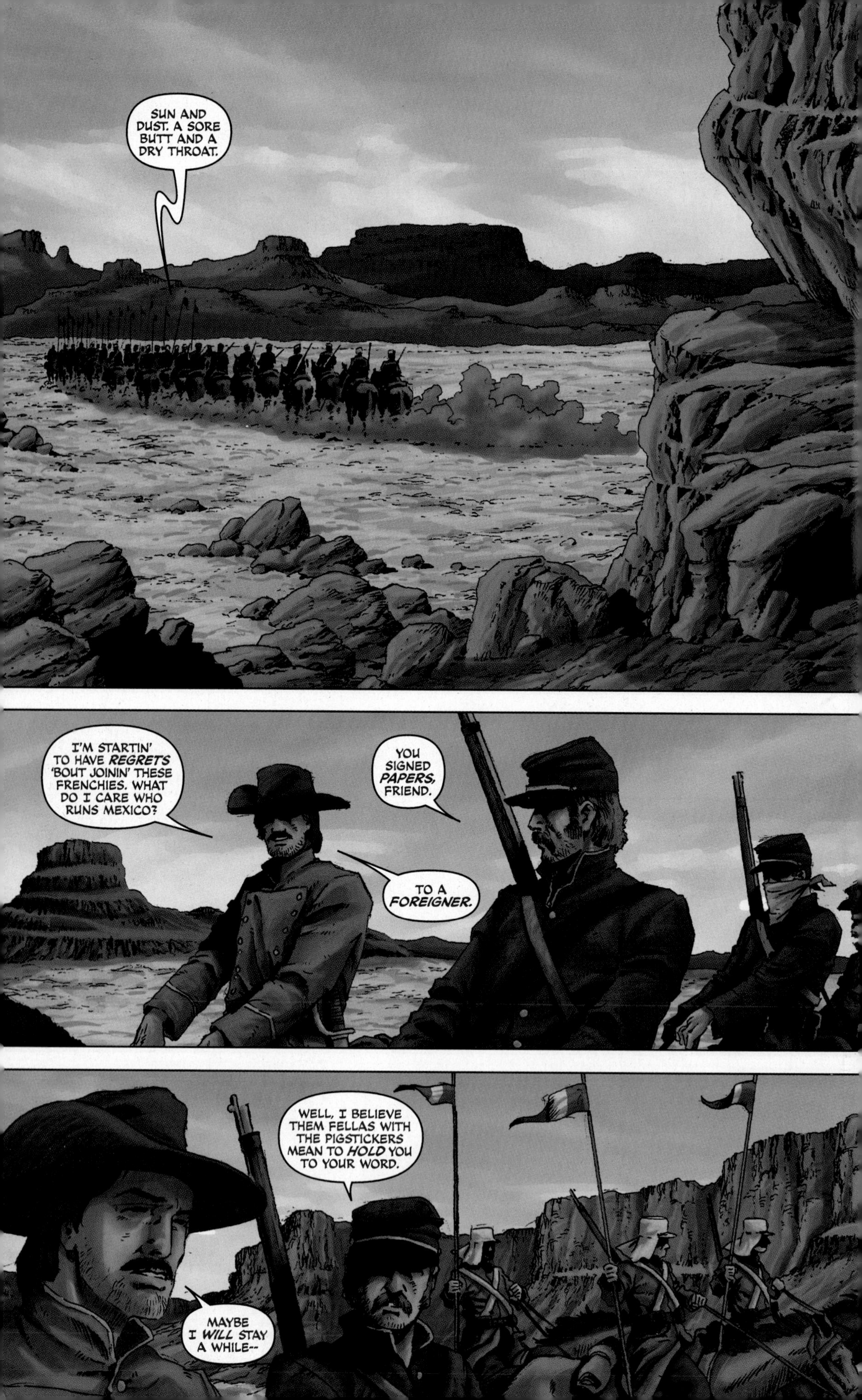
SUN AND DUST. A SORE BUTT AND A DRY THROAT.
I'M STARTIN' TO HAVE *REGRETS* 'BOUT JOININ' THESE FRENCHIES. WHAT DO I CARE WHO RUNS MEXICO?
YOU SIGNED *PAPERS,* FRIEND.
TO A *FOREIGNER.*
WELL, I BELIEVE THEM FELLAS WITH THE PIGSTICKERS MEAN TO *HOLD* YOU TO YOUR WORD.
MAYBE I *WILL* STAY A WHILE--

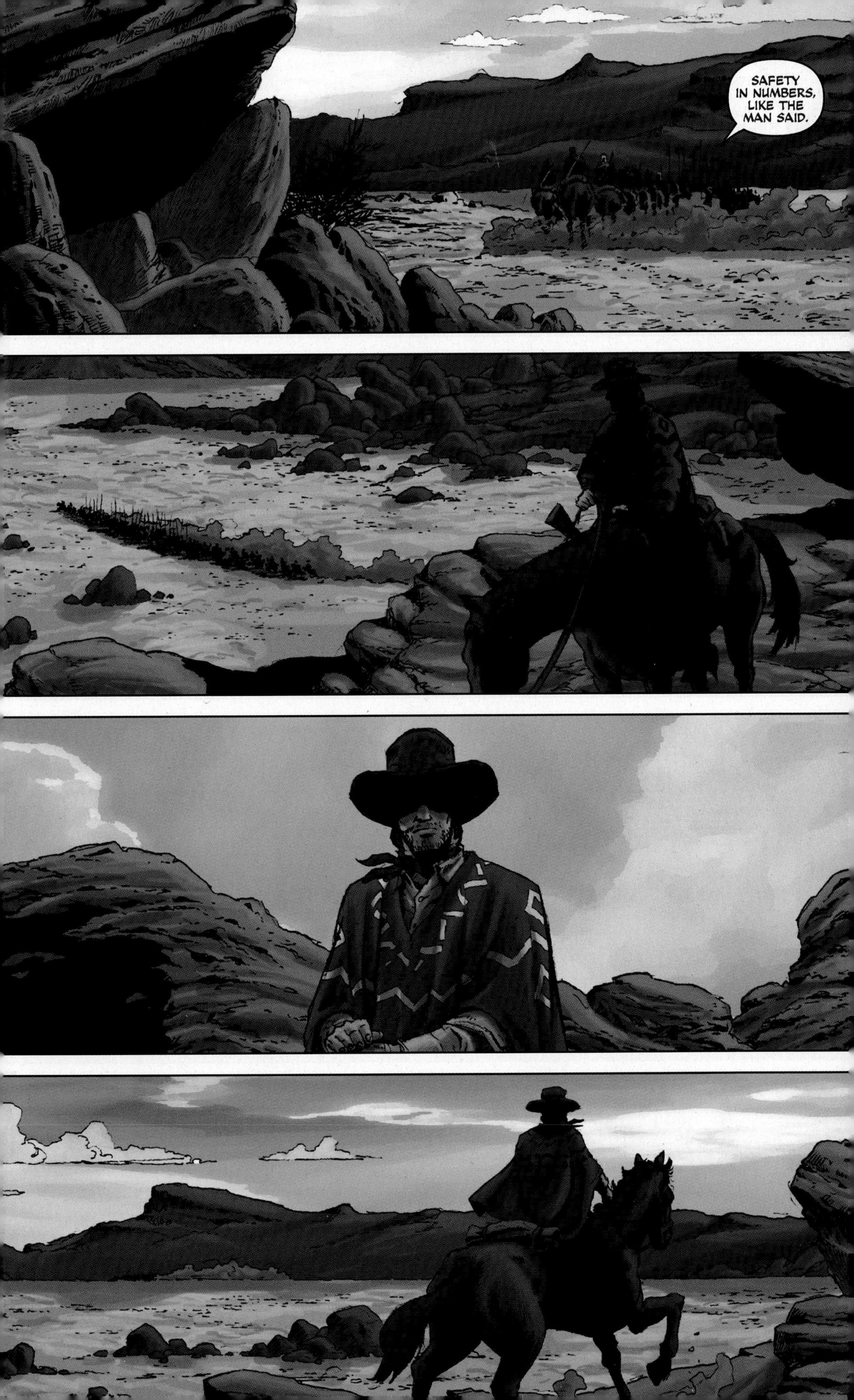
SAFETY IN NUMBERS, LIKE THE MAN SAID.

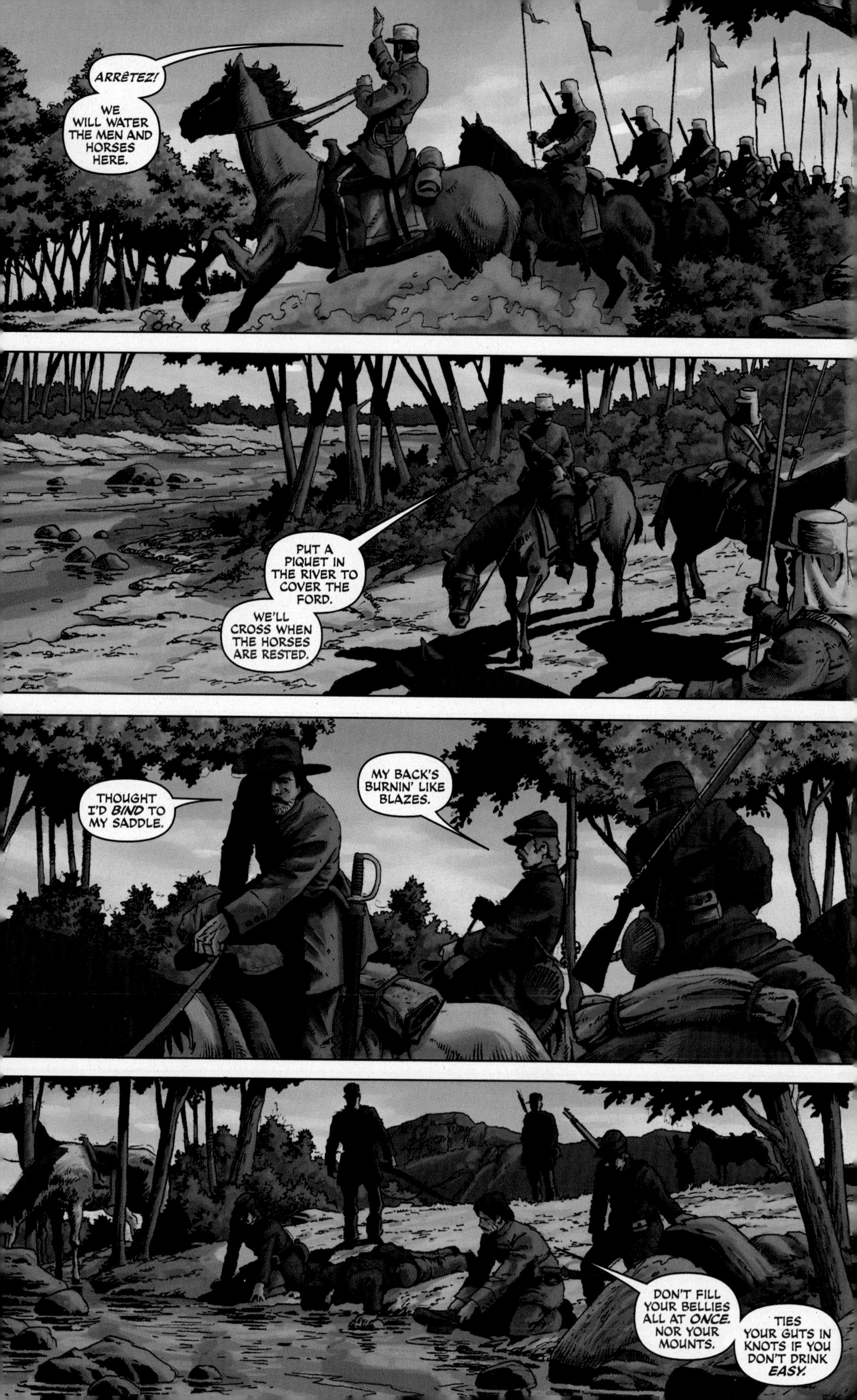
ARRÊTEZ!
WE WILL WATER THE MEN AND HORSES HERE.
PUT A PIQUET IN THE RIVER TO COVER THE FORD.
WE'LL CROSS WHEN THE HORSES ARE RESTED.
THOUGHT I'D *BIND* TO MY SADDLE.
MY BACK'S BURNIN' LIKE BLAZES.
DON'T FILL YOUR BELLIES ALL AT *ONCE.* NOR YOUR MOUNTS.
TIES YOUR GUTS IN KNOTS IF YOU DON'T DRINK *EASY.*

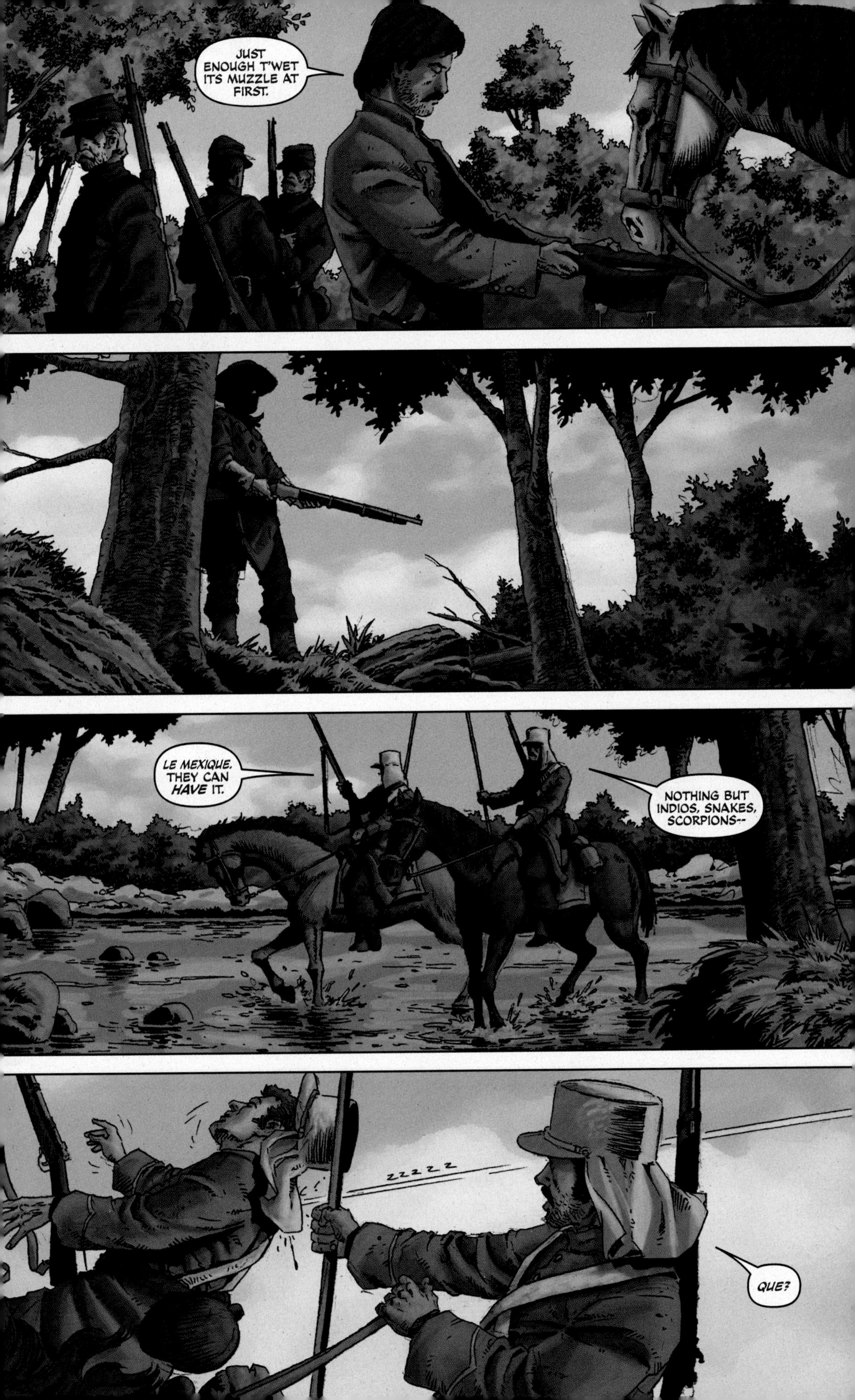
JUST ENOUGH T'WET ITS MUZZLE AT FIRST.
LE MEXIQUE. THEY CAN *HAVE* IT.
NOTHING BUT INDIOS, SNAKES, SCORPIONS--
ZZZZZ
QUE?

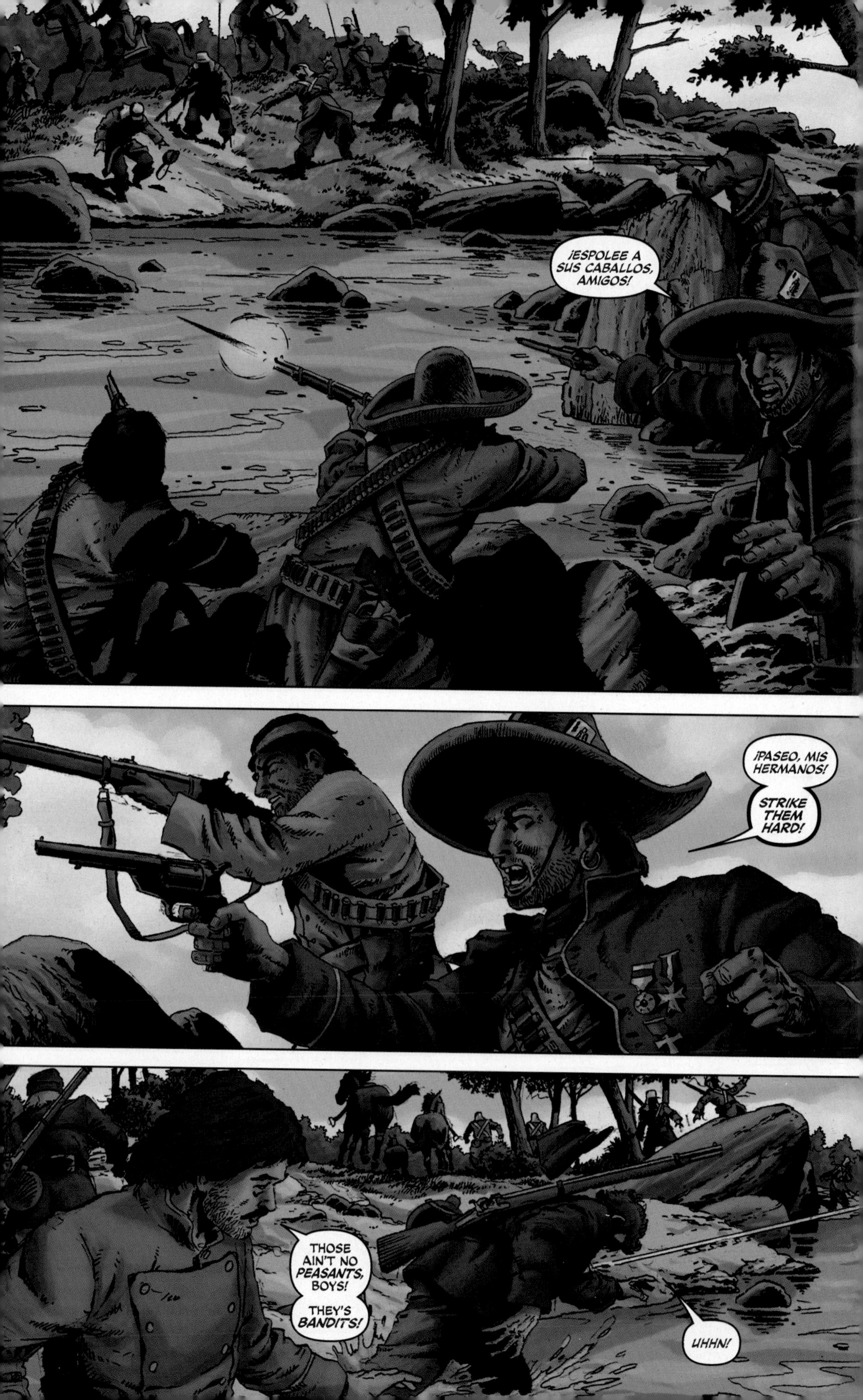
¡ESPOLEE A SUS CABALLOS, AMIGOS!
¡PASEO, MIS HERMANOS!
STRIKE THEM HARD!
THOSE AIN'T NO PEASANTS, BOYS!
THEY'S BANDITS!
UHHN!

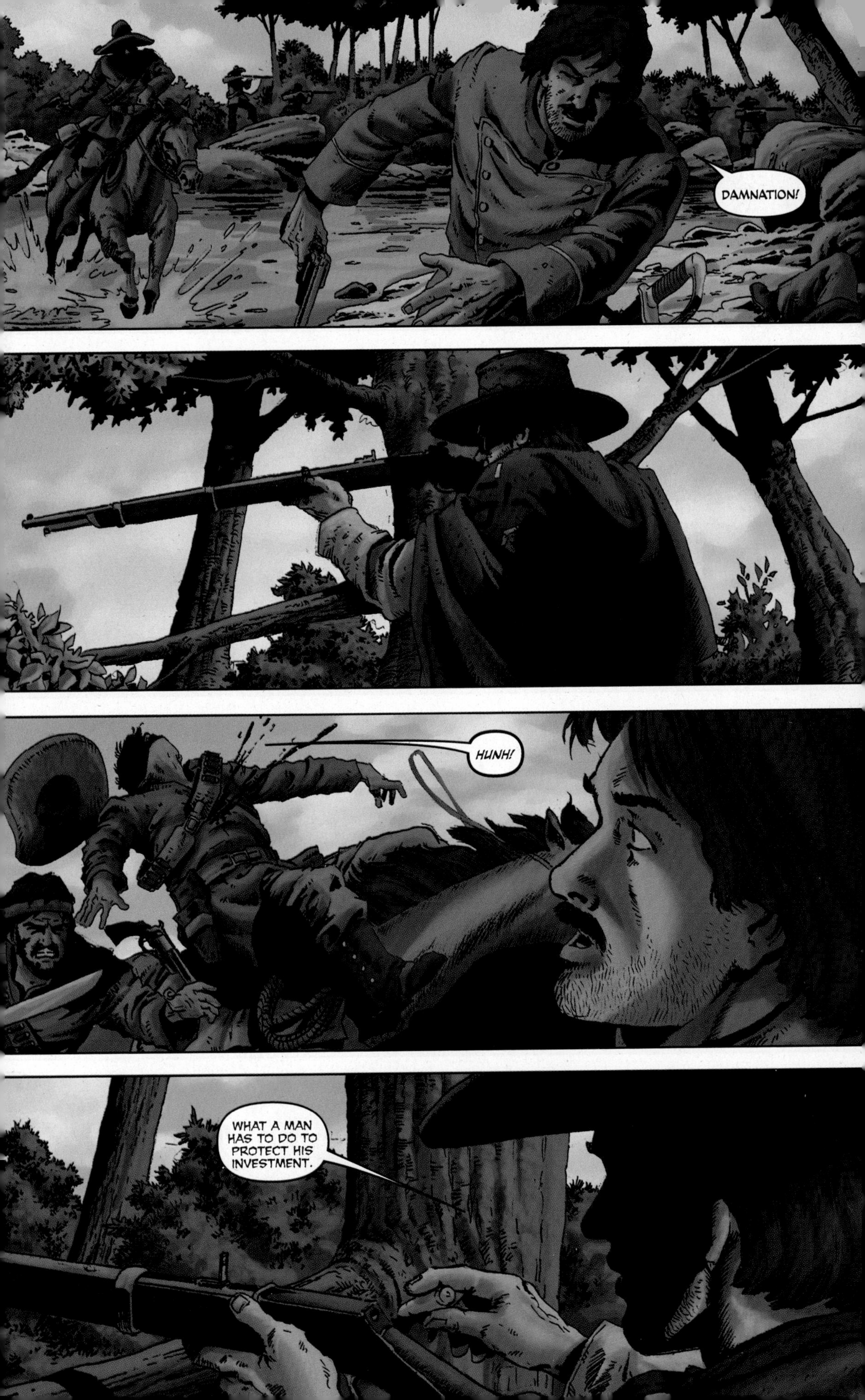
DAMNATION!
HUNH!
WHAT A MAN HAS TO DO TO PROTECT HIS INVESTMENT.

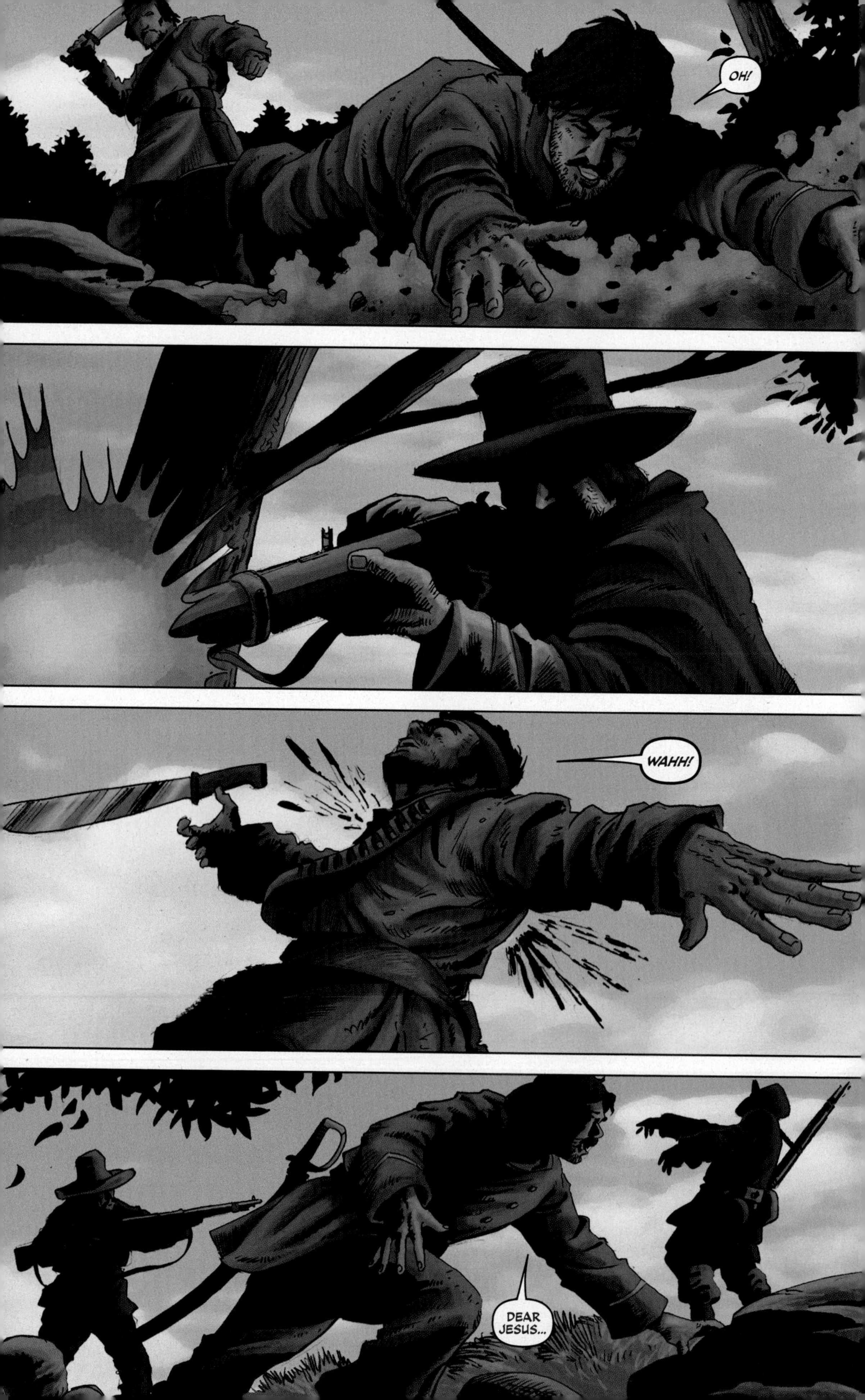
OH!
WAHH!
DEAR JESUS...

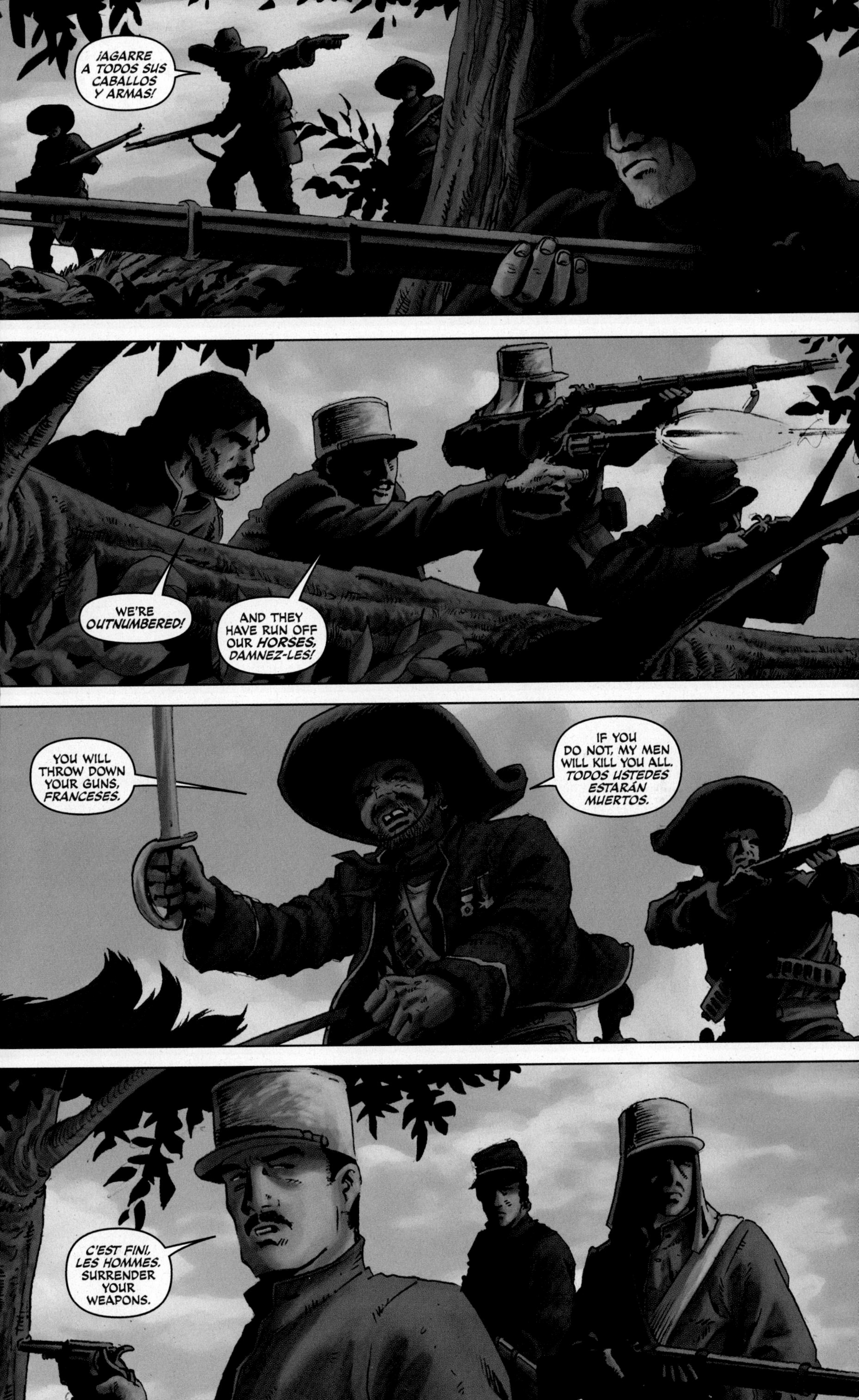
¡AGARRE A TODOS SUS CABALLOS Y ARMAS!
WE'RE OUTNUMBERED!
AND THEY HAVE RUN OFF OUR HORSES, DAMNEZ-LES!
YOU WILL THROW DOWN YOUR GUNS, FRANCESES.
IF YOU DO NOT, MY MEN WILL KILL YOU ALL. TODOS USTEDES ESTARÁN MUERTOS.
C'EST FINI, LES HOMMES. SURRENDER YOUR WEAPONS.

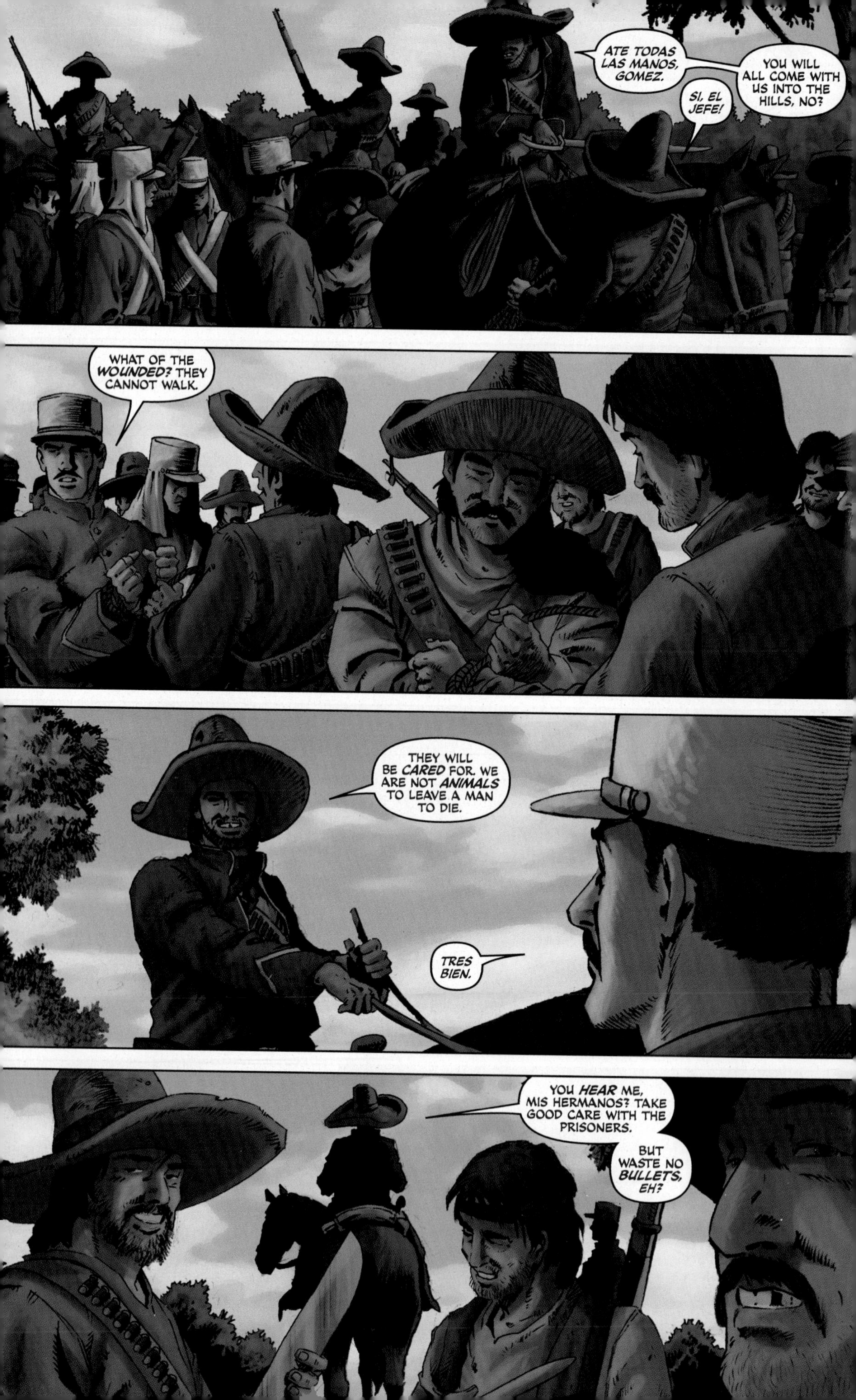
ATE TODAS LAS MANOS, GOMEZ.
SI, EL JEFE!
YOU WILL ALL COME WITH US INTO THE HILLS, NO?
WHAT OF THE WOUNDED? THEY CANNOT WALK.
THEY WILL BE CARED FOR. WE ARE NOT ANIMALS TO LEAVE A MAN TO DIE.
TRES BIEN.
YOU HEAR ME, MIS HERMANOS? TAKE GOOD CARE WITH THE PRISONERS.
BUT WASTE NO BULLETS, EH?

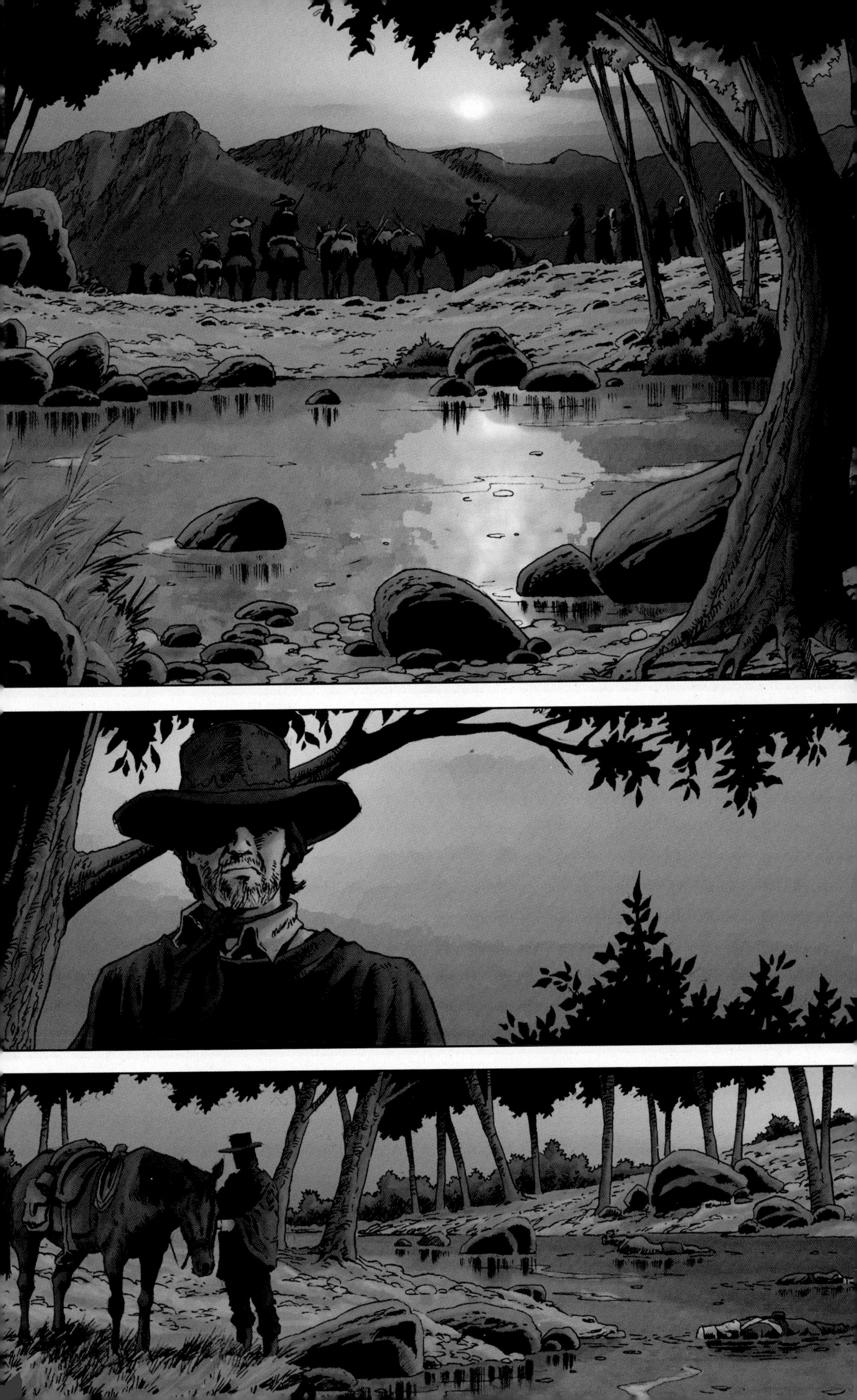

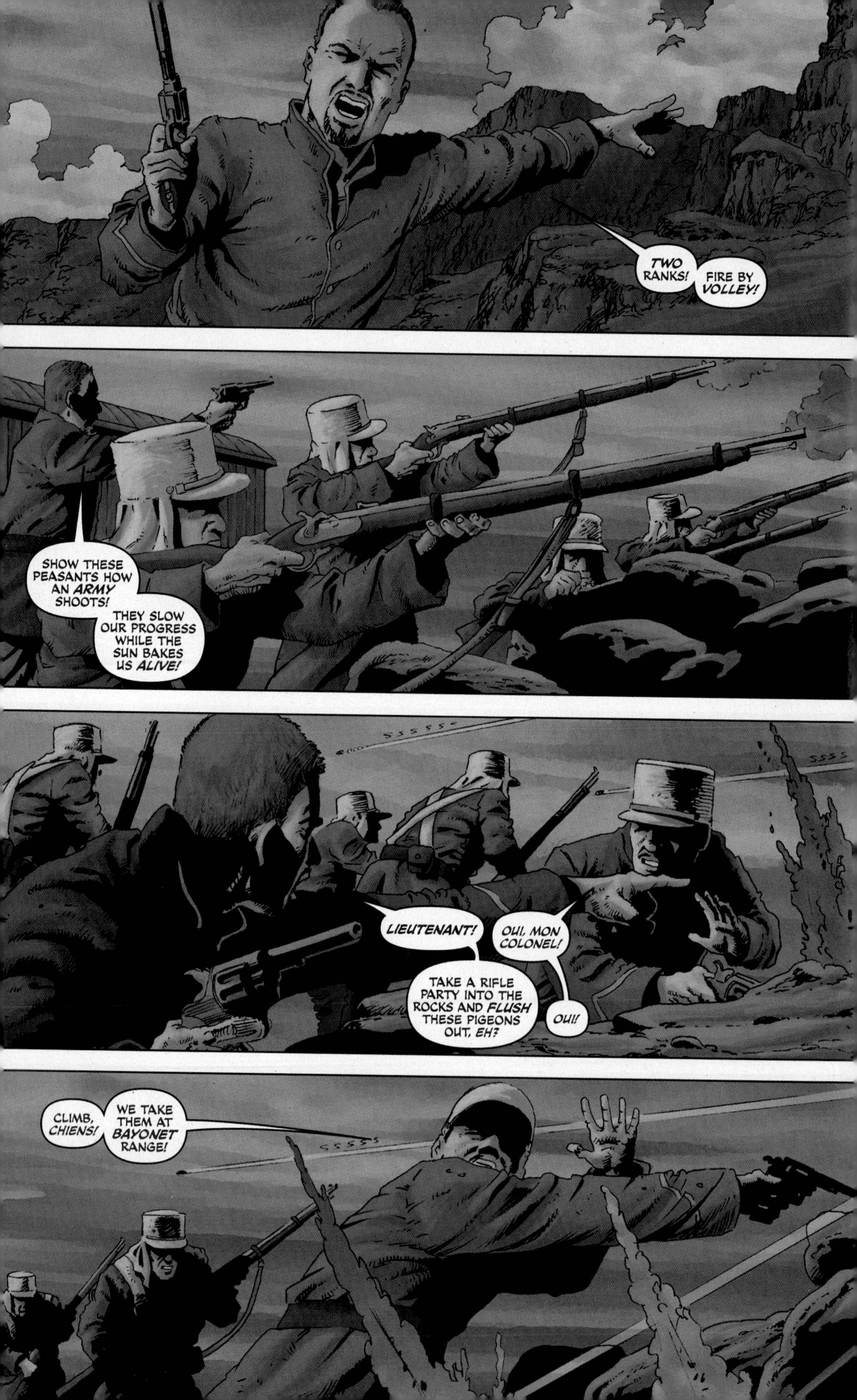
TWO RANKS!
FIRE BY VOLLEY!
SHOW THESE PEASANTS HOW AN ARMY SHOOTS!
THEY SLOW OUR PROGRESS WHILE THE SUN BAKES US ALIVE!
LIEUTENANT!
OUI, MON COLONEL!
TAKE A RIFLE PARTY INTO THE ROCKS AND FLUSH THESE PIGEONS OUT, EH?
OUI!
CLIMB, CHIENS!
WE TAKE THEM AT BAYONET RANGE!

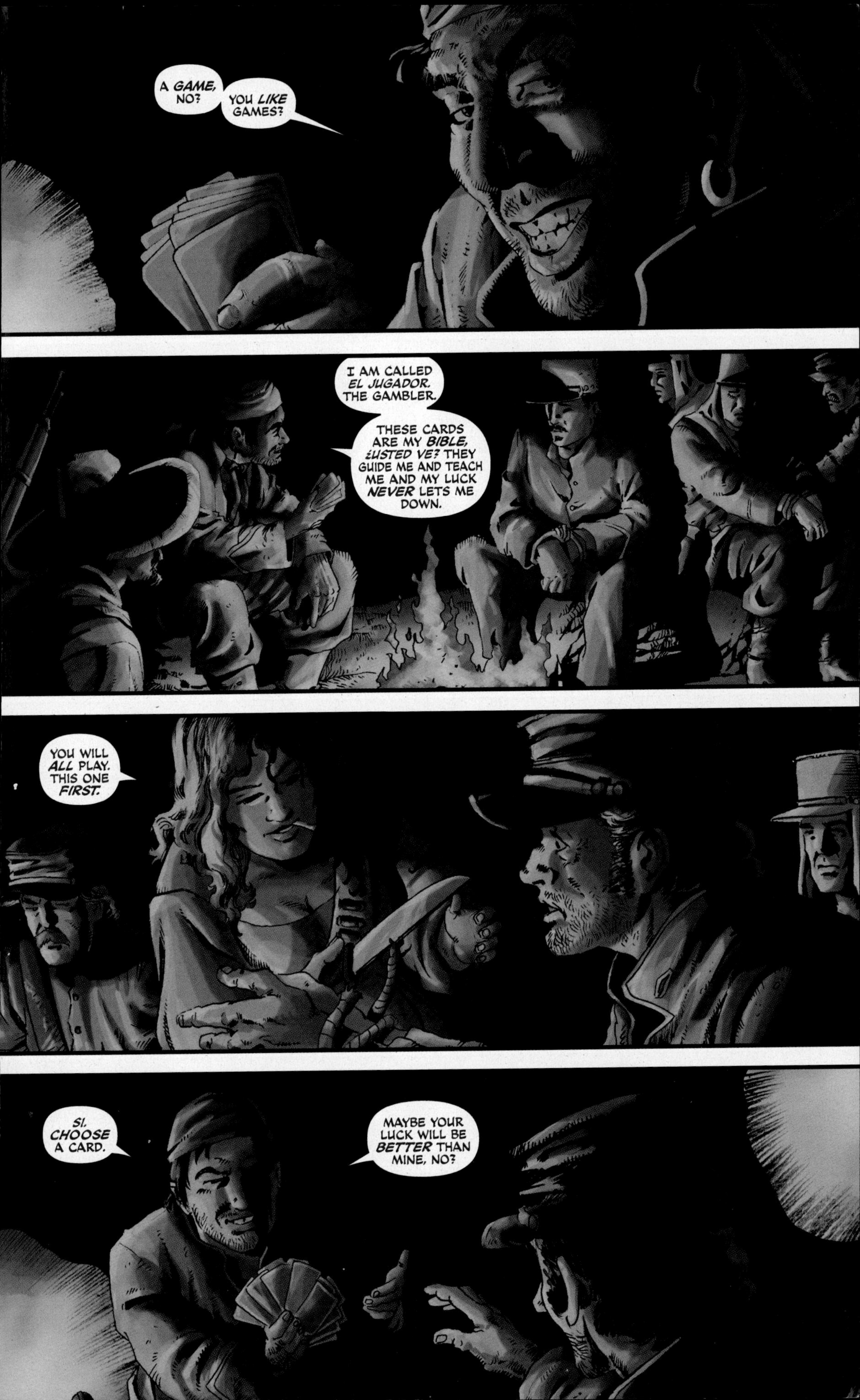
A GAME, NO?
YOU LIKE GAMES?
I AM CALLED EL JUGADOR. THE GAMBLER.
THESE CARDS ARE MY BIBLE, ¿USTED VE? THEY GUIDE ME AND TEACH ME AND MY LUCK NEVER LETS ME DOWN.
YOU WILL ALL PLAY. THIS ONE FIRST.
SI. CHOOSE A CARD.
MAYBE YOUR LUCK WILL BE BETTER THAN MINE, NO?

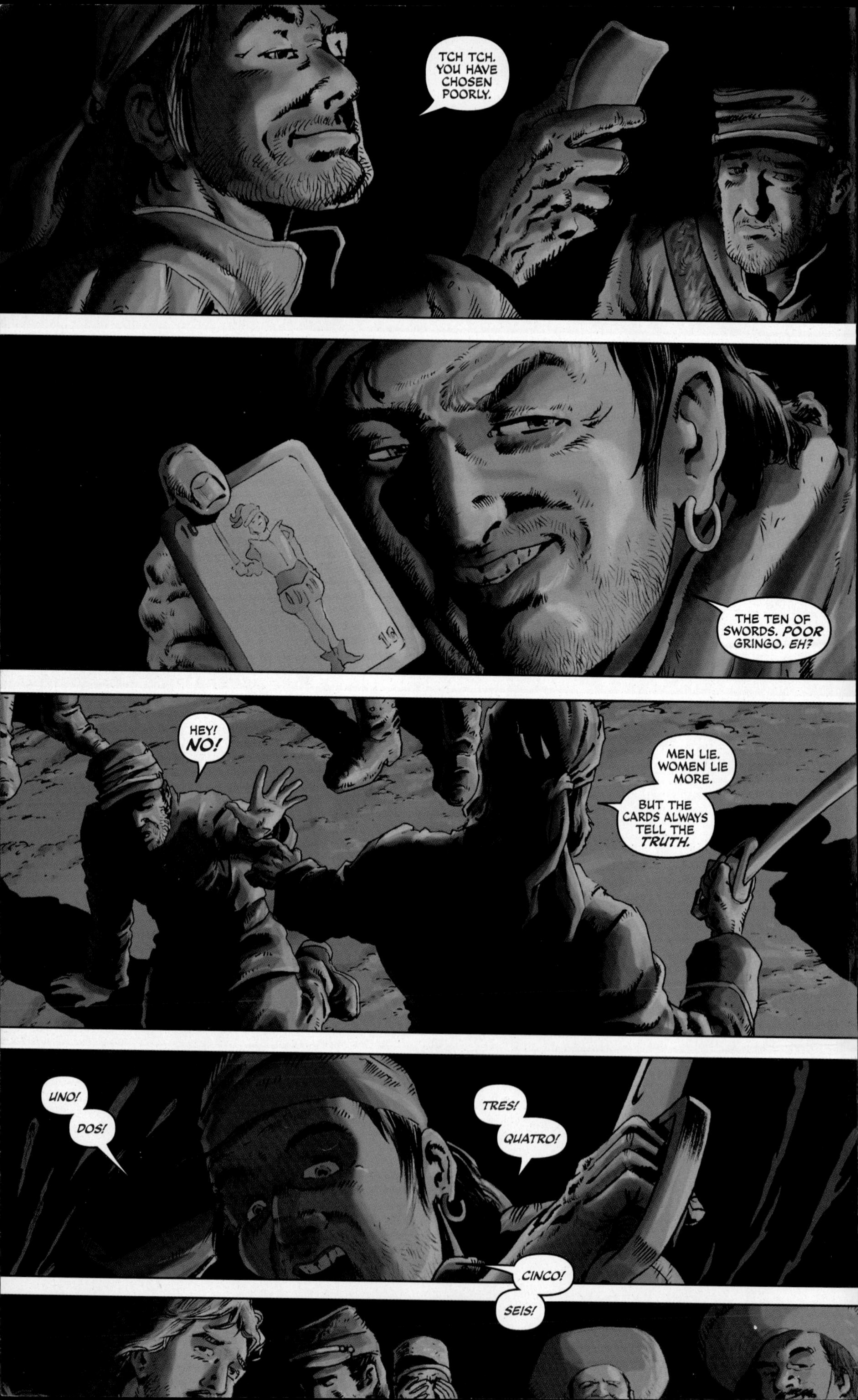
TCH TCH. YOU HAVE CHOSEN POORLY.
THE TEN OF SWORDS. *POOR* GRINGO, *EH?*
HEY! **NO!**
MEN LIE. WOMEN LIE MORE.
BUT THE CARDS ALWAYS TELL THE *TRUTH.*
UNO!
DOS!
TRES!
QUATRO!
CINCO!
SEIS!

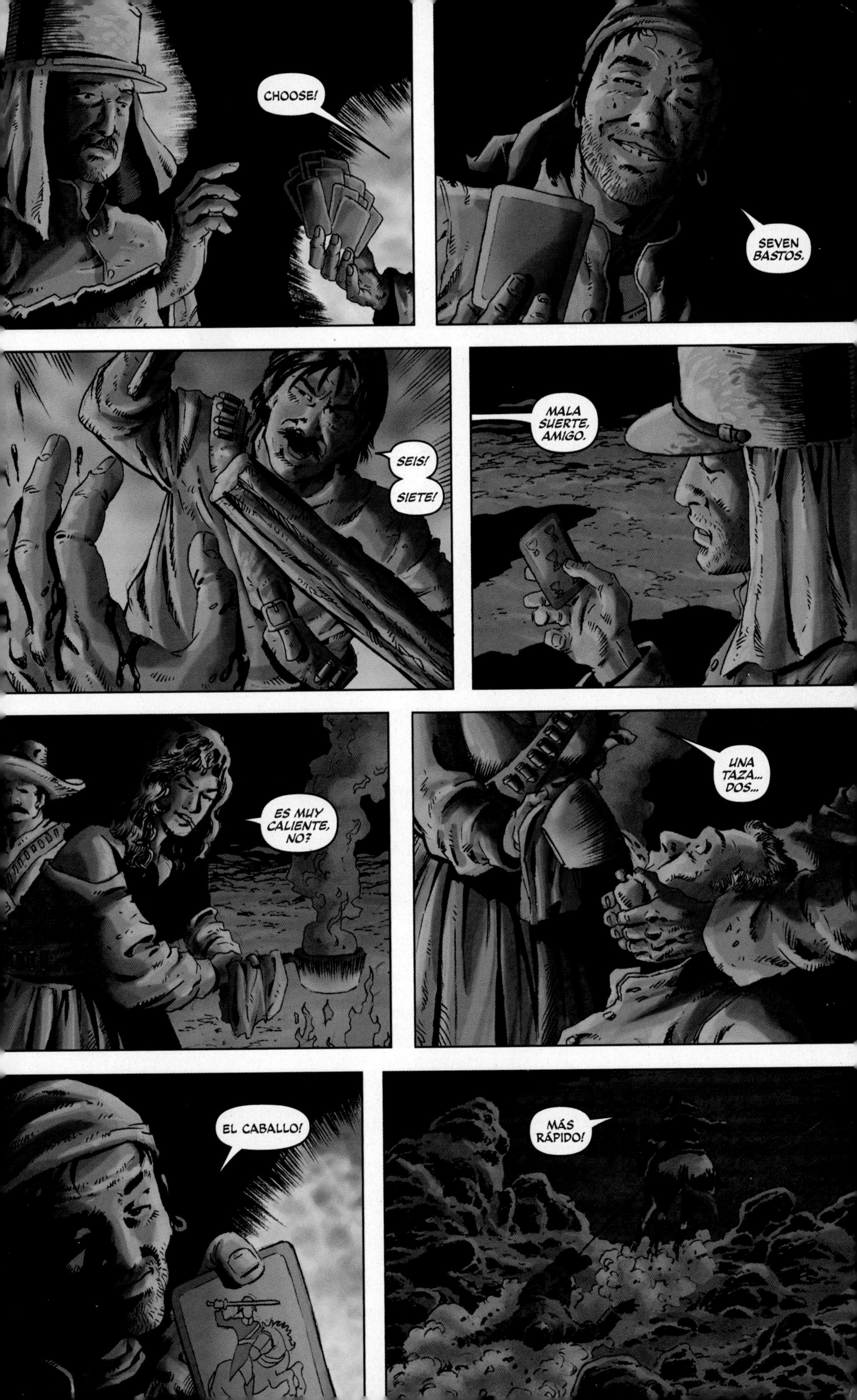
CHOOSE!
SEVEN BASTOS.
SEIS!
SIETE!
MALA SUERTE, AMIGO.
ES MUY CALIENTE, NO?
UNA TAZA... DOS...
EL CABALLO!
MÁS RÁPIDO!

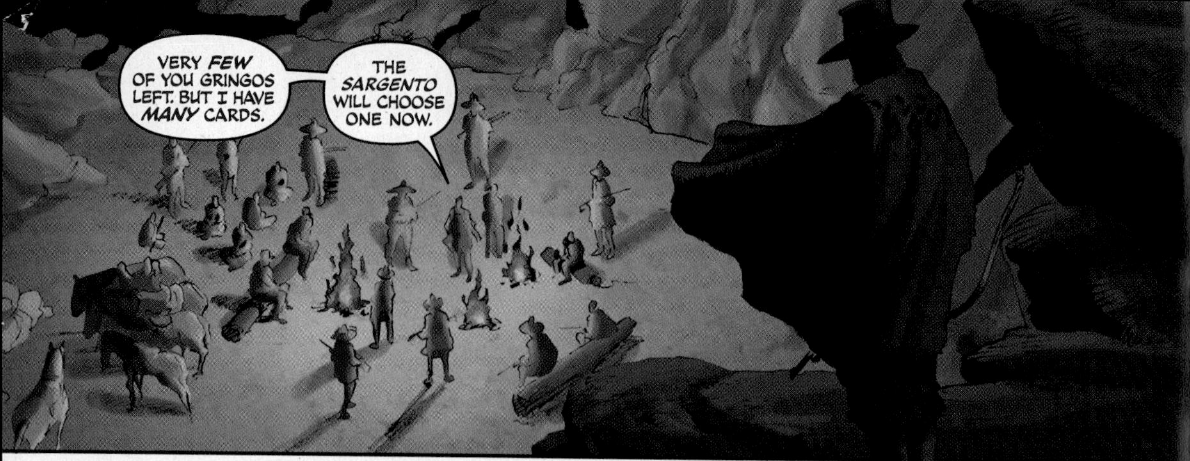
VERY *FEW* OF YOU GRINGOS LEFT. BUT I HAVE *MANY* CARDS.
THE *SARGENTO* WILL CHOOSE ONE NOW.

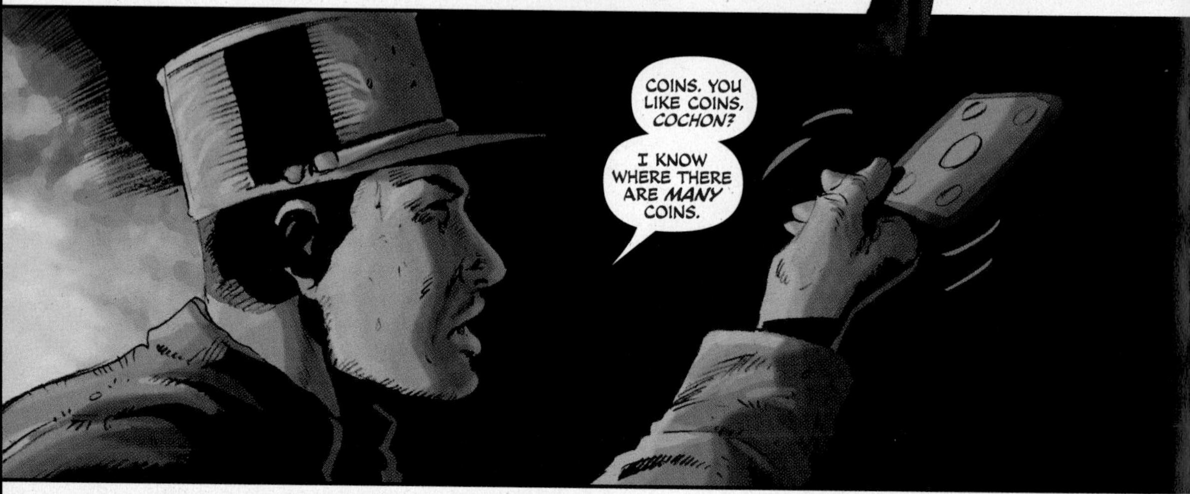
COINS. YOU LIKE COINS, *COCHON?*
I KNOW WHERE THERE ARE *MANY* COINS.

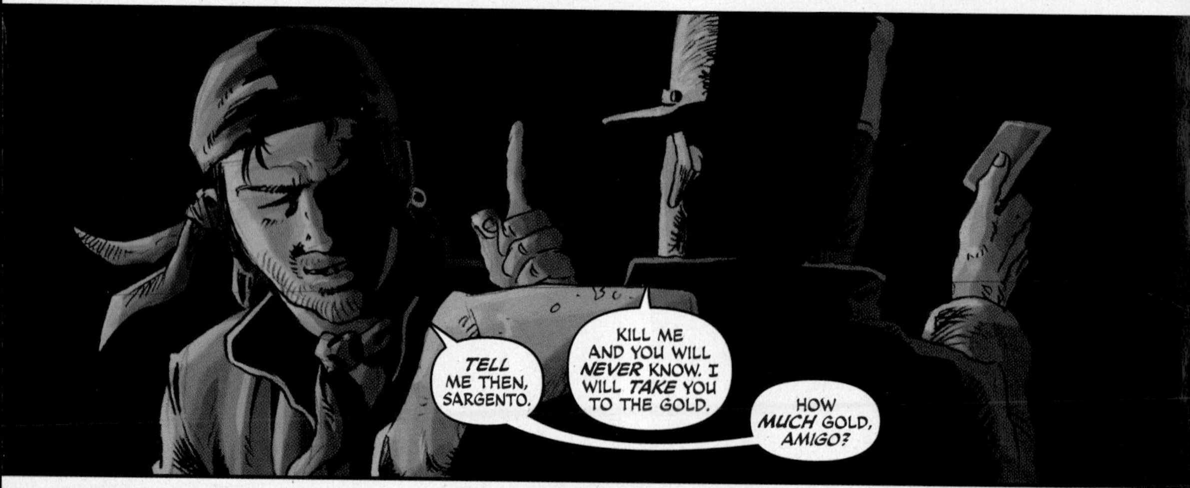
KILL ME AND YOU WILL ***NEVER*** KNOW. I WILL *TAKE* YOU TO THE GOLD.
TELL ME THEN, SARGENTO.
HOW *MUCH* GOLD, *AMIGO?*

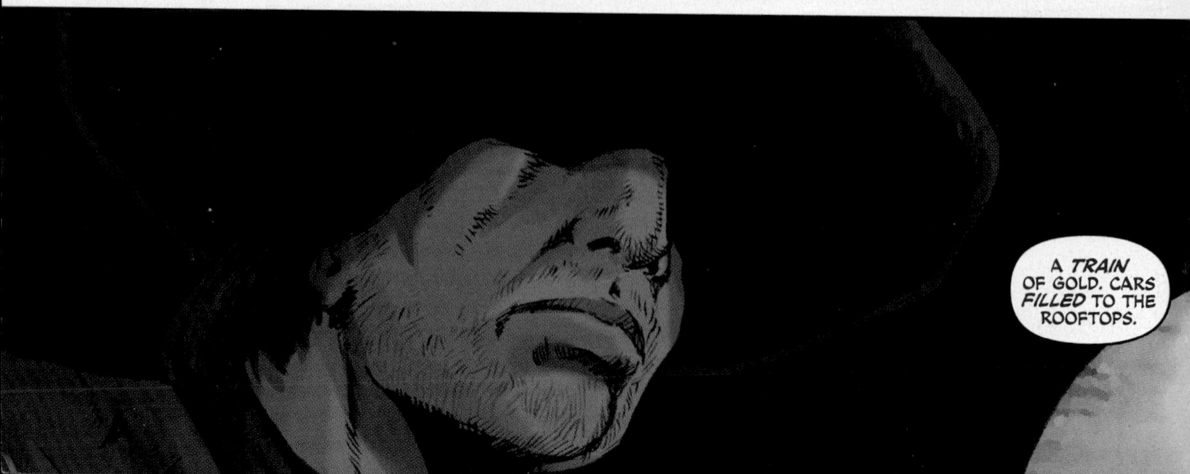
A *TRAIN* OF GOLD. CARS *FILLED* TO THE ROOFTOPS.

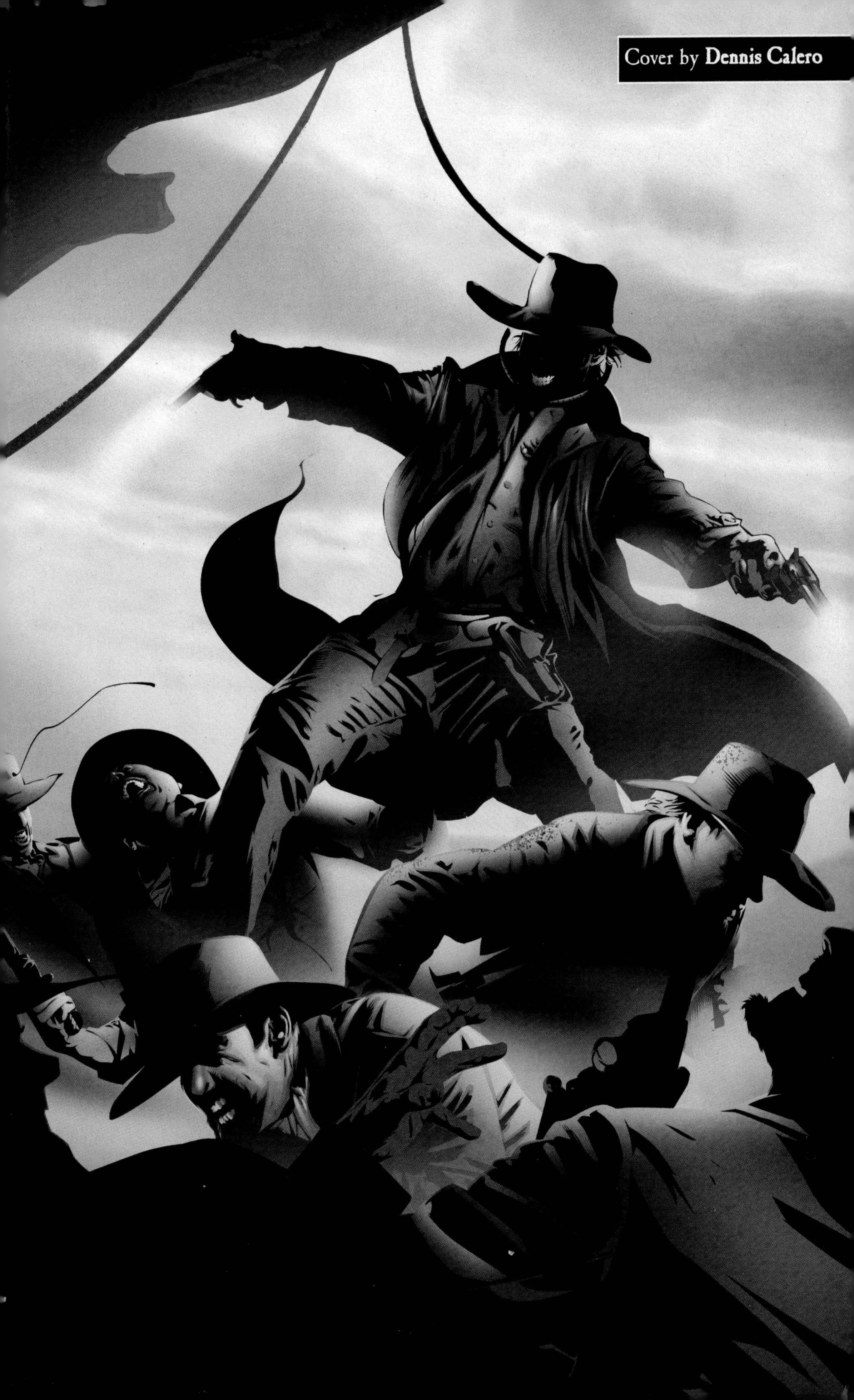
Cover by **Dennis Calero**

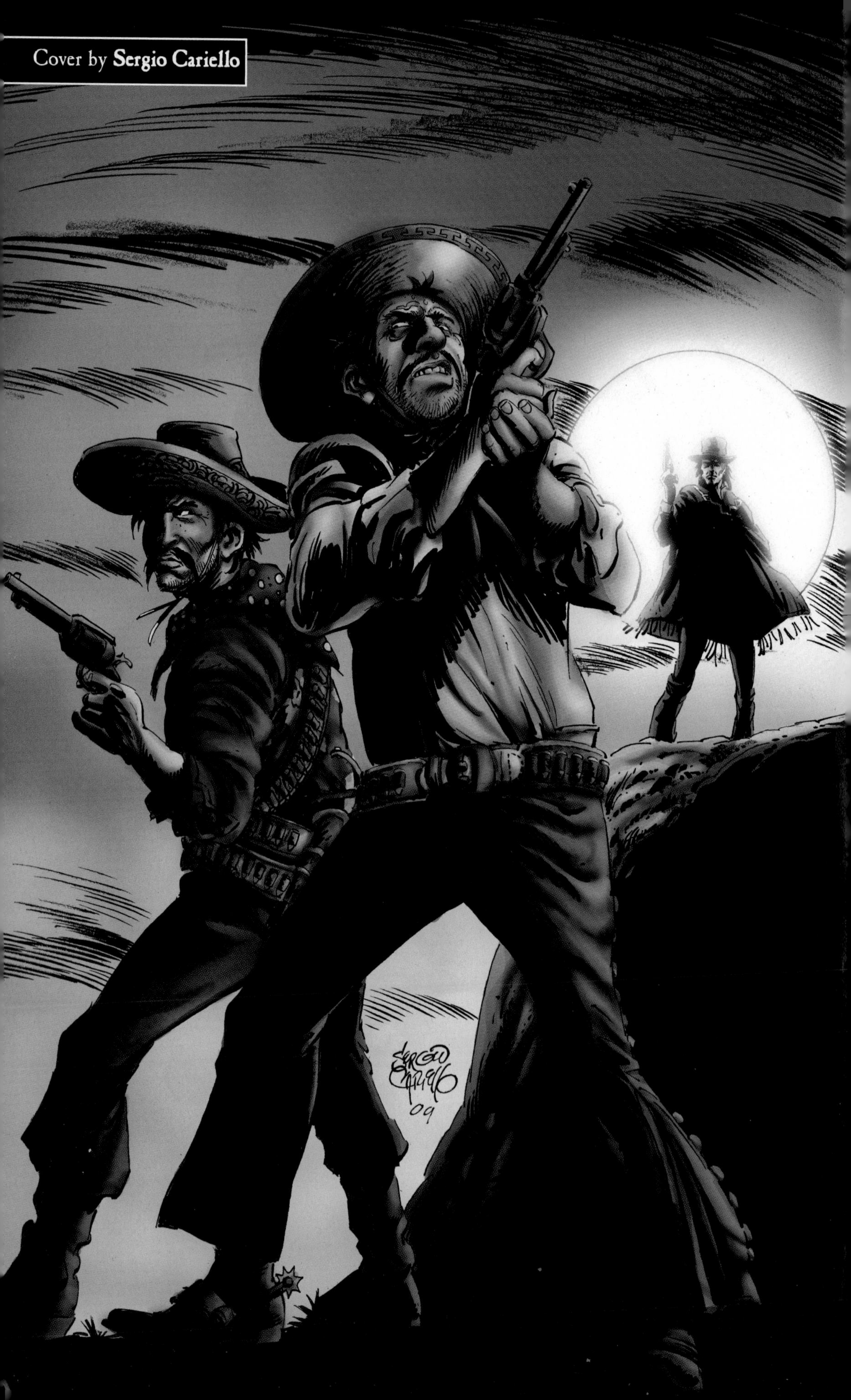

Cover by **Sergio Cariello**

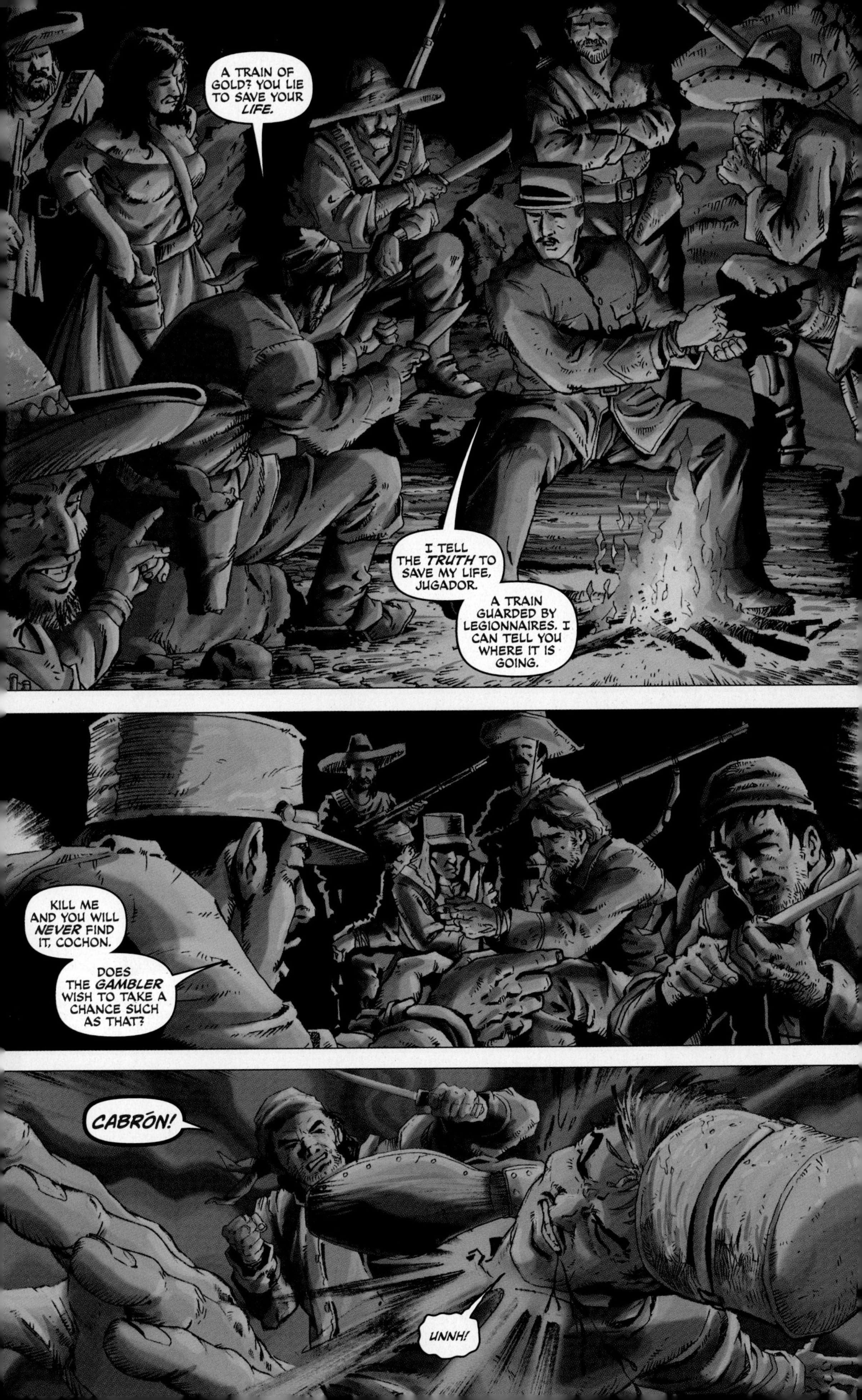
A TRAIN OF GOLD? YOU LIE TO SAVE YOUR *LIFE.*
I TELL THE *TRUTH* TO SAVE MY LIFE, JUGADOR.
A TRAIN GUARDED BY LEGIONNAIRES. I CAN TELL YOU WHERE IT IS GOING.
KILL ME AND YOU WILL *NEVER* FIND IT, COCHON.
DOES THE *GAMBLER* WISH TO TAKE A CHANCE SUCH AS THAT?
CABRÓN!
UNNH!

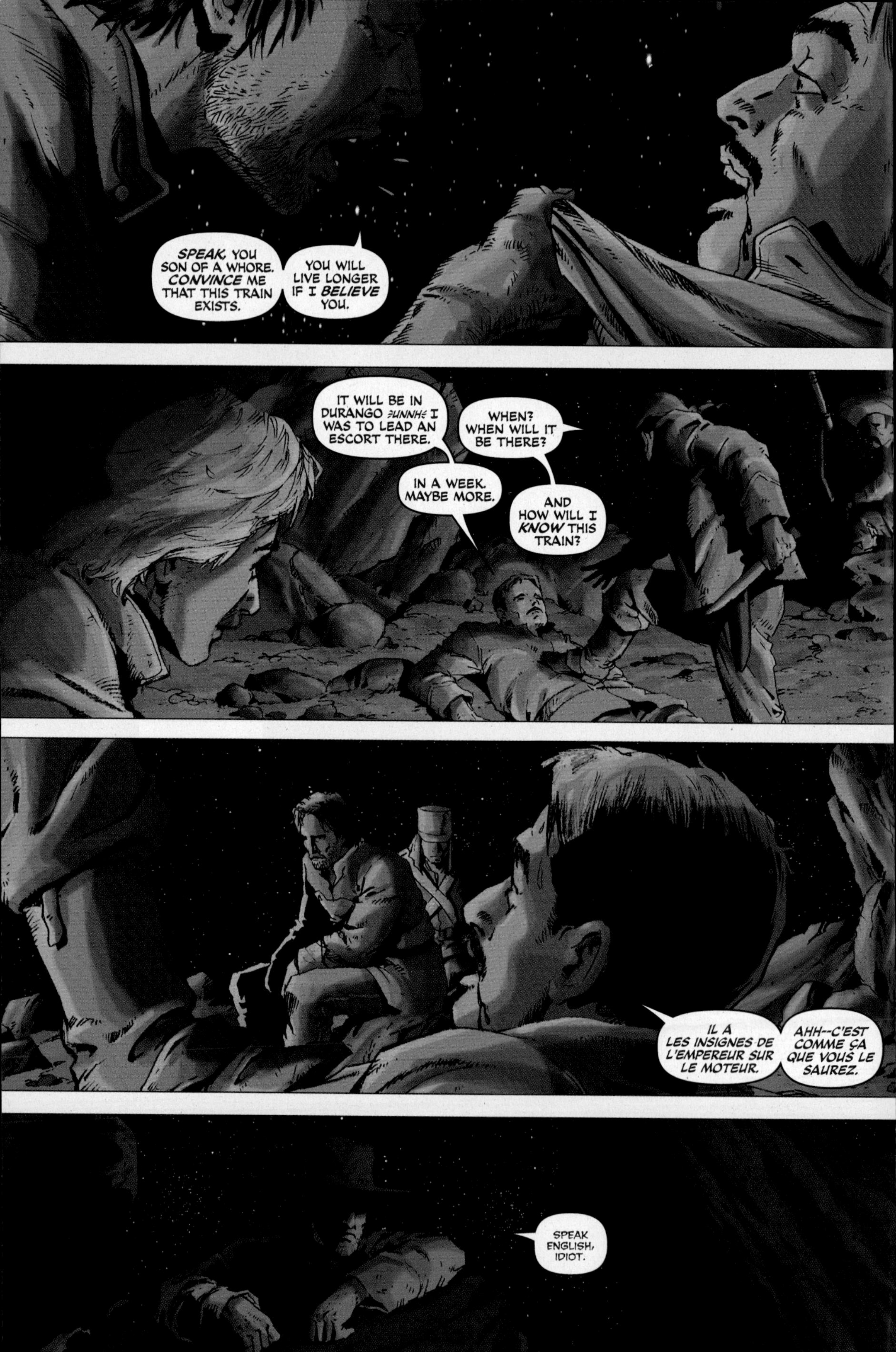

SPEAK, YOU SON OF A WHORE. *CONVINCE* ME THAT THIS TRAIN EXISTS.
YOU WILL LIVE LONGER IF I *BELIEVE* YOU.
IT WILL BE IN DURANGO *UNNH* I WAS TO LEAD AN ESCORT THERE.
IN A WEEK. MAYBE MORE.
WHEN? WHEN WILL IT BE THERE?
AND HOW WILL I *KNOW* THIS TRAIN?
IL A LES INSIGNES DE L'EMPEREUR SUR LE MOTEUR.
AHH--C'EST COMME ÇA QUE VOUS LE SAUREZ.
SPEAK ENGLISH, IDIOT.

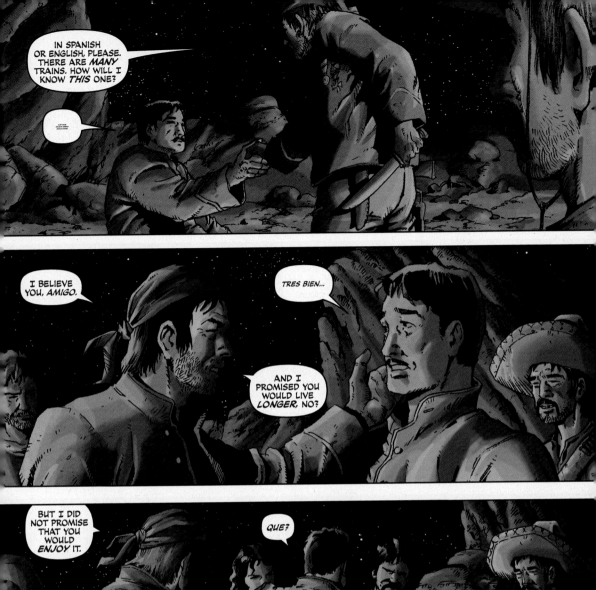

IN SPANISH OR ENGLISH, PLEASE. THERE ARE *MANY* TRAINS. HOW WILL I KNOW *THIS* ONE?

I BELIEVE YOU, *AMIGO.*

TRES BIEN...

AND I PROMISED YOU WOULD LIVE *LONGER*, NO?

BUT I DID NOT PROMISE THAT YOU WOULD *ENJOY* IT.

QUE?

BUT I *TOLD* YOU OF THE TRAIN! I MADE YOU *RICH*, YOU *COCHON!*

HA HA!

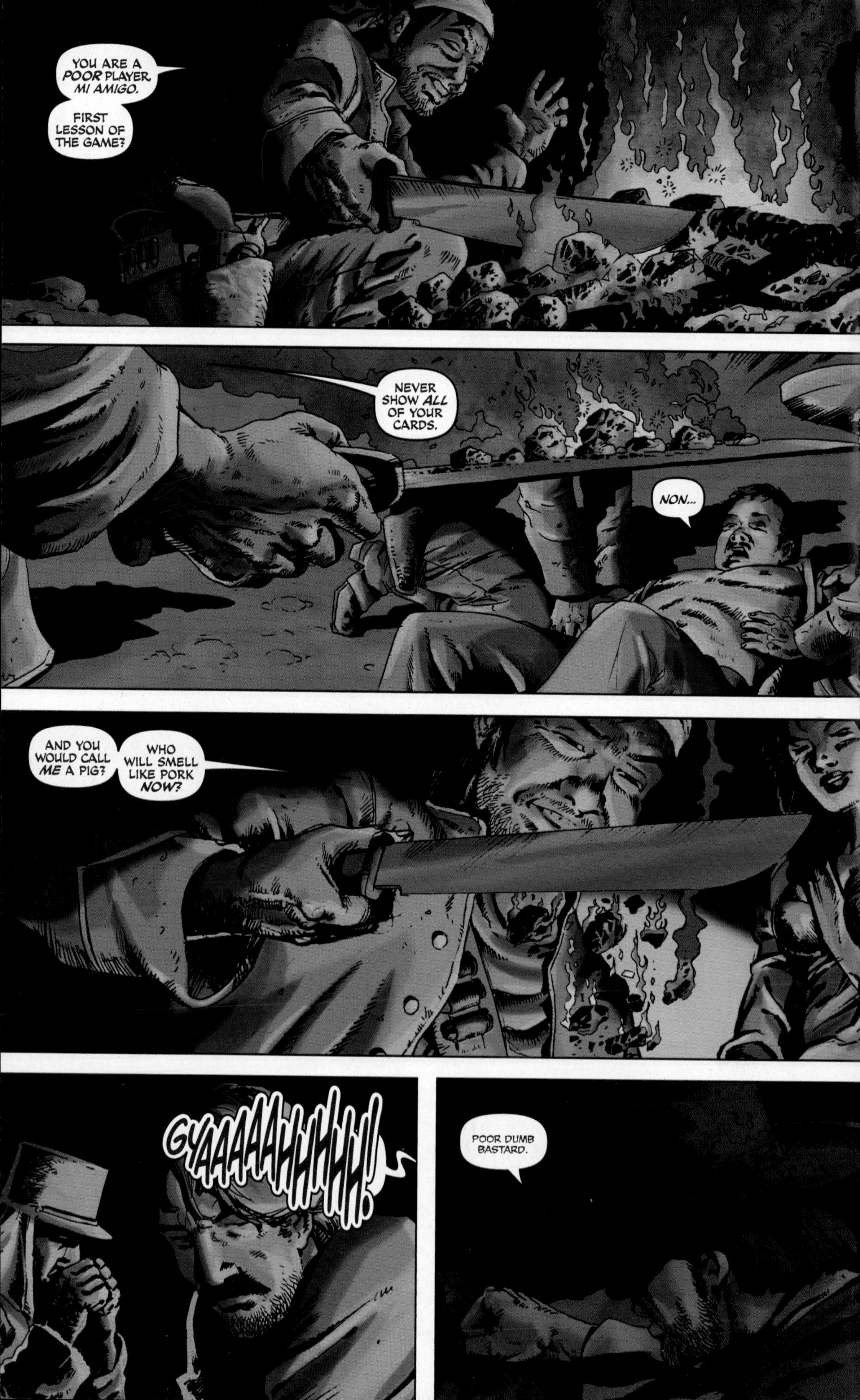
YOU ARE A POOR PLAYER, MI AMIGO.
FIRST LESSON OF THE GAME?
NEVER SHOW ALL OF YOUR CARDS.
NON...
AND YOU WOULD CALL ME A PIG?
WHO WILL SMELL LIKE PORK NOW?
GYAAAAAHHHHH!
POOR DUMB BASTARD.

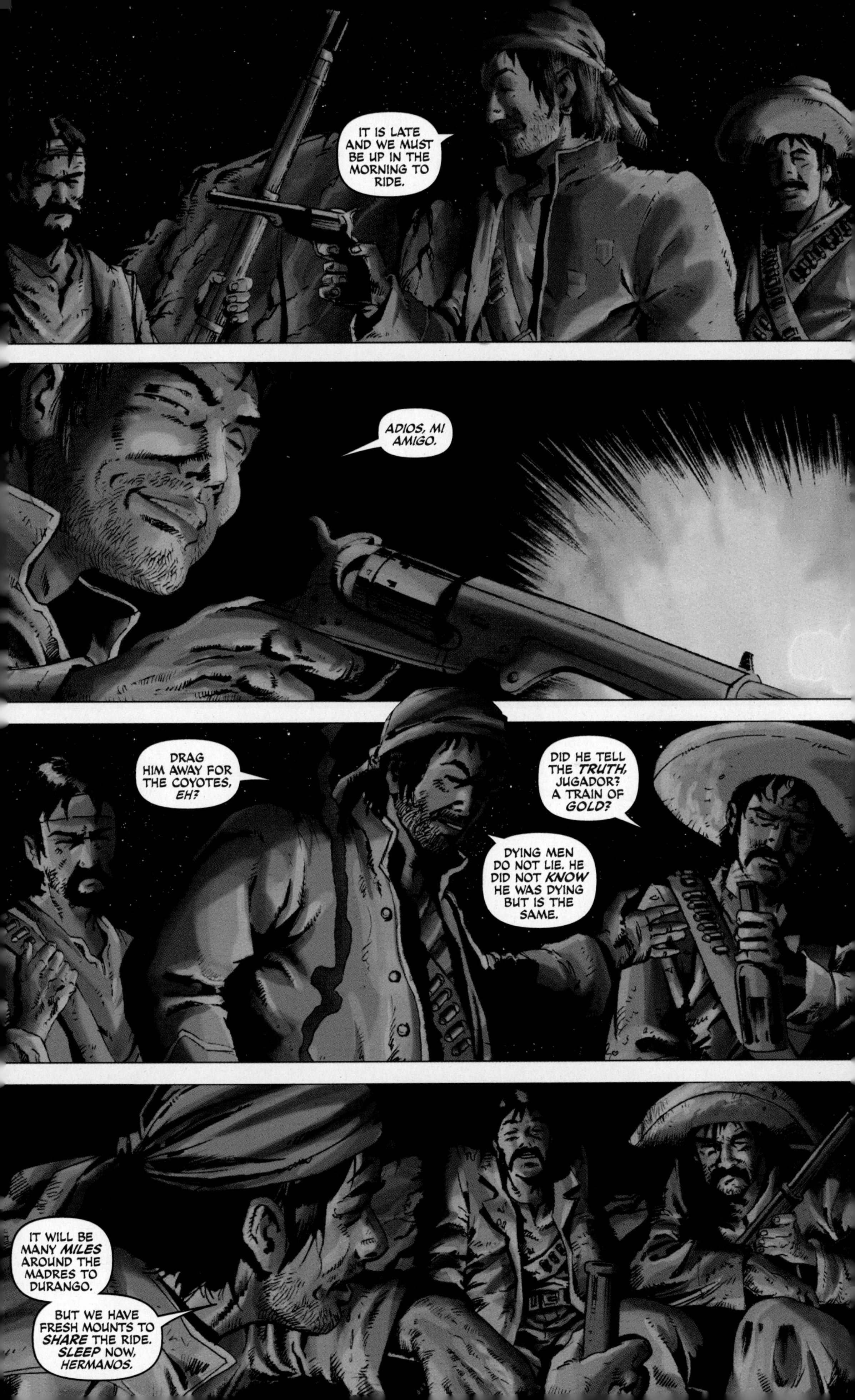
IT IS LATE AND WE MUST BE UP IN THE MORNING TO RIDE.
ADIOS, MI AMIGO.
DRAG HIM AWAY FOR THE COYOTES, EH?
DID HE TELL THE TRUTH, JUGADOR? A TRAIN OF GOLD?
DYING MEN DO NOT LIE. HE DID NOT KNOW HE WAS DYING BUT IS THE SAME.
IT WILL BE MANY MILES AROUND THE MADRES TO DURANGO.
BUT WE HAVE FRESH MOUNTS TO SHARE THE RIDE. SLEEP NOW, HERMANOS.

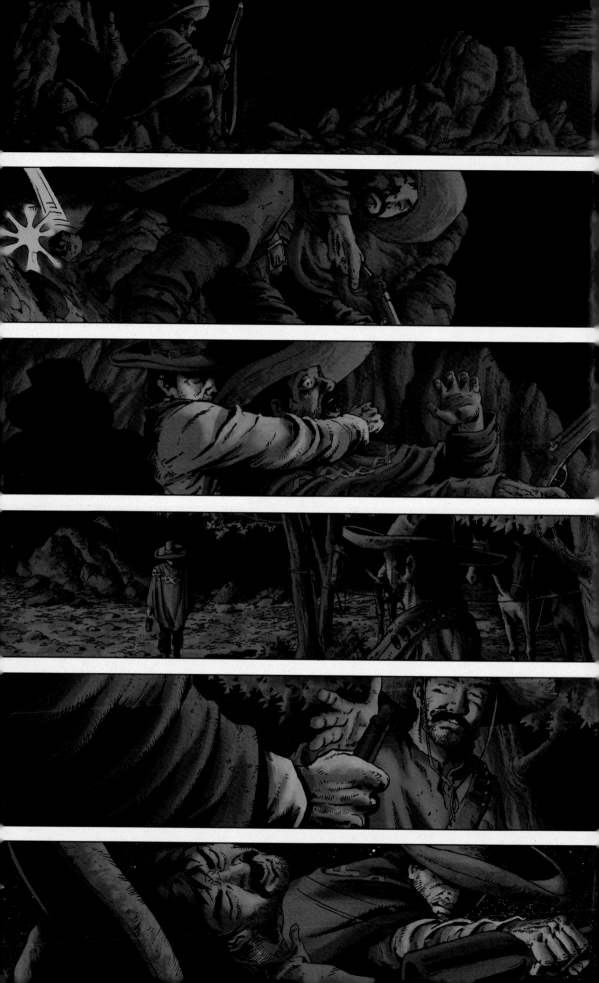

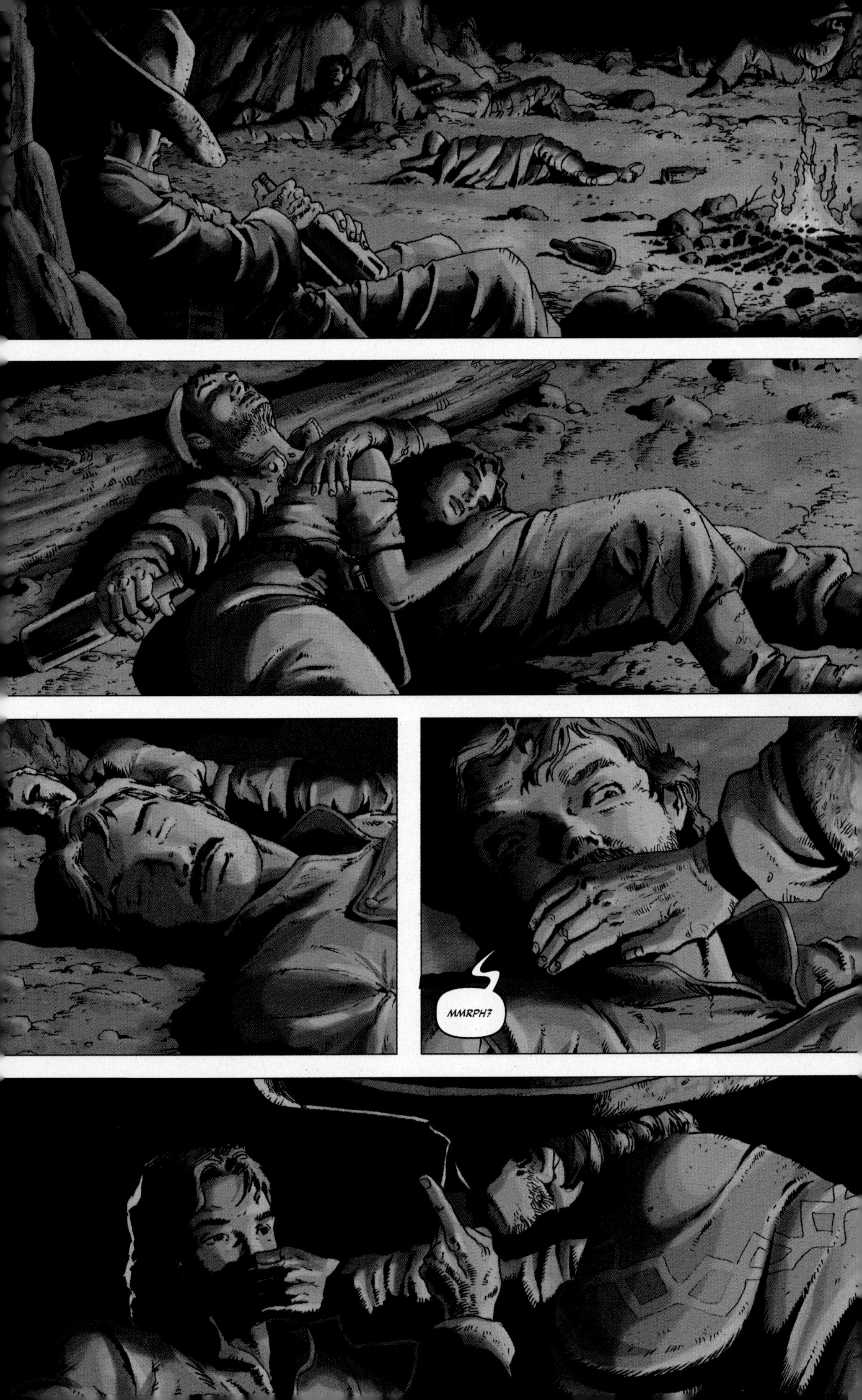
MMRPH?

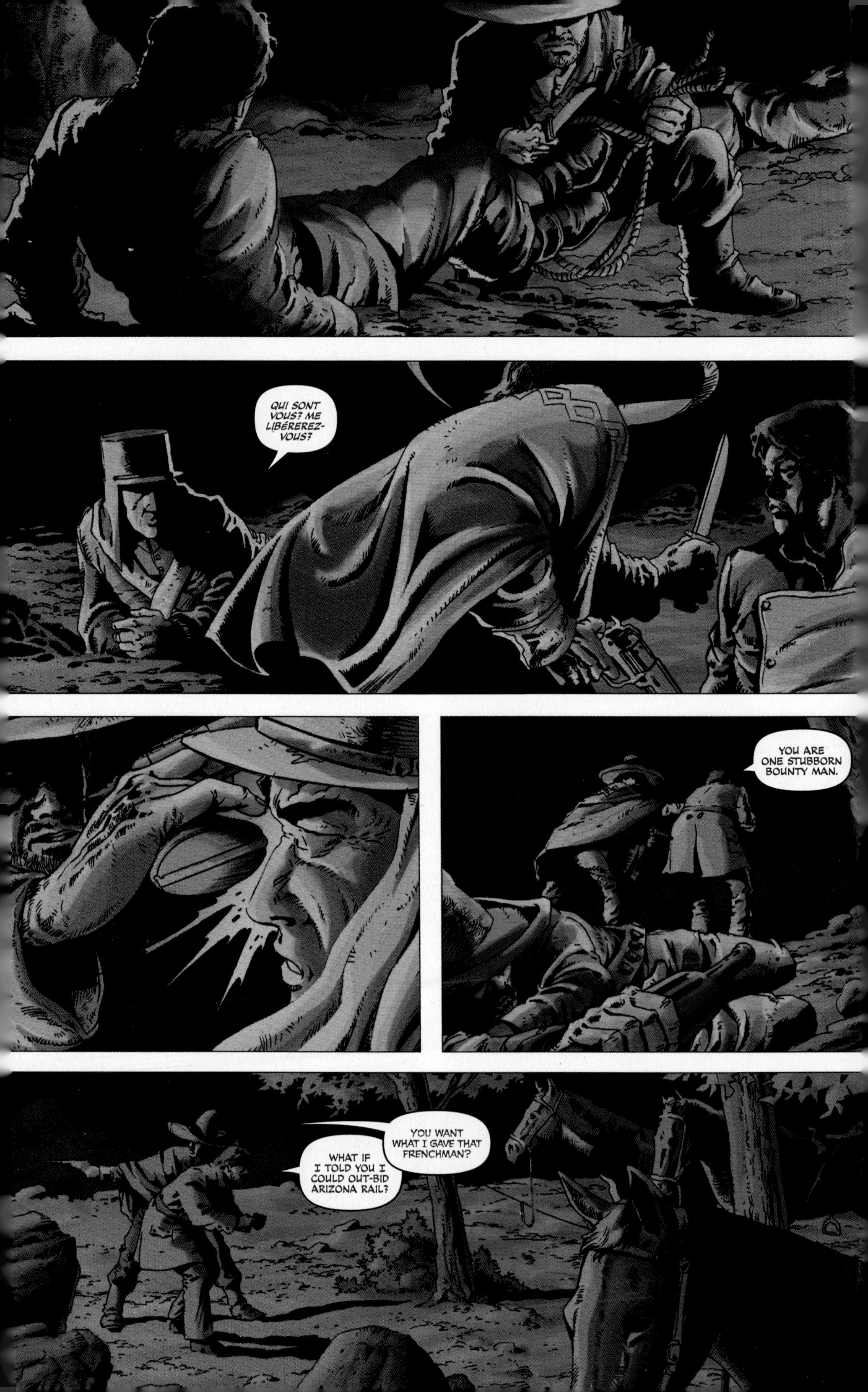
QUI SONT VOUS? ME LIBÉREREZ-VOUS?
YOU ARE ONE STUBBORN BOUNTY MAN.
YOU WANT WHAT I GAVE THAT FRENCHMAN?
WHAT IF I TOLD YOU I COULD OUT-BID ARIZONA RAIL?

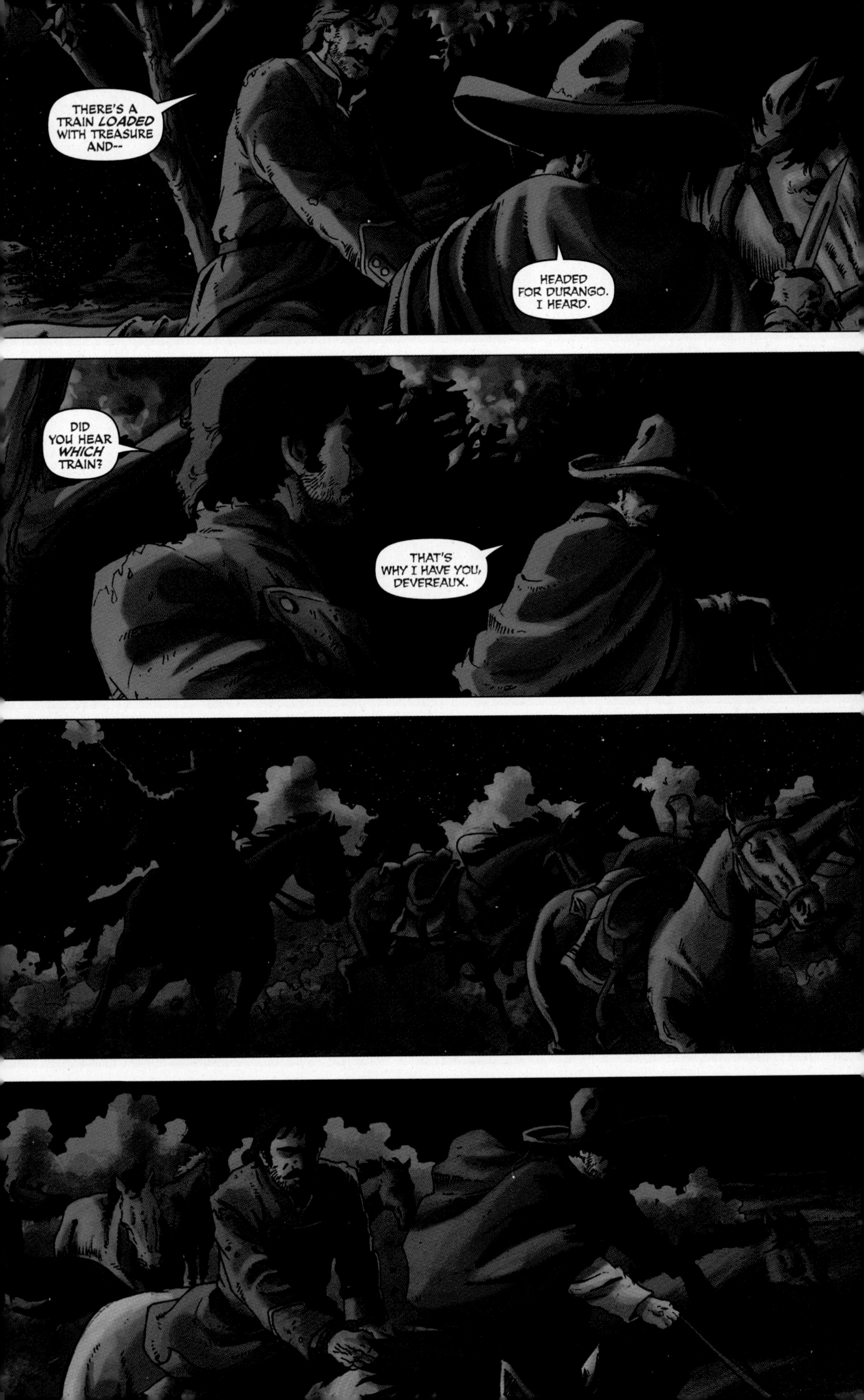
THERE'S A TRAIN *LOADED* WITH TREASURE AND--
HEADED FOR DURANGO. I HEARD.
DID YOU HEAR *WHICH* TRAIN?
THAT'S WHY I HAVE YOU, DEVEREAUX.

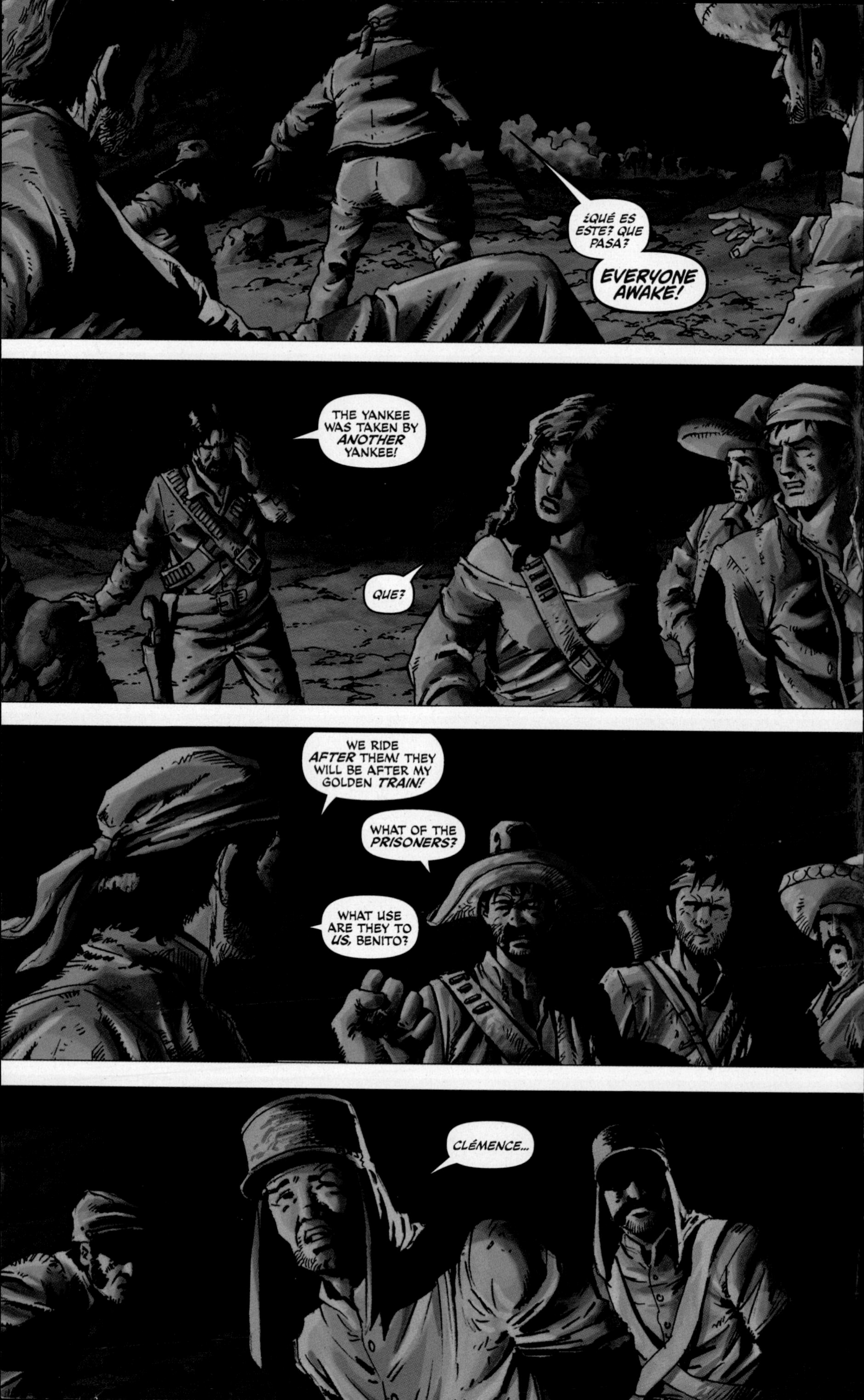
¿QUÉ ES ESTE? QUE PASA?
EVERYONE AWAKE!
THE YANKEE WAS TAKEN BY ANOTHER YANKEE!
QUE?
WE RIDE AFTER THEM! THEY WILL BE AFTER MY GOLDEN TRAIN!
WHAT OF THE PRISONERS?
WHAT USE ARE THEY TO US, BENITO?
CLÉMENCE...

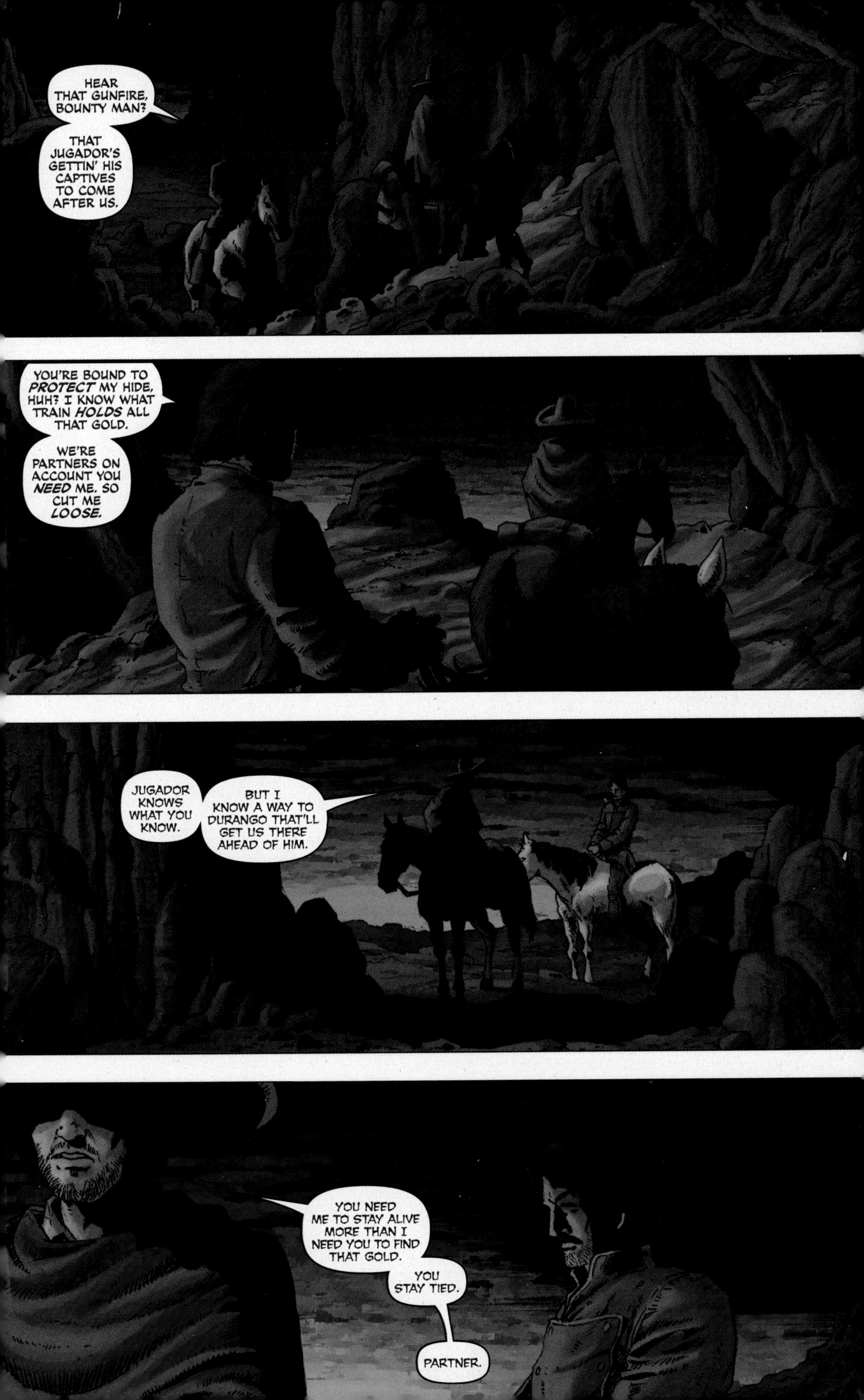
HEAR THAT GUNFIRE, BOUNTY MAN?
THAT JUGADOR'S GETTIN' HIS CAPTIVES TO COME AFTER US.
YOU'RE BOUND TO PROTECT MY HIDE, HUH? I KNOW WHAT TRAIN HOLDS ALL THAT GOLD.
WE'RE PARTNERS ON ACCOUNT YOU NEED ME. SO CUT ME LOOSE.
JUGADOR KNOWS WHAT YOU KNOW.
BUT I KNOW A WAY TO DURANGO THAT'LL GET US THERE AHEAD OF HIM.
YOU NEED ME TO STAY ALIVE MORE THAN I NEED YOU TO FIND THAT GOLD.
YOU STAY TIED.
PARTNER.

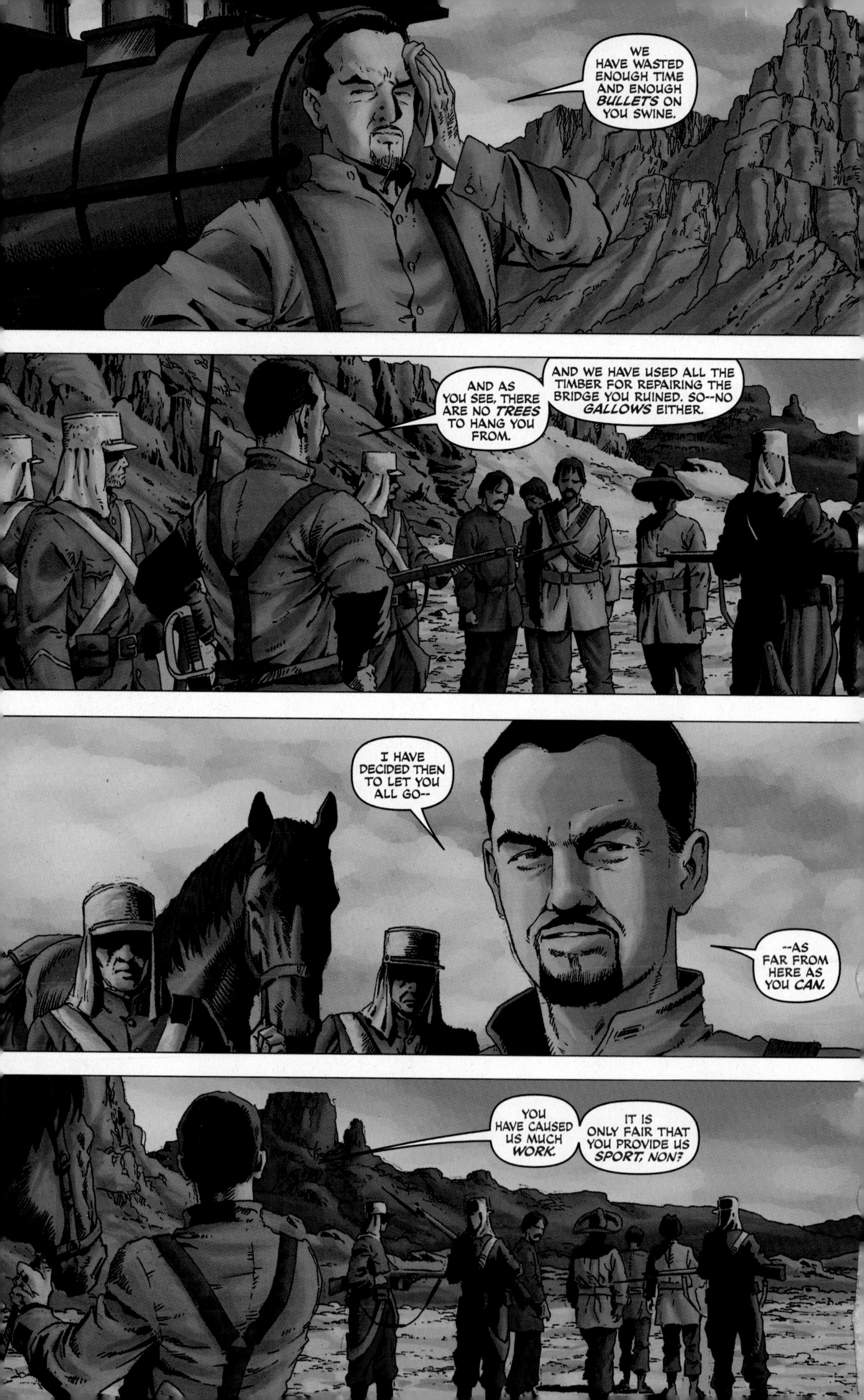
WE HAVE WASTED ENOUGH TIME AND ENOUGH BULLETS ON YOU SWINE.
AND AS YOU SEE, THERE ARE NO TREES TO HANG YOU FROM.
AND WE HAVE USED ALL THE TIMBER FOR REPAIRING THE BRIDGE YOU RUINED. SO--NO GALLOWS EITHER.
I HAVE DECIDED THEN TO LET YOU ALL GO--
--AS FAR FROM HERE AS YOU CAN.
YOU HAVE CAUSED US MUCH WORK.
IT IS ONLY FAIR THAT YOU PROVIDE US SPORT, NON?

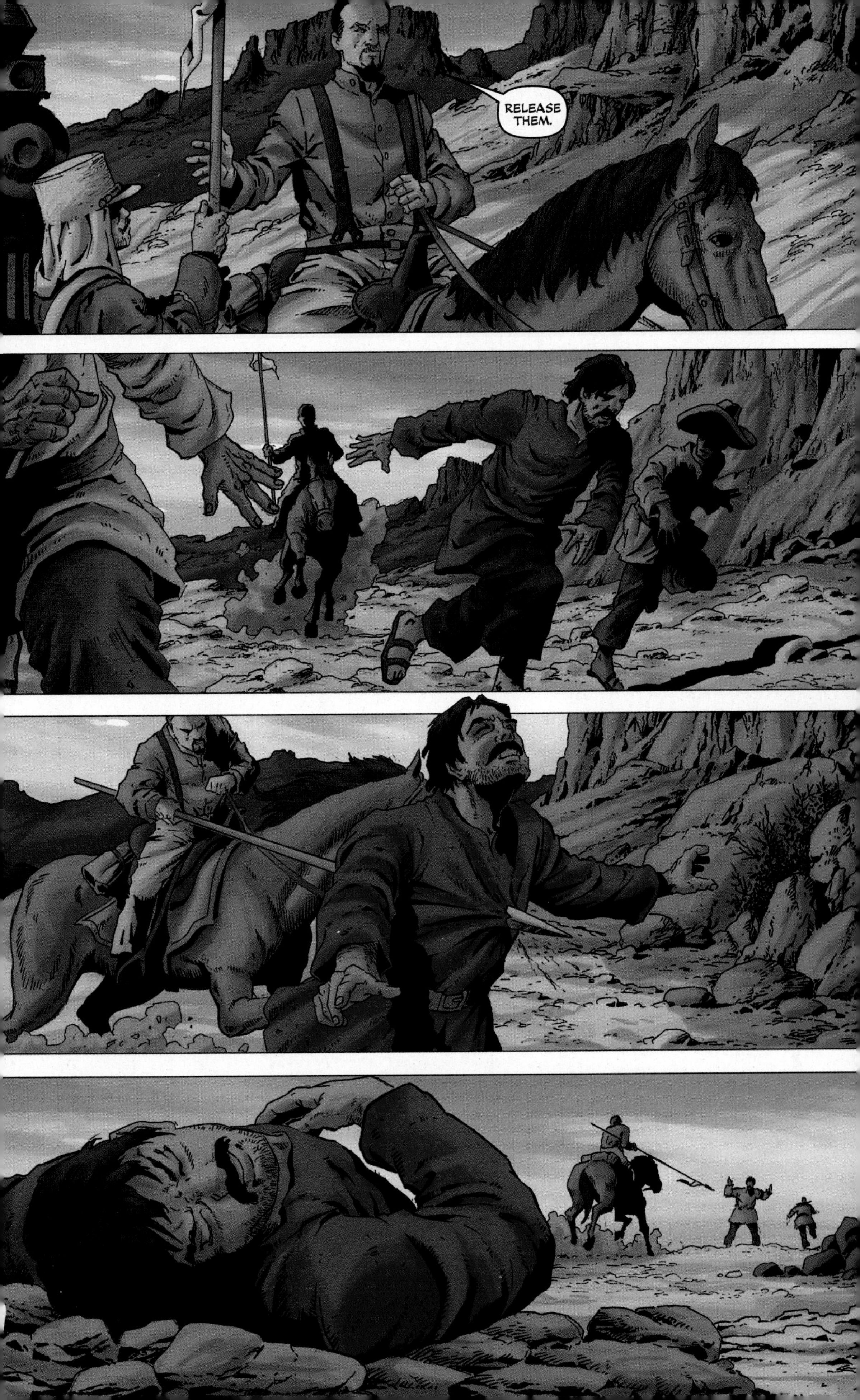
RELEASE THEM.

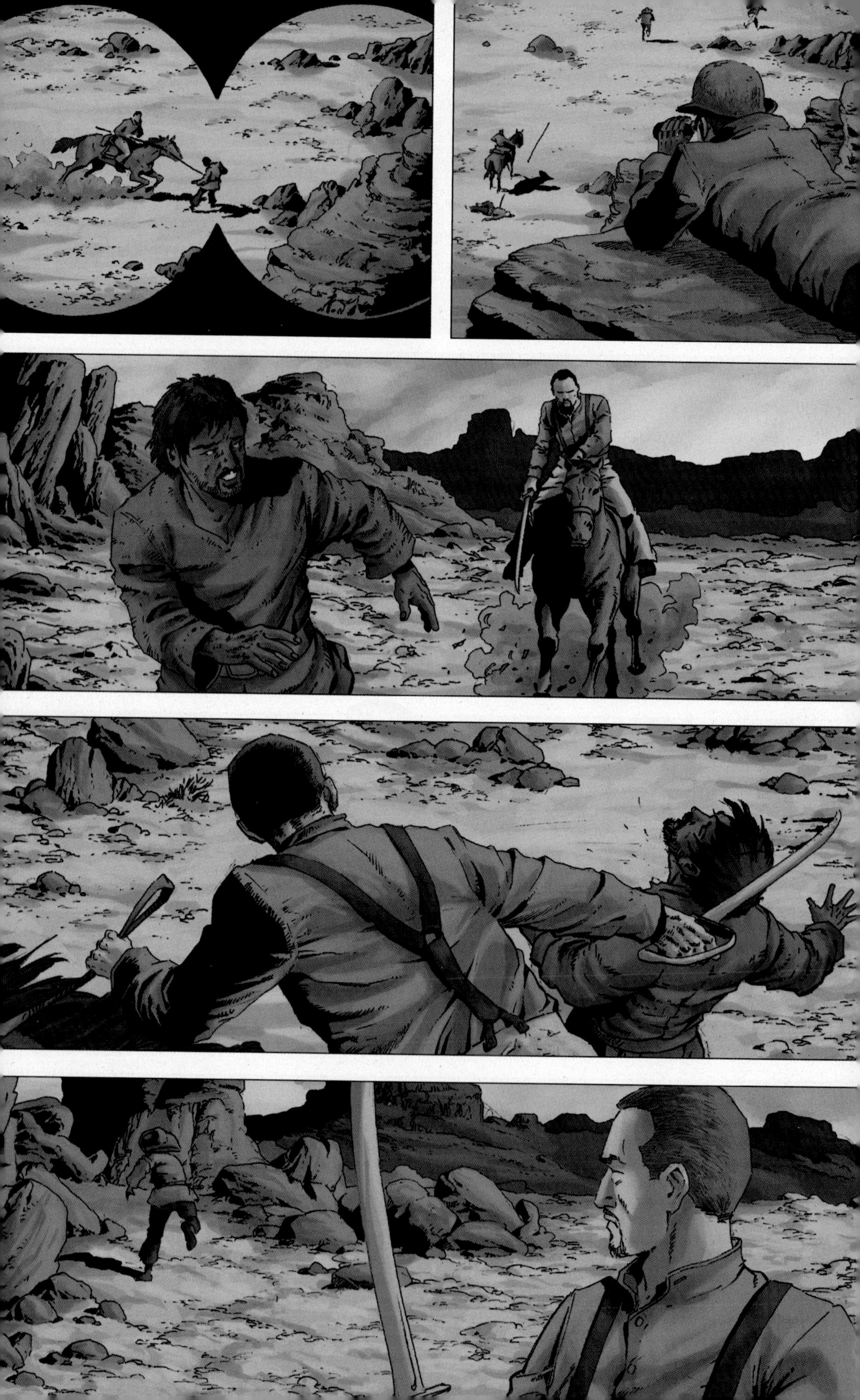

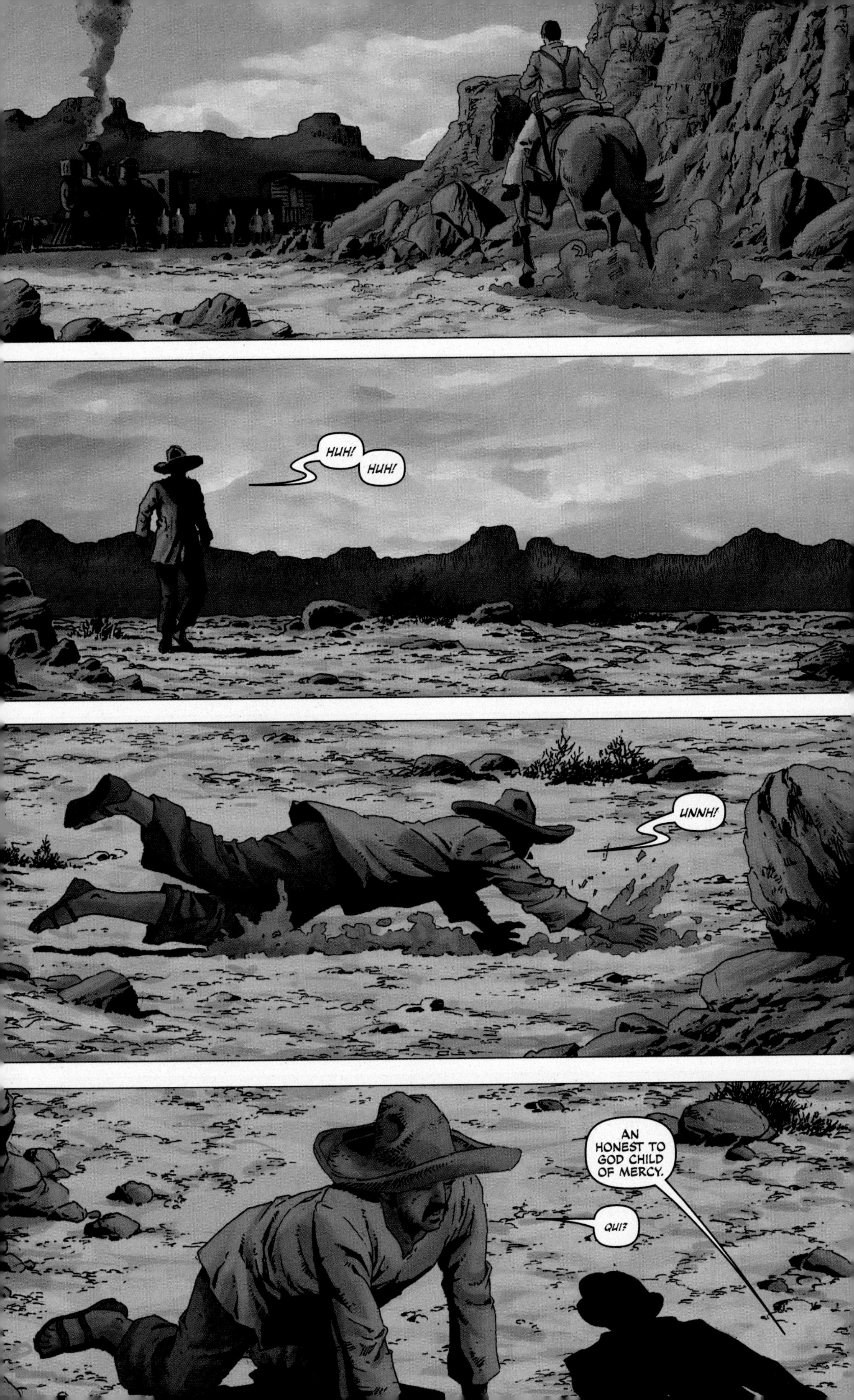
HUH!
HUH!
UNNH!
AN HONEST TO GOD CHILD OF MERCY.
QUI?

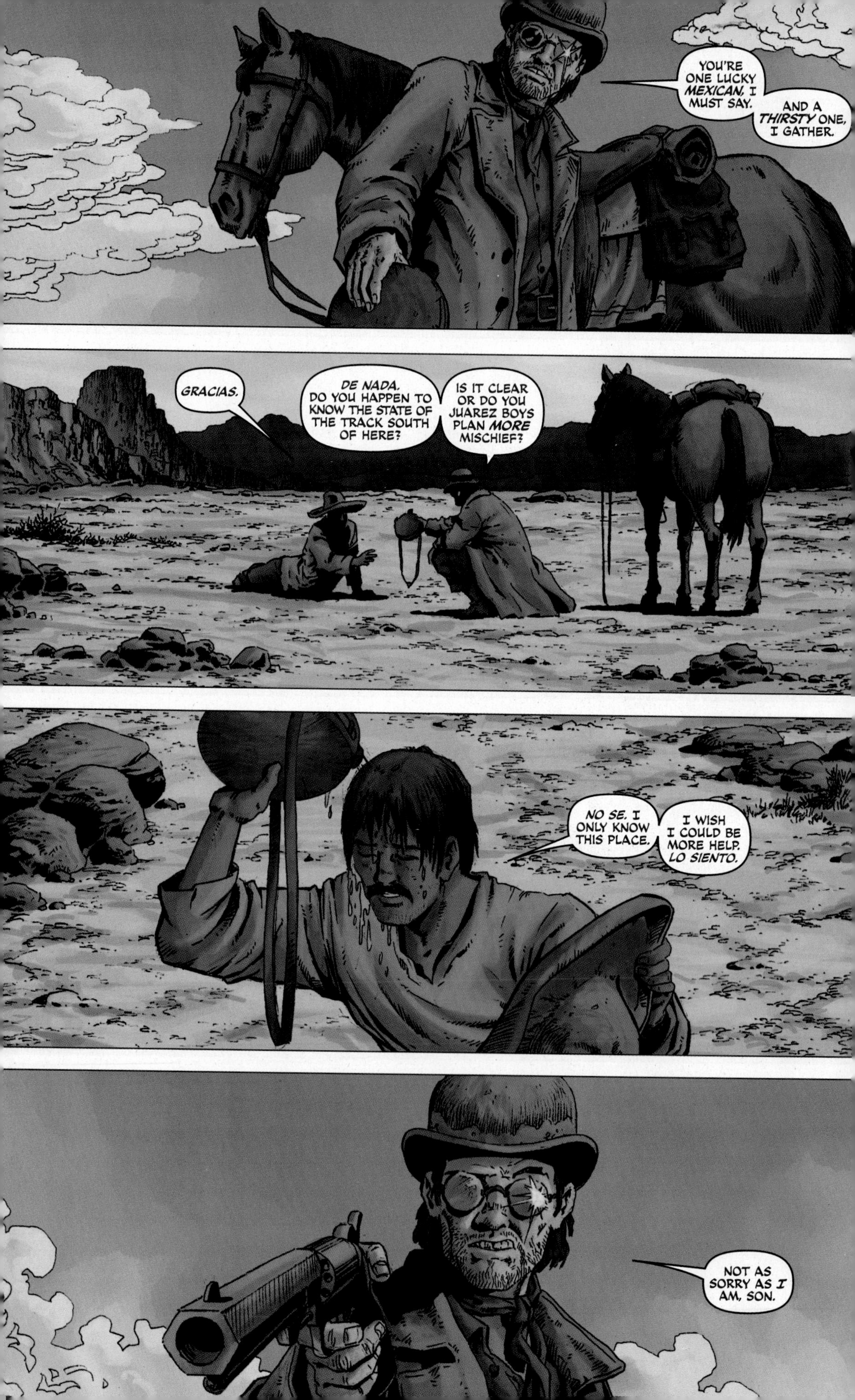
YOU'RE ONE LUCKY MEXICAN, I MUST SAY.
AND A THIRSTY ONE, I GATHER.
GRACIAS.
DE NADA. DO YOU HAPPEN TO KNOW THE STATE OF THE TRACK SOUTH OF HERE?
IS IT CLEAR OR DO YOU JUAREZ BOYS PLAN MORE MISCHIEF?
NO SE. I ONLY KNOW THIS PLACE.
I WISH I COULD BE MORE HELP. LO SIENTO.
NOT AS SORRY AS I AM, SON.

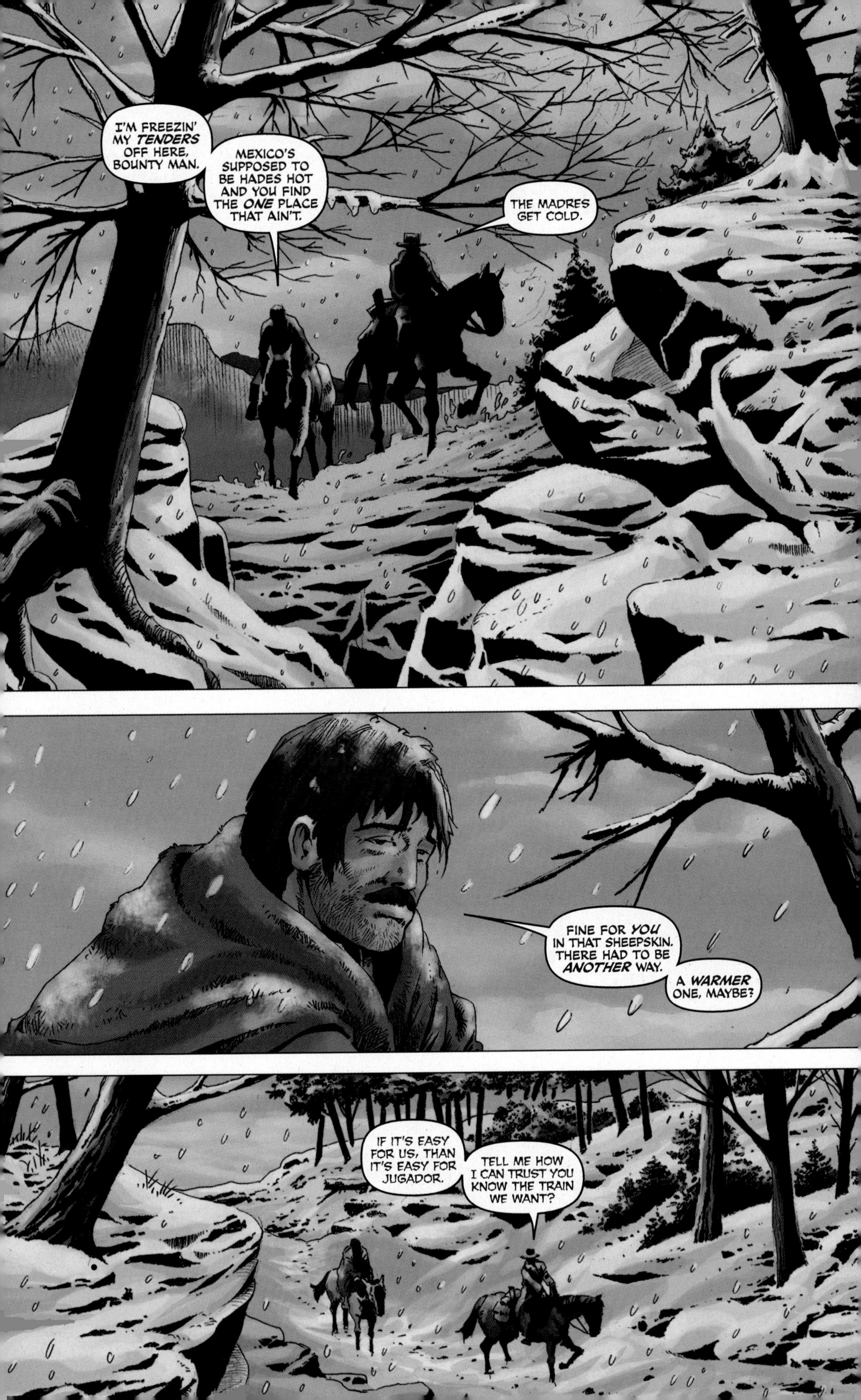
I'M FREEZIN' MY *TENDERS* OFF HERE, BOUNTY MAN.
MEXICO'S SUPPOSED TO BE HADES HOT AND YOU FIND THE *ONE* PLACE THAT AIN'T.
THE MADRES GET COLD.
FINE FOR *YOU* IN THAT SHEEPSKIN. THERE HAD TO BE *ANOTHER* WAY.
A *WARMER* ONE, MAYBE?
IF IT'S EASY FOR US, THAN IT'S EASY FOR JUGADOR.
TELL ME HOW I CAN TRUST YOU KNOW THE TRAIN WE WANT?

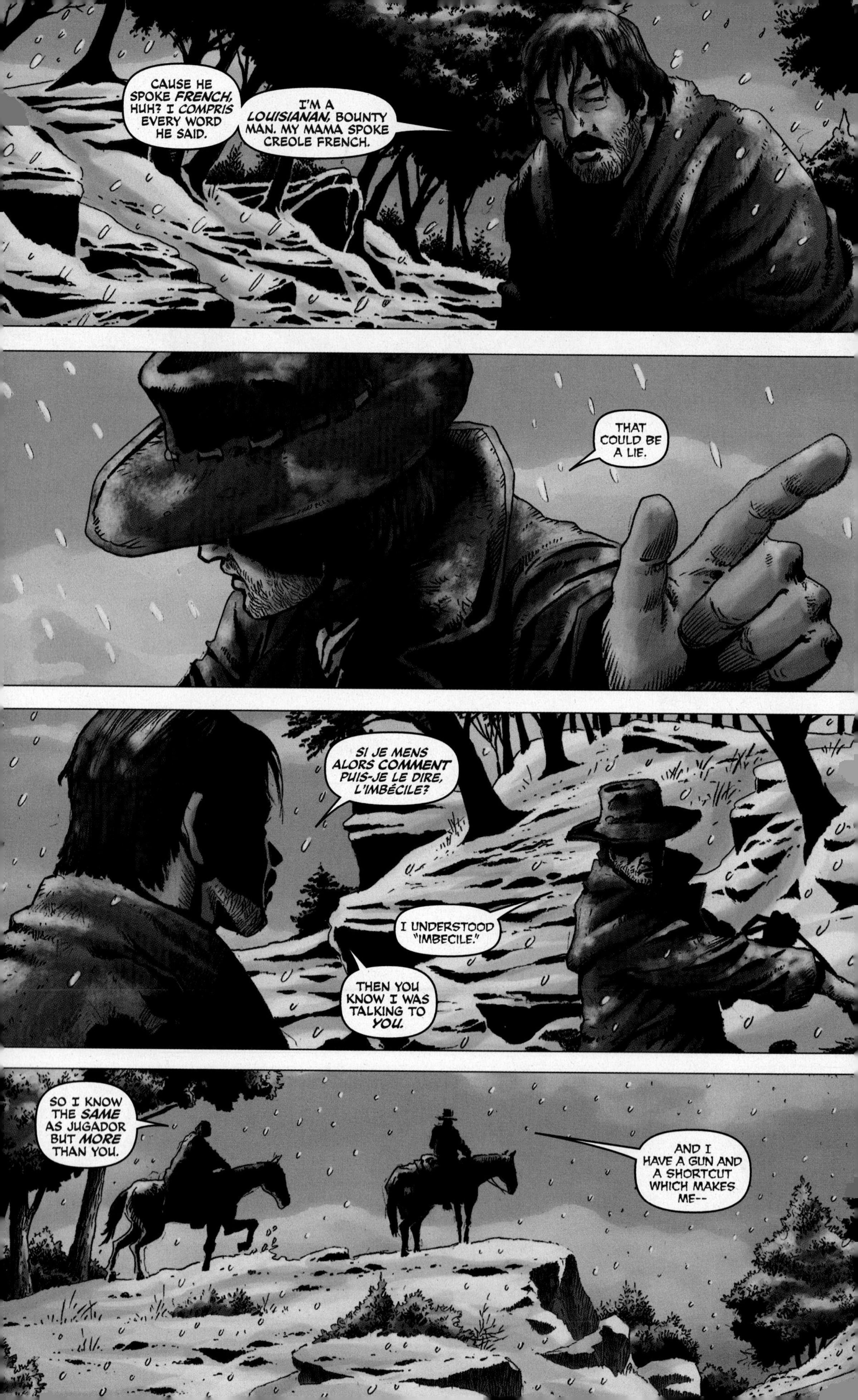
CAUSE HE SPOKE FRENCH, HUH? I COMPRIS EVERY WORD HE SAID.
I'M A LOUISIANAN, BOUNTY MAN. MY MAMA SPOKE CREOLE FRENCH.
THAT COULD BE A LIE.
SI JE MENS ALORS COMMENT PUIS-JE LE DIRE, L'IMBÉCILE?
I UNDERSTOOD "IMBECILE."
THEN YOU KNOW I WAS TALKING TO YOU.
SO I KNOW THE SAME AS JUGADOR BUT MORE THAN YOU.
AND I HAVE A GUN AND A SHORTCUT WHICH MAKES ME--

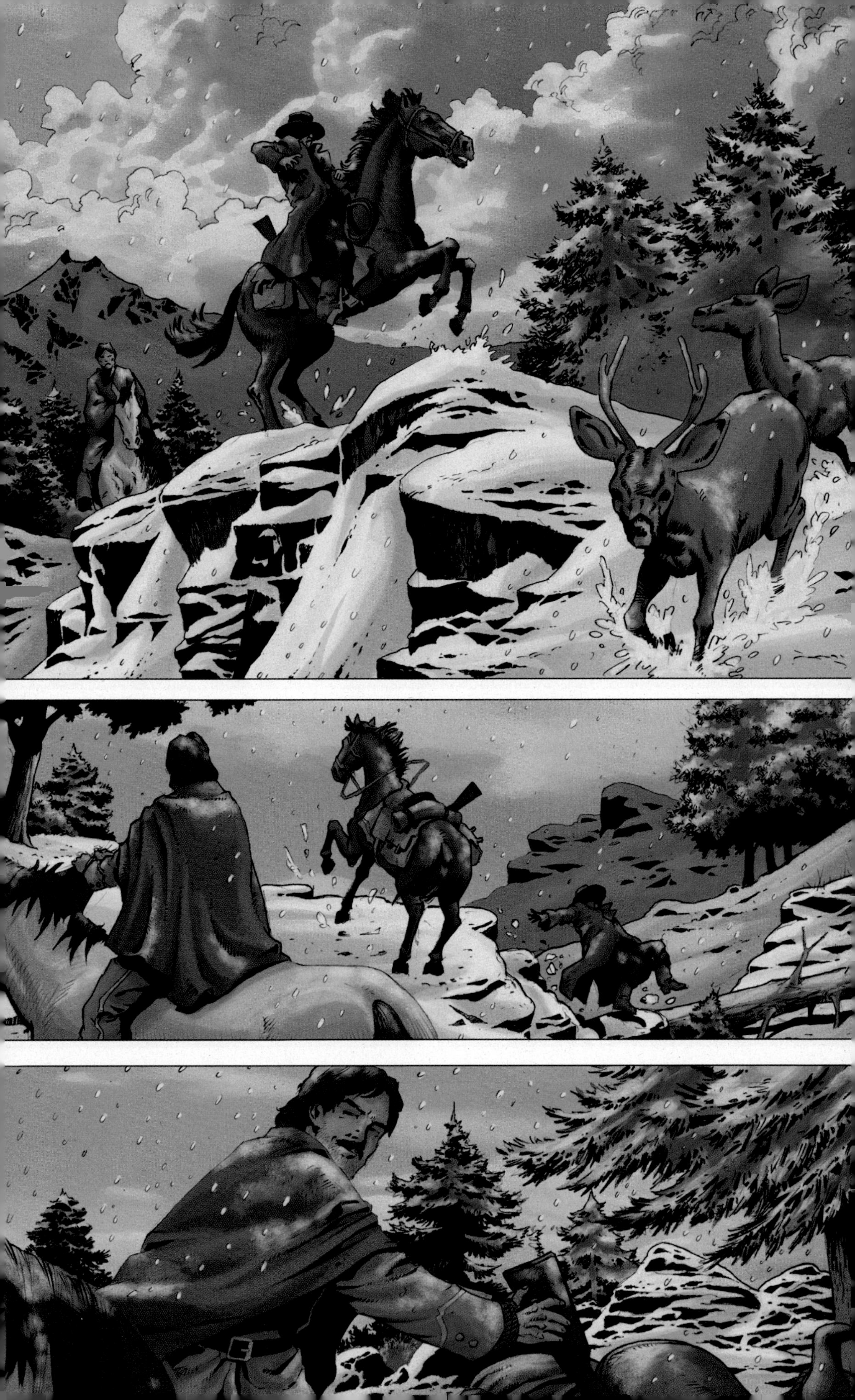

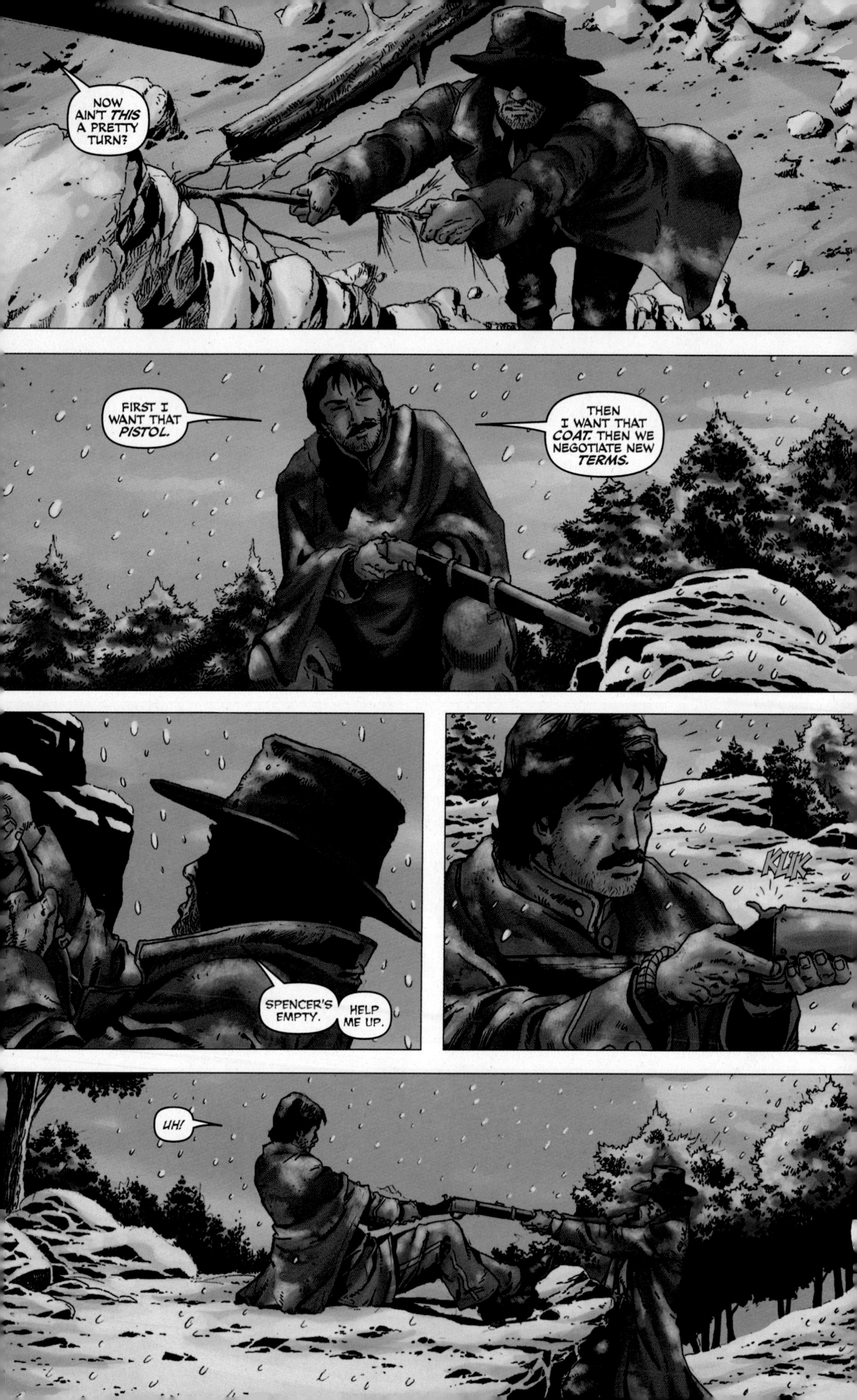
NOW AIN'T THIS A PRETTY TURN?
FIRST I WANT THAT PISTOL.
THEN I WANT THAT COAT. THEN WE NEGOTIATE NEW TERMS.
SPENCER'S EMPTY.
HELP ME UP.
KLIK
UH!

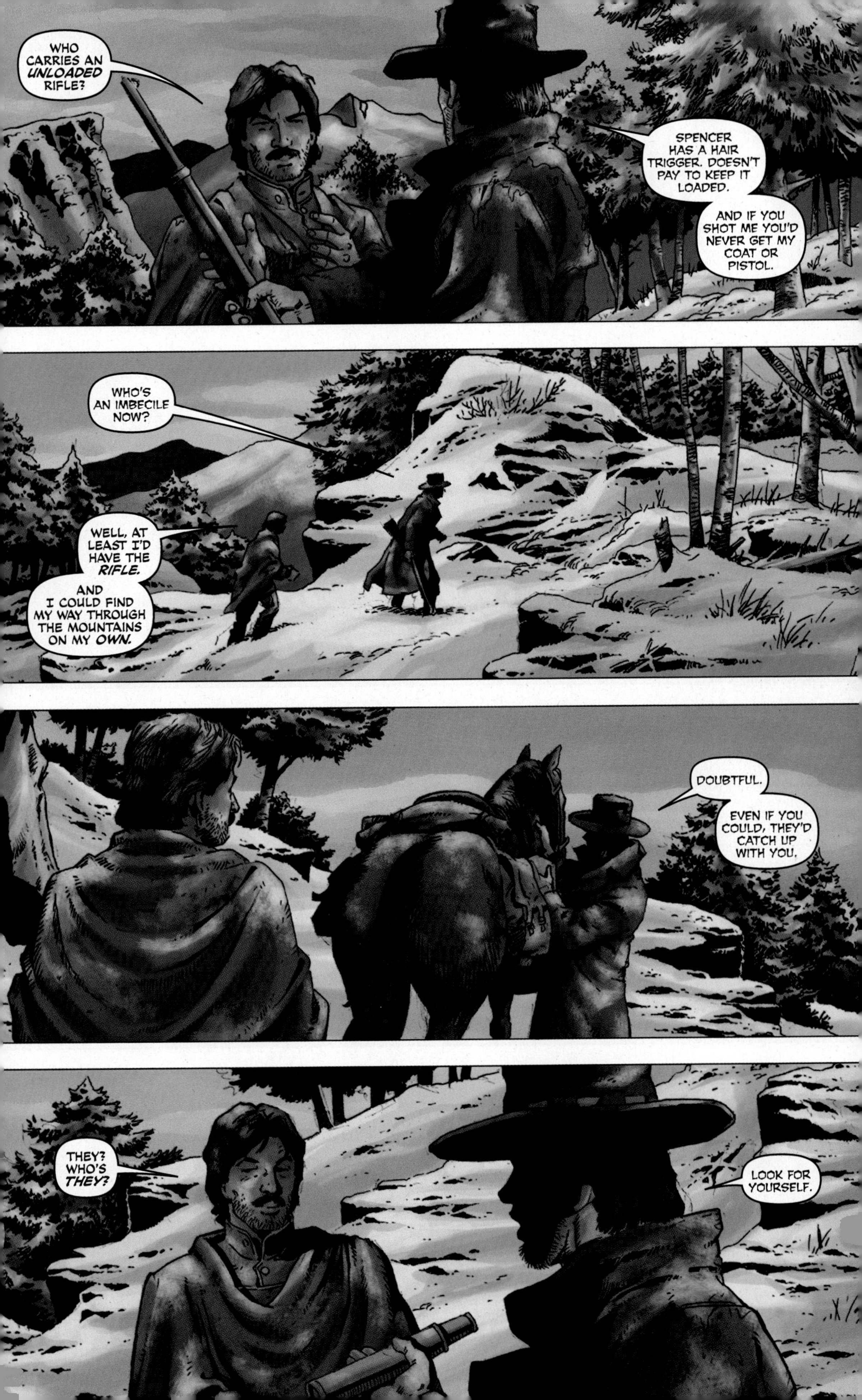
WHO CARRIES AN *UNLOADED* RIFLE?
SPENCER HAS A HAIR TRIGGER. DOESN'T PAY TO KEEP IT LOADED.
AND IF YOU SHOT ME YOU'D NEVER GET MY COAT OR PISTOL.
WHO'S AN IMBECILE NOW?
WELL, AT LEAST I'D HAVE THE *RIFLE.*
AND I COULD FIND MY WAY THROUGH THE MOUNTAINS ON MY *OWN.*
DOUBTFUL.
EVEN IF YOU COULD, THEY'D CATCH UP WITH YOU.
THEY? WHO'S *THEY?*
LOOK FOR YOURSELF.

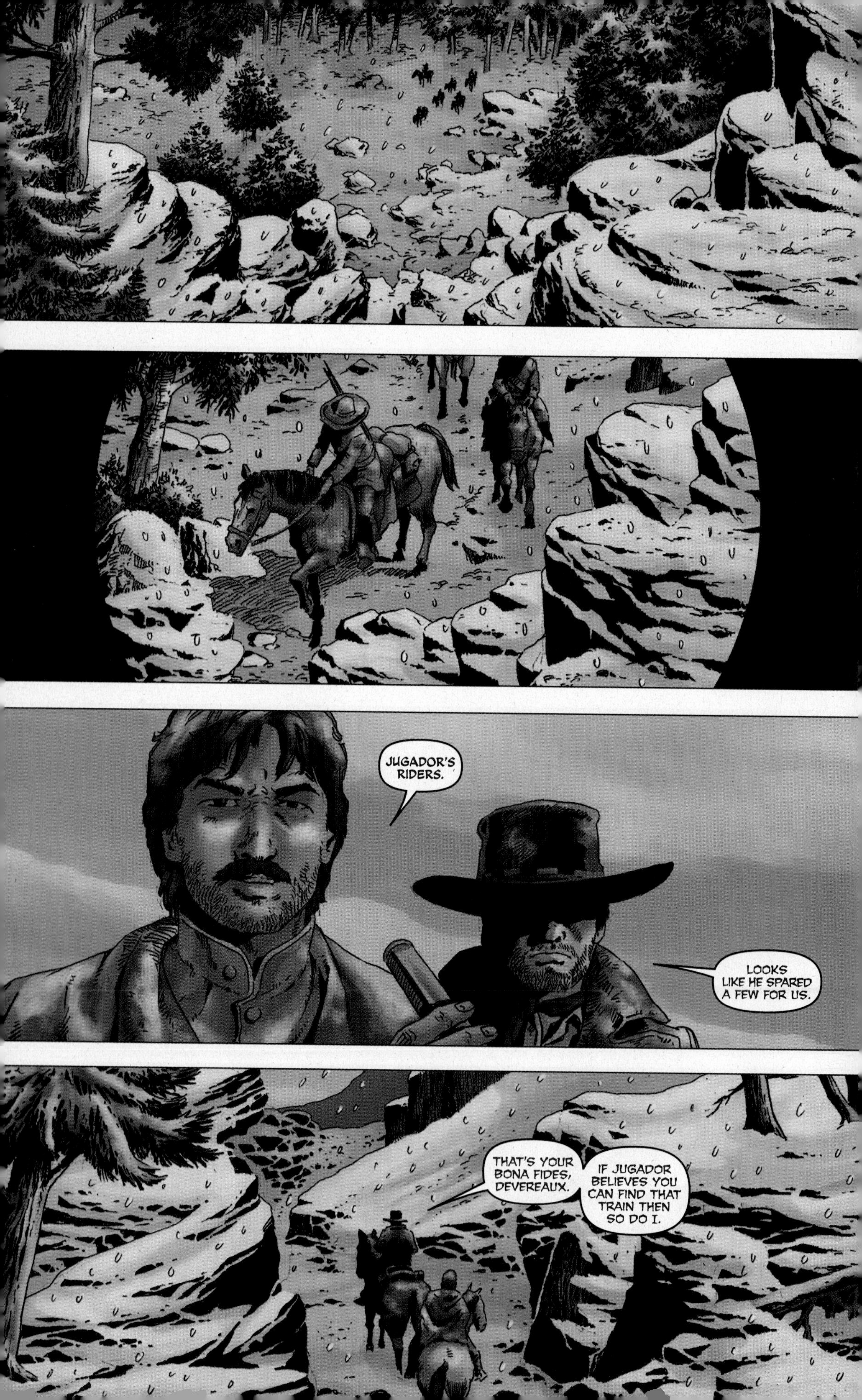
JUGADOR'S RIDERS.
LOOKS LIKE HE SPARED A FEW FOR US.
THAT'S YOUR BONA FIDES, DEVEREAUX.
IF JUGADOR BELIEVES YOU CAN FIND THAT TRAIN THEN SO DO I.

Cover by **Dennis Calero**

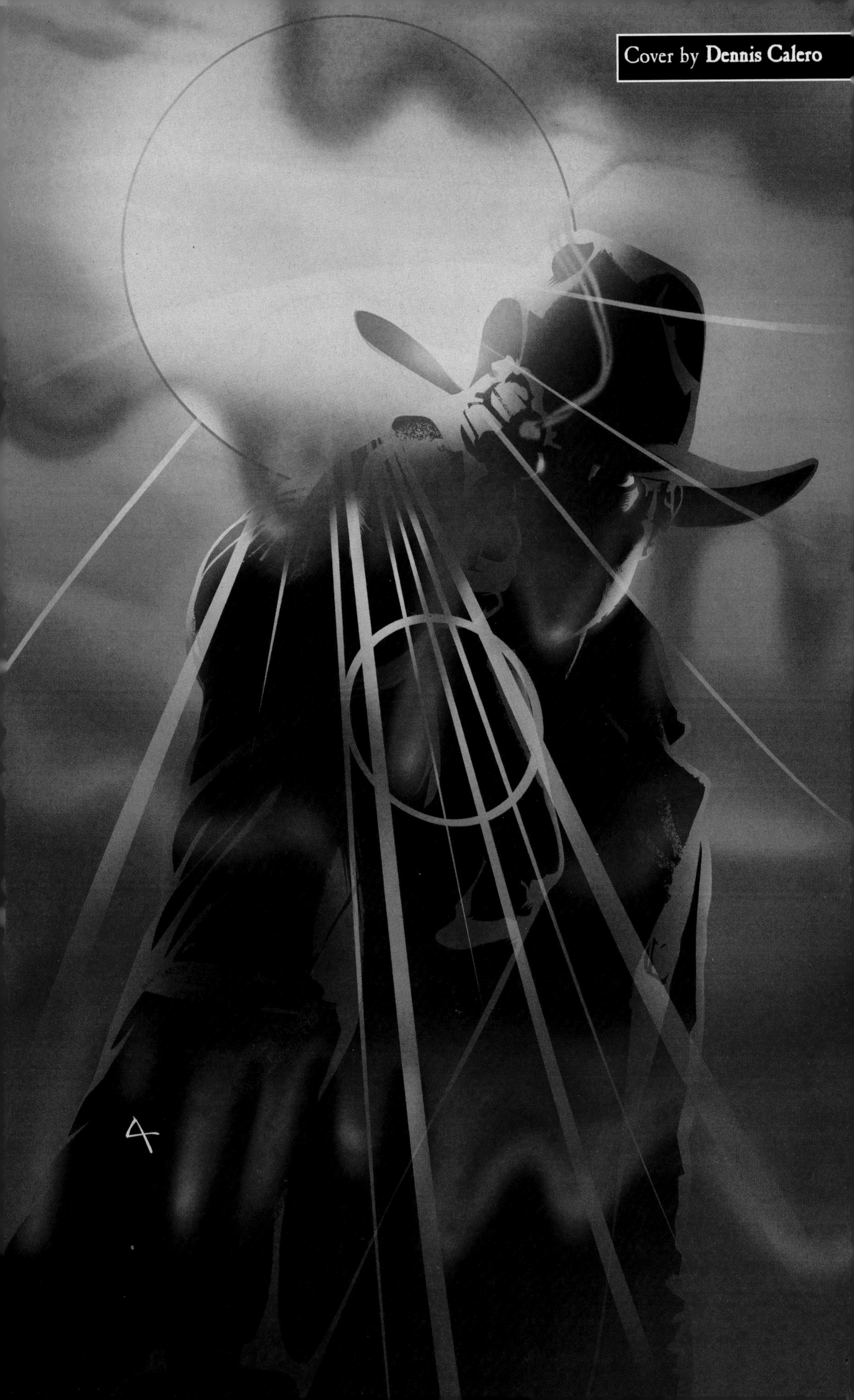
4

Cover by **Sergio Cariello**

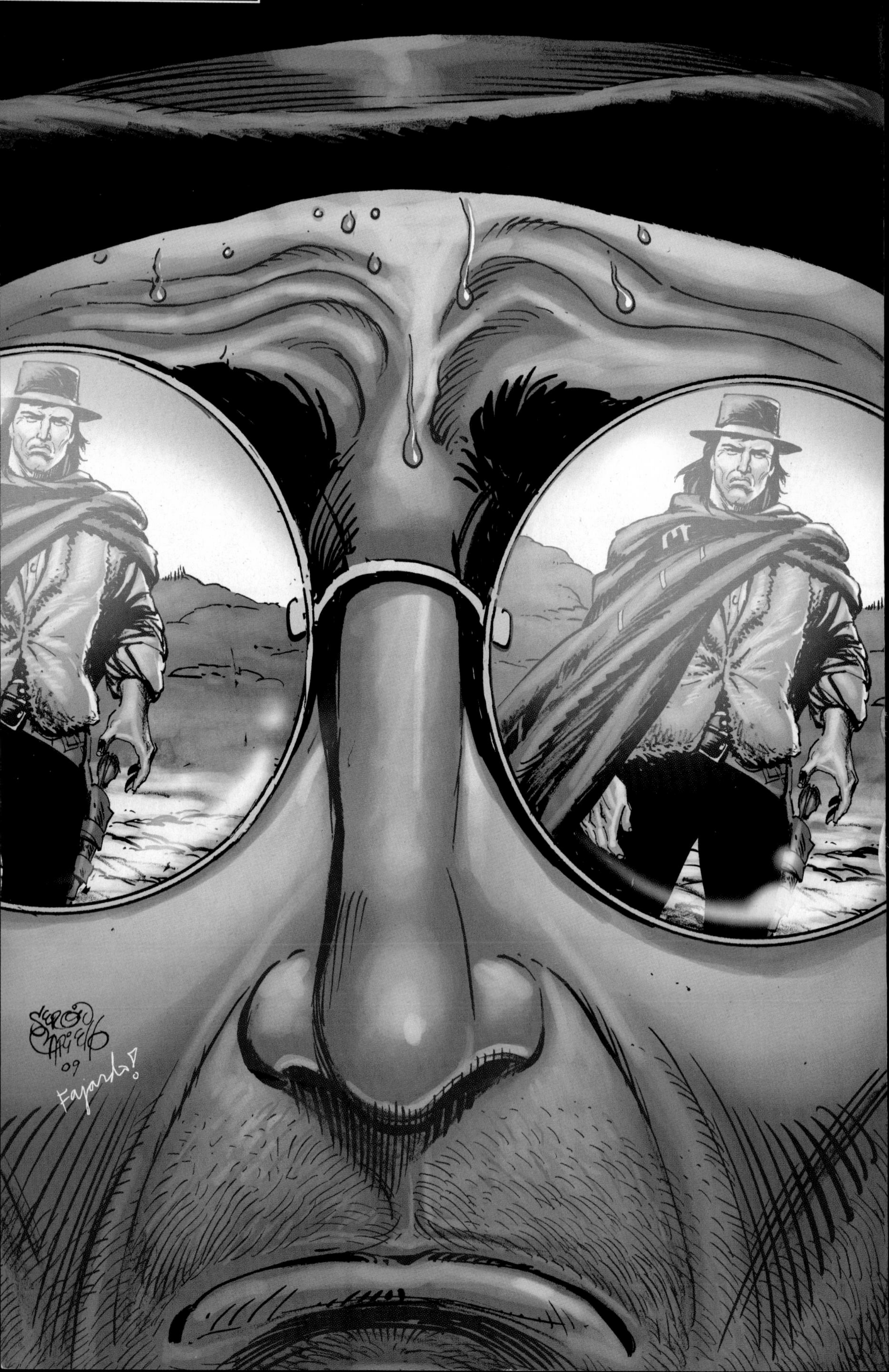

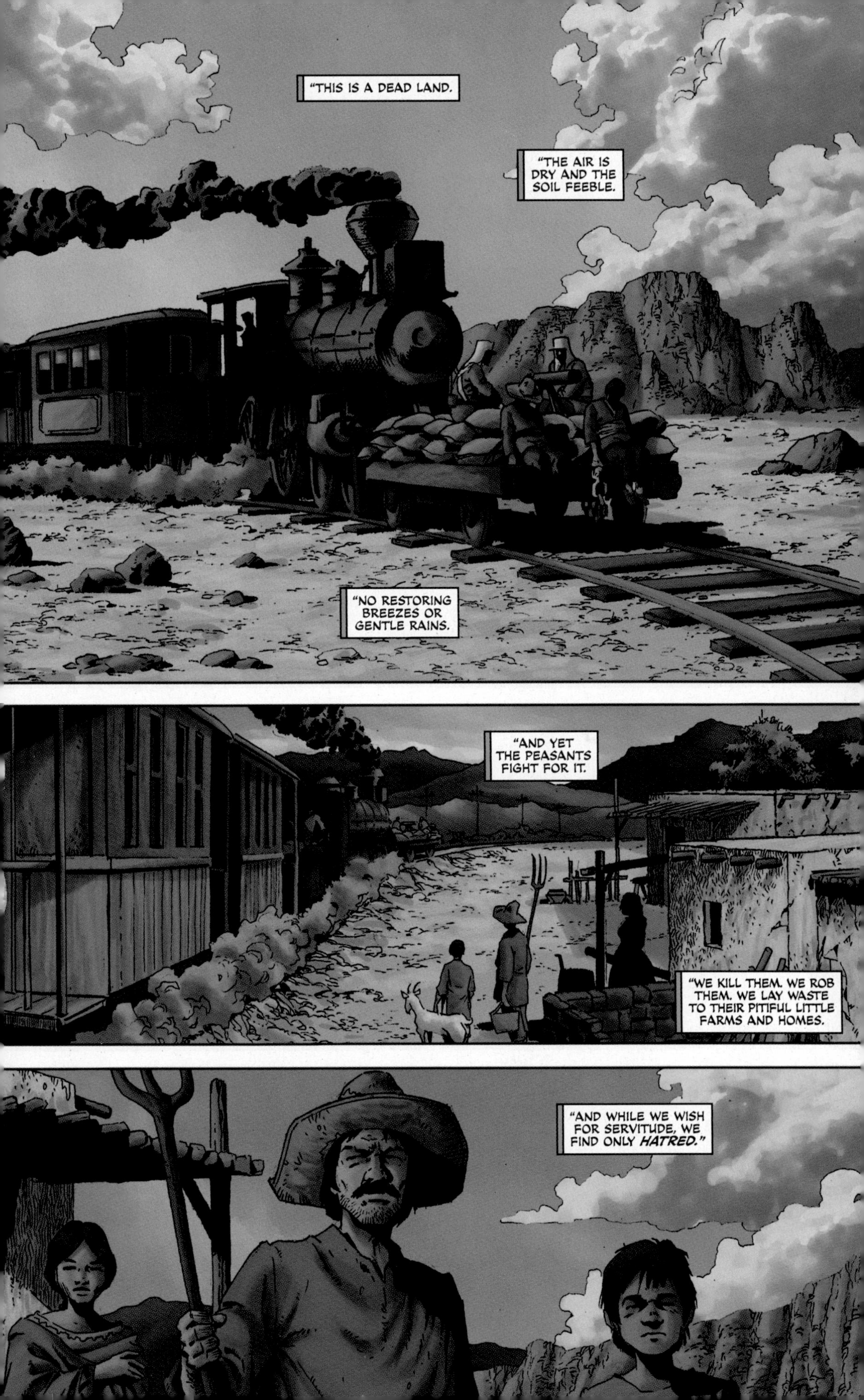
"THIS IS A DEAD LAND.
"THE AIR IS DRY AND THE SOIL FEEBLE.
"NO RESTORING BREEZES OR GENTLE RAINS.
"AND YET THE PEASANTS FIGHT FOR IT.
"WE KILL THEM. WE ROB THEM. WE LAY WASTE TO THEIR PITIFUL LITTLE FARMS AND HOMES.
"AND WHILE WE WISH FOR SERVITUDE, WE FIND ONLY HATRED."

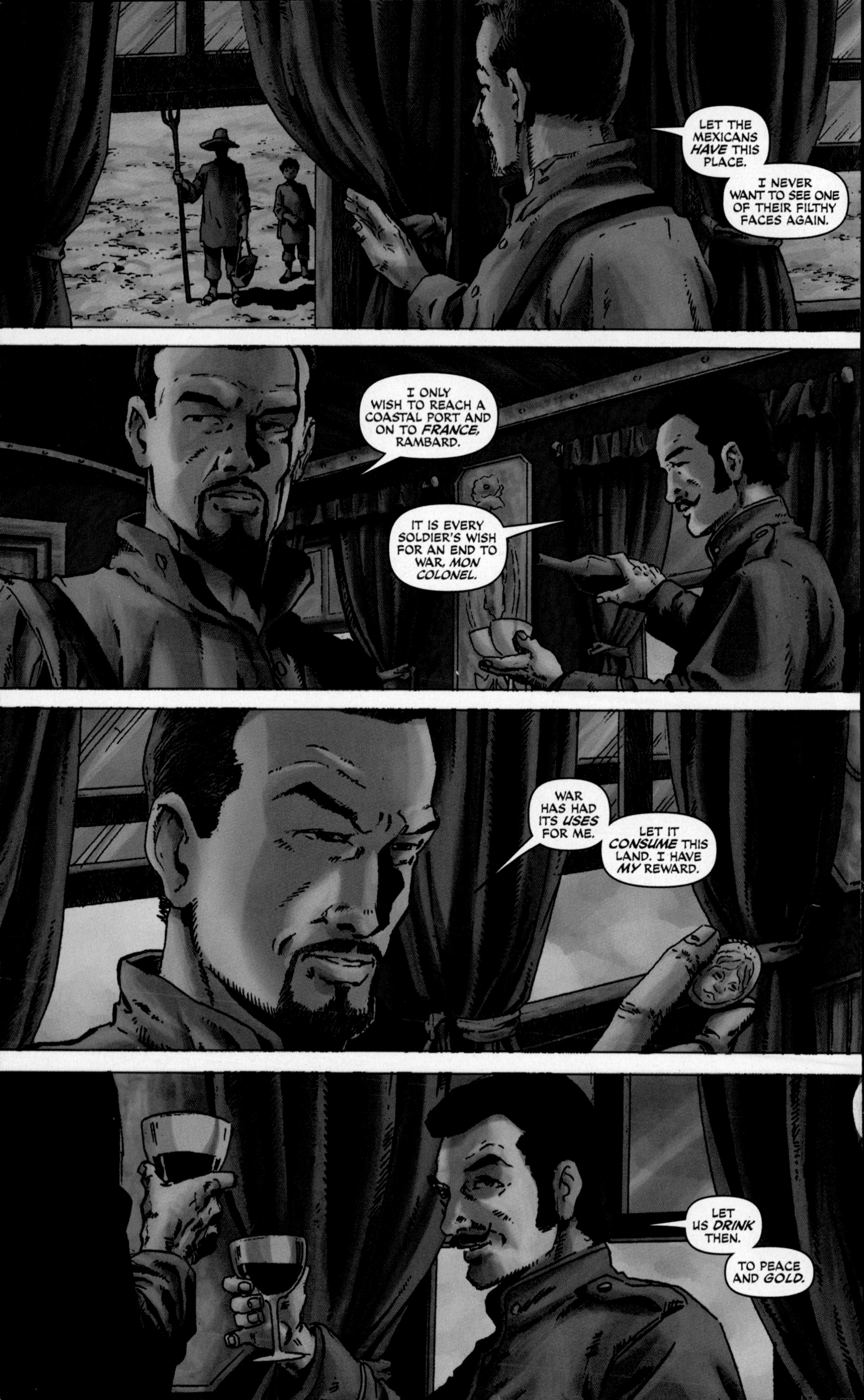
LET THE MEXICANS HAVE THIS PLACE.
I NEVER WANT TO SEE ONE OF THEIR FILTHY FACES AGAIN.
I ONLY WISH TO REACH A COASTAL PORT AND ON TO FRANCE, RAMBARD.
IT IS EVERY SOLDIER'S WISH FOR AN END TO WAR, MON COLONEL.
WAR HAS HAD ITS USES FOR ME.
LET IT CONSUME THIS LAND. I HAVE MY REWARD.
LET US DRINK THEN.
TO PEACE AND GOLD.

"AND LEAVE MEXICO FOR THE *DEVIL*."

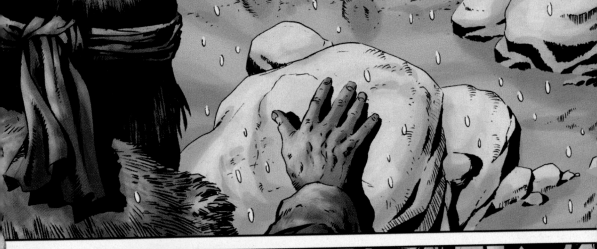

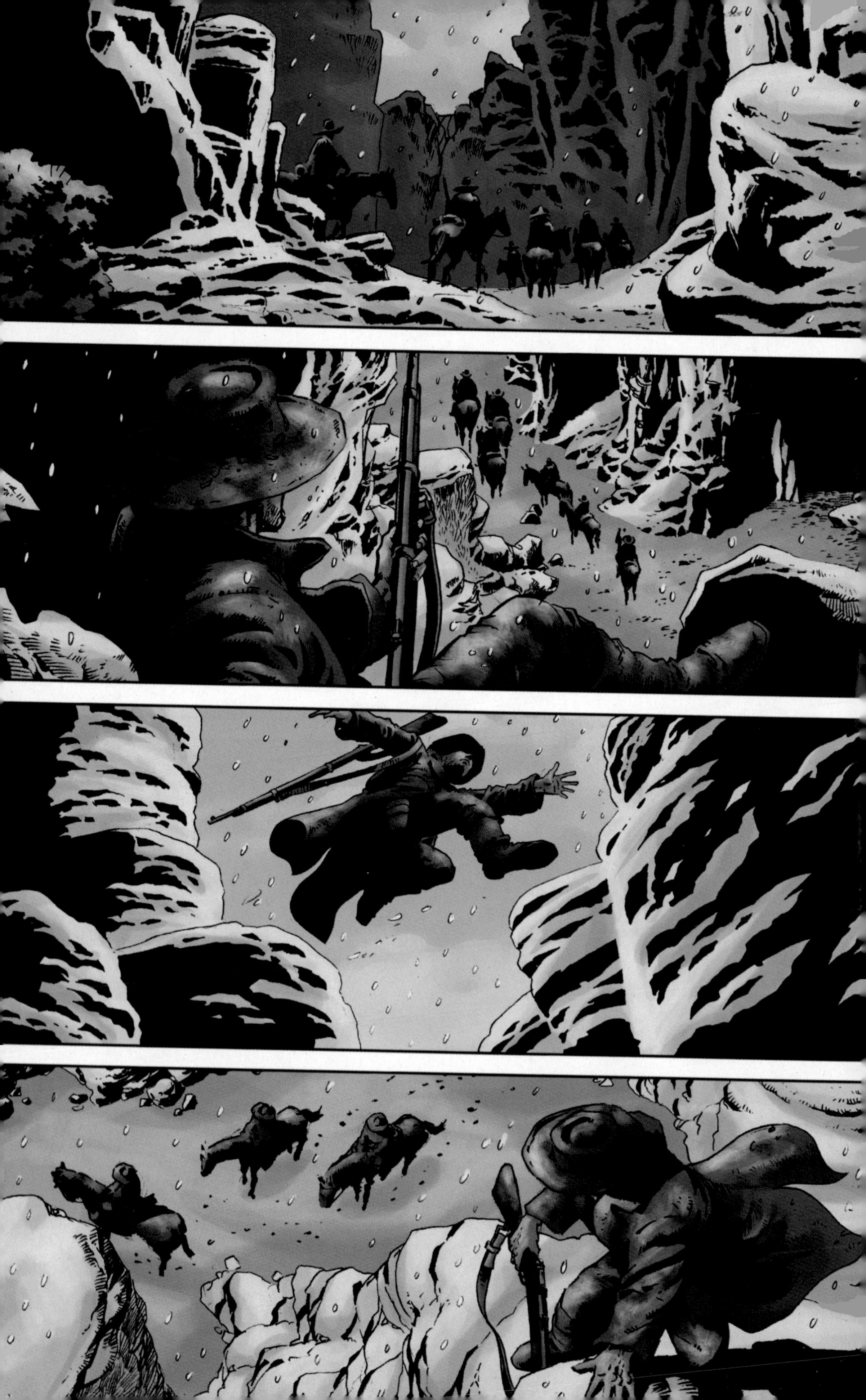

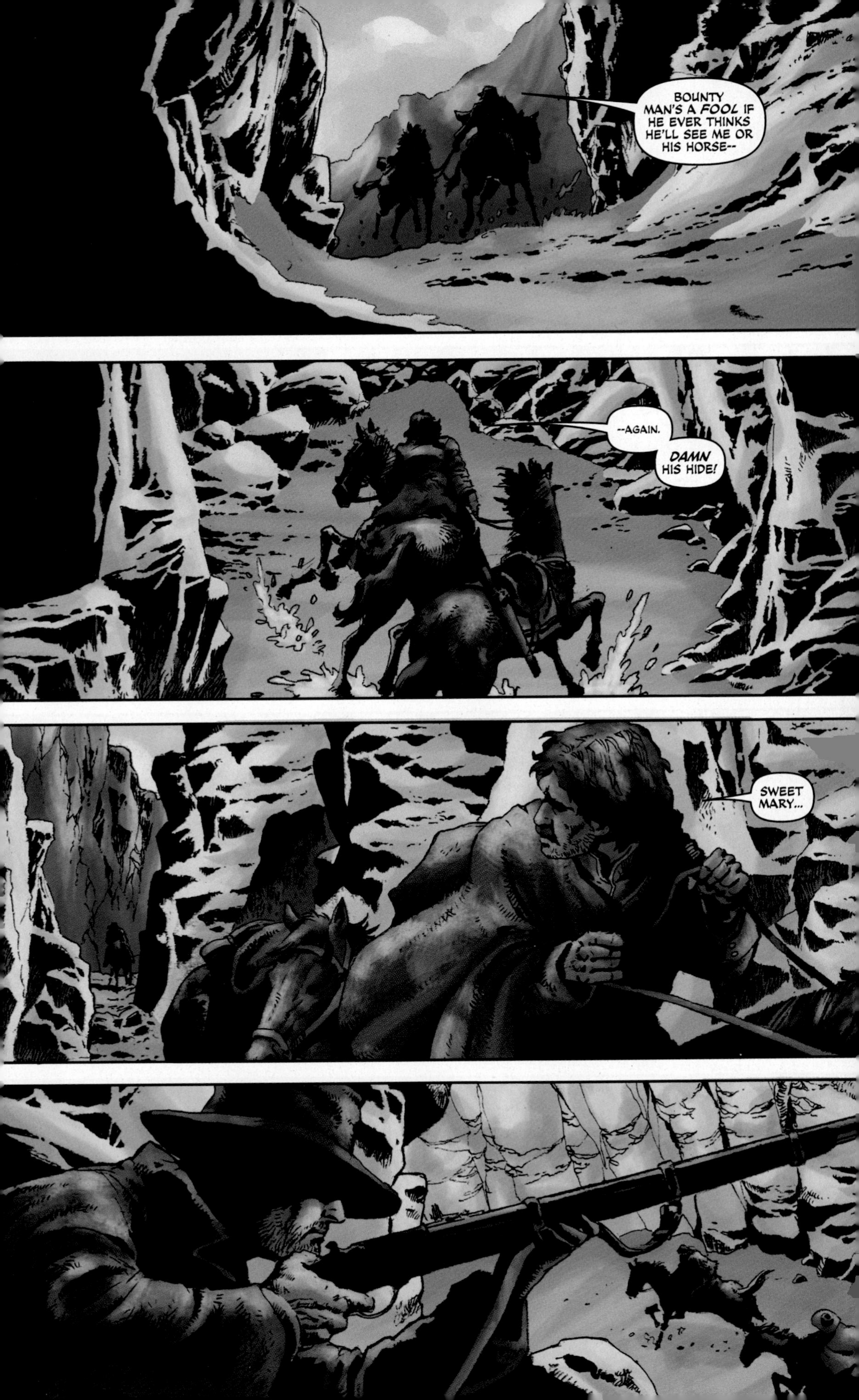
BOUNTY MAN'S A *FOOL* IF HE EVER THINKS HE'LL SEE ME OR HIS HORSE--
--AGAIN.
DAMN HIS HIDE!
SWEET MARY...

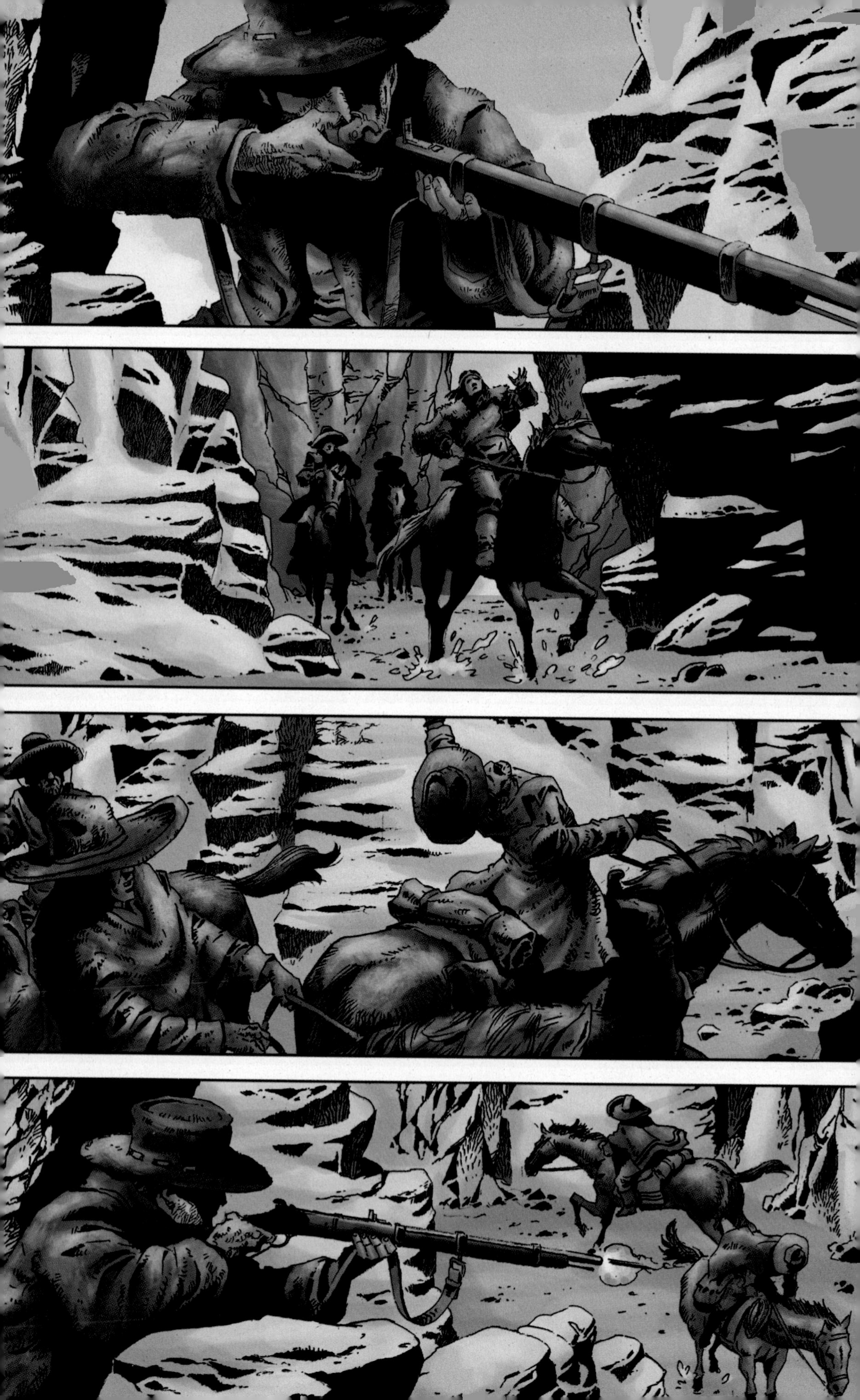

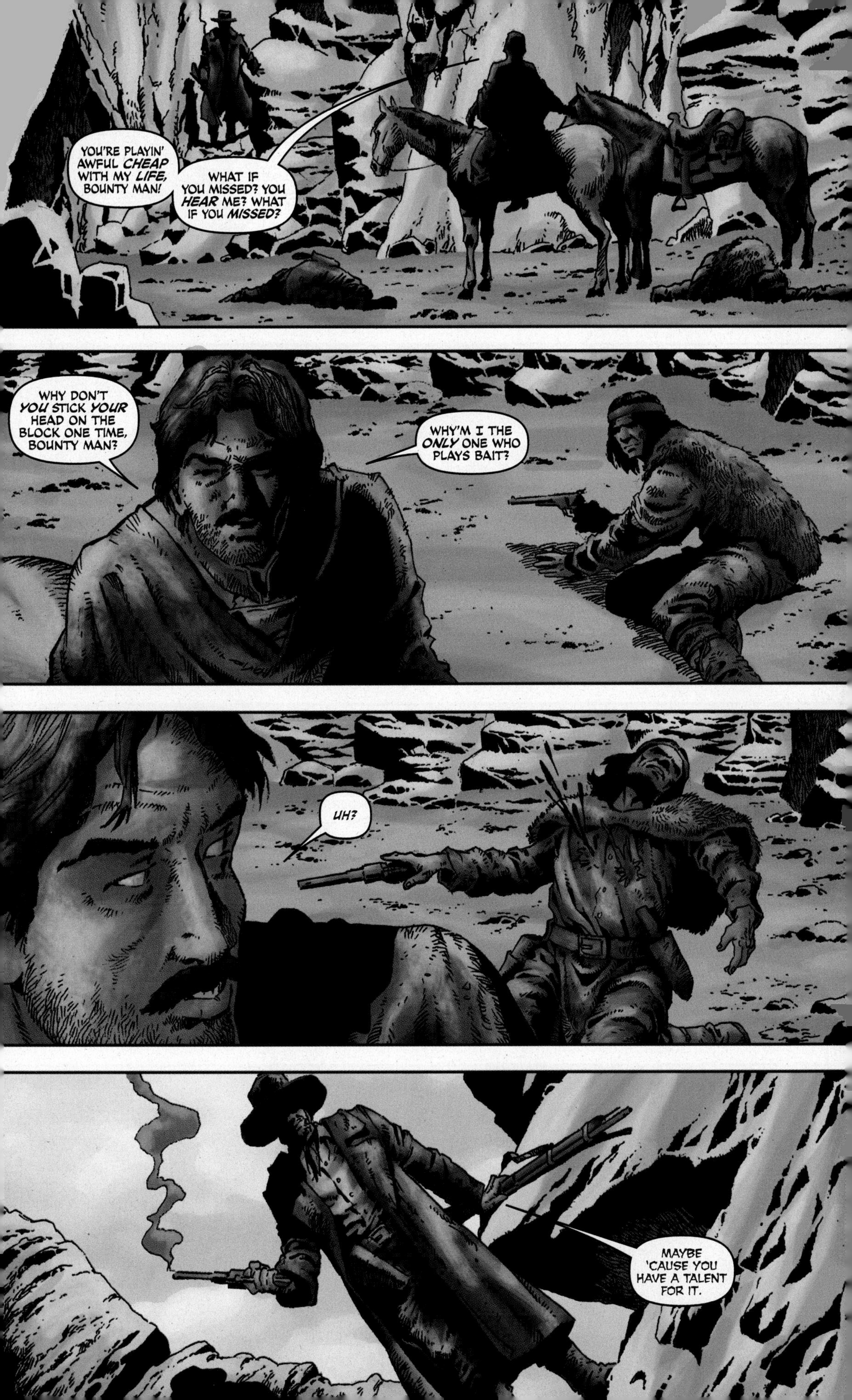
YOU'RE PLAYIN' AWFUL CHEAP WITH MY LIFE, BOUNTY MAN!
WHAT IF YOU MISSED? YOU HEAR ME? WHAT IF YOU MISSED?
WHY DON'T YOU STICK YOUR HEAD ON THE BLOCK ONE TIME, BOUNTY MAN?
WHY'M I THE ONLY ONE WHO PLAYS BAIT?
UH?
MAYBE 'CAUSE YOU HAVE A TALENT FOR IT.

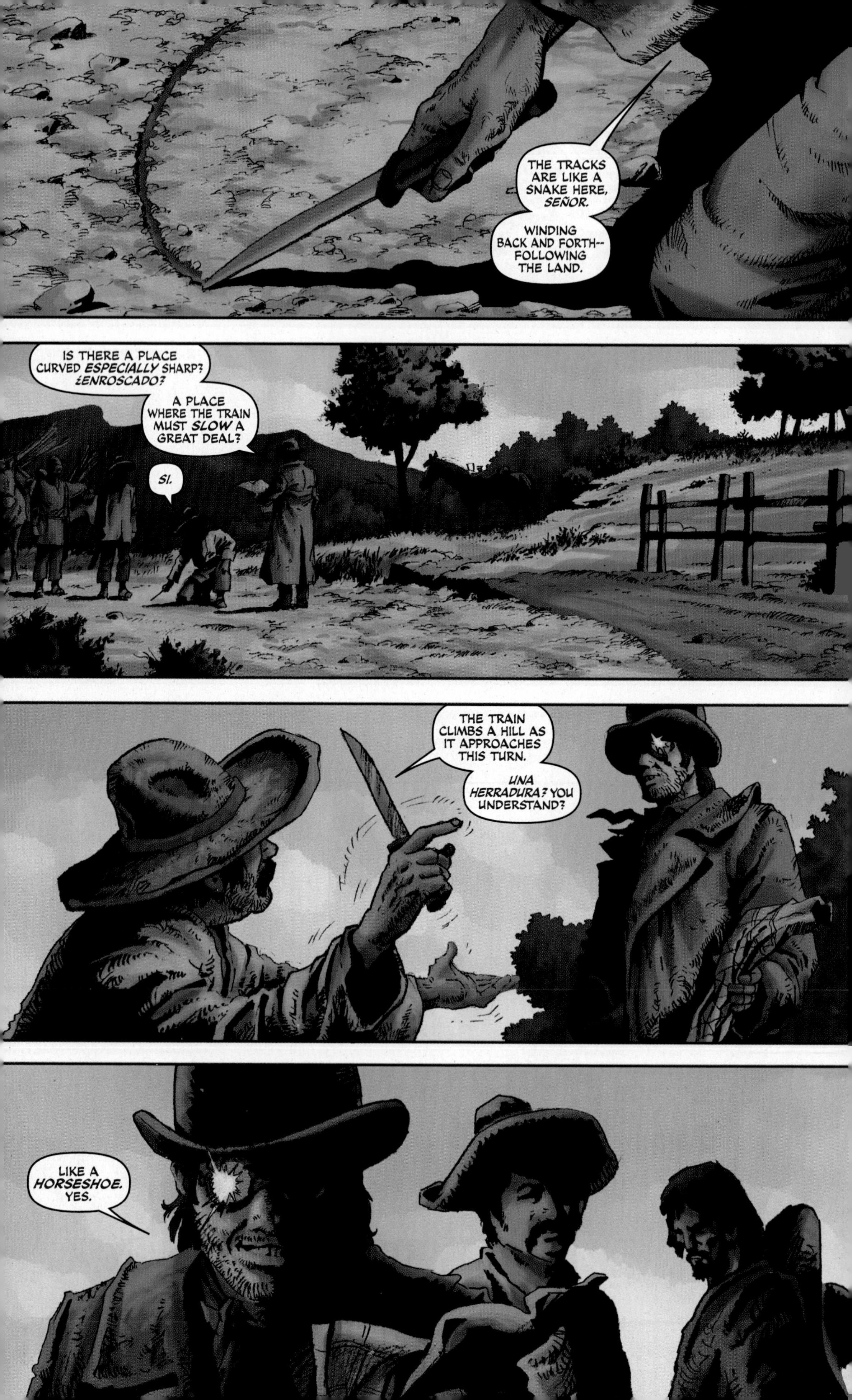
THE TRACKS ARE LIKE A SNAKE HERE, SEÑOR.
WINDING BACK AND FORTH-- FOLLOWING THE LAND.
IS THERE A PLACE CURVED ESPECIALLY SHARP? ¿ENROSCADO?
A PLACE WHERE THE TRAIN MUST SLOW A GREAT DEAL?
SÍ.
THE TRAIN CLIMBS A HILL AS IT APPROACHES THIS TURN.
UNA HERRADURA? YOU UNDERSTAND?
LIKE A HORSESHOE. YES.

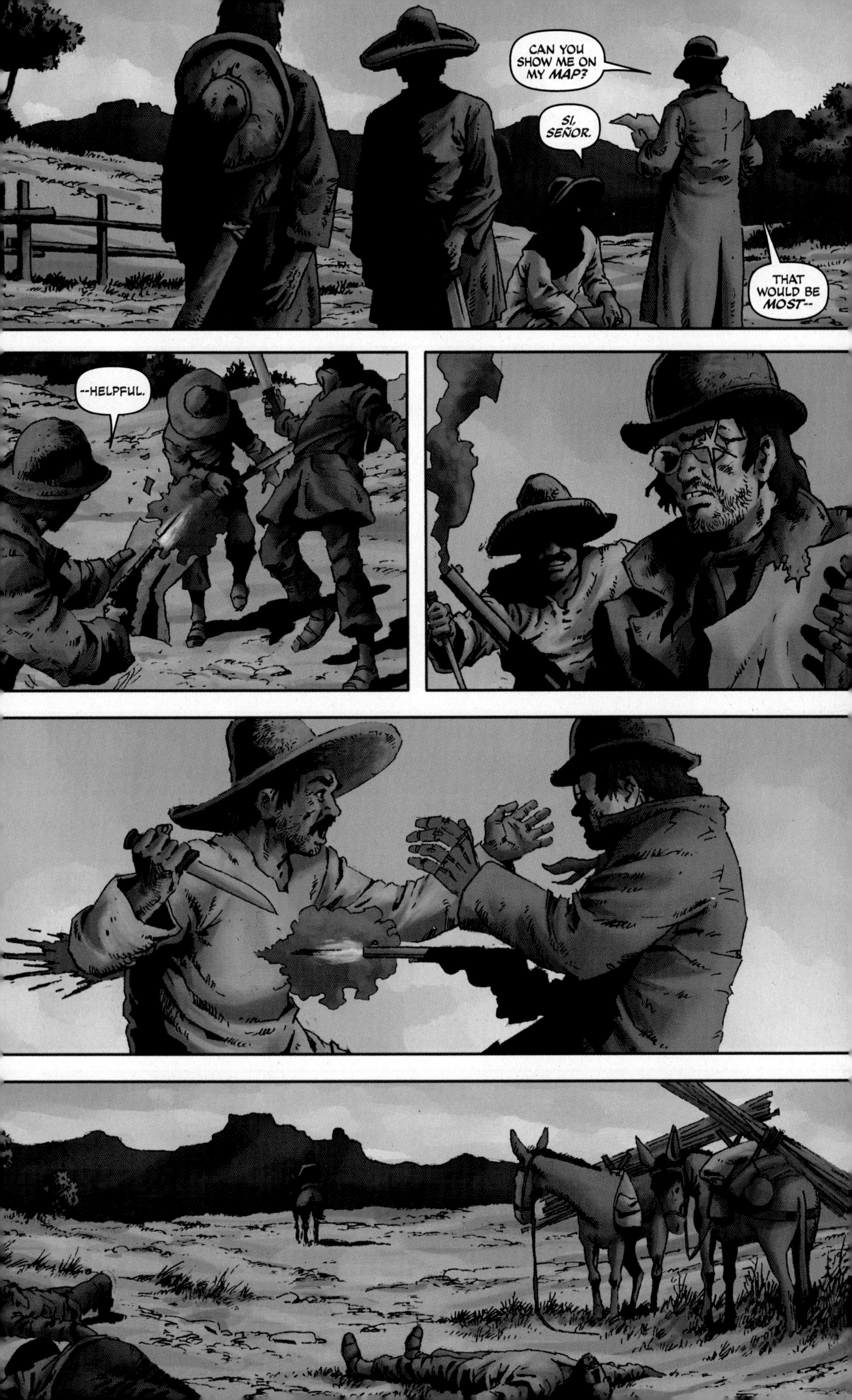
CAN YOU SHOW ME ON MY *MAP?*
SI, SEÑOR.
THAT WOULD BE *MOST*--
--HELPFUL.

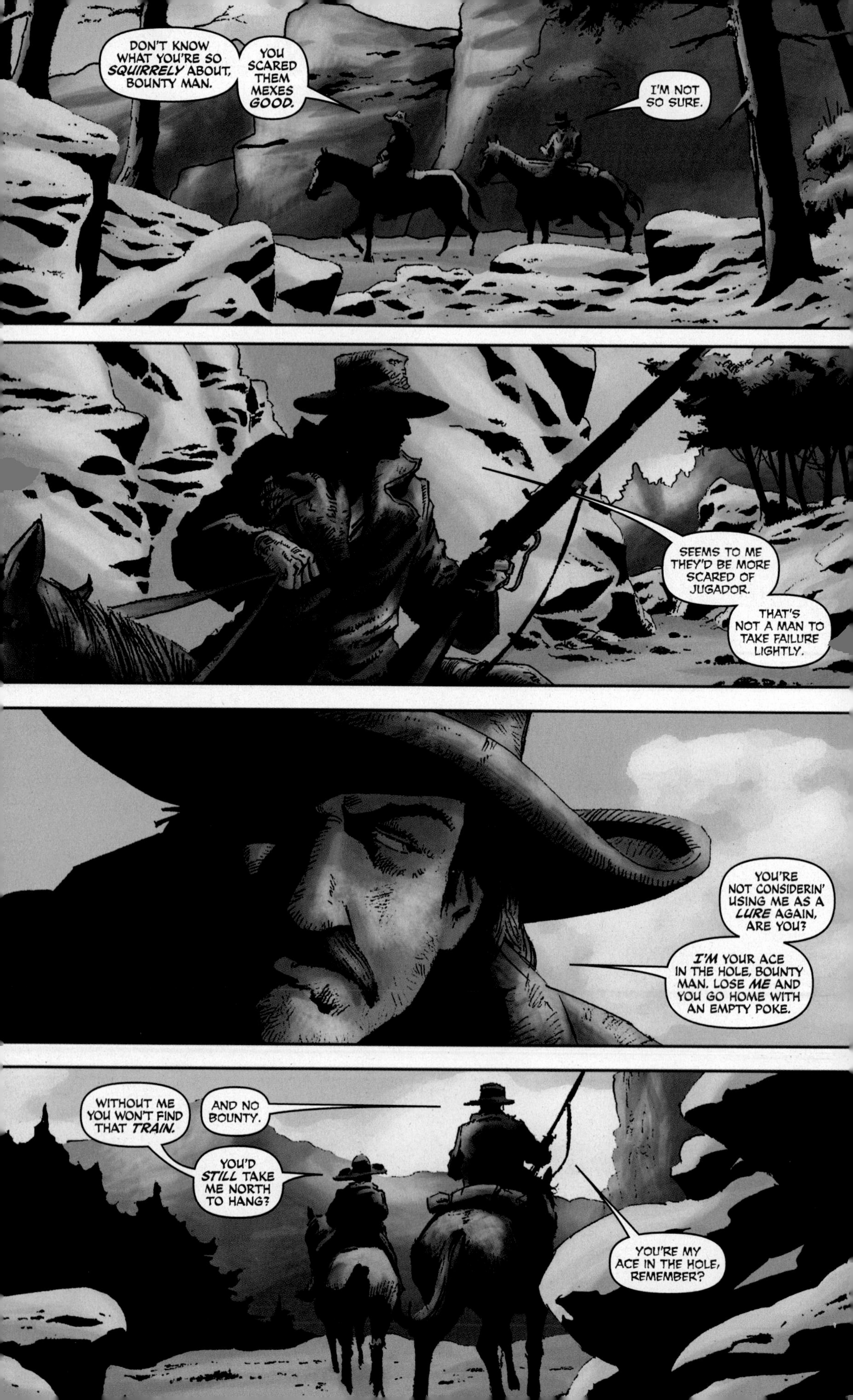
DON'T KNOW WHAT YOU'RE SO *SQUIRRELY* ABOUT, BOUNTY MAN.
YOU SCARED THEM MEXES *GOOD.*
I'M NOT SO SURE.
SEEMS TO ME THEY'D BE MORE SCARED OF JUGADOR.
THAT'S NOT A MAN TO TAKE FAILURE LIGHTLY.
YOU'RE NOT CONSIDERIN' USING ME AS A *LURE* AGAIN, ARE YOU?
I'M YOUR ACE IN THE HOLE, BOUNTY MAN. LOSE *ME* AND YOU GO HOME WITH AN EMPTY POKE.
WITHOUT ME YOU WON'T FIND THAT *TRAIN.*
AND NO BOUNTY.
YOU'D *STILL* TAKE ME NORTH TO HANG?
YOU'RE MY ACE IN THE HOLE, REMEMBER?

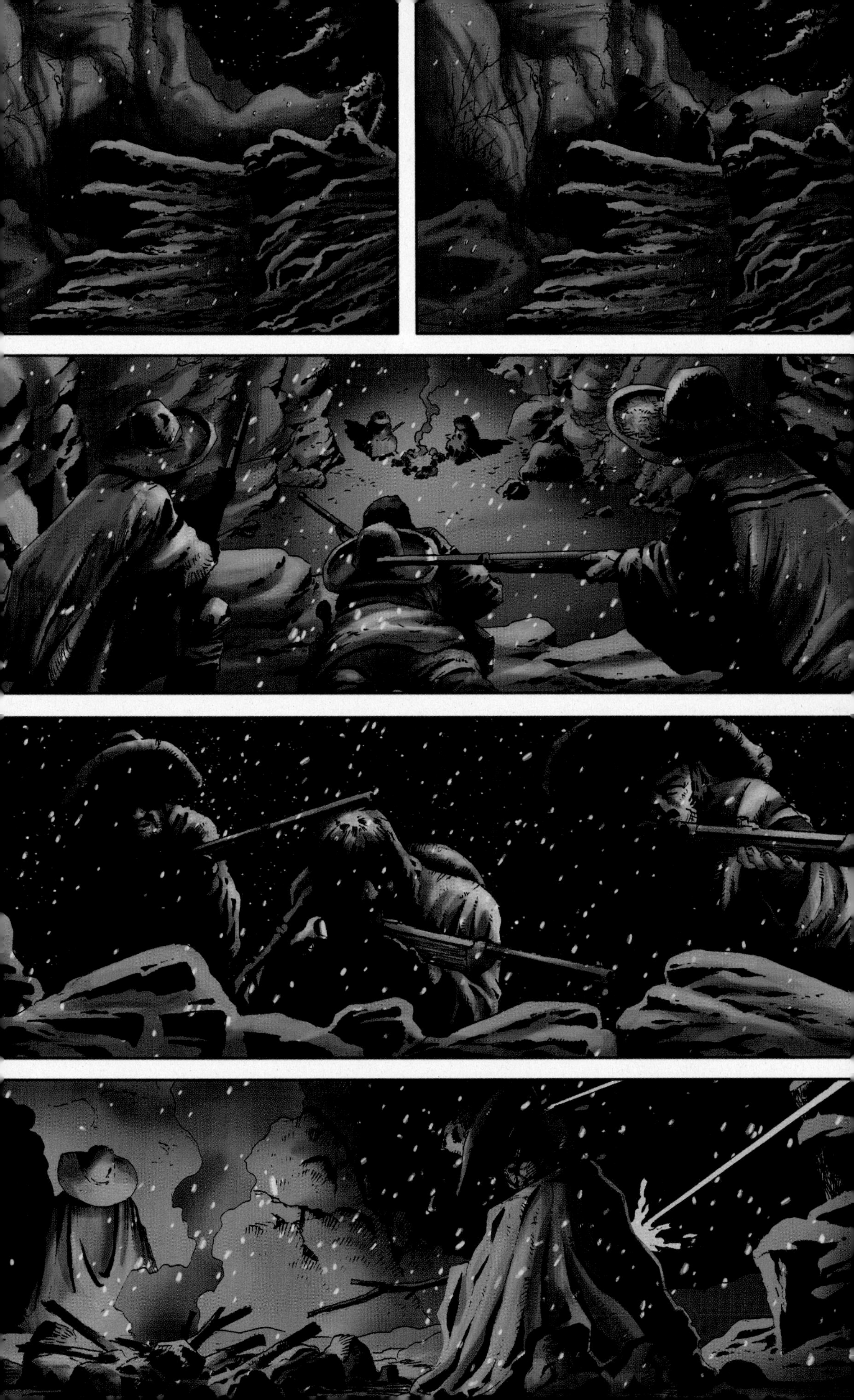

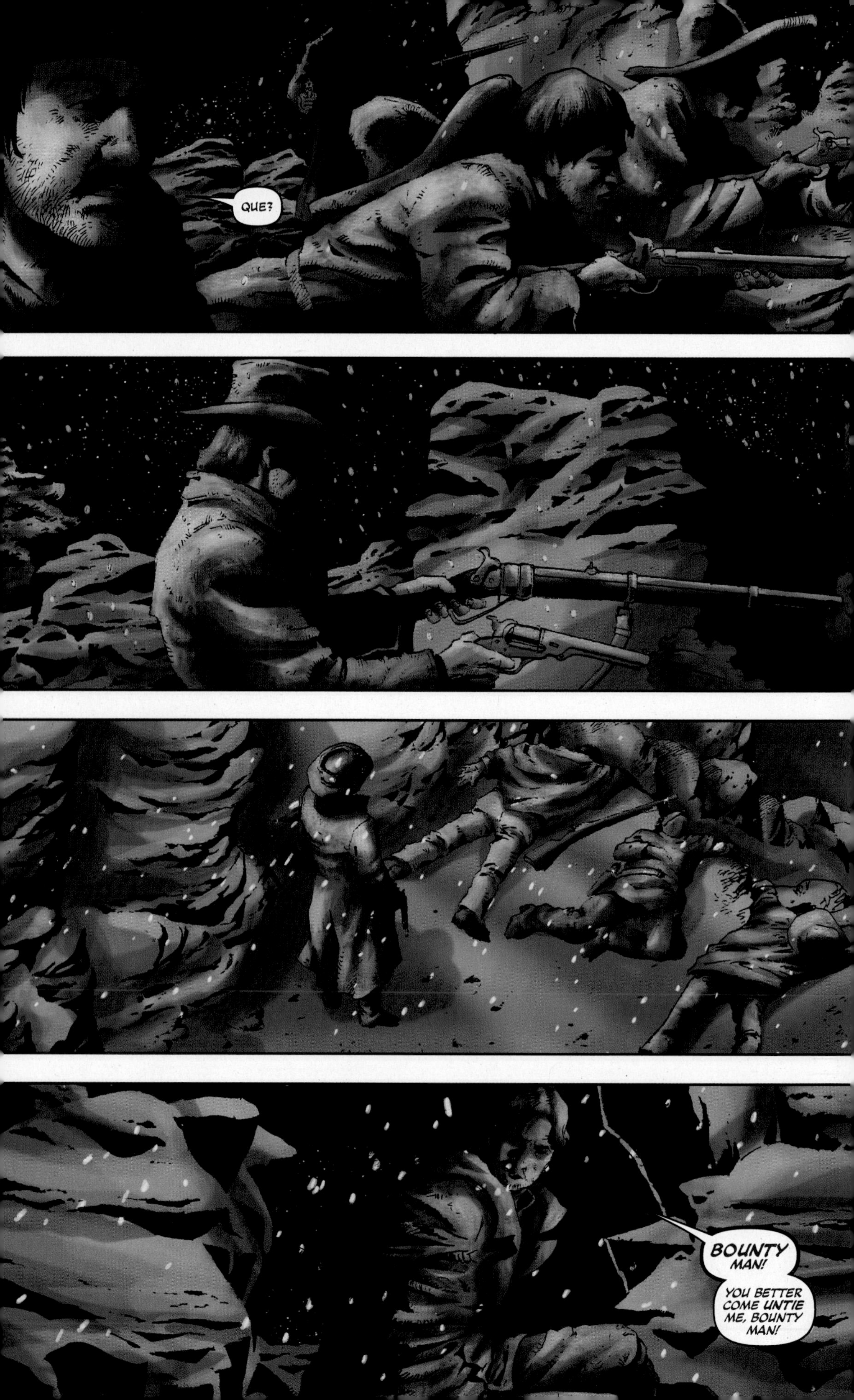
QUE?
BOUNTY MAN!
YOU BETTER COME UNTIE ME, BOUNTY MAN!

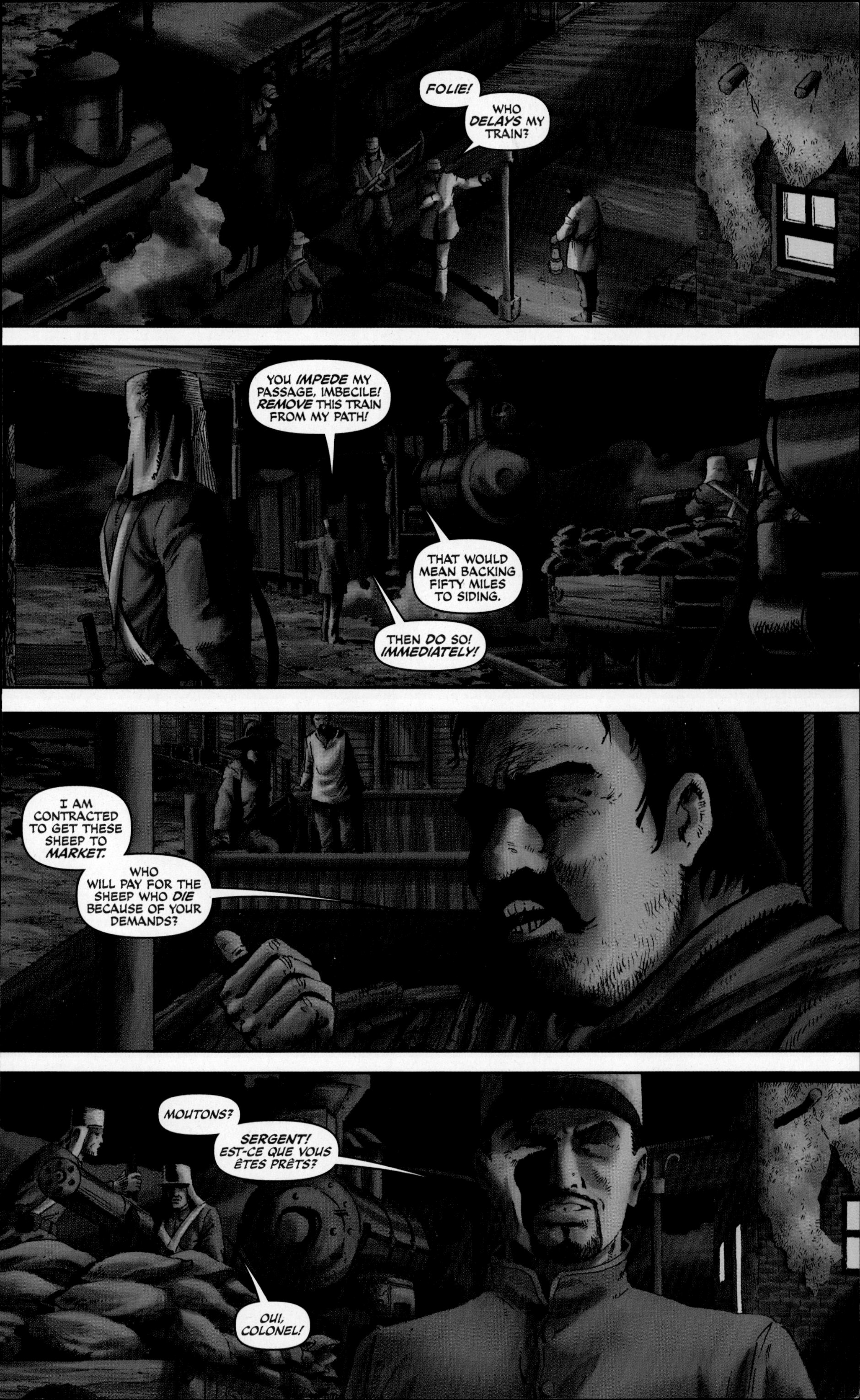
FOLIE!
WHO DELAYS MY TRAIN?
YOU IMPEDE MY PASSAGE, IMBECILE! REMOVE THIS TRAIN FROM MY PATH!
THAT WOULD MEAN BACKING FIFTY MILES TO SIDING.
THEN DO SO! IMMEDIATELY!
I AM CONTRACTED TO GET THESE SHEEP TO MARKET.
WHO WILL PAY FOR THE SHEEP WHO DIE BECAUSE OF YOUR DEMANDS?
MOUTONS?
SERGENT! EST-CE QUE VOUS ÊTES PRÊTS?
OUI, COLONEL!

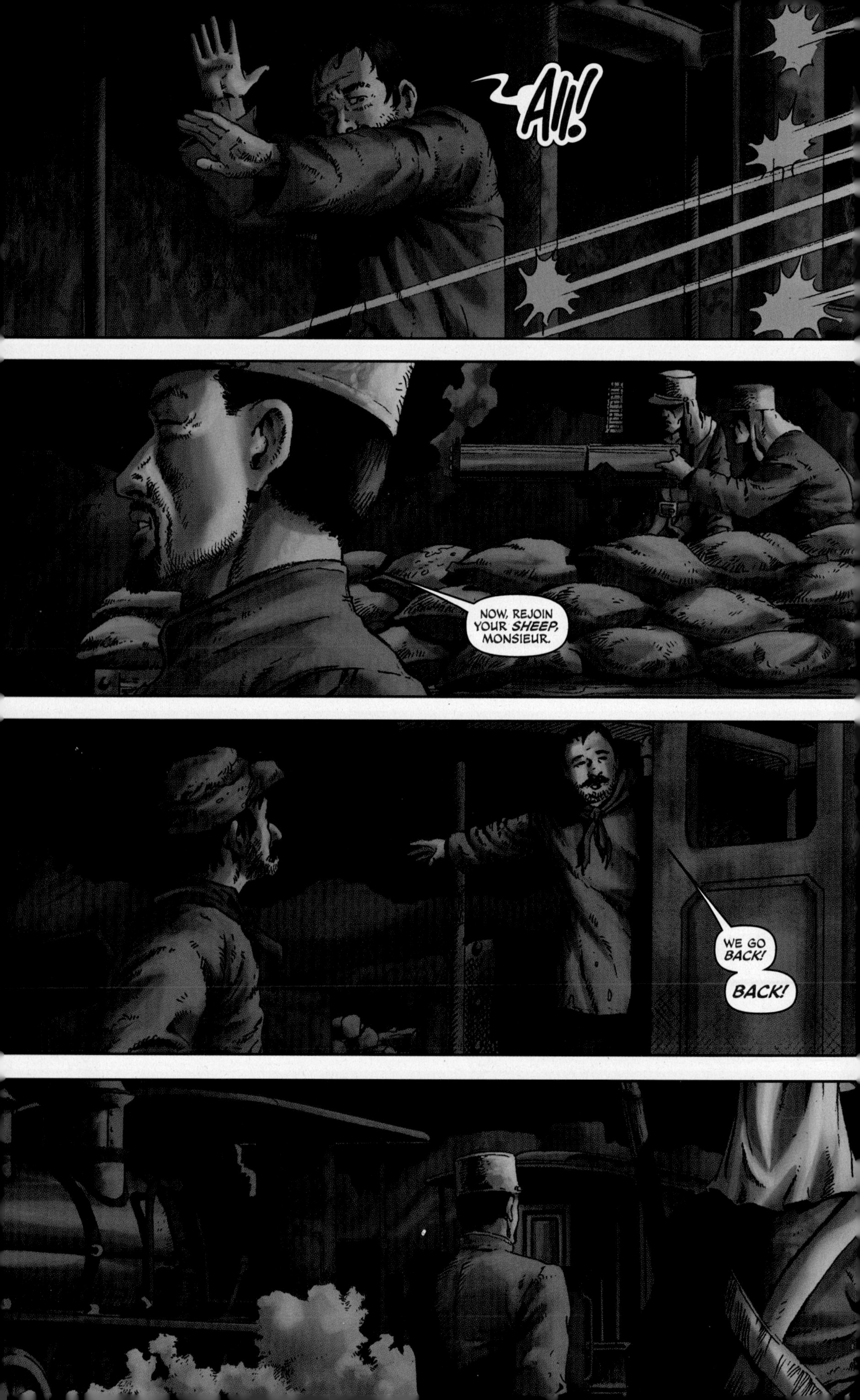
AII!
NOW, REJOIN YOUR SHEEP, MONSIEUR.
WE GO BACK!
BACK!

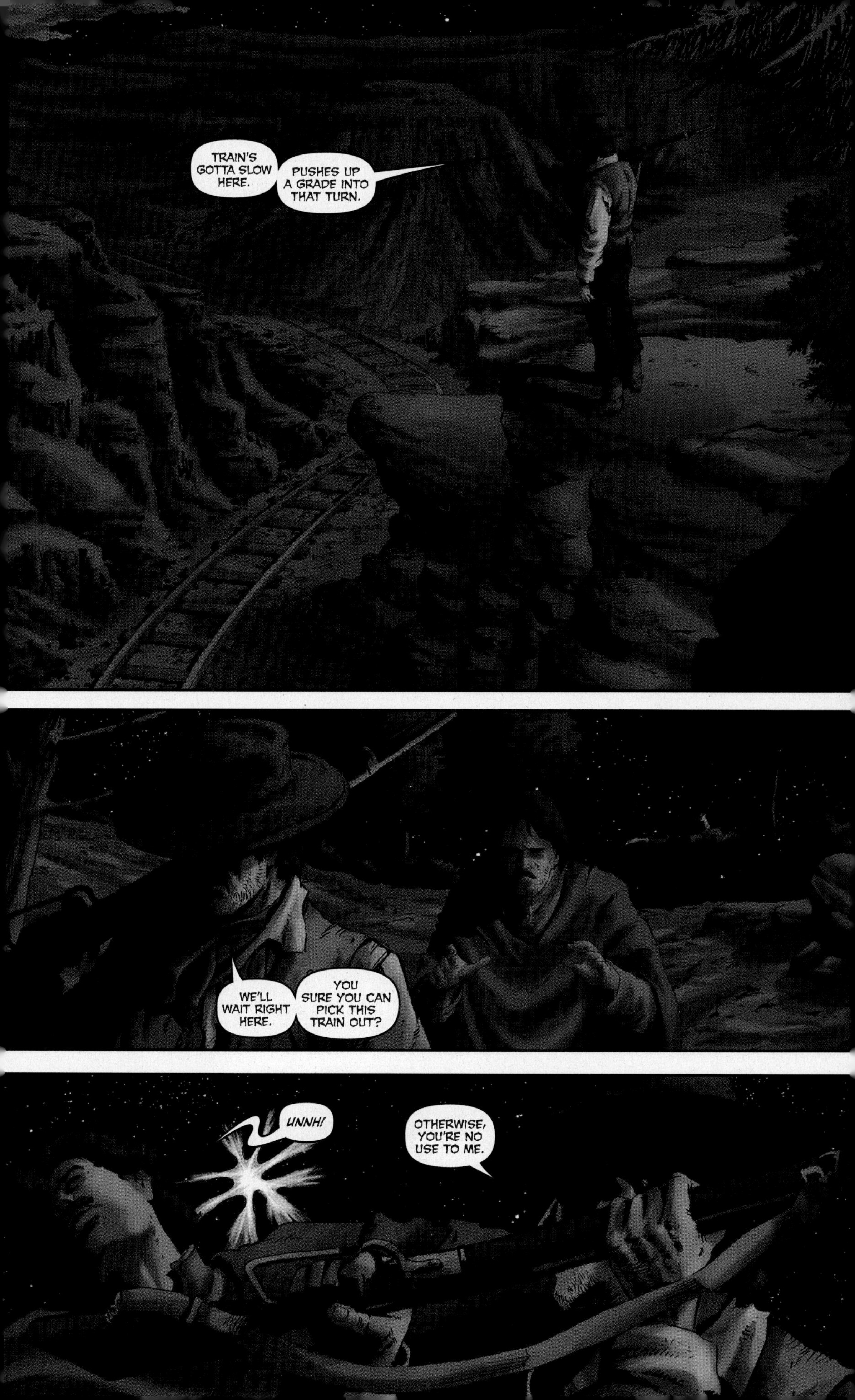
TRAIN'S GOTTA SLOW HERE.
PUSHES UP A GRADE INTO THAT TURN.
WE'LL WAIT RIGHT HERE.
YOU SURE YOU CAN PICK THIS TRAIN OUT?
UNNH!
OTHERWISE, YOU'RE NO USE TO ME.

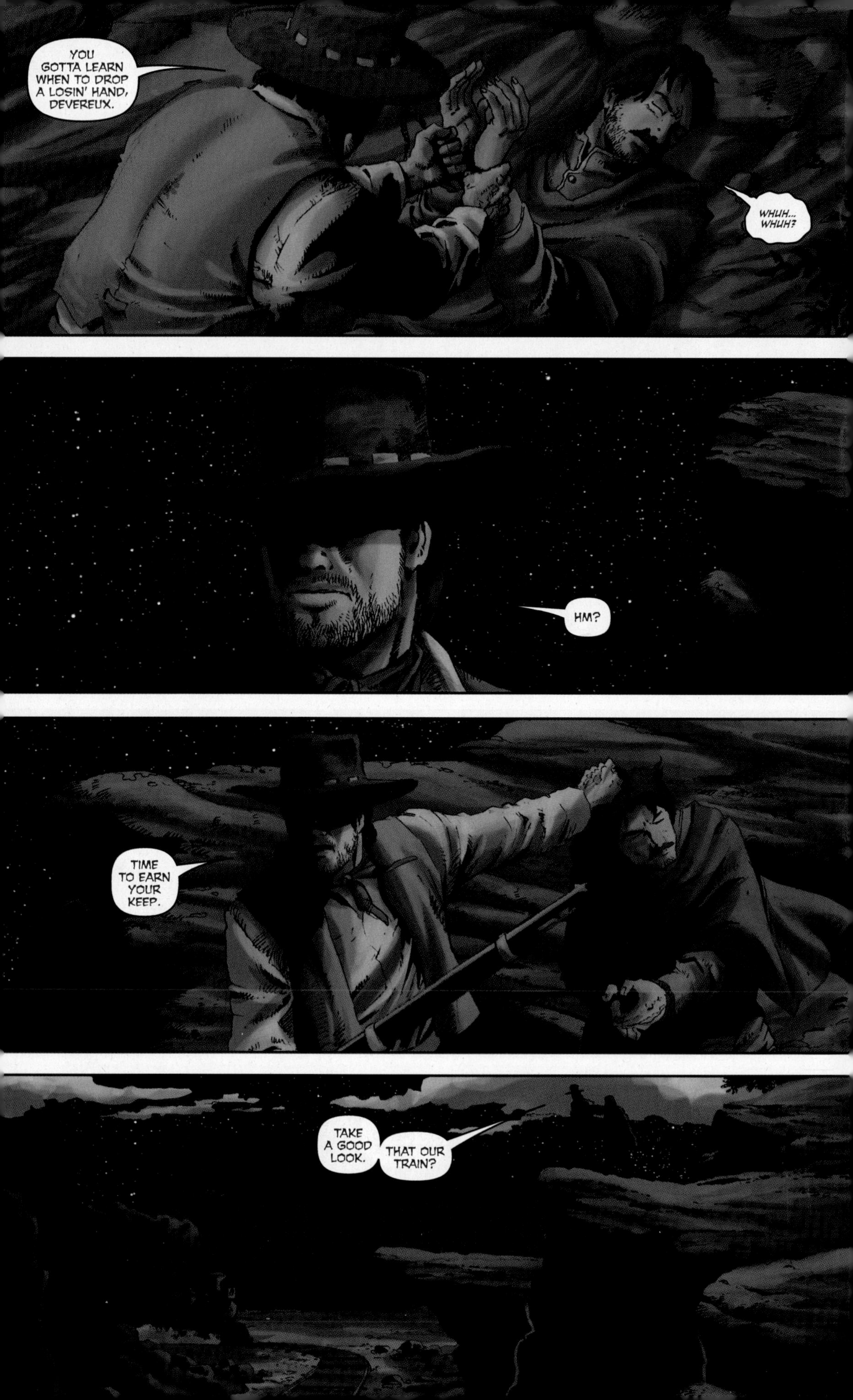
YOU GOTTA LEARN WHEN TO DROP A LOSIN' HAND, DEVEREUX.
WHUH... WHUH?
HM?
TIME TO EARN YOUR KEEP.
TAKE A GOOD LOOK.
THAT OUR TRAIN?

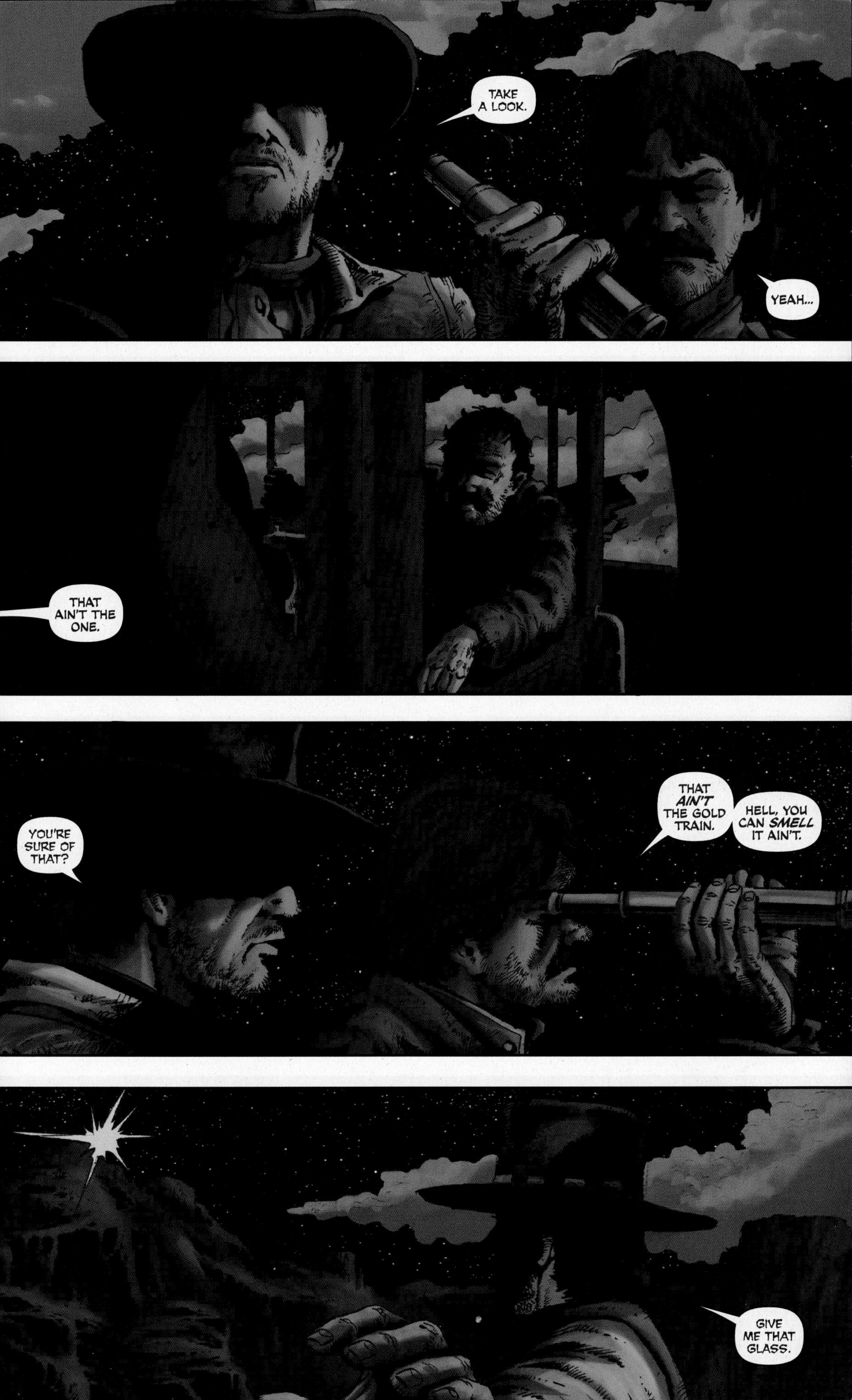
TAKE A LOOK.
YEAH...
THAT AIN'T THE ONE.
YOU'RE SURE OF THAT?
THAT *AIN'T* THE GOLD TRAIN.
HELL, YOU CAN *SMELL* IT AIN'T.
GIVE ME THAT GLASS.

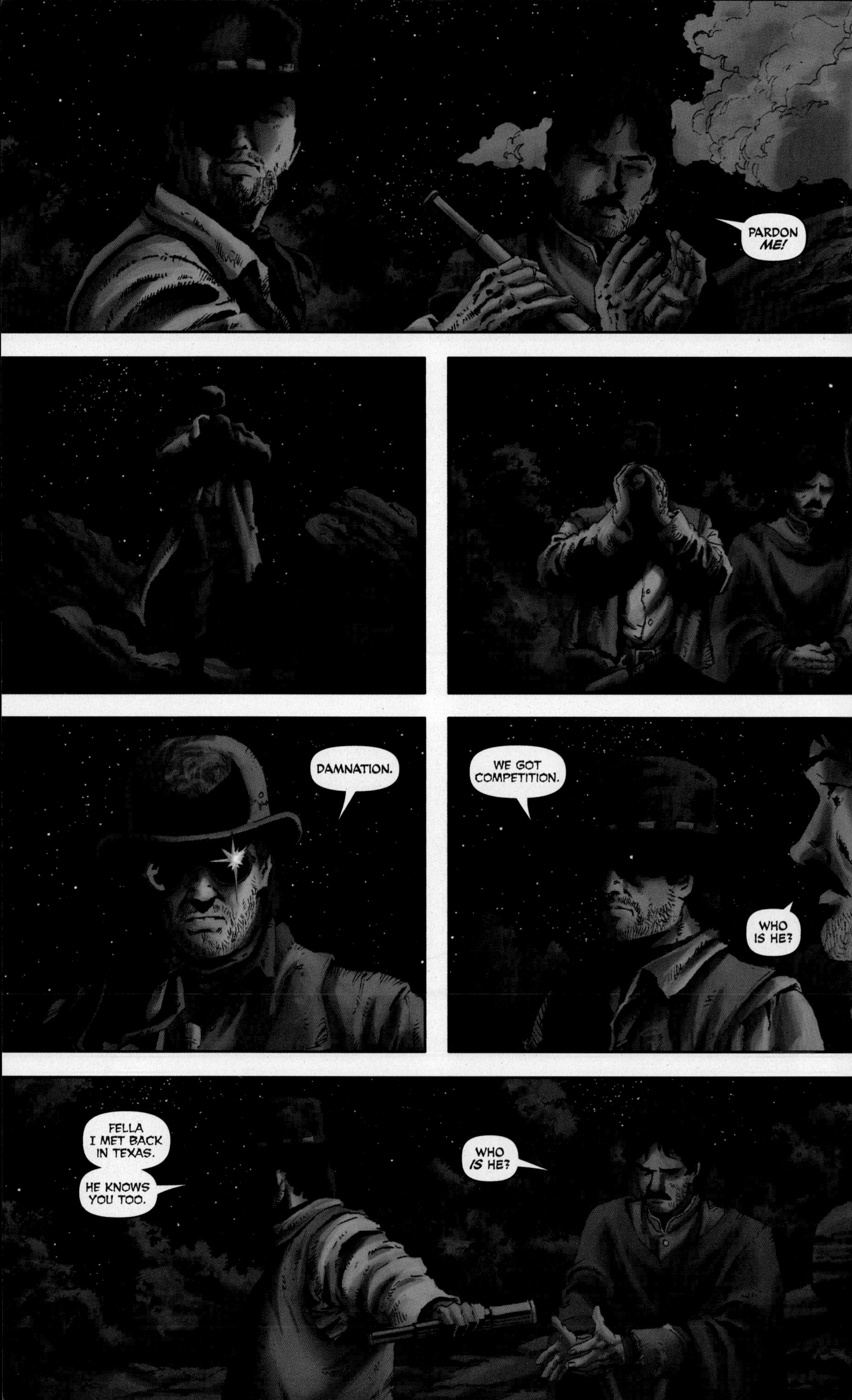
PARDON ME!
DAMNATION.
WE GOT COMPETITION.
WHO IS HE?
FELLA I MET BACK IN TEXAS.
HE KNOWS YOU TOO.
WHO IS HE?

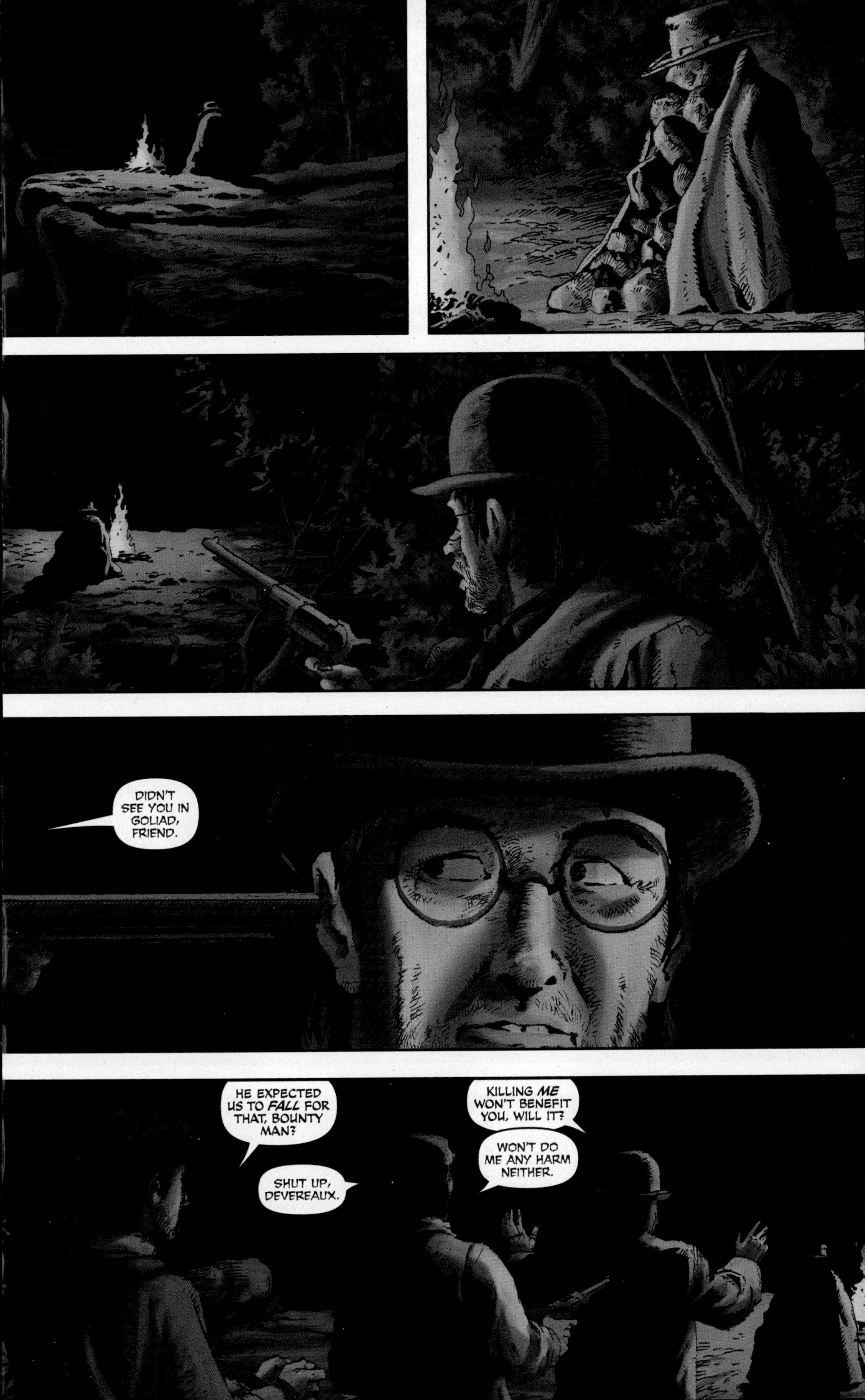
DIDN'T SEE YOU IN GOLIAD, FRIEND.
HE EXPECTED US TO FALL FOR THAT, BOUNTY MAN?
SHUT UP, DEVEREAUX.
KILLING ME WON'T BENEFIT YOU, WILL IT?
WON'T DO ME ANY HARM NEITHER.

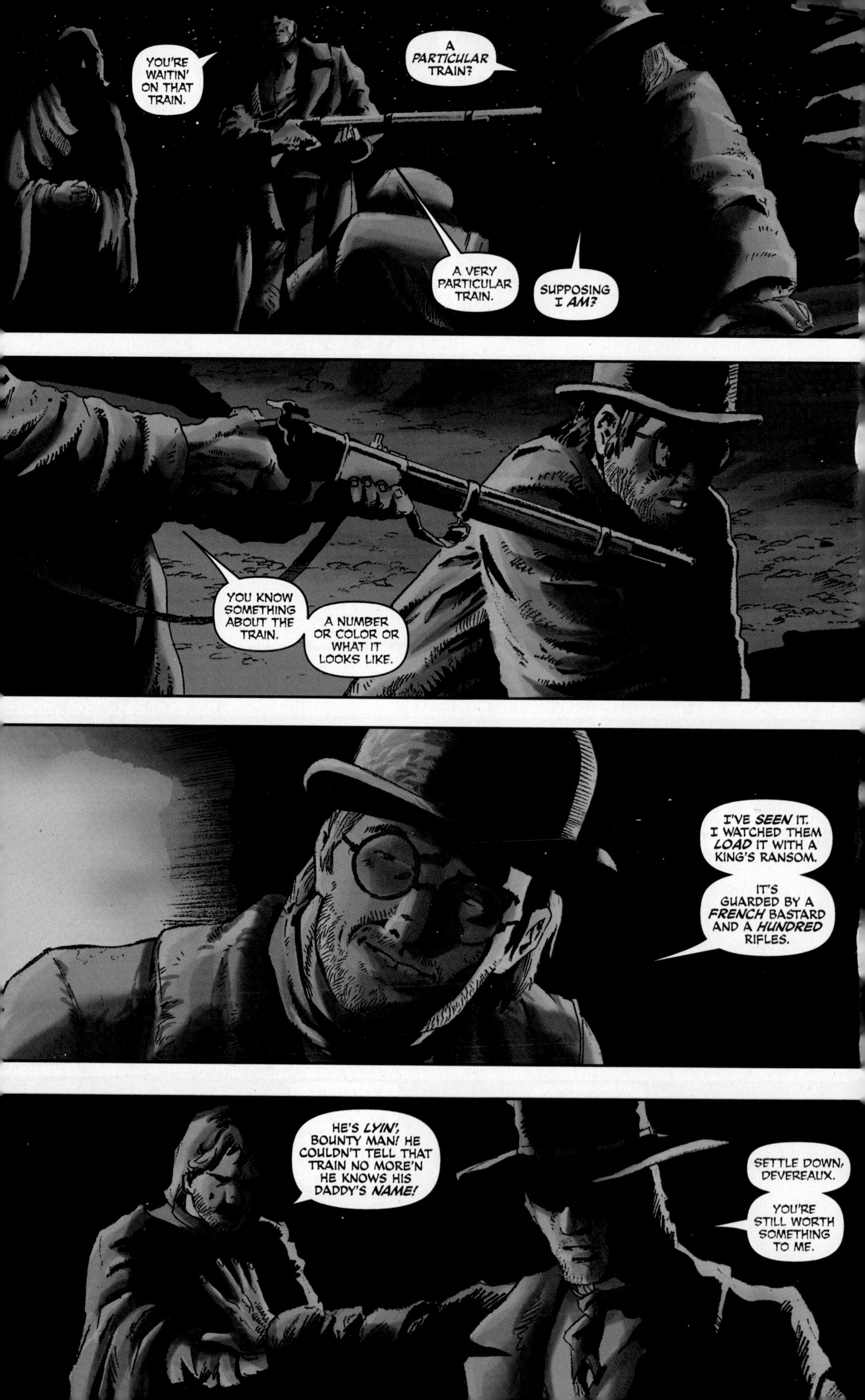
YOU'RE WAITIN' ON THAT TRAIN.
A PARTICULAR TRAIN?
A VERY PARTICULAR TRAIN.
SUPPOSING I AM?
YOU KNOW SOMETHING ABOUT THE TRAIN.
A NUMBER OR COLOR OR WHAT IT LOOKS LIKE.
I'VE SEEN IT. I WATCHED THEM LOAD IT WITH A KING'S RANSOM.
IT'S GUARDED BY A FRENCH BASTARD AND A HUNDRED RIFLES.
HE'S LYIN', BOUNTY MAN! HE COULDN'T TELL THAT TRAIN NO MORE'N HE KNOWS HIS DADDY'S NAME!
SETTLE DOWN, DEVEREAUX.
YOU'RE STILL WORTH SOMETHING TO ME.

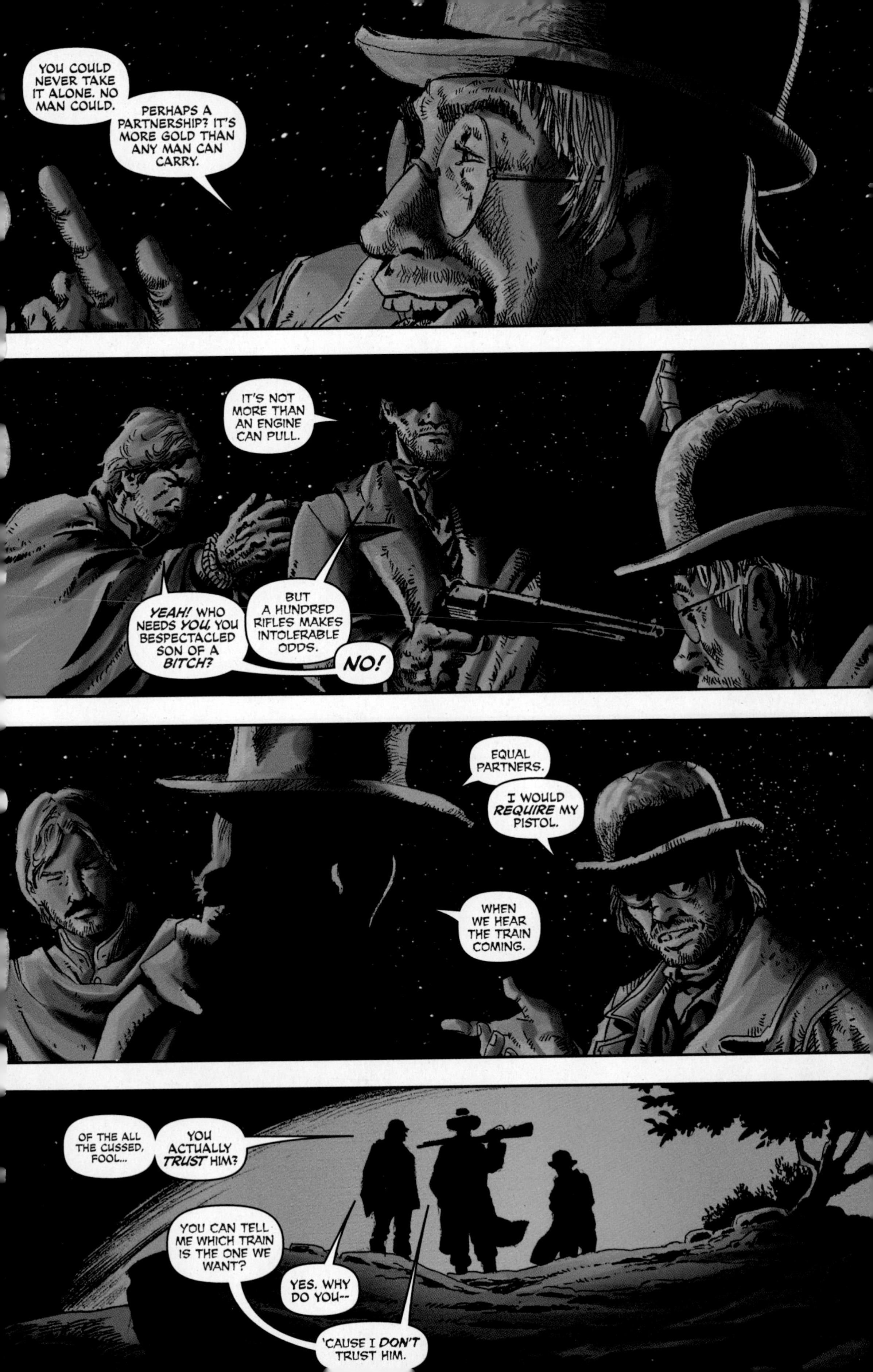
YOU COULD NEVER TAKE IT ALONE. NO MAN COULD.
PERHAPS A PARTNERSHIP? IT'S MORE GOLD THAN ANY MAN CAN CARRY.
IT'S NOT MORE THAN AN ENGINE CAN PULL.
YEAH! WHO NEEDS YOU, YOU BESPECTACLED SON OF A BITCH?
BUT A HUNDRED RIFLES MAKES INTOLERABLE ODDS.
NO!
EQUAL PARTNERS.
I WOULD REQUIRE MY PISTOL.
WHEN WE HEAR THE TRAIN COMING.
OF THE ALL THE CUSSED, FOOL...
YOU ACTUALLY TRUST HIM?
YOU CAN TELL ME WHICH TRAIN IS THE ONE WE WANT?
YES. WHY DO YOU--
'CAUSE I DON'T TRUST HIM.

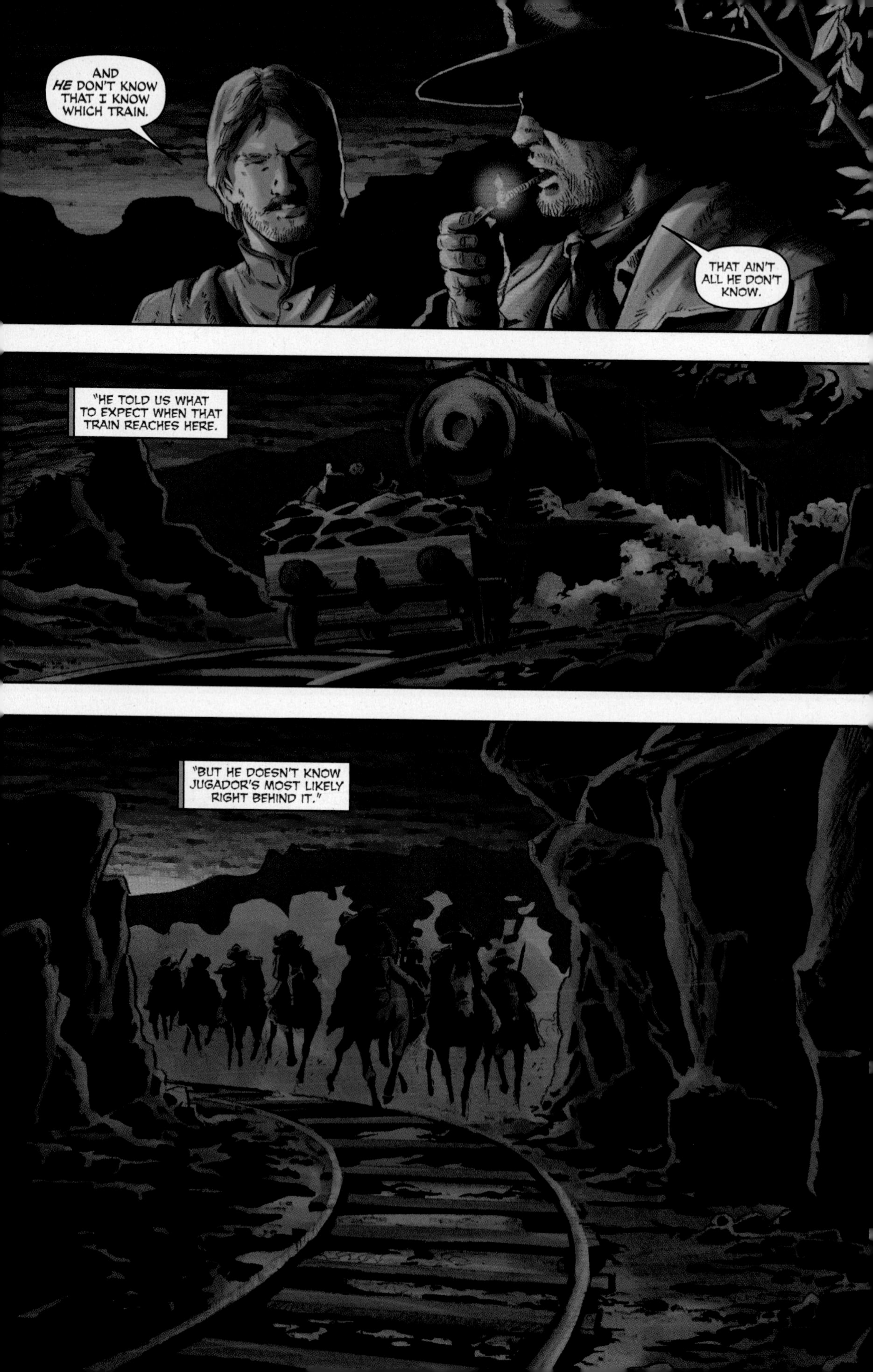
AND HE DON'T KNOW THAT I KNOW WHICH TRAIN.
THAT AIN'T ALL HE DON'T KNOW.
"HE TOLD US WHAT TO EXPECT WHEN THAT TRAIN REACHES HERE.
"BUT HE DOESN'T KNOW JUGADOR'S MOST LIKELY RIGHT BEHIND IT."

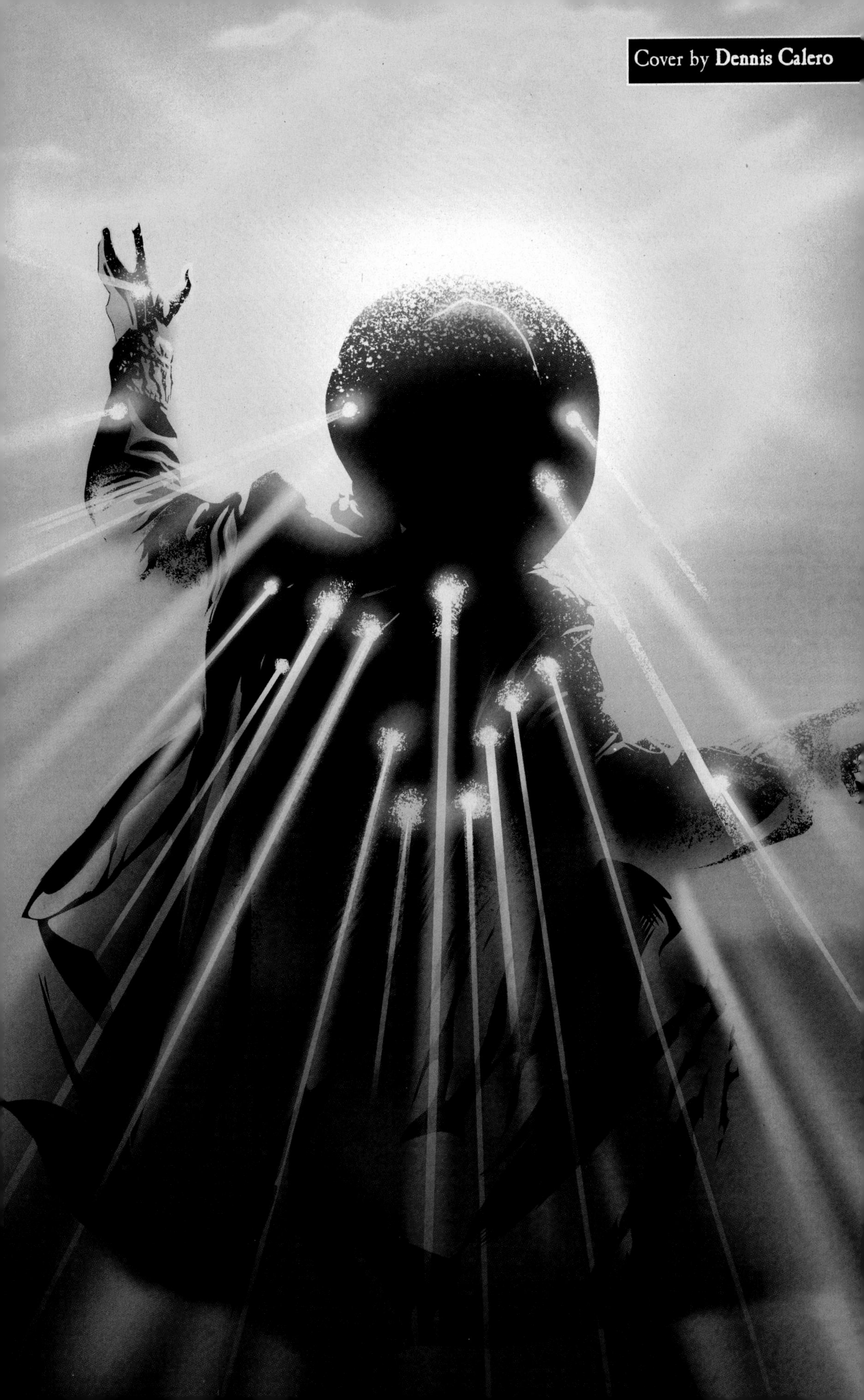
Cover by **Dennis Calero**

Cover by **Sergio Cariello**

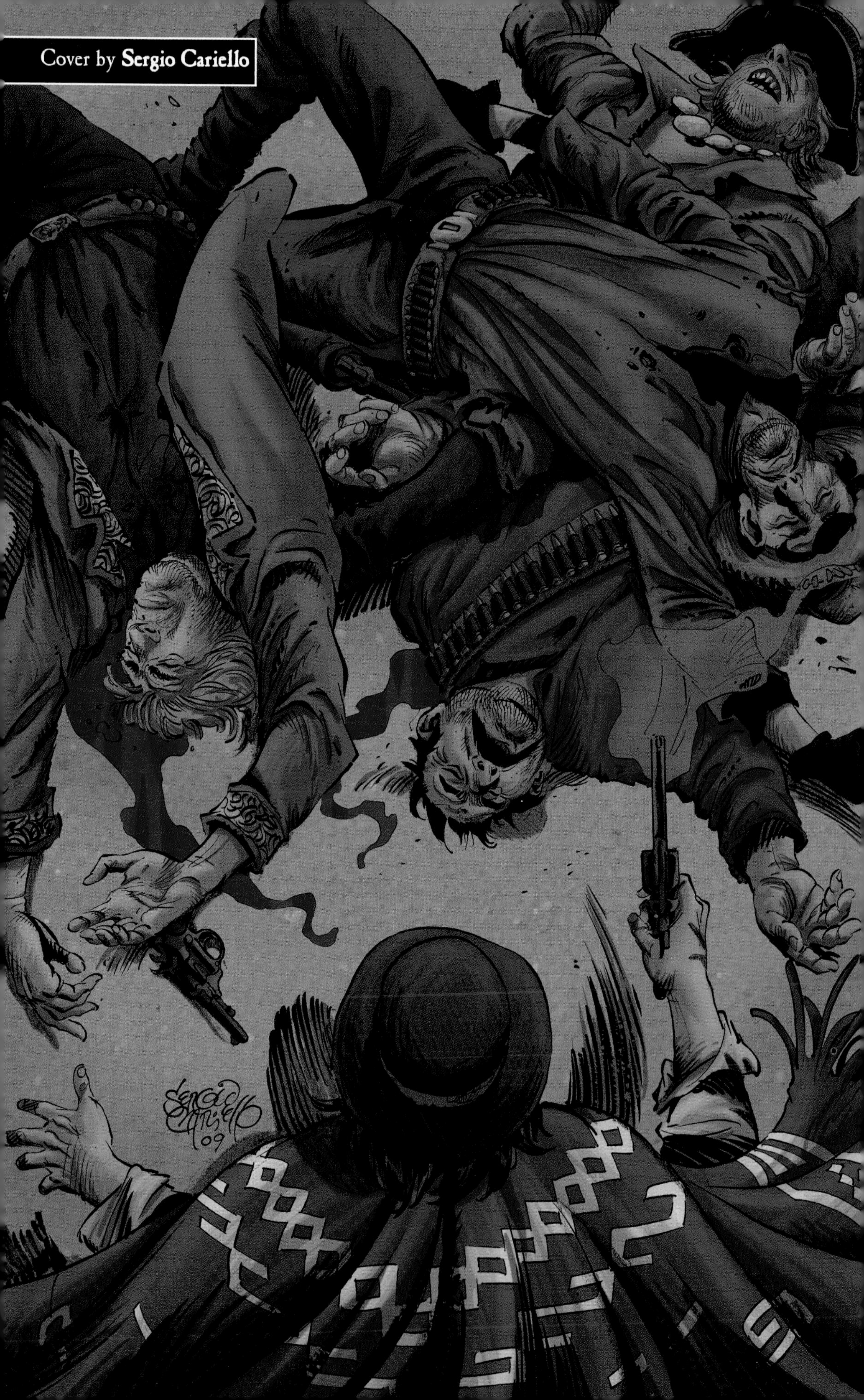

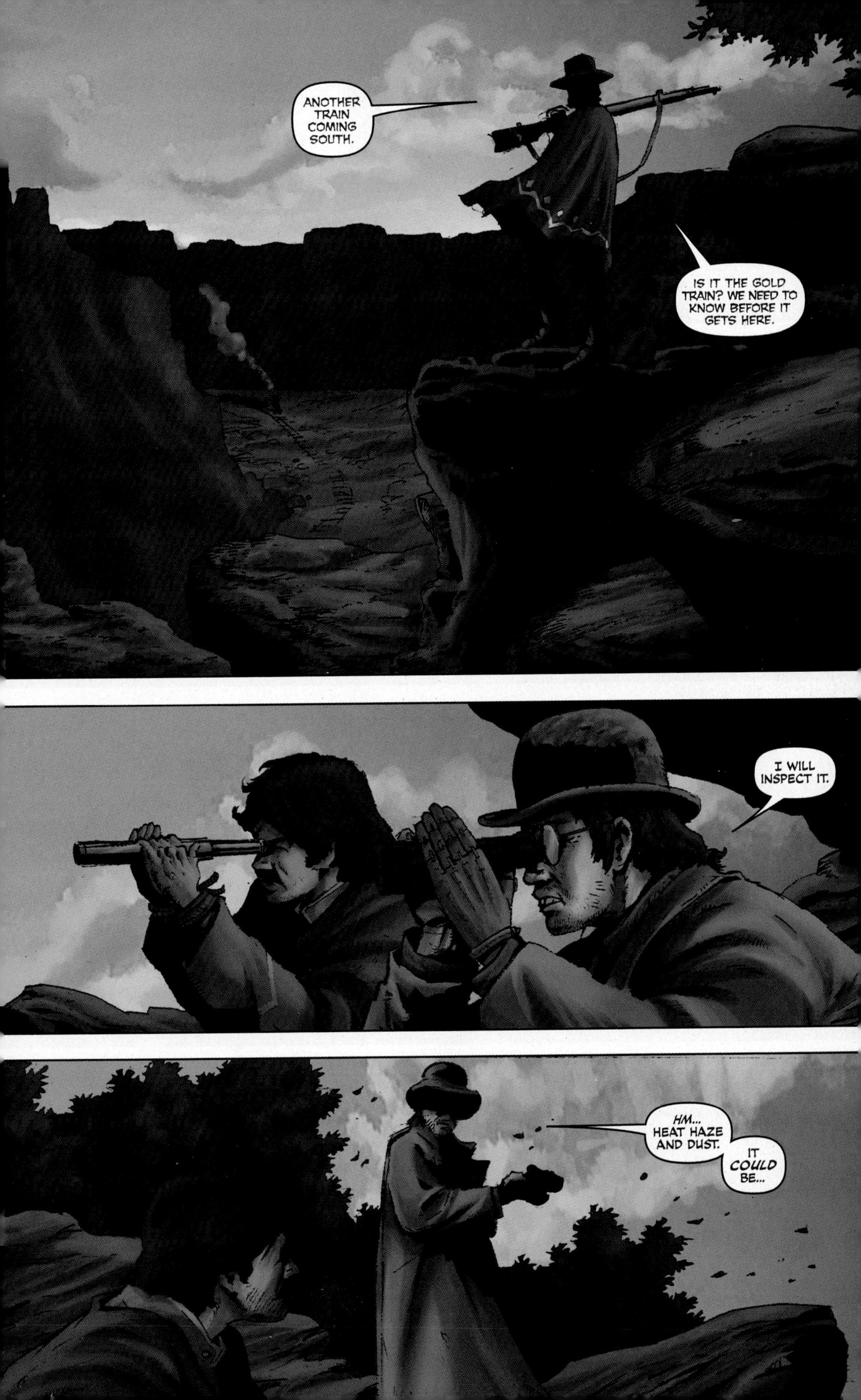
ANOTHER TRAIN COMING SOUTH.
IS IT THE GOLD TRAIN? WE NEED TO KNOW BEFORE IT GETS HERE.
I WILL INSPECT IT.
HM... HEAT HAZE AND DUST.
IT COULD BE...

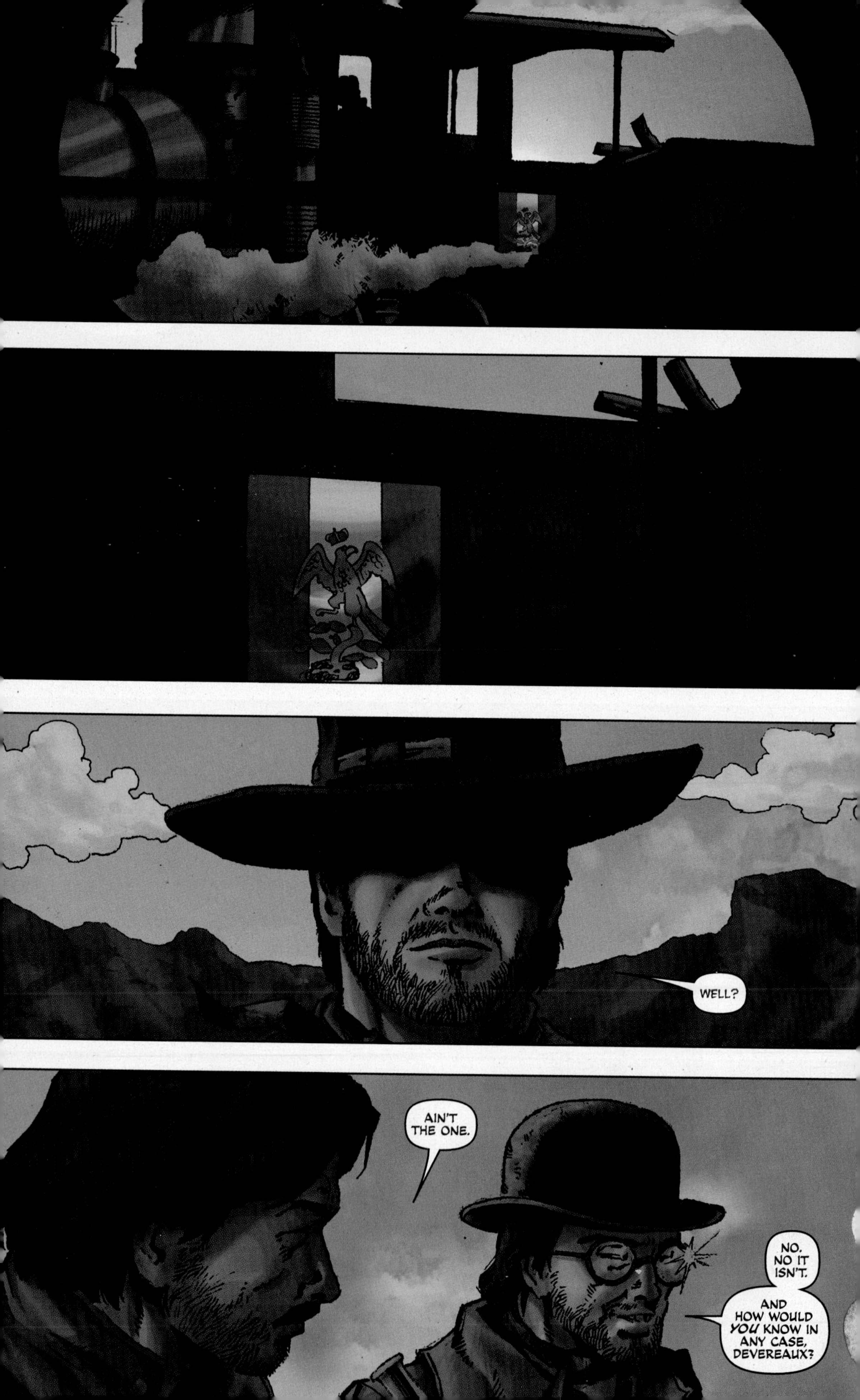
WELL?
AIN'T THE ONE.
NO. NO IT ISN'T.
AND HOW WOULD *YOU* KNOW IN ANY CASE, DEVEREAUX?

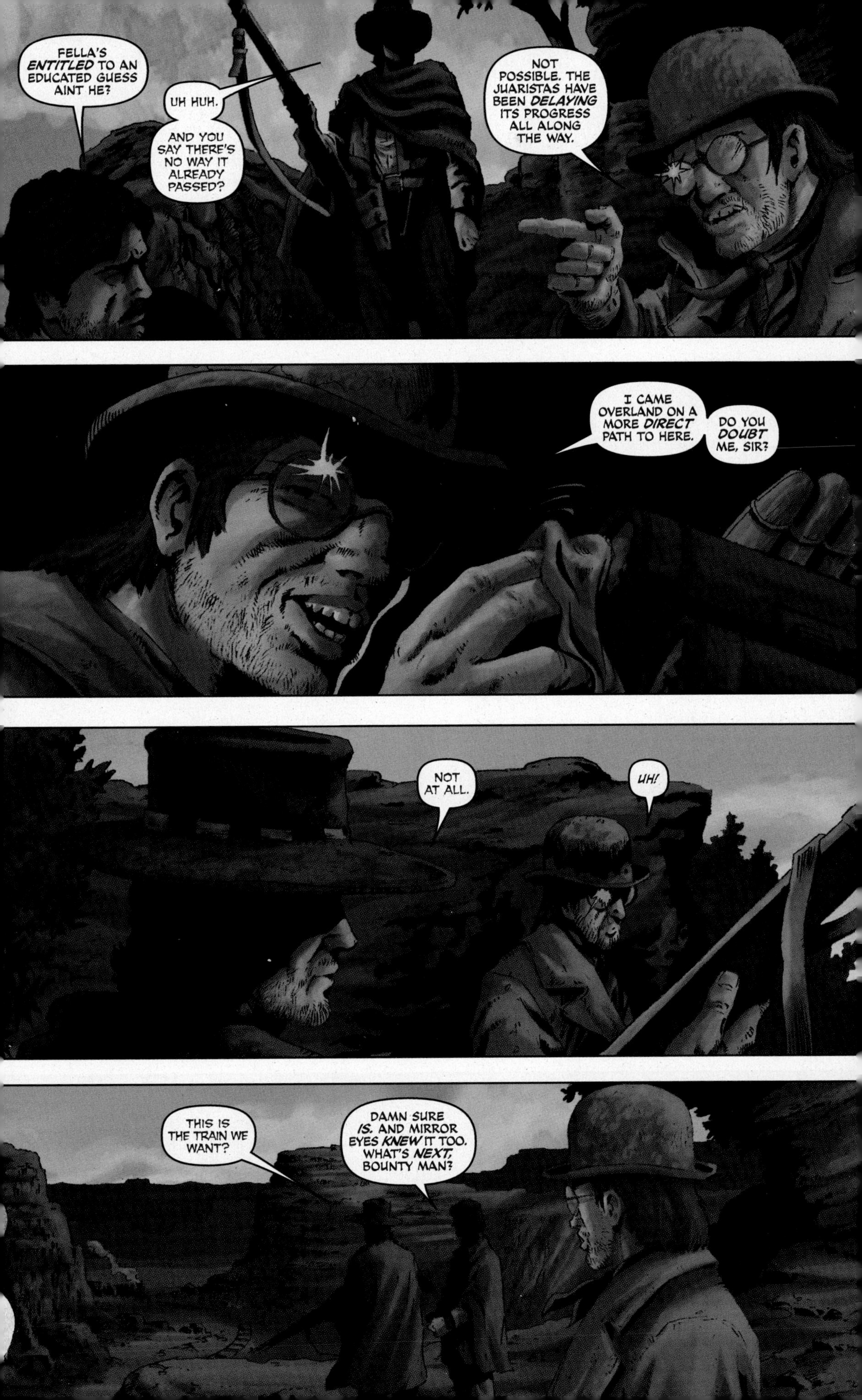
FELLA'S *ENTITLED* TO AN EDUCATED GUESS AINT HE?
UH HUH.
AND YOU SAY THERE'S NO WAY IT ALREADY PASSED?
NOT POSSIBLE. THE JUARISTAS HAVE BEEN *DELAYING* ITS PROGRESS ALL ALONG THE WAY.
I CAME OVERLAND ON A MORE *DIRECT* PATH TO HERE.
DO YOU *DOUBT* ME, SIR?
NOT AT ALL.
UH!
THIS IS THE TRAIN WE WANT?
DAMN SURE *IS.* AND MIRROR EYES *KNEW* IT TOO. WHAT'S *NEXT,* BOUNTY MAN?

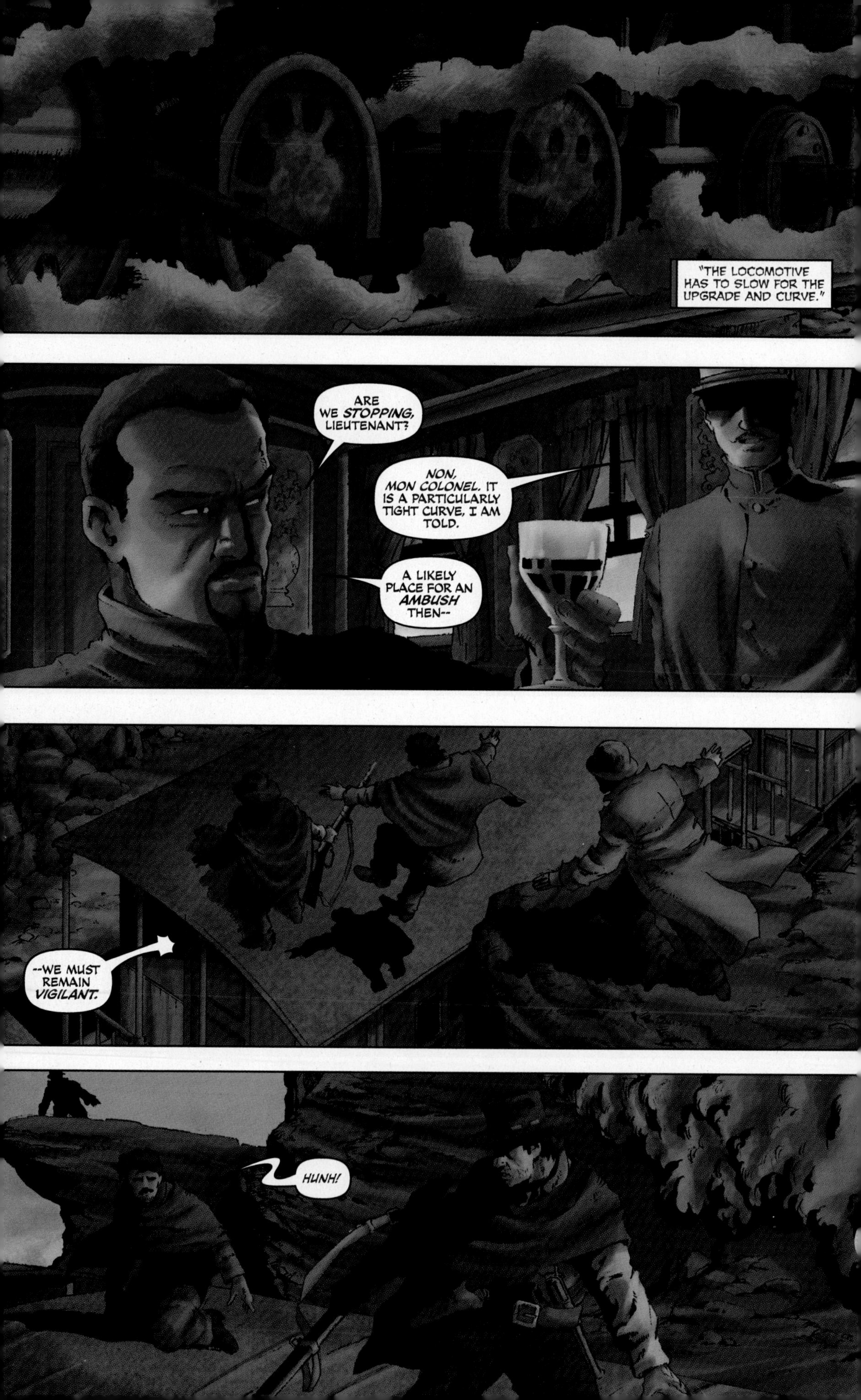
"THE LOCOMOTIVE HAS TO SLOW FOR THE UPGRADE AND CURVE."
ARE WE STOPPING, LIEUTENANT?
NON, MON COLONEL. IT IS A PARTICULARLY TIGHT CURVE, I AM TOLD.
A LIKELY PLACE FOR AN AMBUSH THEN--
--WE MUST REMAIN VIGILANT.
HUNH!

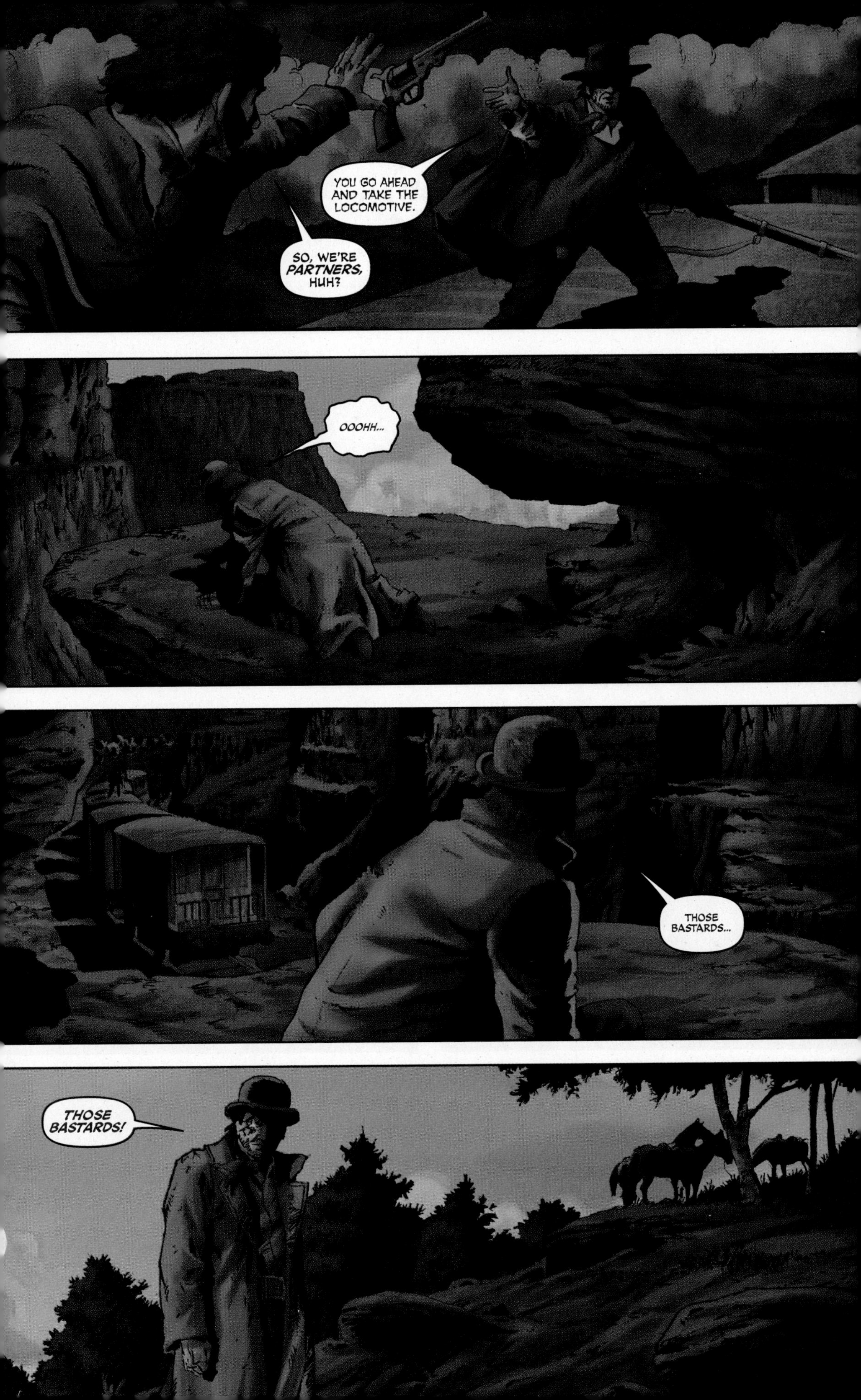
SO, WE'RE *PARTNERS*, HUH?
YOU GO AHEAD AND TAKE THE LOCOMOTIVE.
OOOHH...
THOSE BASTARDS...
THOSE BASTARDS!

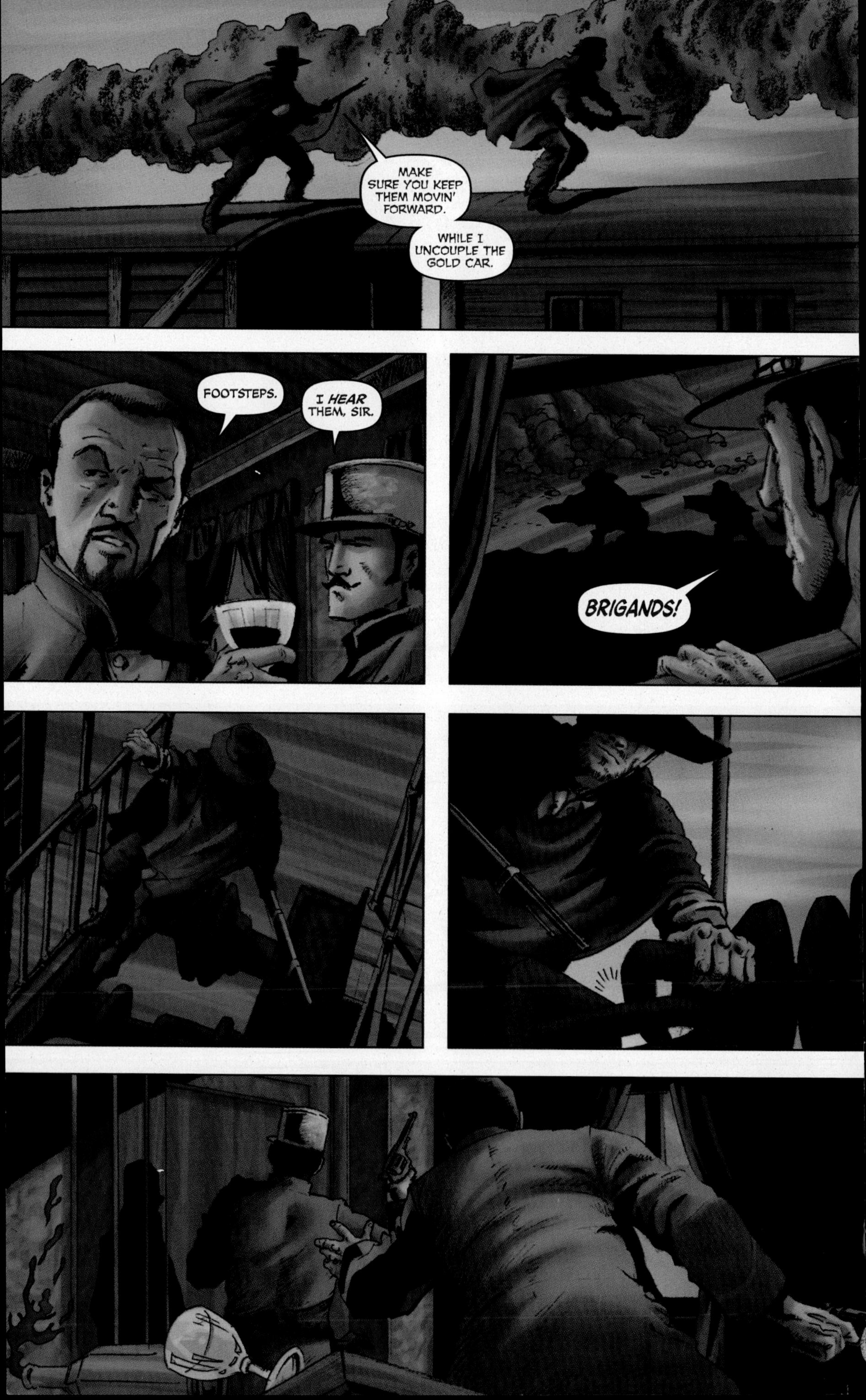
MAKE SURE YOU KEEP THEM MOVIN' FORWARD.
WHILE I UNCOUPLE THE GOLD CAR.
FOOTSTEPS.
I *HEAR* THEM, SIR.
BRIGANDS!

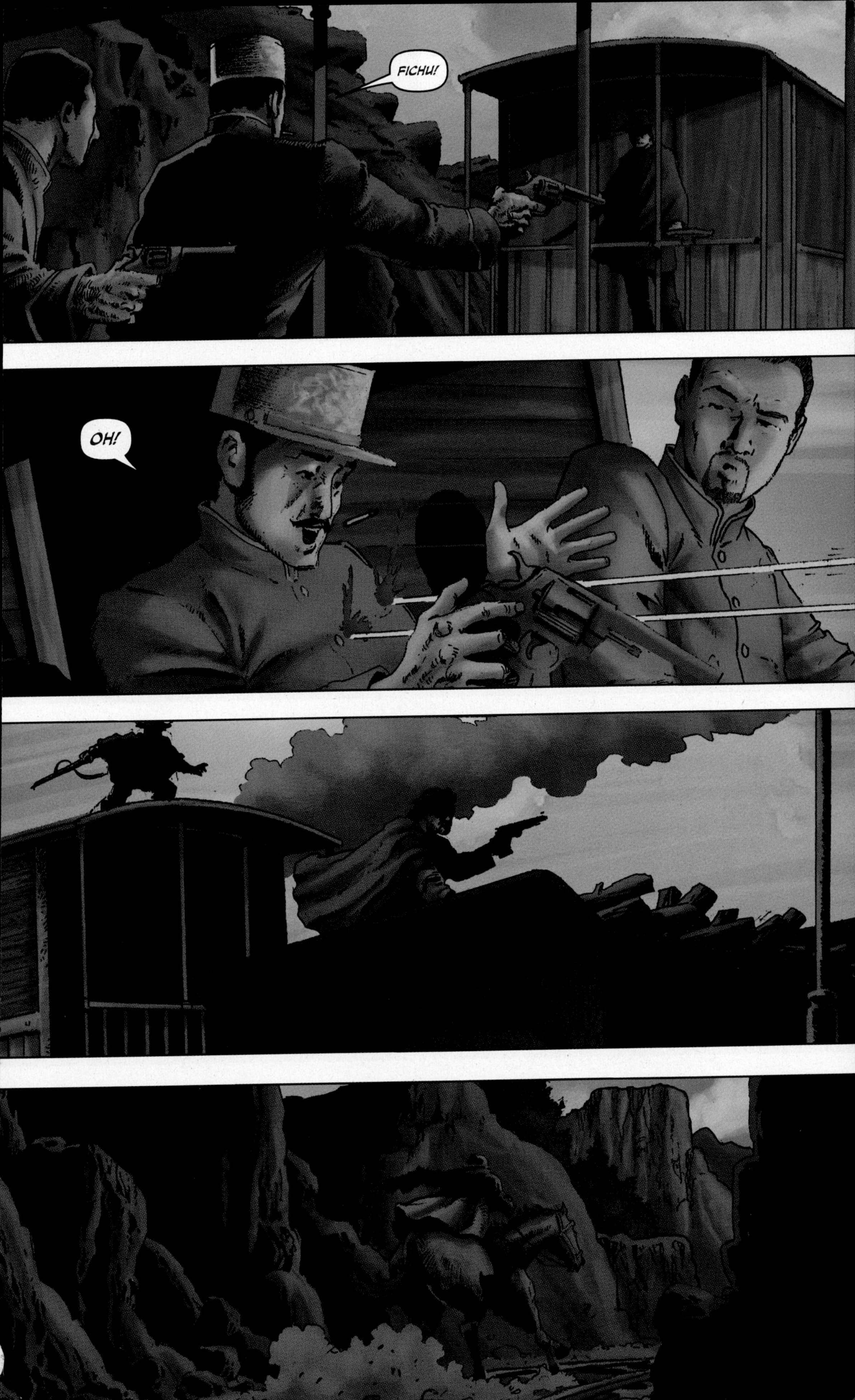
FICHU!
OH!

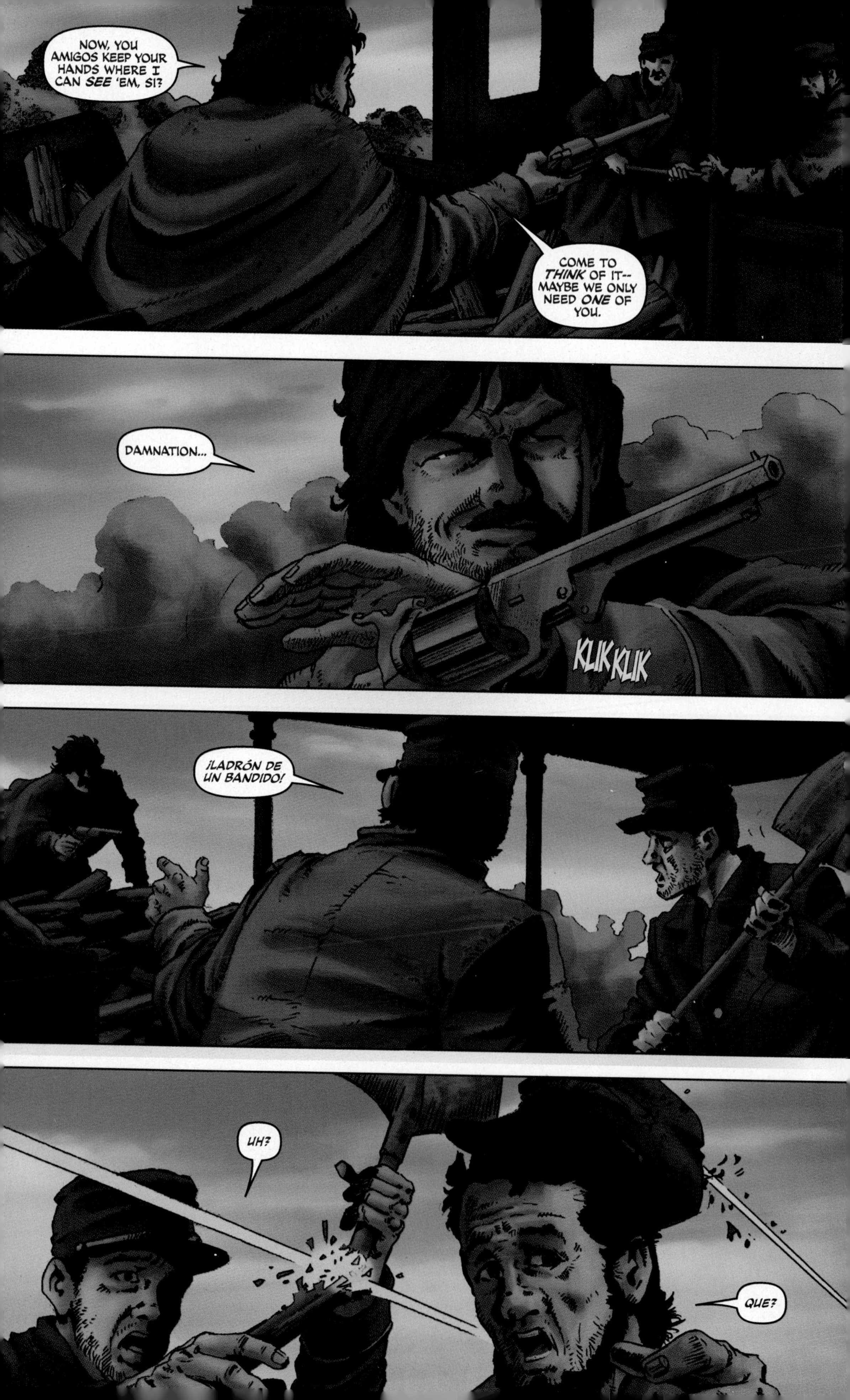
NOW, YOU AMIGOS KEEP YOUR HANDS WHERE I CAN SEE 'EM, SI?
COME TO THINK OF IT-- MAYBE WE ONLY NEED ONE OF YOU.
DAMNATION...
KLIK KLIK
¡LADRÓN DE UN BANDIDO!
UH?
QUE?

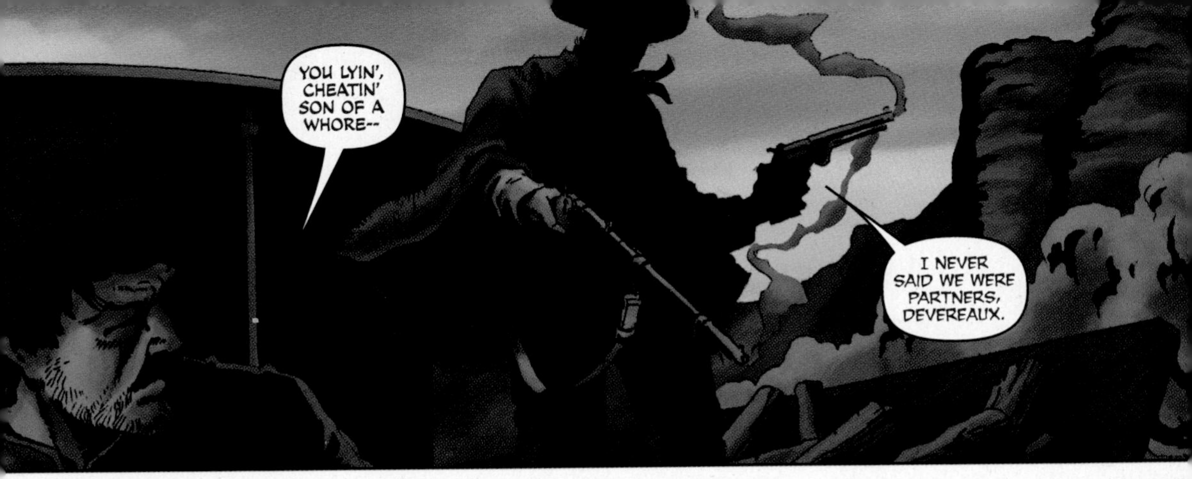
YOU LYIN', CHEATIN' SON OF A WHORE--
I NEVER SAID WE WERE PARTNERS, DEVEREAUX.

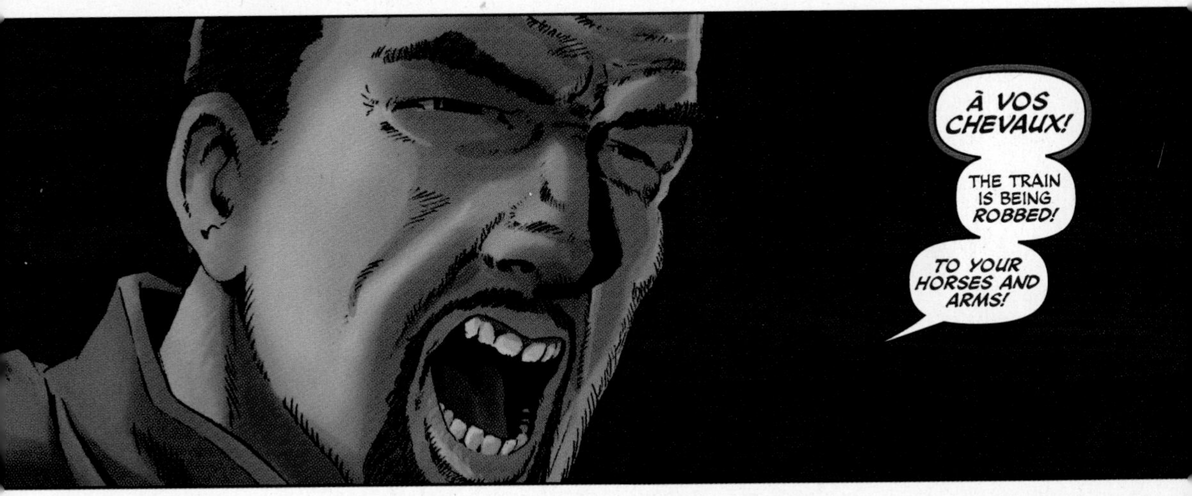
À VOS CHEVAUX!
THE TRAIN IS BEING ROBBED!
TO YOUR HORSES AND ARMS!

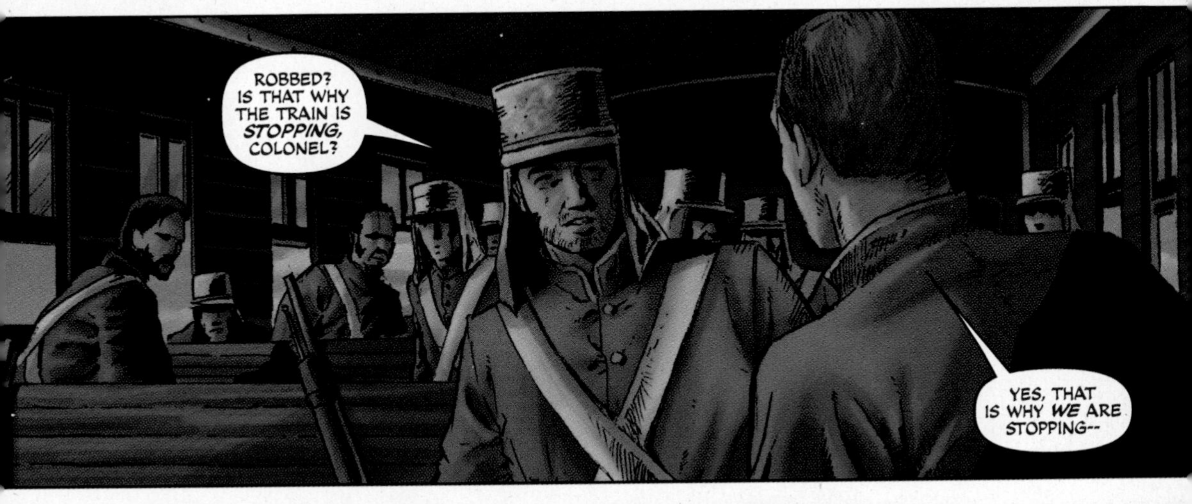
ROBBED? IS THAT WHY THE TRAIN IS STOPPING, COLONEL?
YES, THAT IS WHY WE ARE STOPPING--

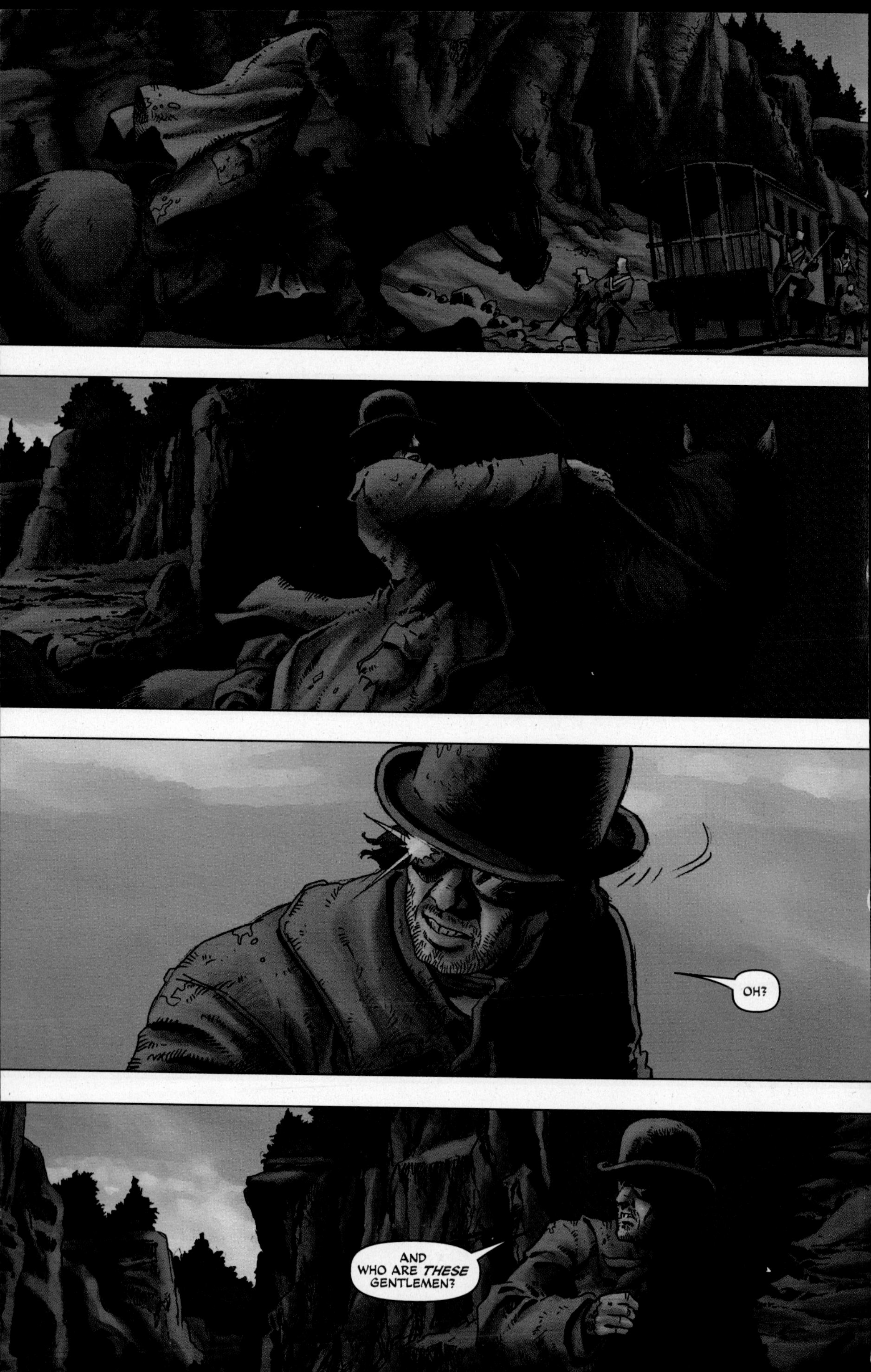
OH?
AND WHO ARE *THESE* GENTLEMEN?

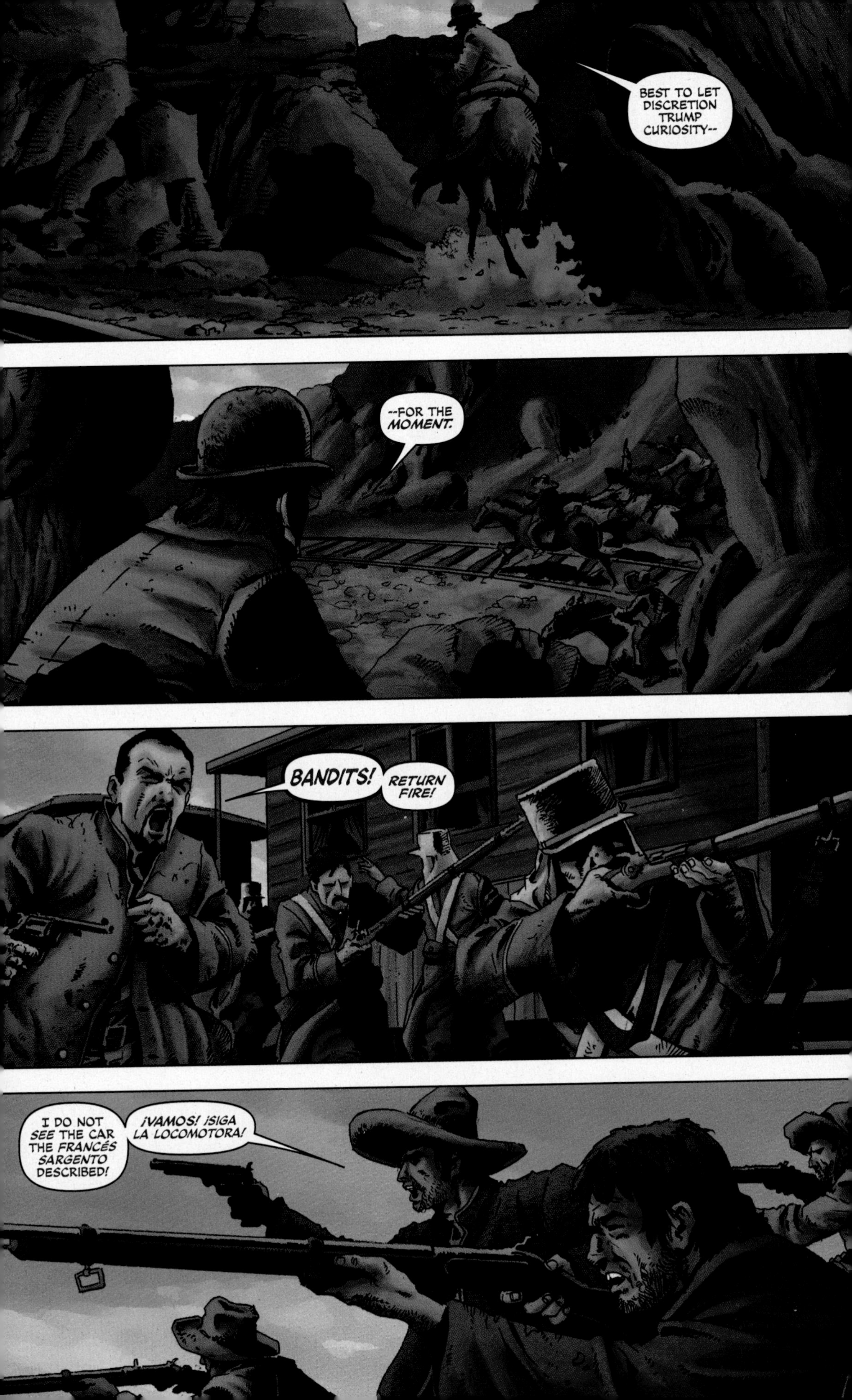

BEST TO LET DISCRETION TRUMP CURIOSITY--
--FOR THE MOMENT.
BANDITS!
RETURN FIRE!
I DO NOT SEE THE CAR THE FRANCÉS SARGENTO DESCRIBED!
¡VAMOS! ¡SIGA LA LOCOMOTORA!

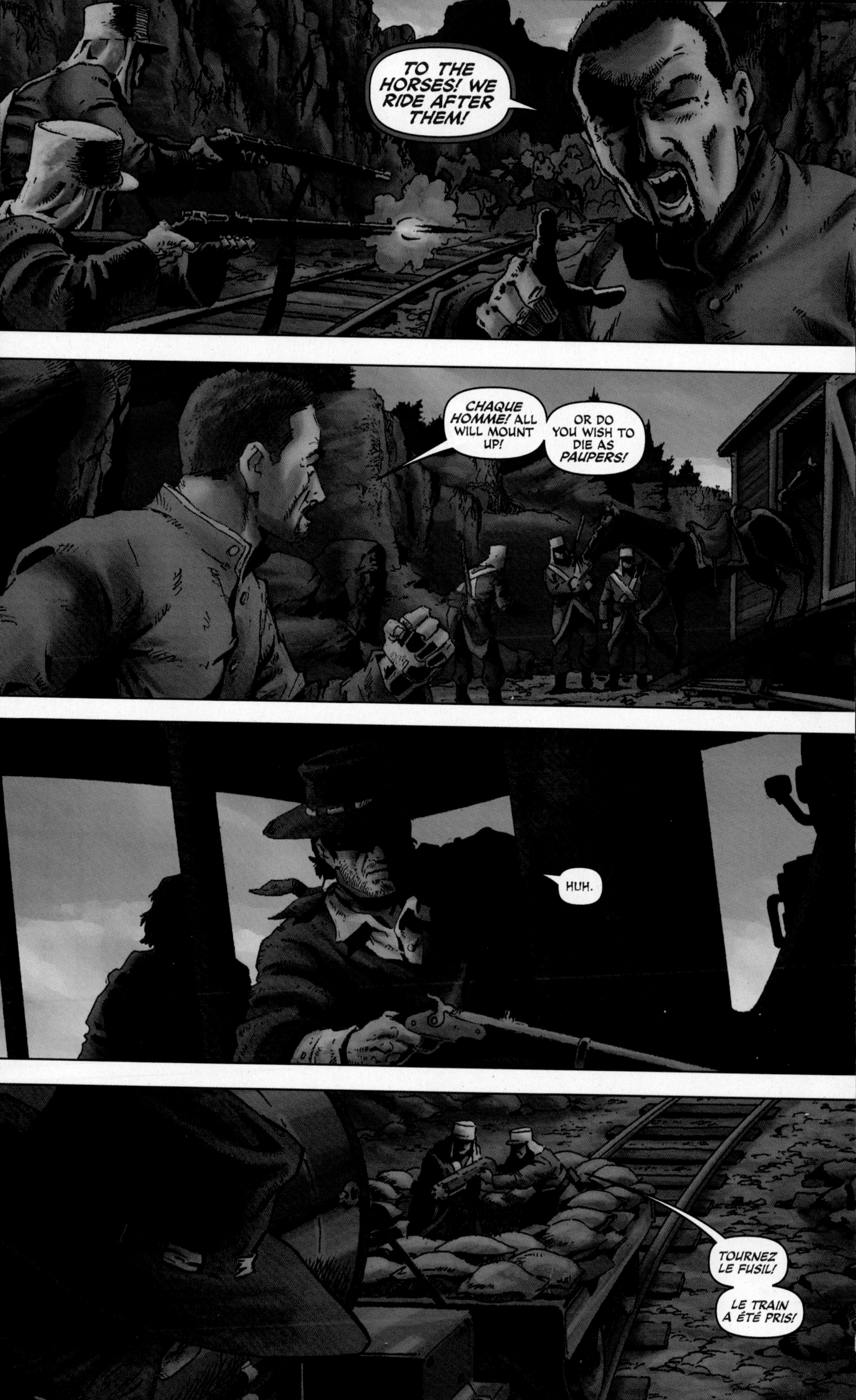
TO THE HORSES! WE RIDE AFTER THEM!
CHAQUE HOMME! ALL WILL MOUNT UP!
OR DO YOU WISH TO DIE AS PAUPERS!
HUH.
TOURNEZ LE FUSIL!
LE TRAIN A ÉTÉ PRIS!

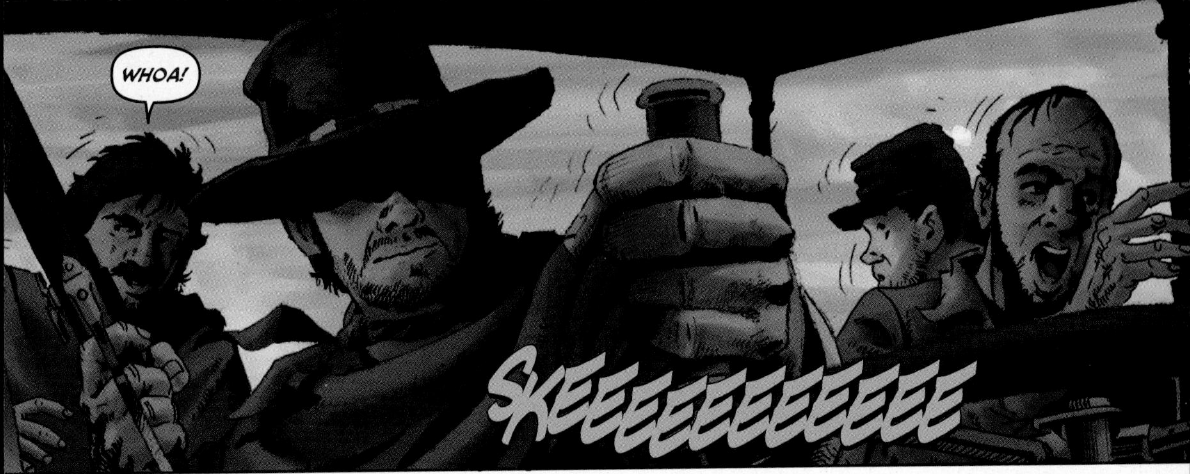
WHOA!
SKEEEEEEEEEEE

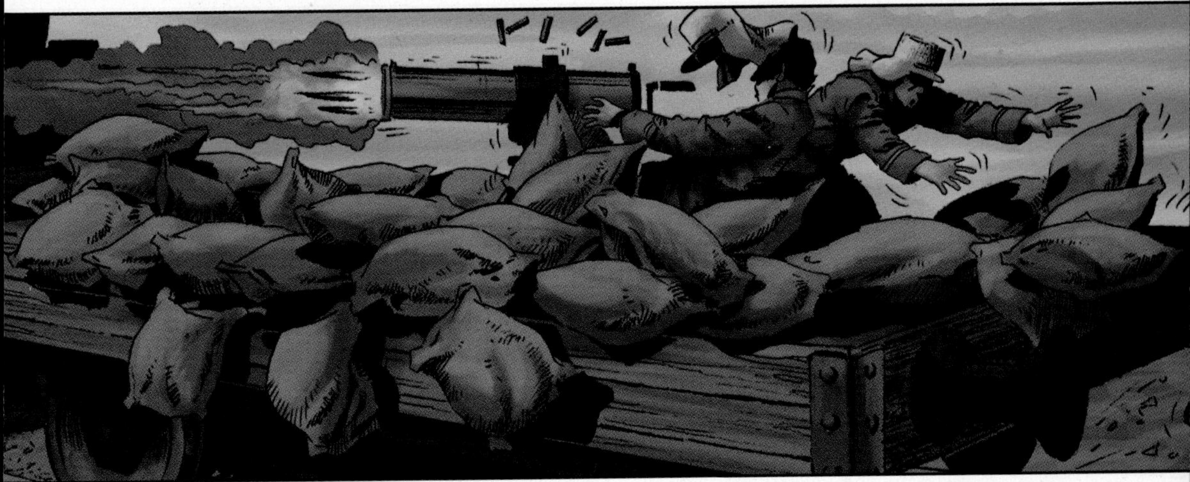

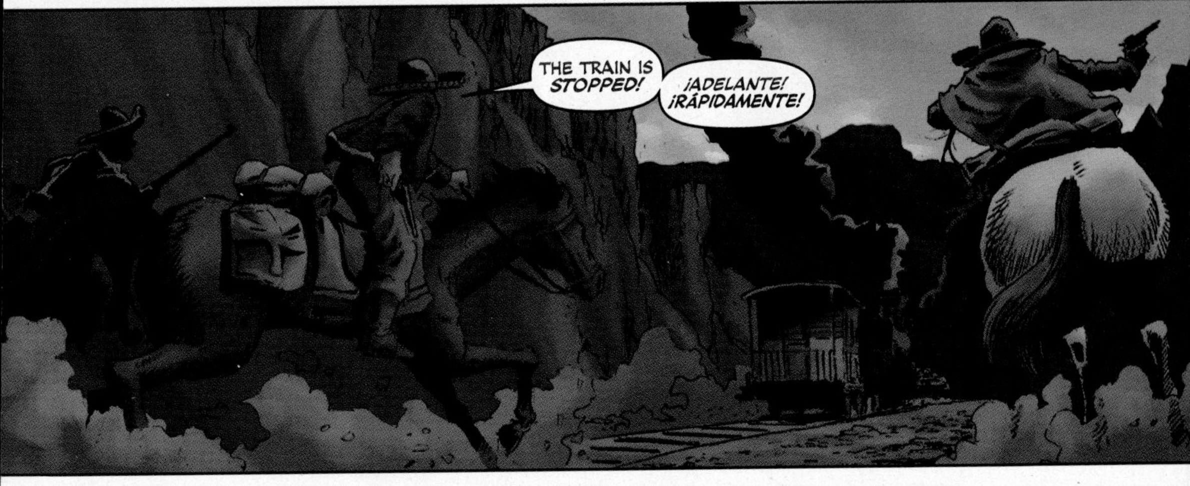
THE TRAIN IS STOPPED!
¡ADELANTE! ¡RÁPIDAMENTE!

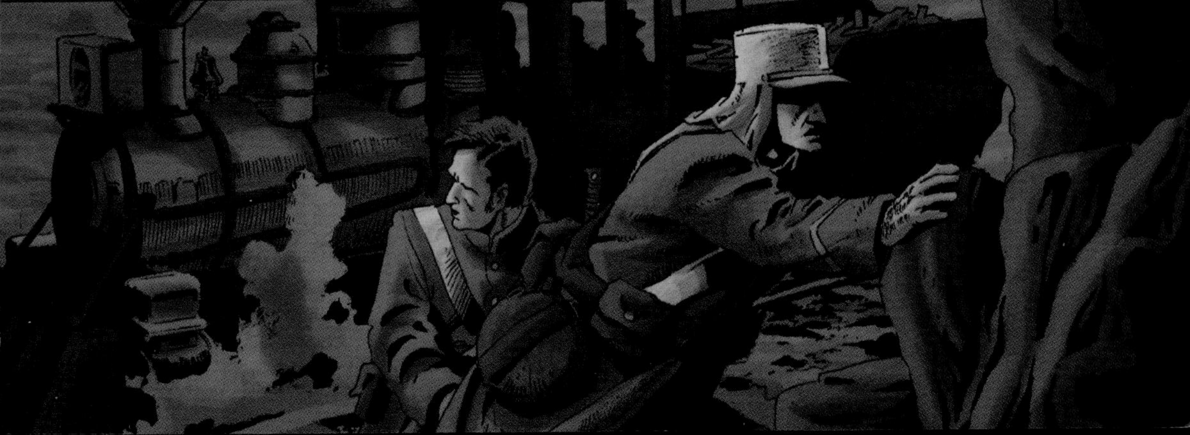

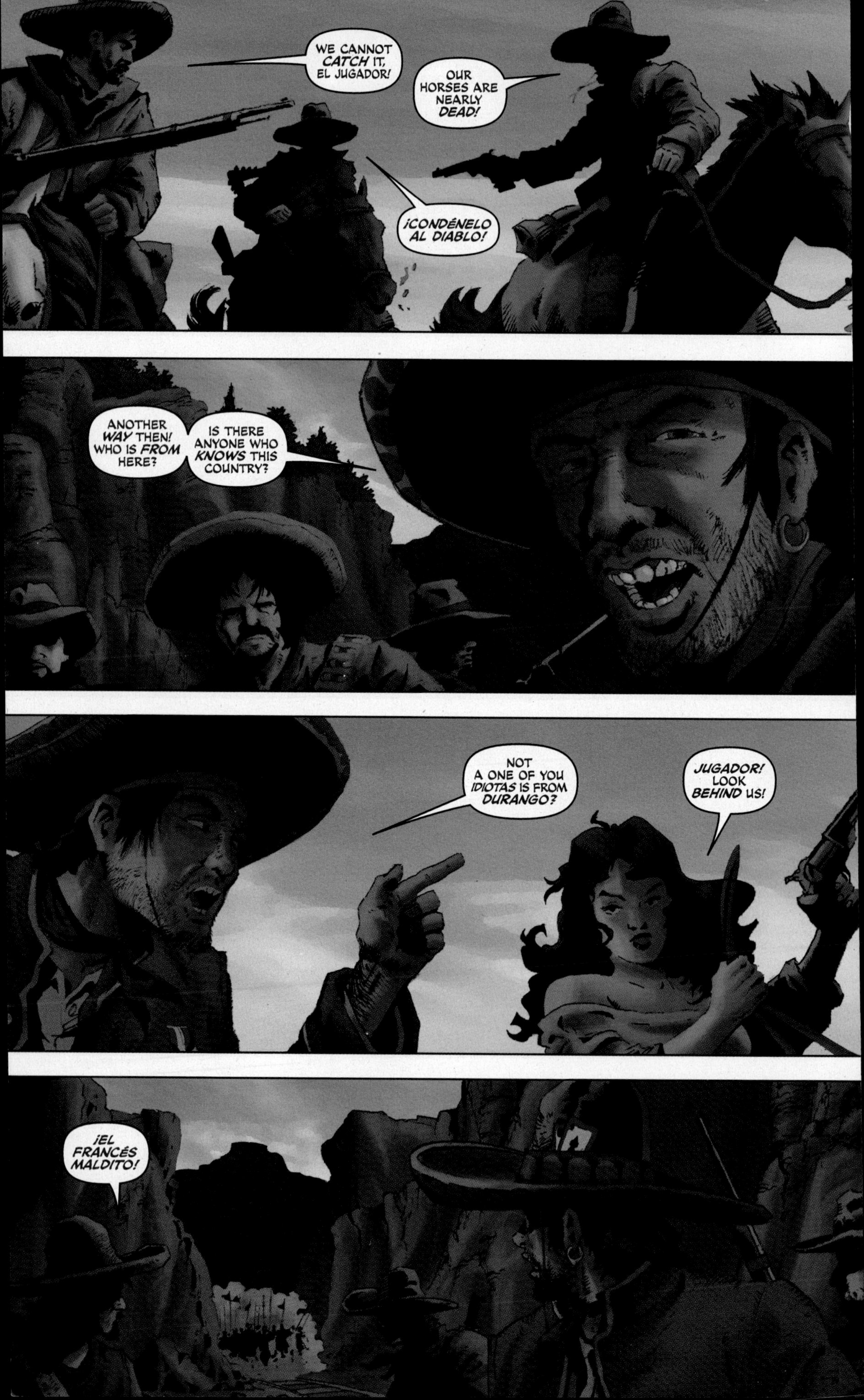

WE CANNOT CATCH IT, EL JUGADOR!
OUR HORSES ARE NEARLY DEAD!
¡CONDÉNELO AL DIABLO!
ANOTHER WAY THEN! WHO IS FROM HERE?
IS THERE ANYONE WHO KNOWS THIS COUNTRY?
NOT A ONE OF YOU IDIOTAS IS FROM DURANGO?
JUGADOR! LOOK BEHIND US!
¡EL FRANCÉS MALDITO!

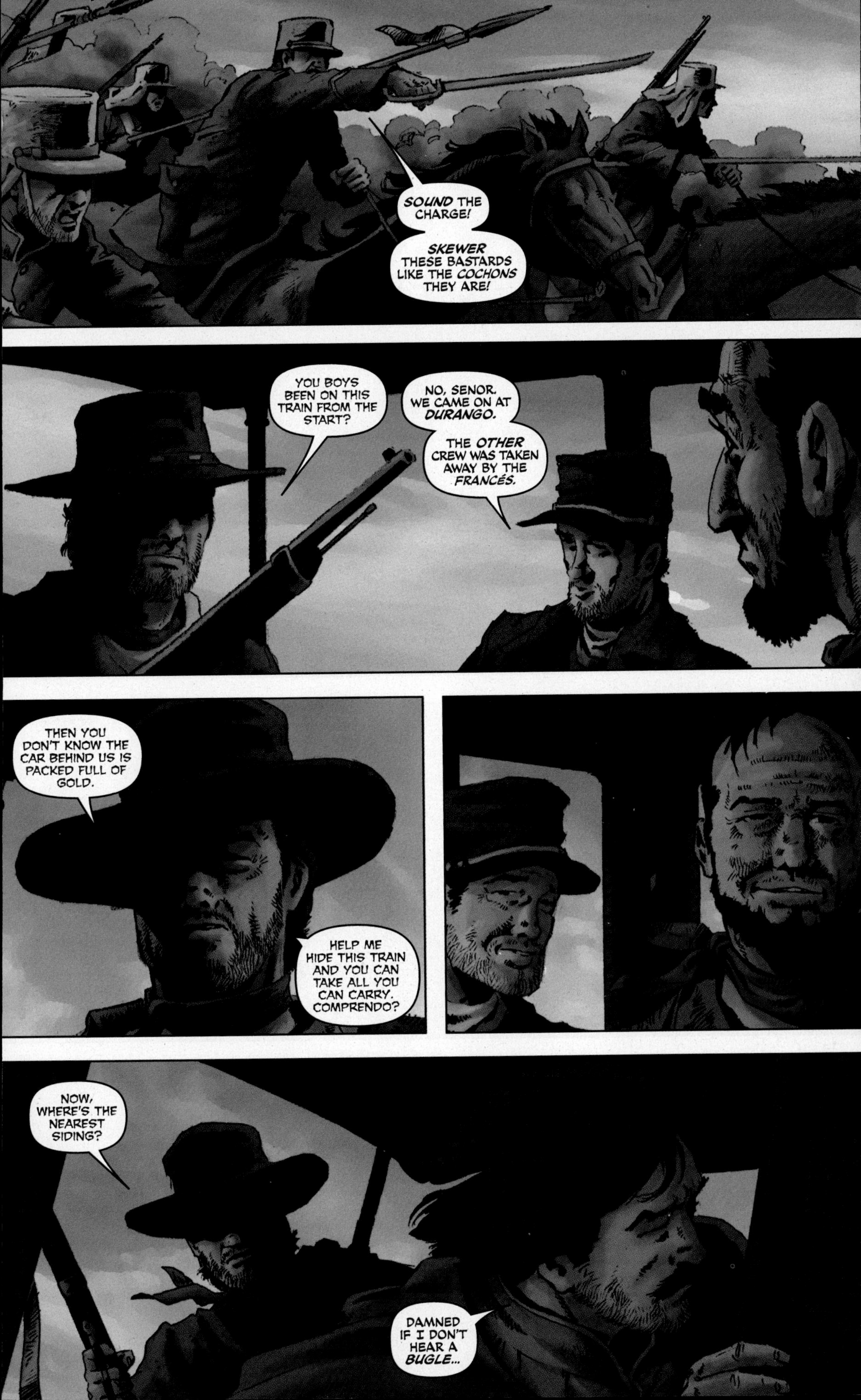
SOUND THE CHARGE!
SKEWER THESE BASTARDS LIKE THE COCHONS THEY ARE!
YOU BOYS BEEN ON THIS TRAIN FROM THE START?
NO, SENOR. WE CAME ON AT DURANGO.
THE OTHER CREW WAS TAKEN AWAY BY THE FRANCÉS.
THEN YOU DON'T KNOW THE CAR BEHIND US IS PACKED FULL OF GOLD.
HELP ME HIDE THIS TRAIN AND YOU CAN TAKE ALL YOU CAN CARRY. COMPRENDO?
NOW, WHERE'S THE NEAREST SIDING?
DAMNED IF I DON'T HEAR A BUGLE...

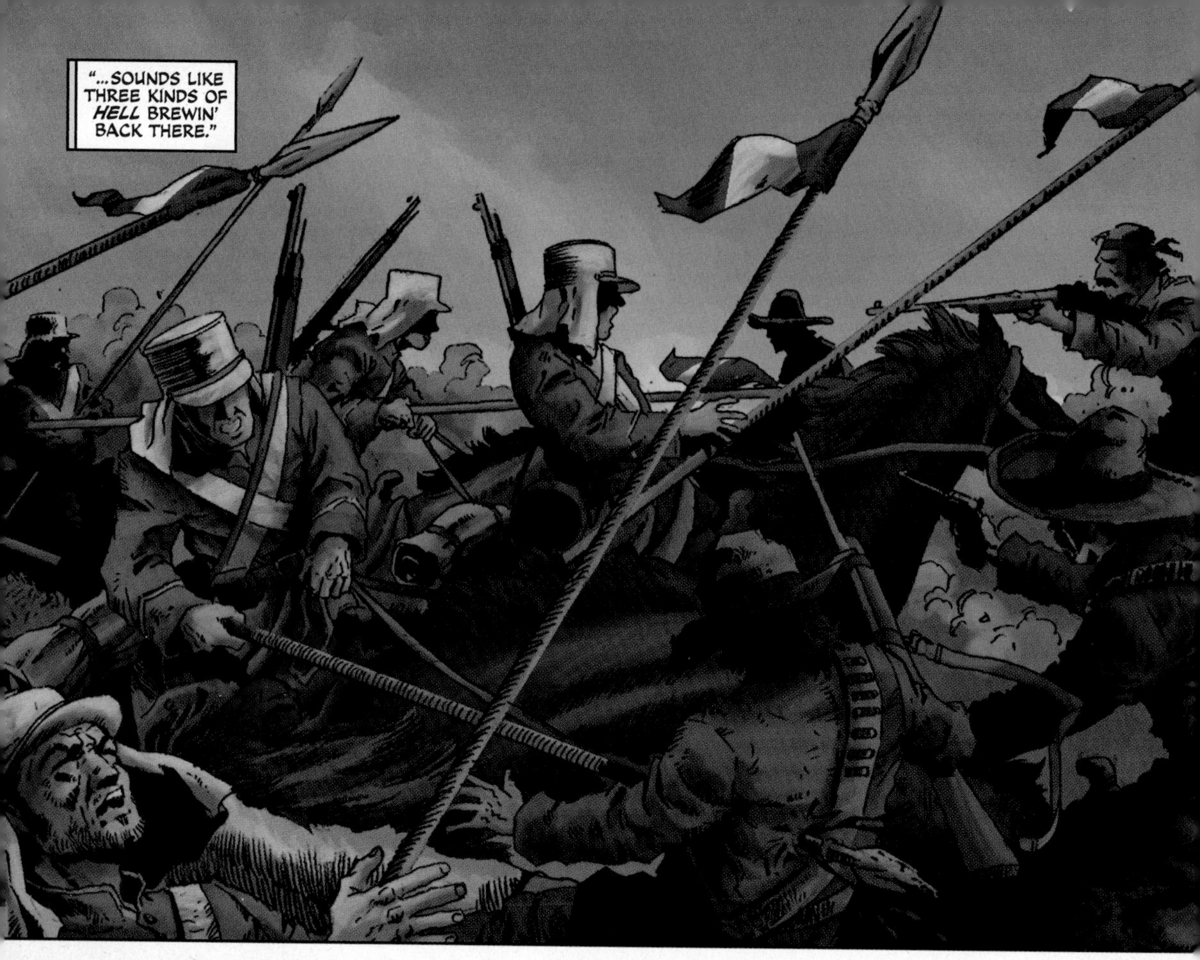
"...SOUNDS LIKE THREE KINDS OF HELL BREWIN' BACK THERE."

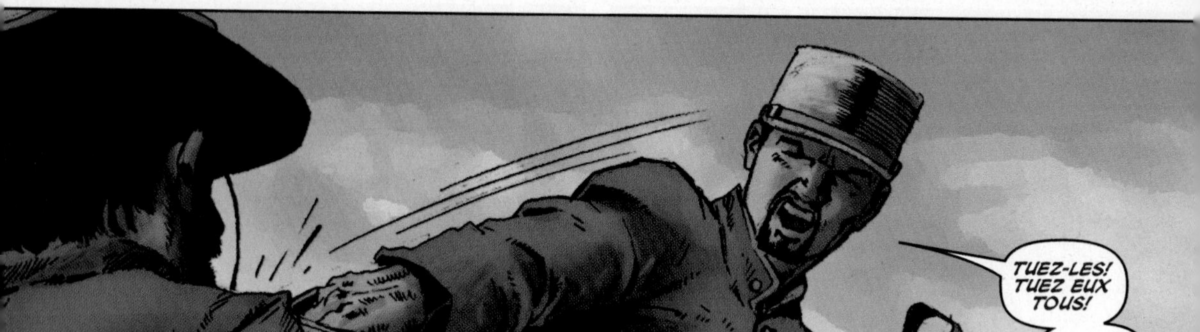
TUEZ-LES! TUEZ EUX TOUS!
THEY ALL WILL DIE!

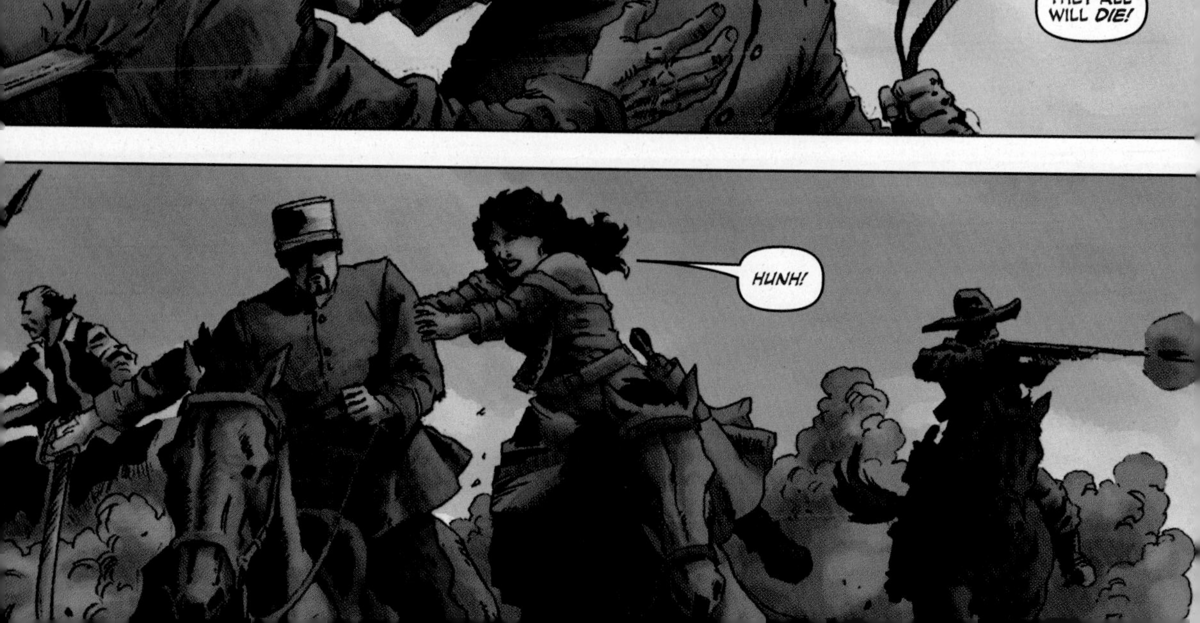
HUNH!

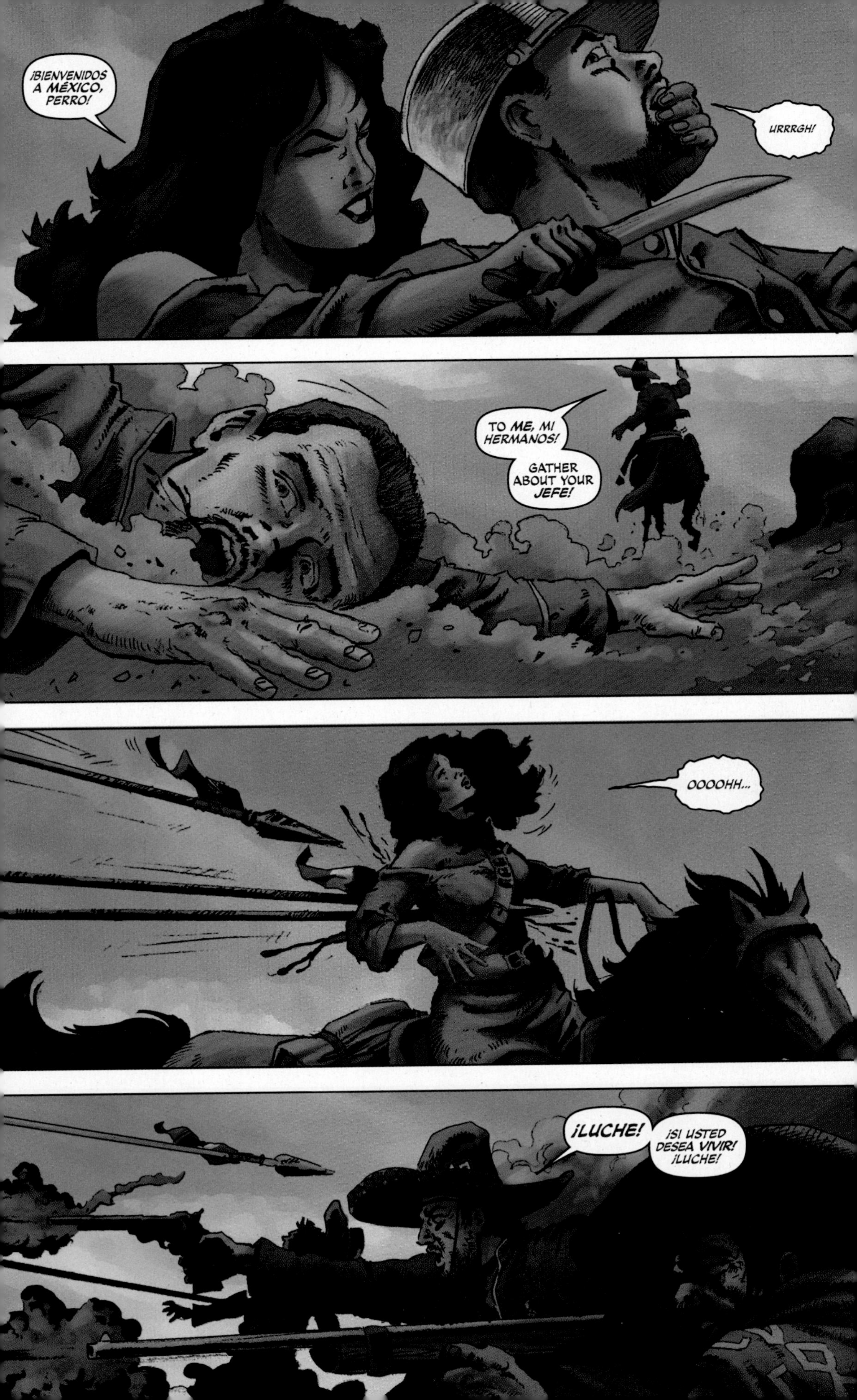
¡BIENVENIDOS A MÉXICO, PERRO!
URRRGH!
TO ME, MI HERMANOS!
GATHER ABOUT YOUR JEFE!
OOOOHH...
¡LUCHE!
¡SI USTED DESEA VIVIR! ¡LUCHE!

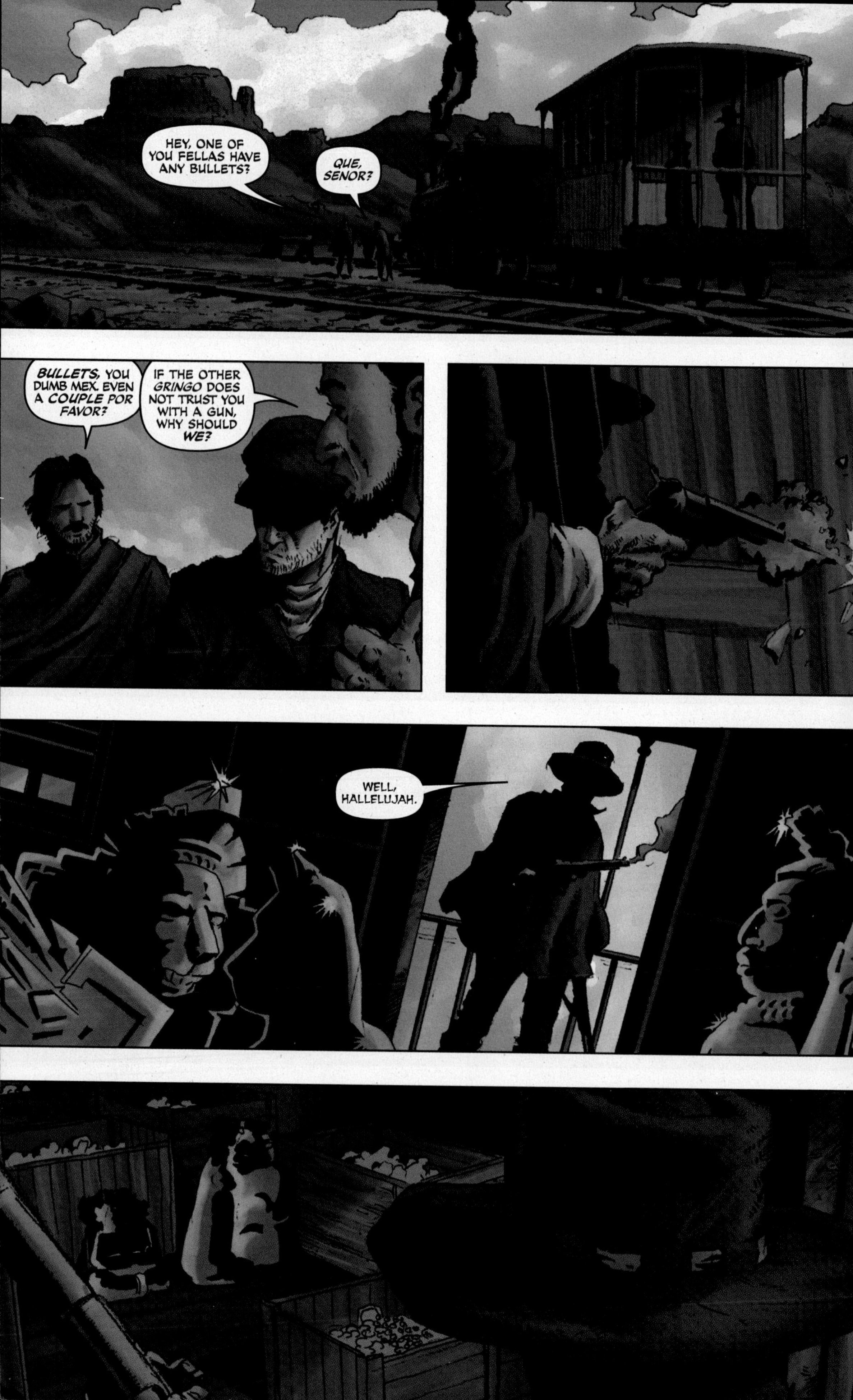
HEY, ONE OF YOU FELLAS HAVE ANY BULLETS?
QUE, SENOR?
BULLETS, YOU DUMB MEX. EVEN A COUPLE POR FAVOR?
IF THE OTHER GRINGO DOES NOT TRUST YOU WITH A GUN, WHY SHOULD WE?
WELL, HALLELUJAH.

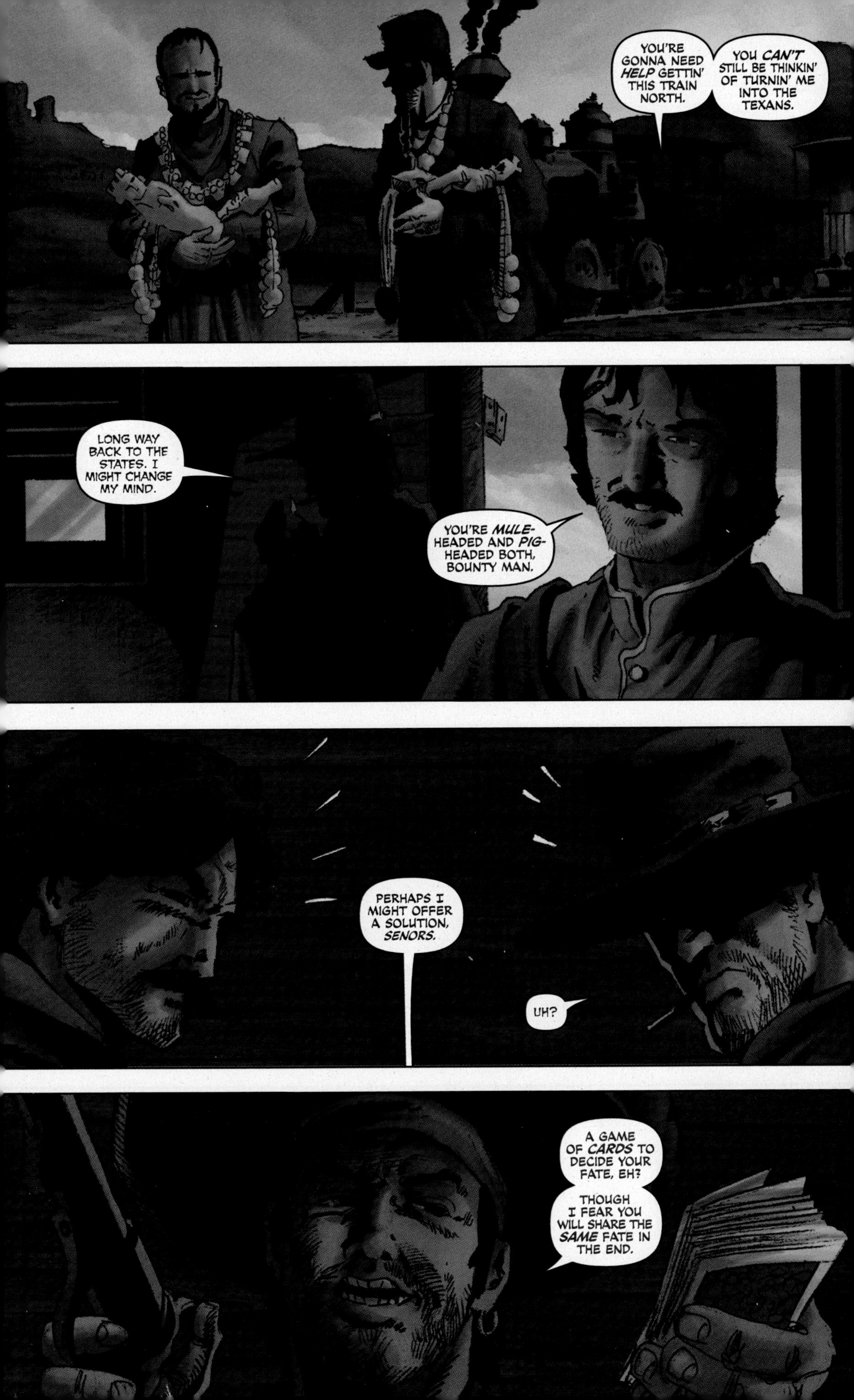
YOU'RE GONNA NEED HELP GETTIN' THIS TRAIN NORTH.
YOU CAN'T STILL BE THINKIN' OF TURNIN' ME INTO THE TEXANS.
LONG WAY BACK TO THE STATES. I MIGHT CHANGE MY MIND.
YOU'RE MULE-HEADED AND PIG-HEADED BOTH, BOUNTY MAN.
PERHAPS I MIGHT OFFER A SOLUTION, SENORS.
UH?
A GAME OF CARDS TO DECIDE YOUR FATE, EH?
THOUGH I FEAR YOU WILL SHARE THE SAME FATE IN THE END.

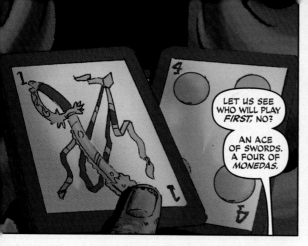

LET US SEE WHO WILL PLAY *FIRST*, NO?

AN ACE OF SWORDS. A FOUR OF *MONEDAS*.

AND I, A SEVEN OF *TAZAS*.

YOU *GRINGOS* WILL GO FIRST.

I AIN'T EVEN GOT A *BULLET*.

HE DOES NOT THINK YOU WILL NEED A *SECOND* BULLET, *SENOR*.

HA HA!

I'LL BE *RETURNIN'* IT TO YOU REAL QUICK, BOUNTY MAN.

NOW WE FIND OUT WHO IS LUCKY AND WHO IS *NOT*, EH?

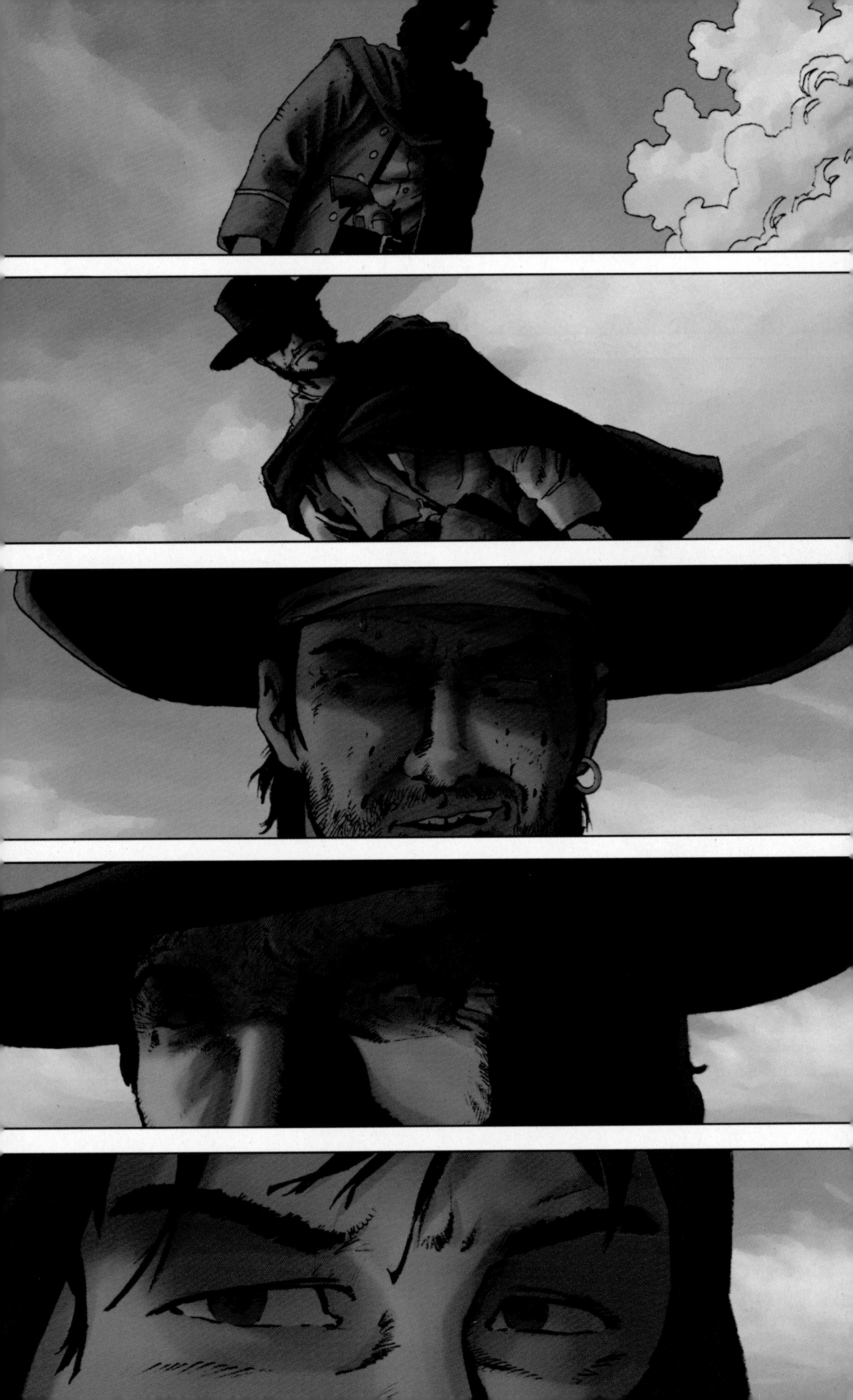

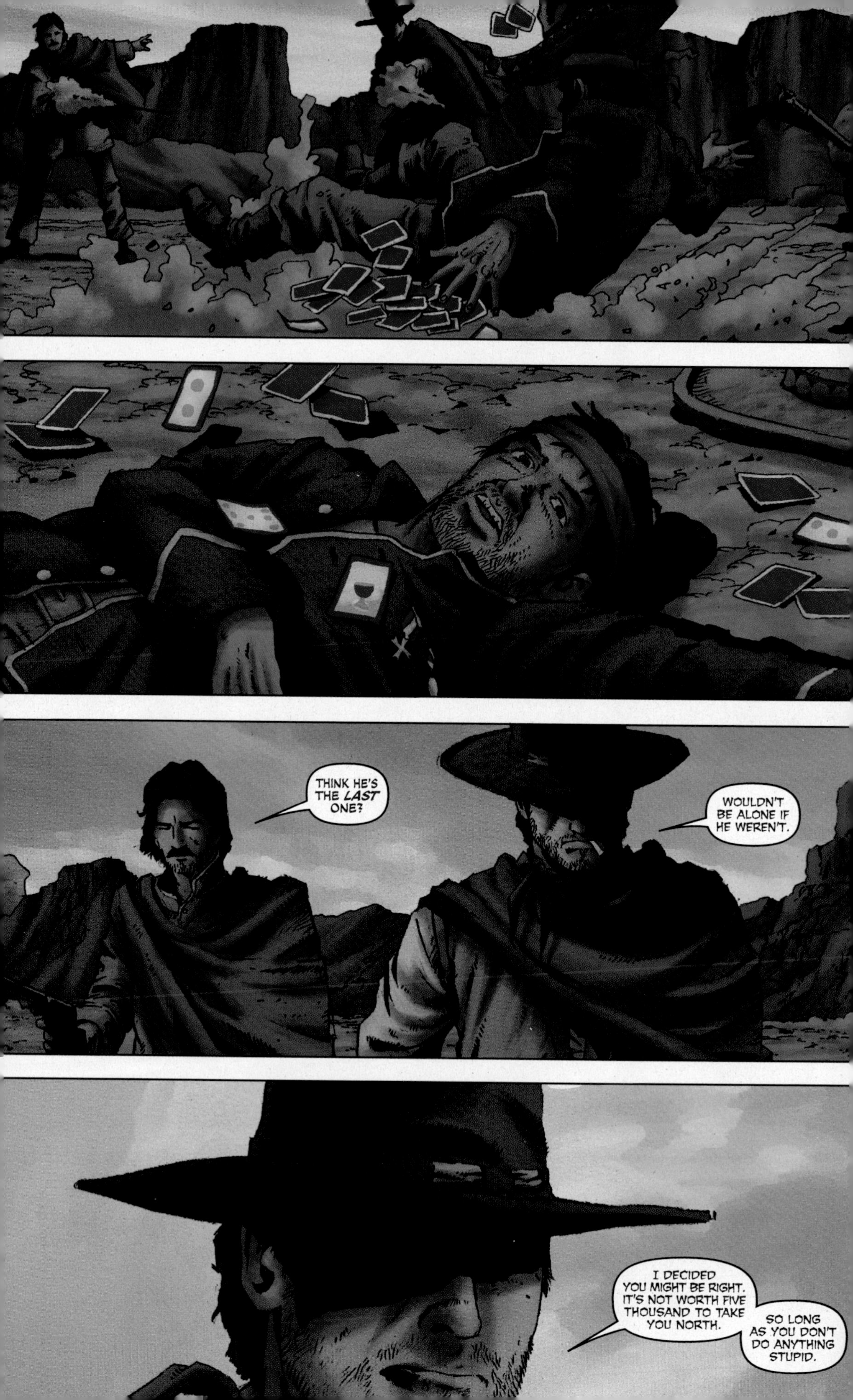
THINK HE'S THE *LAST* ONE?
WOULDN'T BE ALONE IF HE WEREN'T.
I DECIDED YOU MIGHT BE RIGHT. IT'S NOT WORTH FIVE THOUSAND TO TAKE YOU NORTH.
SO LONG AS YOU DON'T DO ANYTHING STUPID.

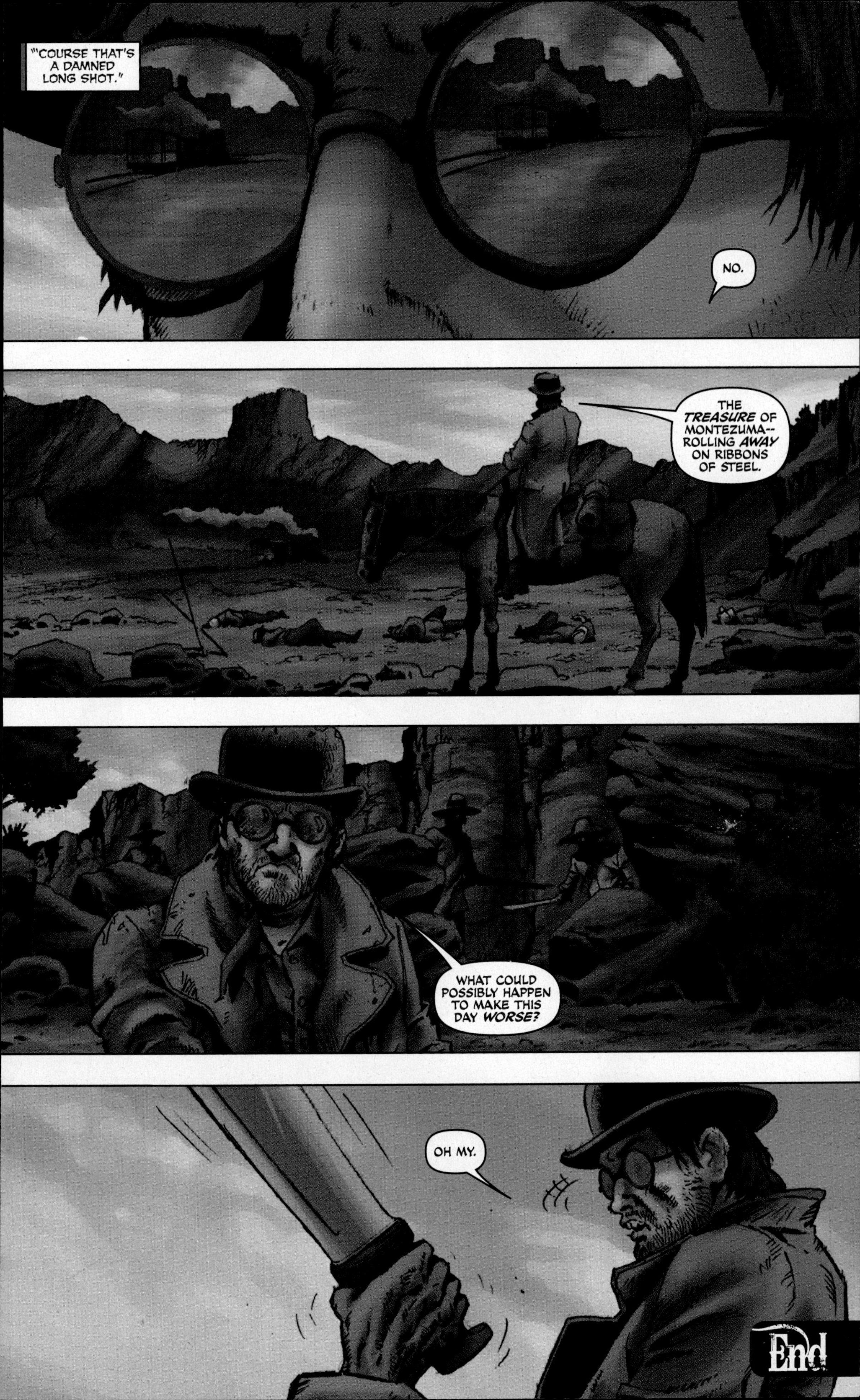
"'COURSE THAT'S A DAMNED LONG SHOT."
NO.
THE *TREASURE* OF MONTEZUMA-- ROLLING *AWAY* ON RIBBONS OF STEEL.
WHAT COULD POSSIBLY HAPPEN TO MAKE THIS DAY *WORSE?*
OH MY.
End

Cover by **Dennis Calero**

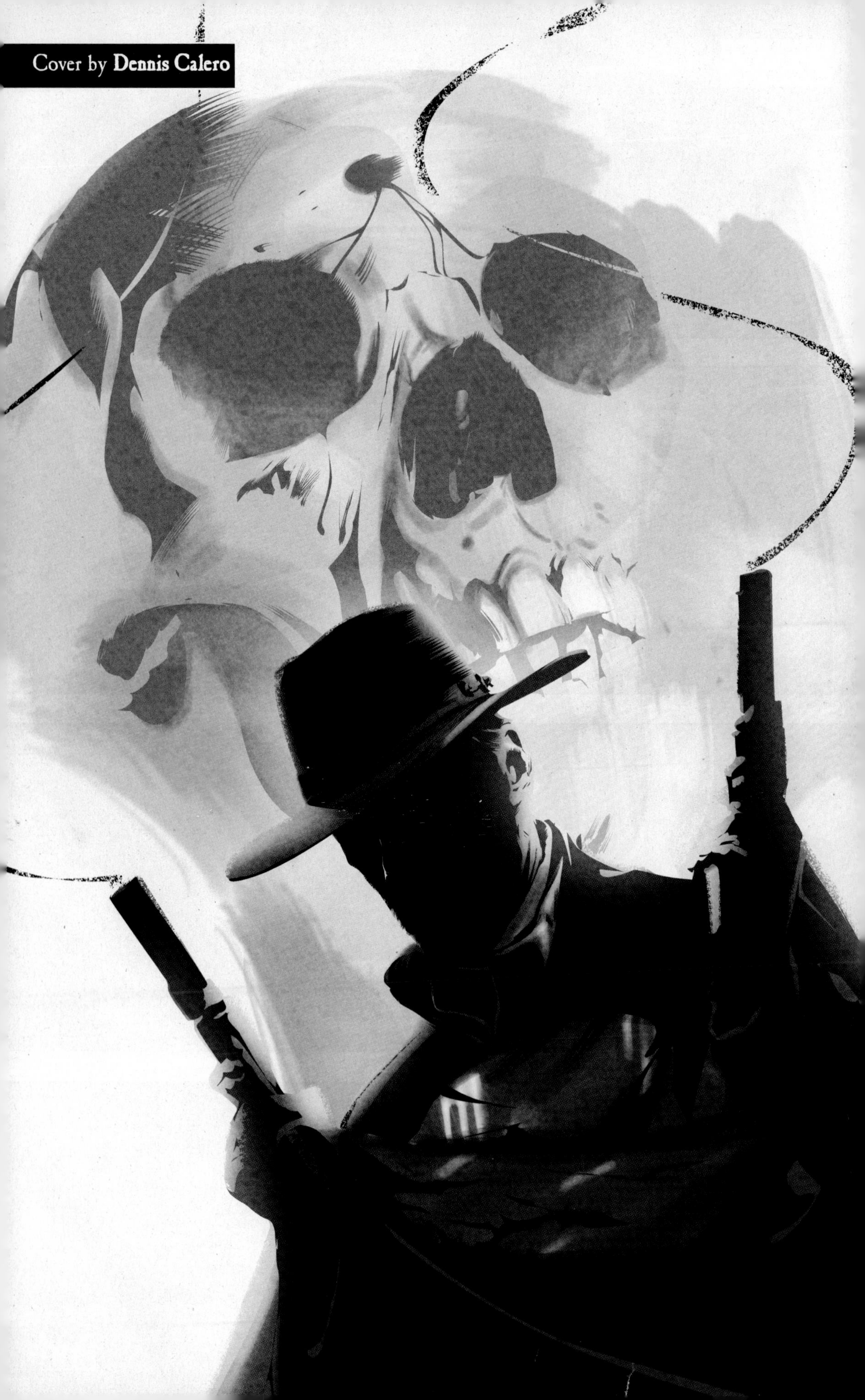

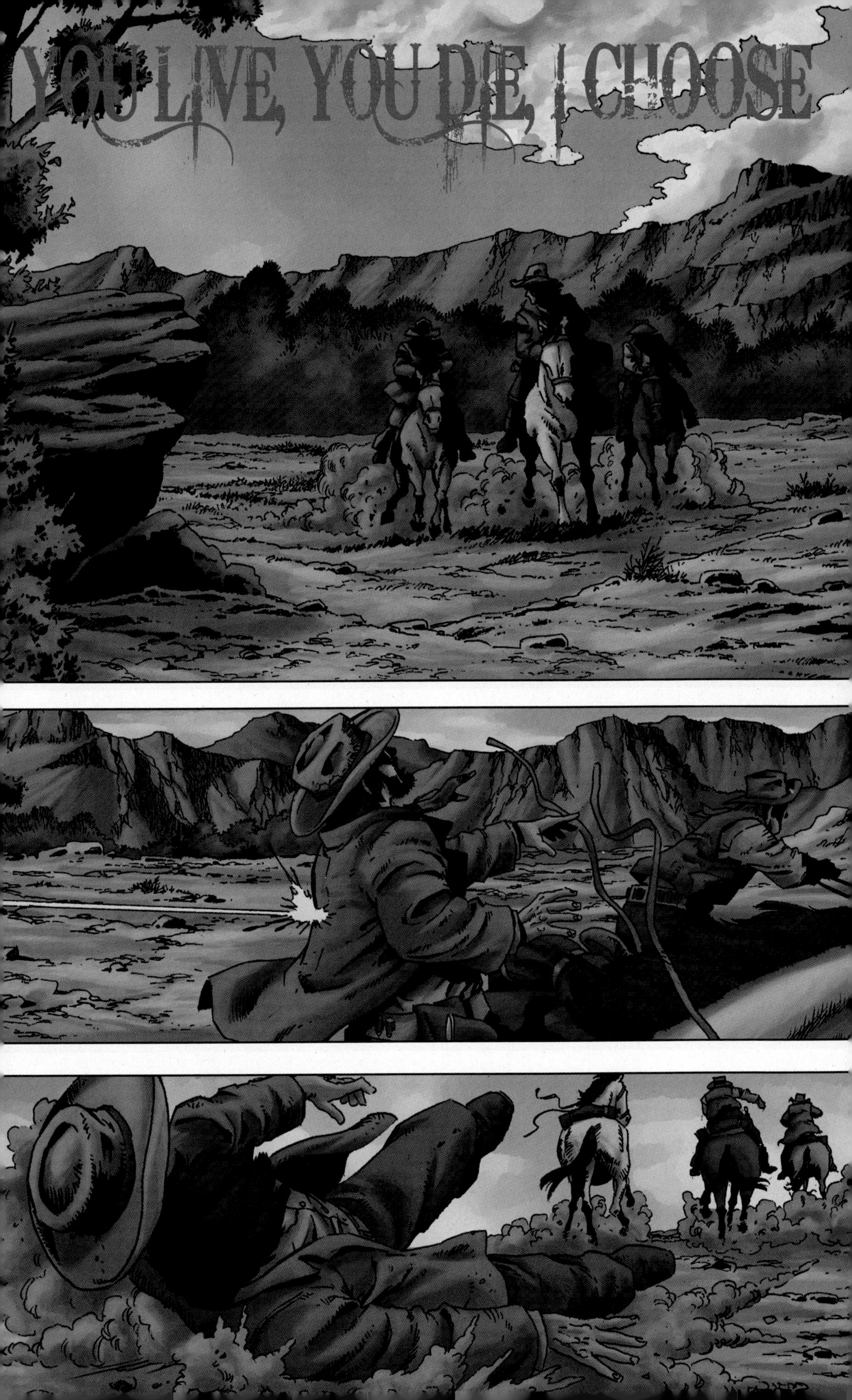
YOU LIVE, YOU DIE, I CHOOSE

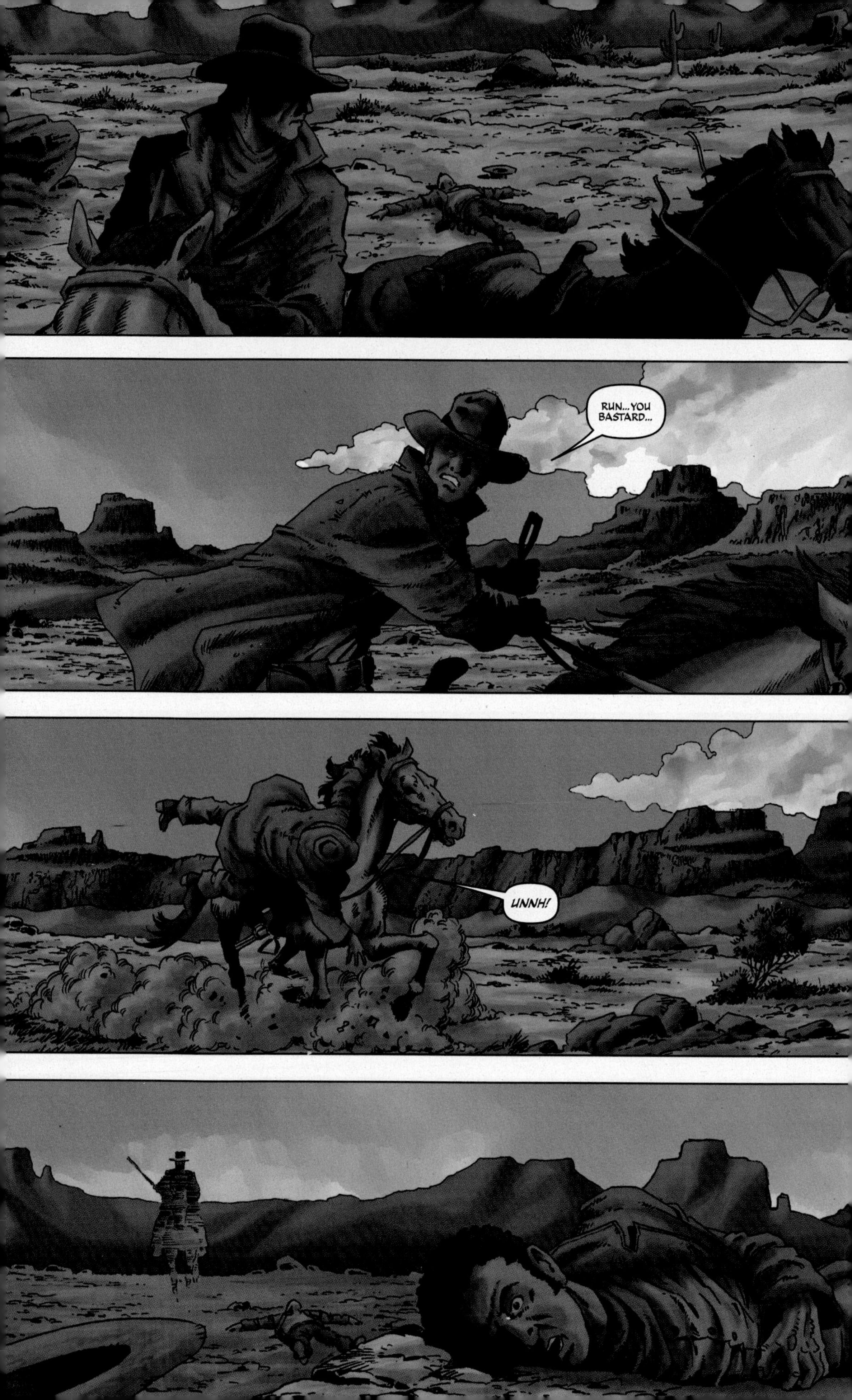
RUN... YOU BASTARD...
UNNH!

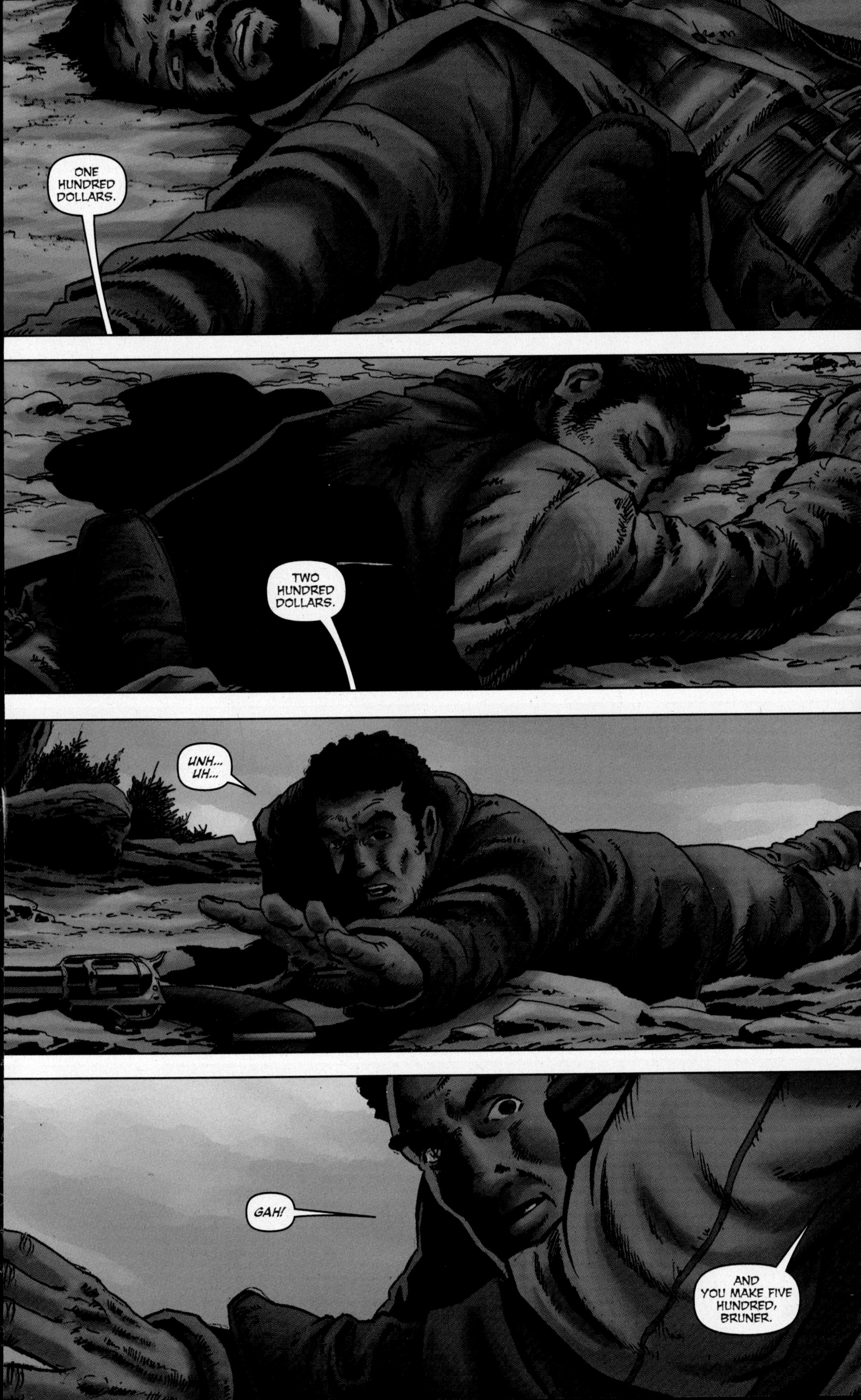
ONE HUNDRED DOLLARS.
TWO HUNDRED DOLLARS.
UNH... UH...
GAH!
AND YOU MAKE FIVE HUNDRED, BRUNER.

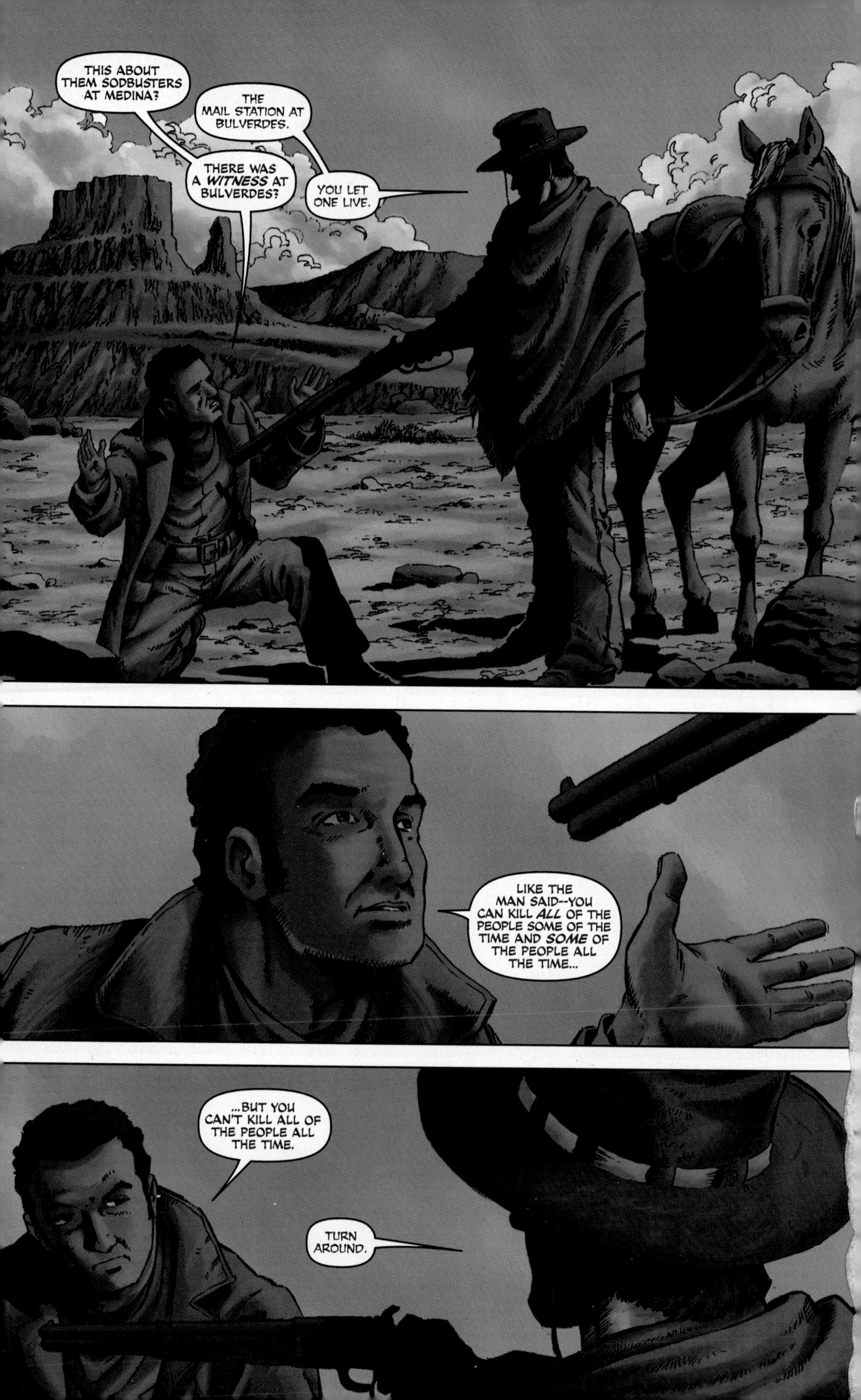
THIS ABOUT THEM SODBUSTERS AT MEDINA?
THE MAIL STATION AT BULVERDES.
THERE WAS A WITNESS AT BULVERDES?
YOU LET ONE LIVE.
LIKE THE MAN SAID--YOU CAN KILL ALL OF THE PEOPLE SOME OF THE TIME AND SOME OF THE PEOPLE ALL THE TIME...
...BUT YOU CAN'T KILL ALL OF THE PEOPLE ALL THE TIME.
TURN AROUND.

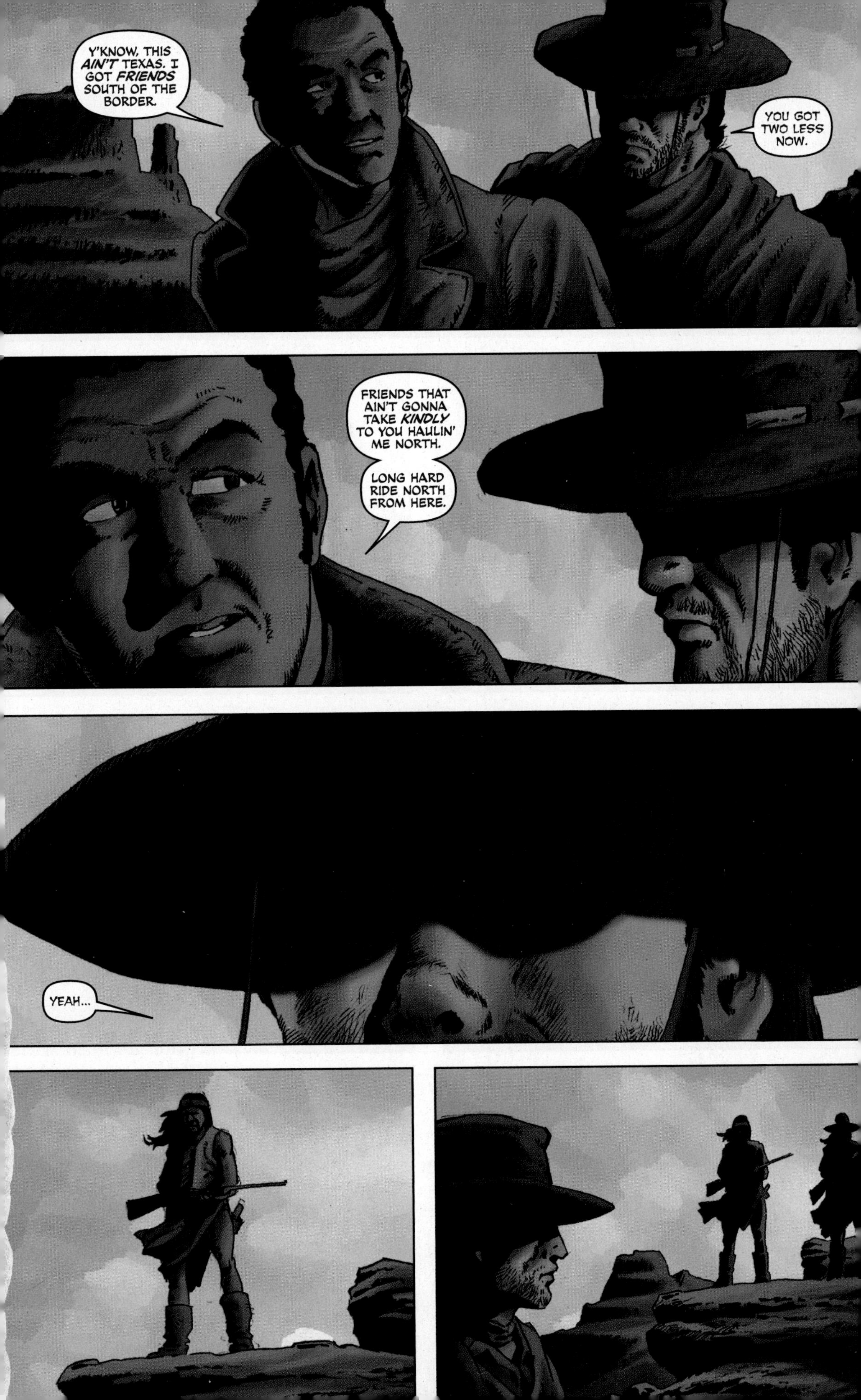
Y'KNOW, THIS AIN'T TEXAS. I GOT FRIENDS SOUTH OF THE BORDER.
YOU GOT TWO LESS NOW.
FRIENDS THAT AIN'T GONNA TAKE KINDLY TO YOU HAULIN' ME NORTH.
LONG HARD RIDE NORTH FROM HERE.
YEAH...

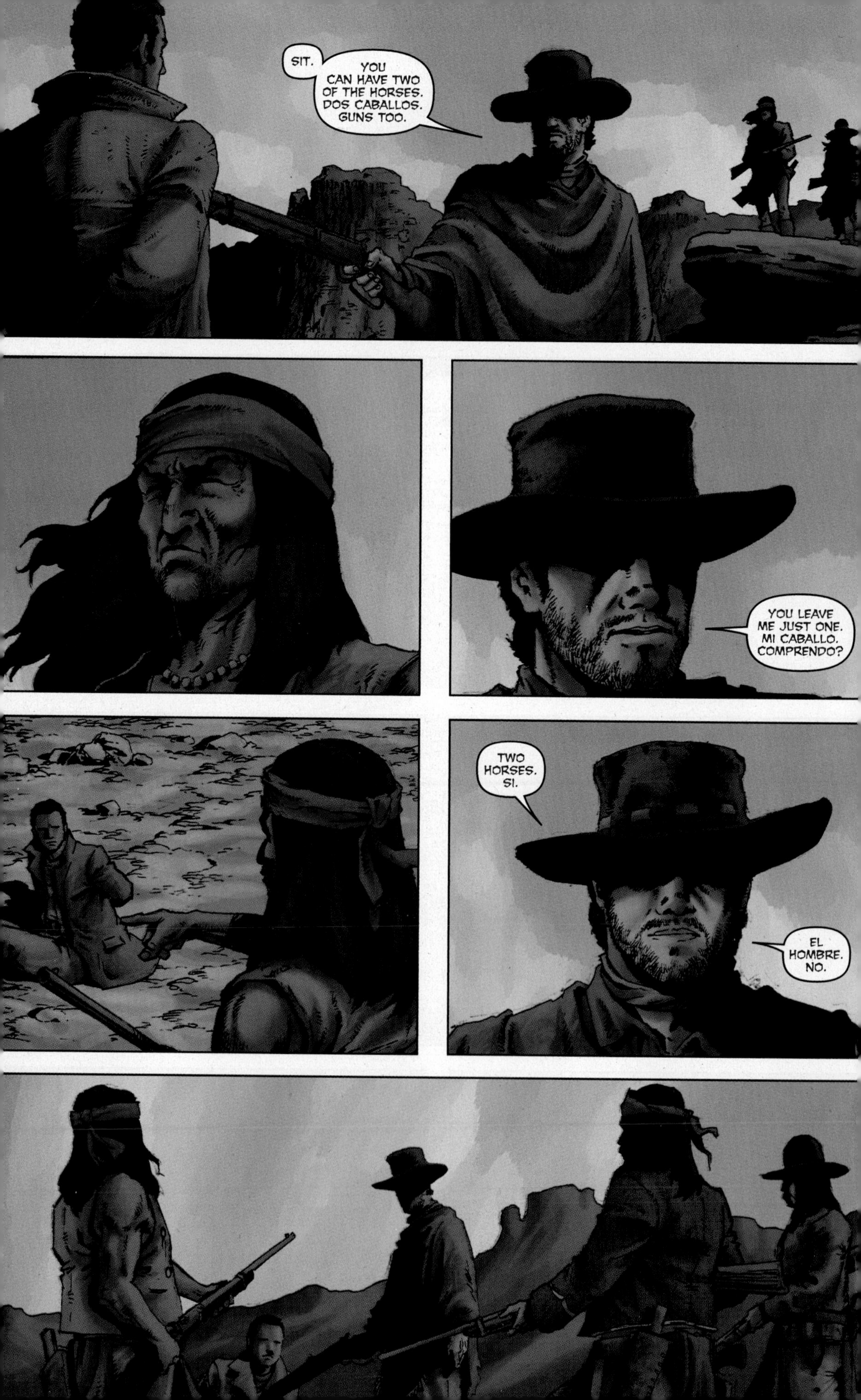
SIT.
YOU CAN HAVE TWO OF THE HORSES. DOS CABALLOS. GUNS TOO.
YOU LEAVE ME JUST ONE. MI CABALLO. COMPRENDO?
TWO HORSES. SI.
EL HOMBRE. NO.

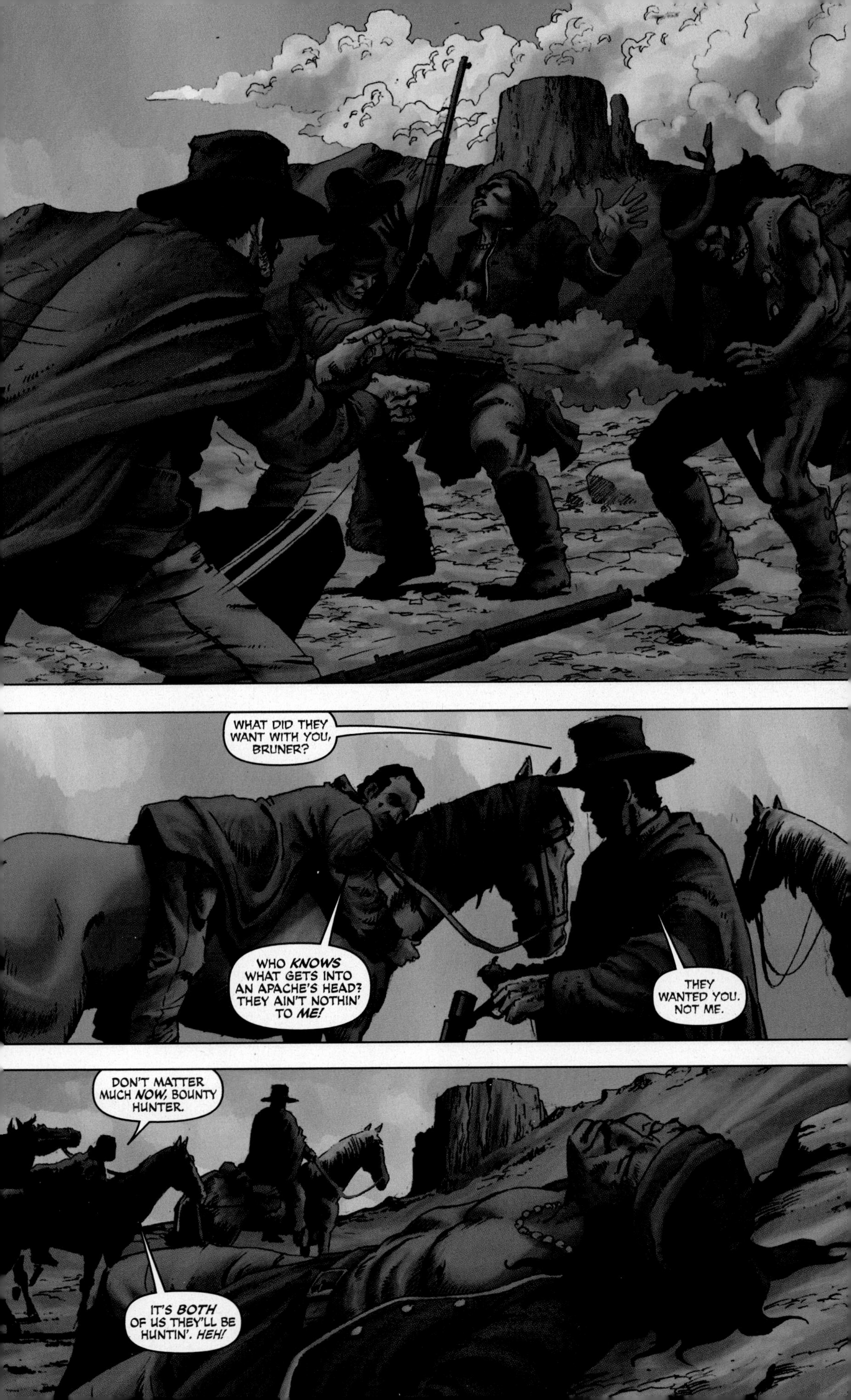
WHAT DID THEY WANT WITH YOU, BRUNER?
WHO *KNOWS* WHAT GETS INTO AN APACHE'S HEAD? THEY AIN'T NOTHIN' TO *ME!*
THEY WANTED YOU. NOT ME.
DON'T MATTER MUCH *NOW*, BOUNTY HUNTER.
IT'S *BOTH* OF US THEY'LL BE HUNTIN'. *HEH!*

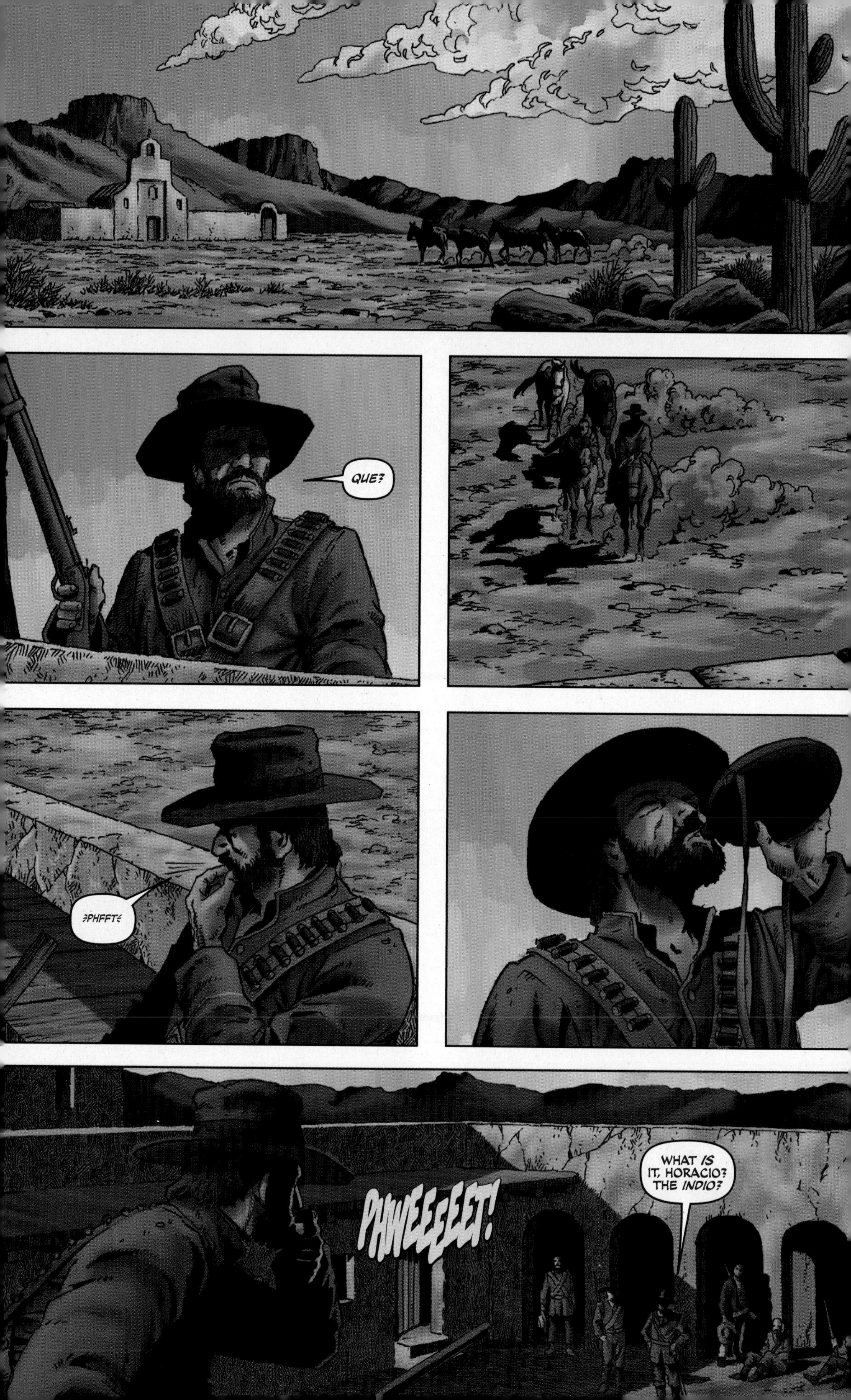
QUE?
PHFFT
PHWEEEEEET!
WHAT IS IT, HORACIO? THE INDIO?

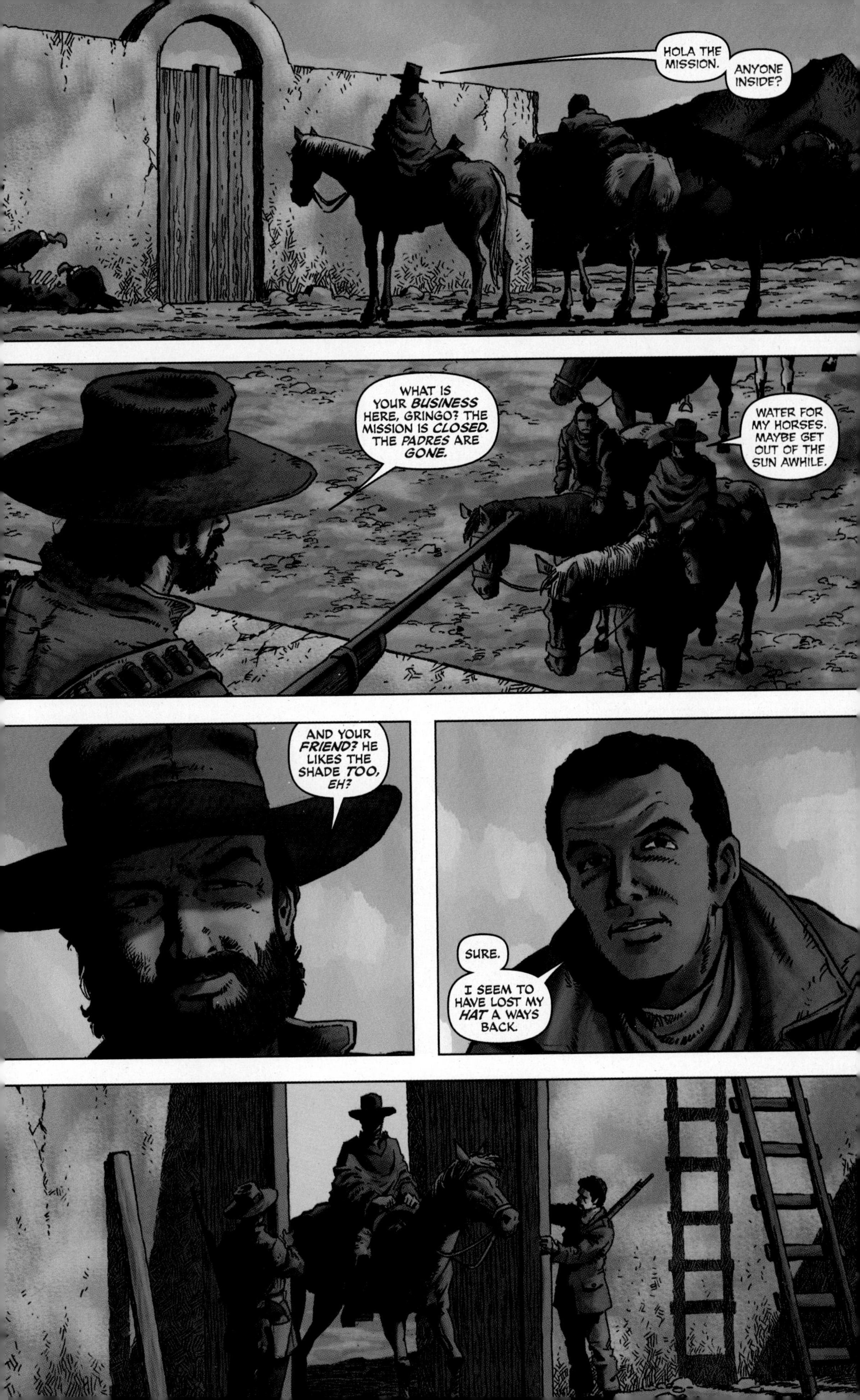
HOLA THE MISSION.
ANYONE INSIDE?
WHAT IS YOUR BUSINESS HERE, GRINGO? THE MISSION IS CLOSED. THE PADRES ARE GONE.
WATER FOR MY HORSES. MAYBE GET OUT OF THE SUN AWHILE.
AND YOUR FRIEND? HE LIKES THE SHADE TOO, EH?
SURE.
I SEEM TO HAVE LOST MY HAT A WAYS BACK.

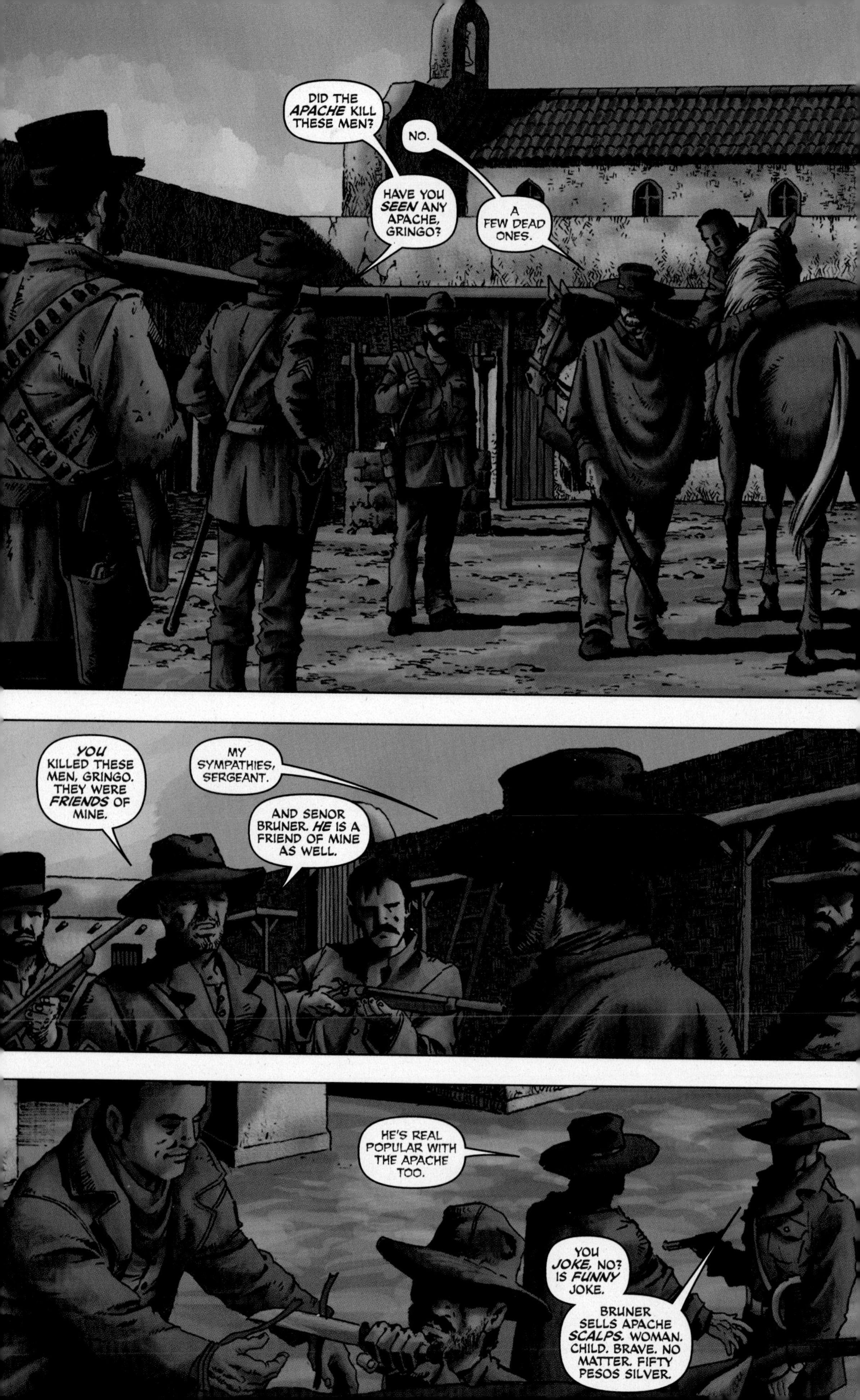
DID THE *APACHE* KILL THESE MEN?
NO.
HAVE YOU *SEEN* ANY APACHE, GRINGO?
A FEW DEAD ONES.
YOU KILLED THESE MEN, GRINGO. THEY WERE *FRIENDS* OF MINE.
MY SYMPATHIES, SERGEANT.
AND SENOR BRUNER. *HE* IS A FRIEND OF MINE AS WELL.
HE'S REAL POPULAR WITH THE APACHE TOO.
YOU *JOKE,* NO? IS *FUNNY* JOKE.
BRUNER SELLS APACHE *SCALPS.* WOMAN. CHILD. BRAVE. NO MATTER. FIFTY PESOS SILVER.

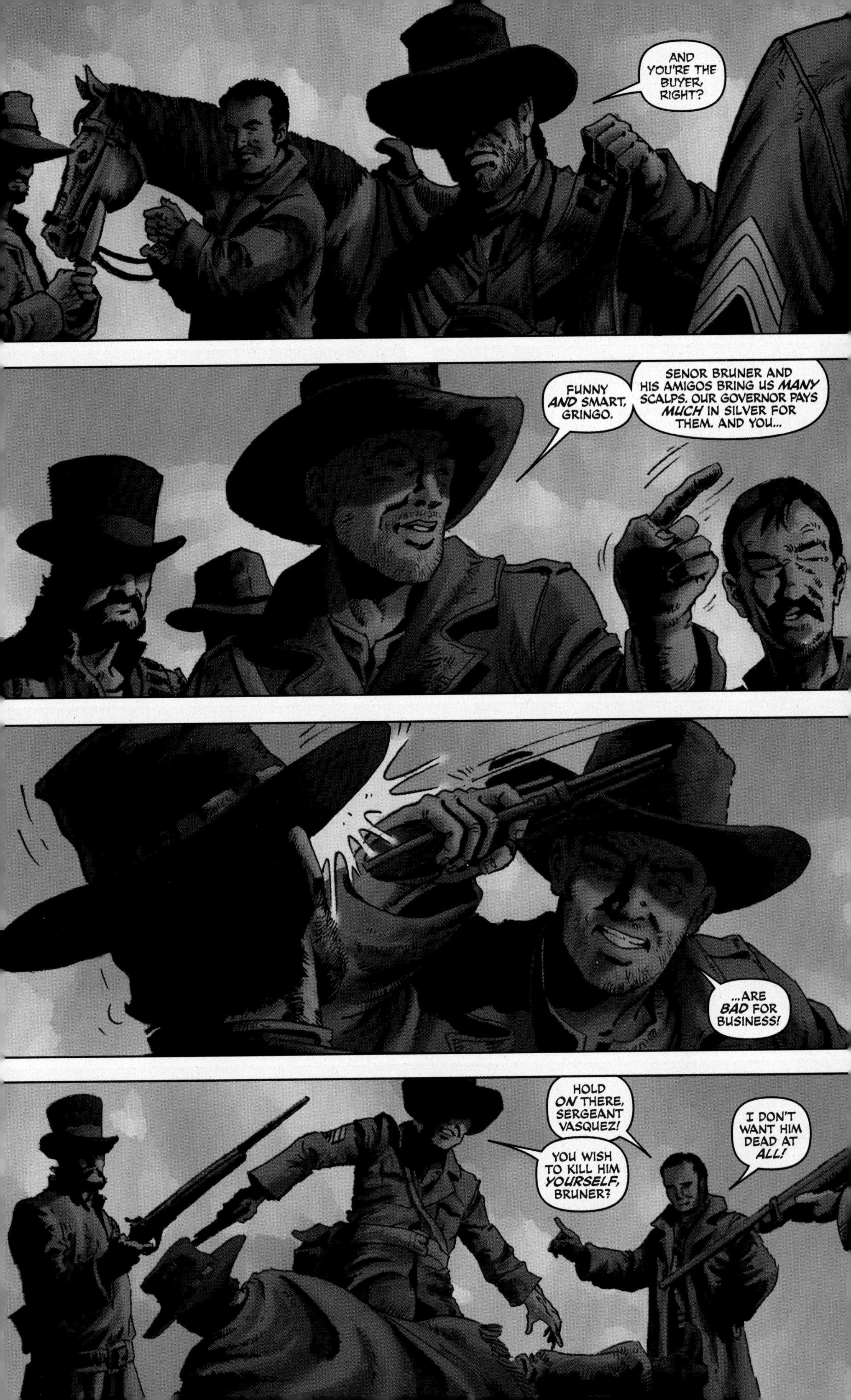
AND YOU'RE THE BUYER, RIGHT?
FUNNY AND SMART, GRINGO.
SENOR BRUNER AND HIS AMIGOS BRING US MANY SCALPS. OUR GOVERNOR PAYS MUCH IN SILVER FOR THEM. AND YOU...
...ARE BAD FOR BUSINESS!
HOLD ON THERE, SERGEANT VASQUEZ!
YOU WISH TO KILL HIM YOURSELF, BRUNER?
I DON'T WANT HIM DEAD AT ALL!

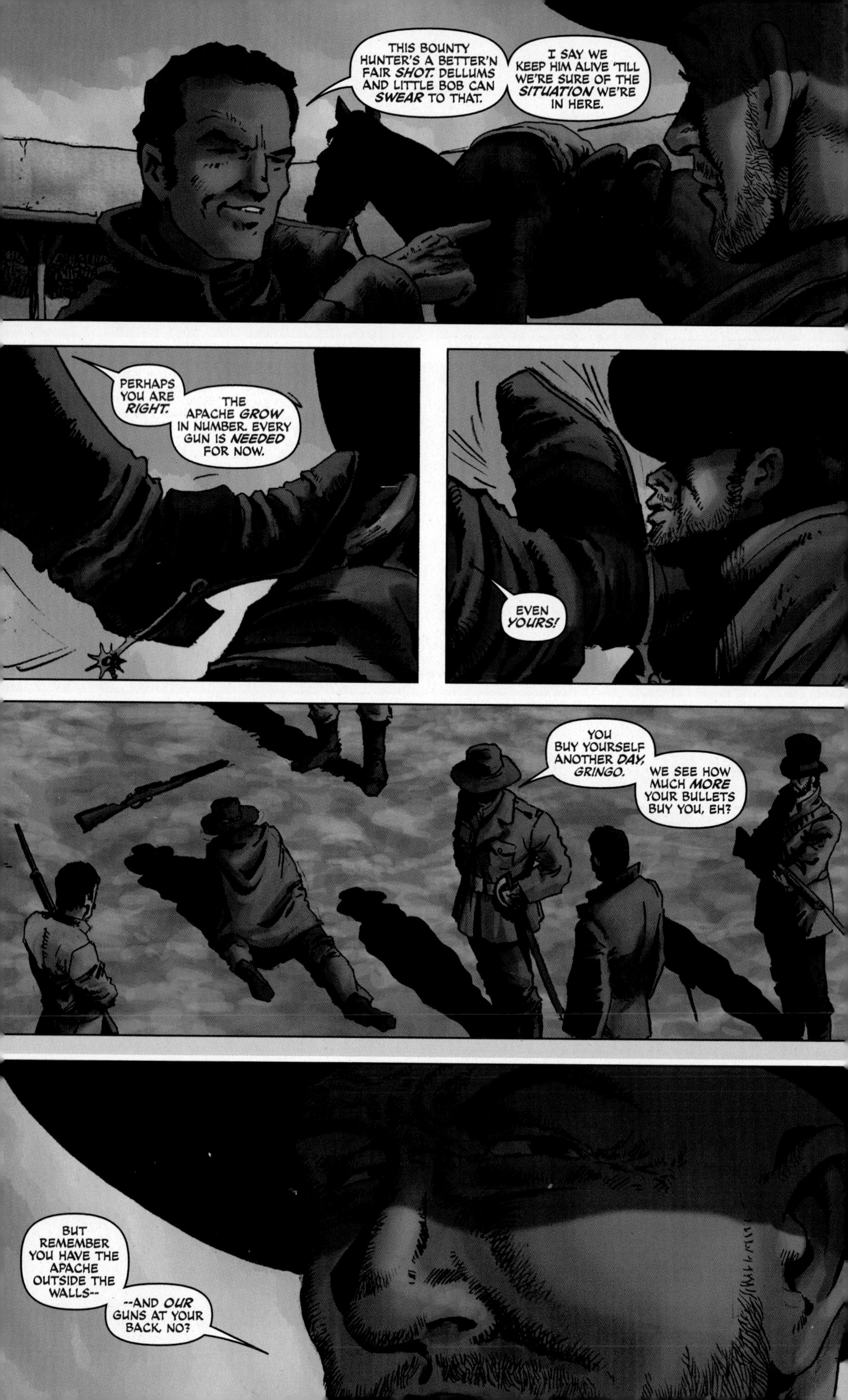
THIS BOUNTY HUNTER'S A BETTER'N FAIR SHOT. DELLUMS AND LITTLE BOB CAN SWEAR TO THAT.
I SAY WE KEEP HIM ALIVE 'TILL WE'RE SURE OF THE SITUATION WE'RE IN HERE.
PERHAPS YOU ARE RIGHT.
THE APACHE GROW IN NUMBER. EVERY GUN IS NEEDED FOR NOW.
EVEN YOURS!
YOU BUY YOURSELF ANOTHER DAY, GRINGO.
WE SEE HOW MUCH MORE YOUR BULLETS BUY YOU, EH?
BUT REMEMBER YOU HAVE THE APACHE OUTSIDE THE WALLS--
--AND OUR GUNS AT YOUR BACK, NO?

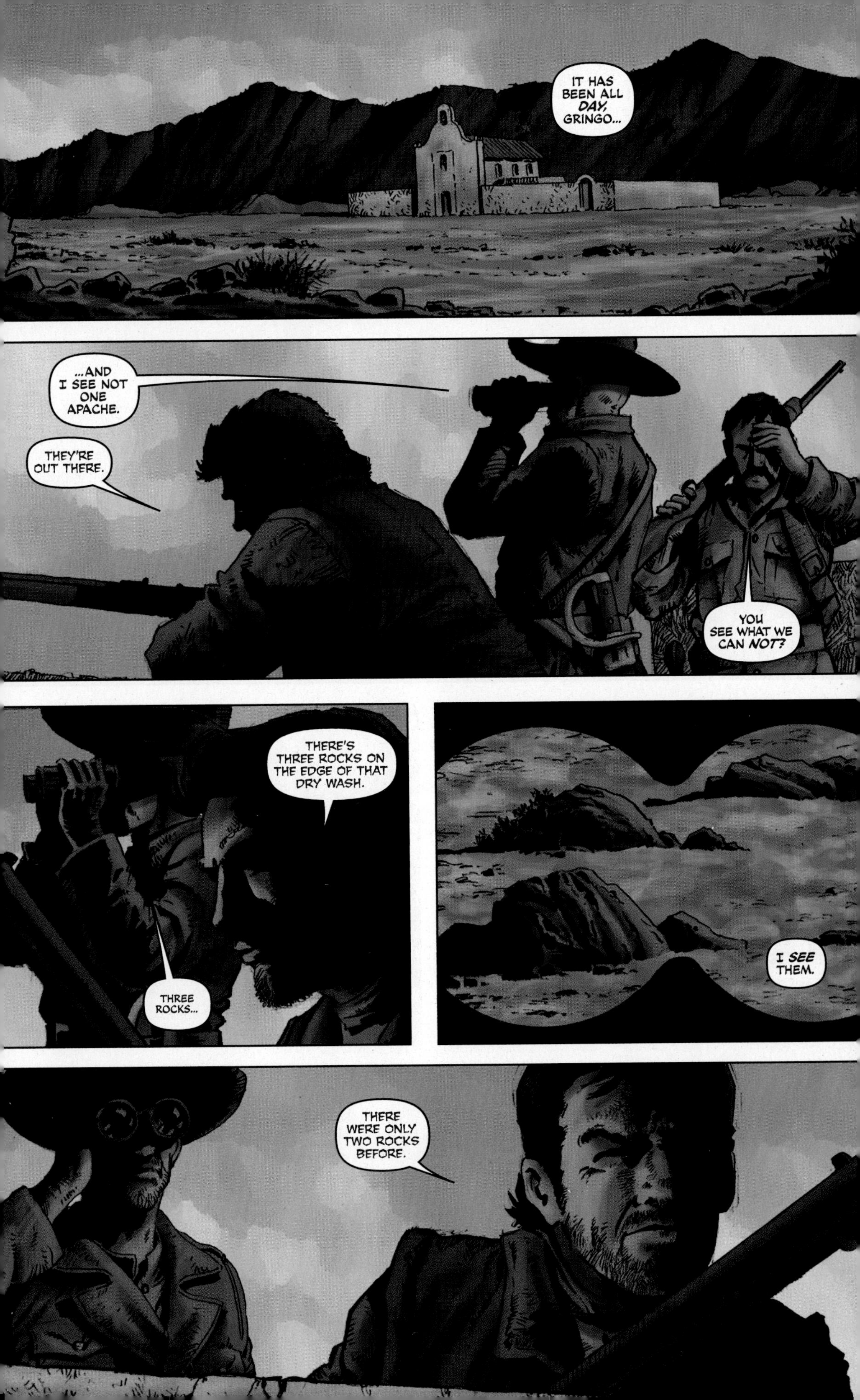
IT HAS BEEN ALL DAY, GRINGO...
...AND I SEE NOT ONE APACHE.
THEY'RE OUT THERE.
YOU SEE WHAT WE CAN NOT?
THERE'S THREE ROCKS ON THE EDGE OF THAT DRY WASH.
THREE ROCKS...
I SEE THEM.
THERE WERE ONLY TWO ROCKS BEFORE.

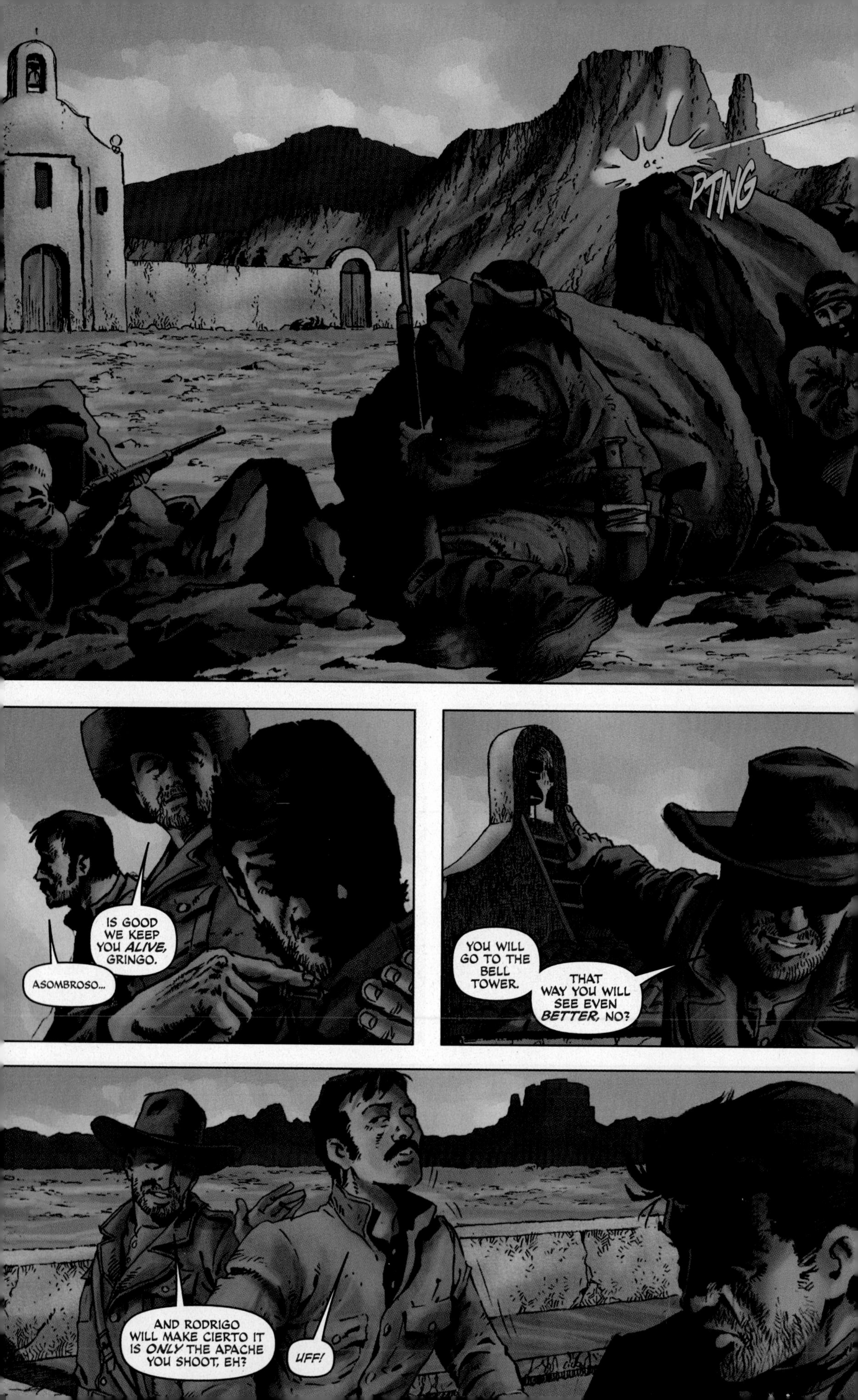
PTING
IS GOOD WE KEEP YOU *ALIVE*, GRINGO.
ASOMBROSO...
YOU WILL GO TO THE BELL TOWER.
THAT WAY YOU WILL SEE EVEN *BETTER*, NO?
AND RODRIGO WILL MAKE CIERTO IT IS *ONLY* THE APACHE YOU SHOOT, EH?
UFF!

THE APACHE HAVE DECIDED TO *WAIT,* BRUNER.

WAIT FOR WHAT?

FOR *YOU,* PERHAPS?

WHAT'RE YOU *DRIVIN'* AT, VASQUEZ?

IT IS *YOU* THEY WANT. THEY KNEW YOU WOULD *COME* HERE.

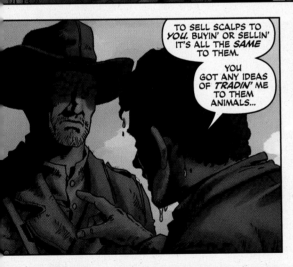

TO SELL SCALPS TO *YOU.* BUYIN' OR SELLIN' IT'S ALL THE *SAME* TO THEM.

YOU GOT ANY IDEAS OF *TRADIN'* ME TO THEM ANIMALS...

YOU ARE RIGHT, BRUNER. *EVERY* GUN COUNTS NOW IF WE ARE TO LIVE.

AND SO LONG AS YOU ARE WORTH MORE *ALIVE* IN TEXAS THAN YOU ARE *DEAD* HERE...

...YOU'LL HAVE A GUARDIAN *ANGEL* WATCHING OVER YOU.

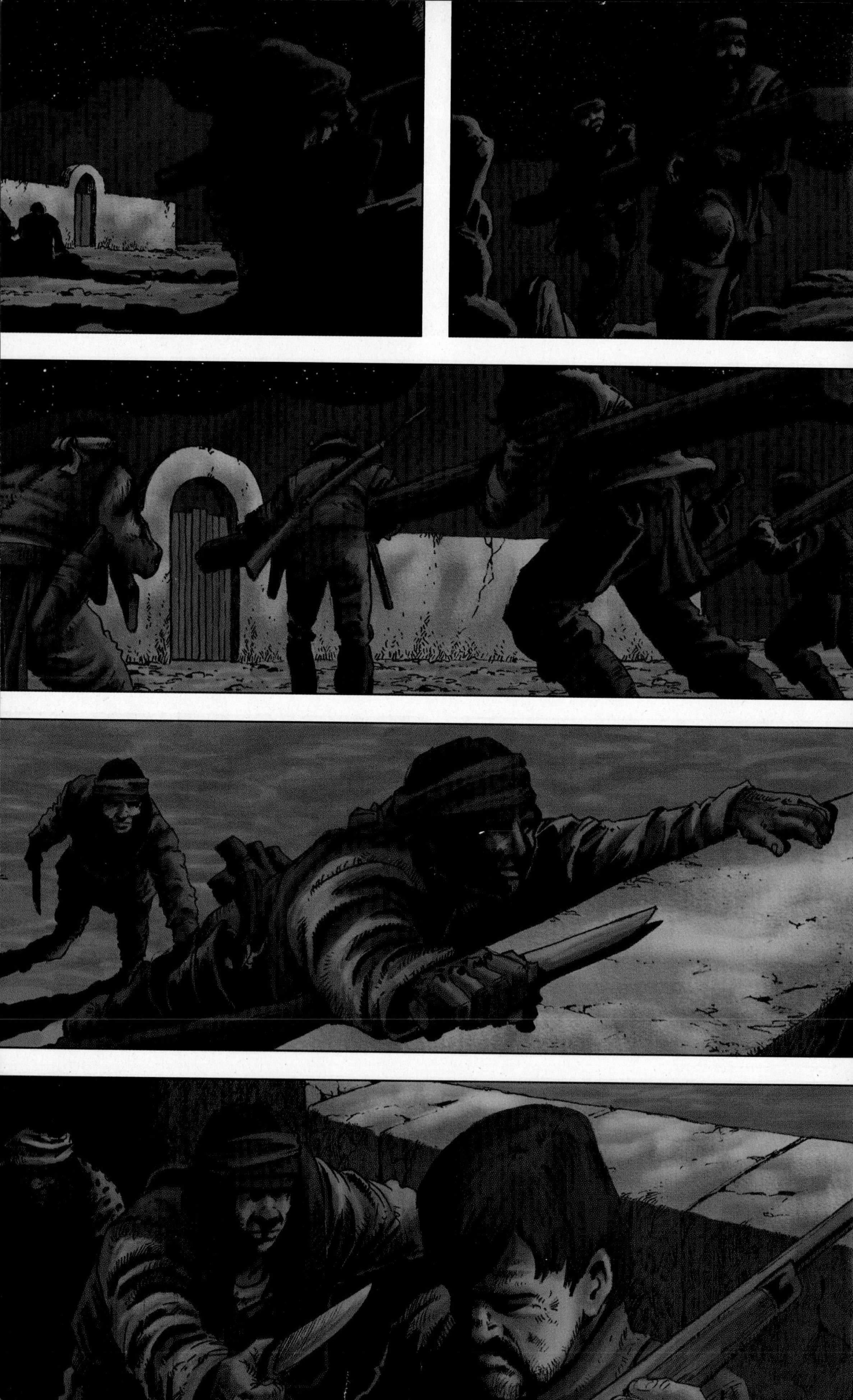

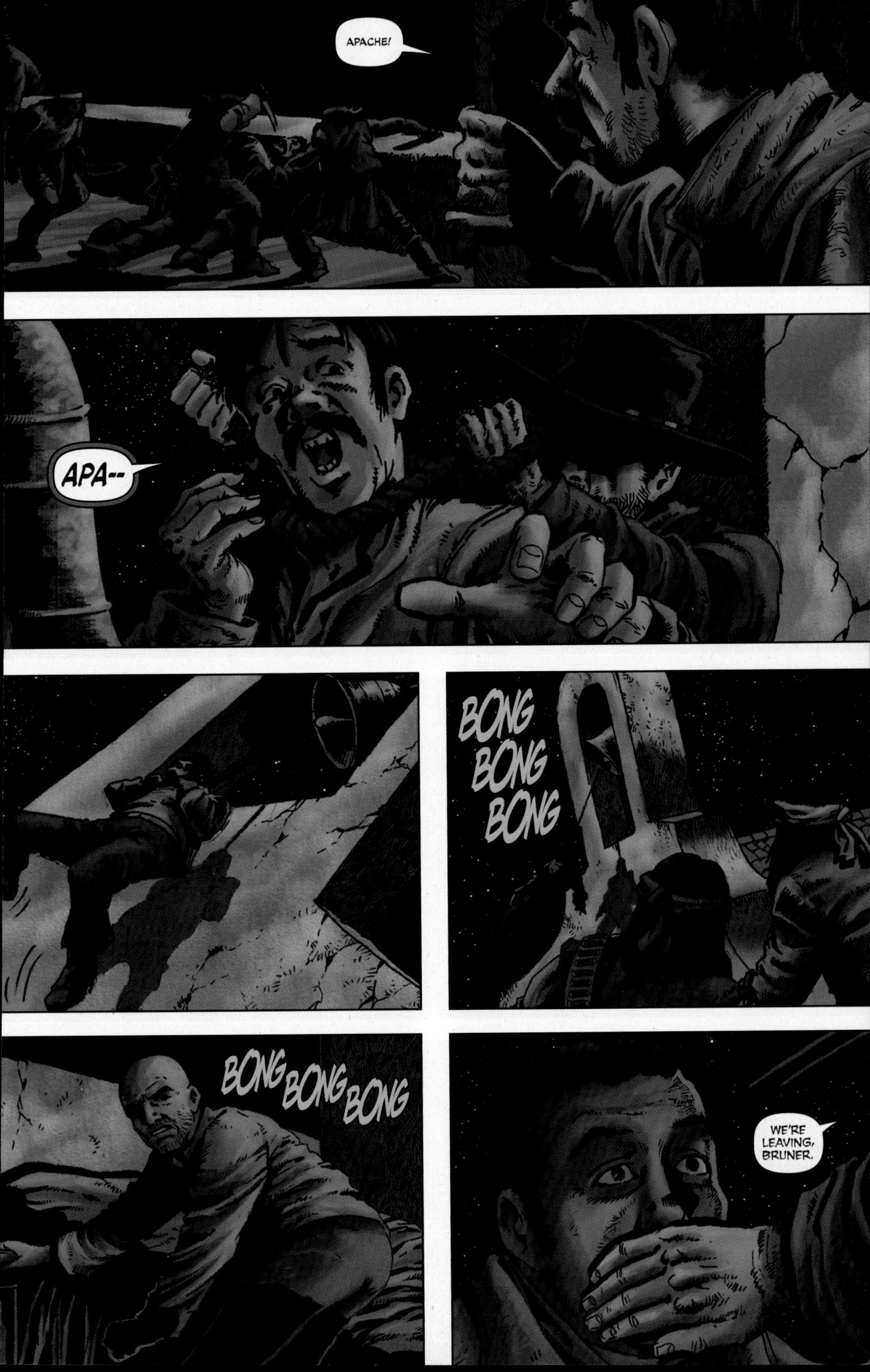
APACHE!
APA--
BONG
BONG
BONG
BONG BONG BONG
WE'RE LEAVING, BRUNER.

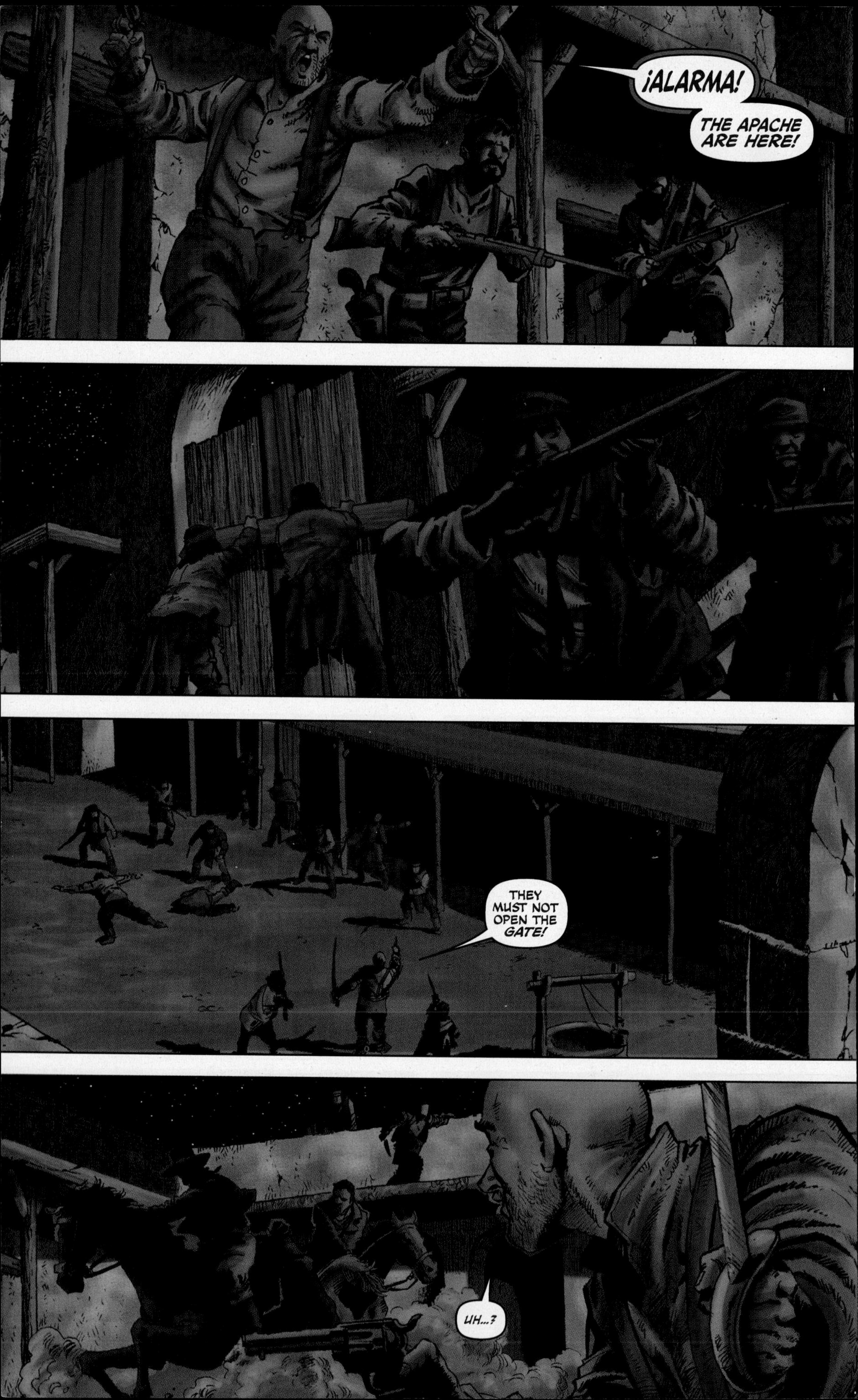
¡ALARMA!
THE APACHE ARE HERE!
THEY MUST NOT OPEN THE GATE!
UH...?

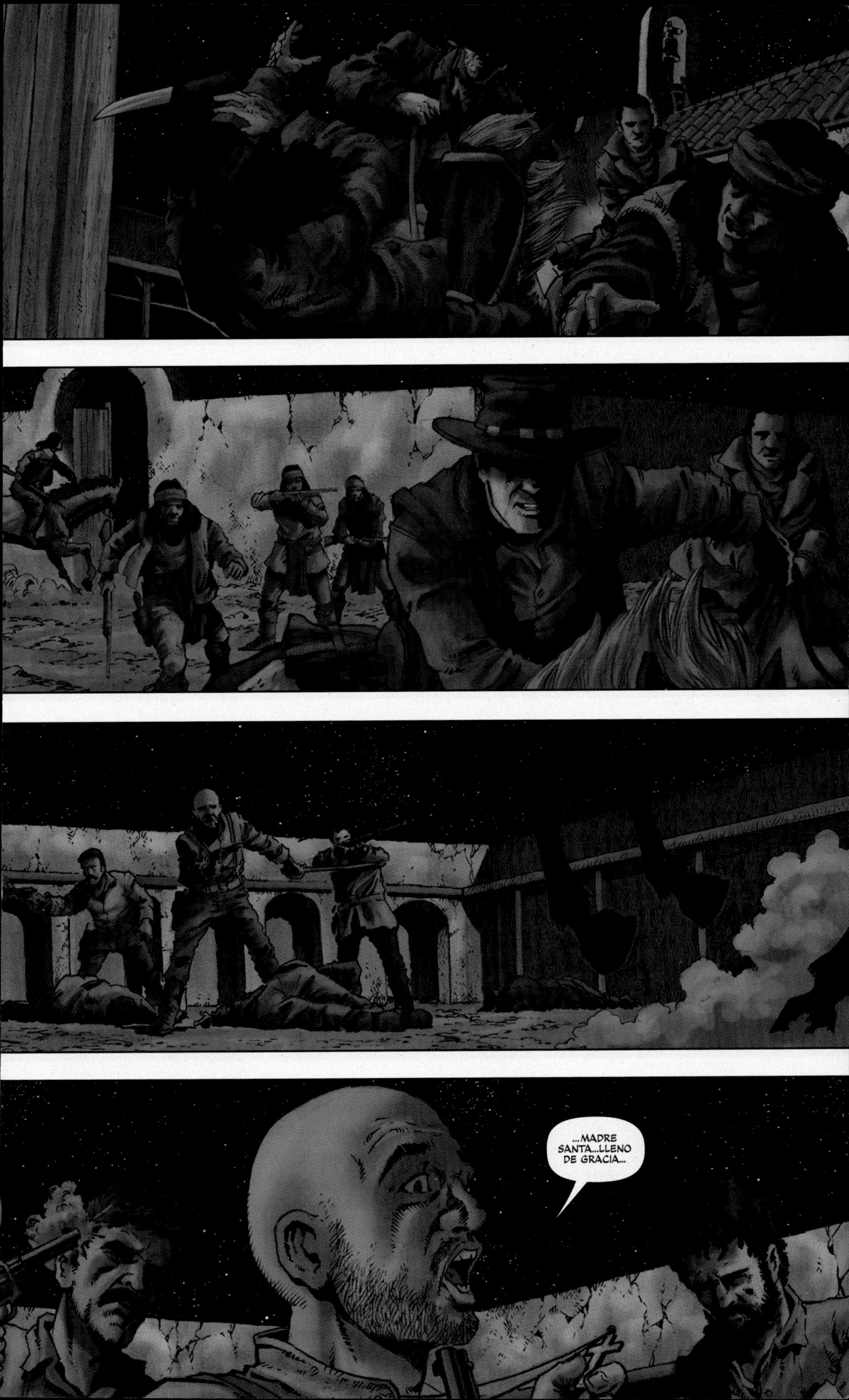
...MADRE SANTA...LLENO DE GRACIA...

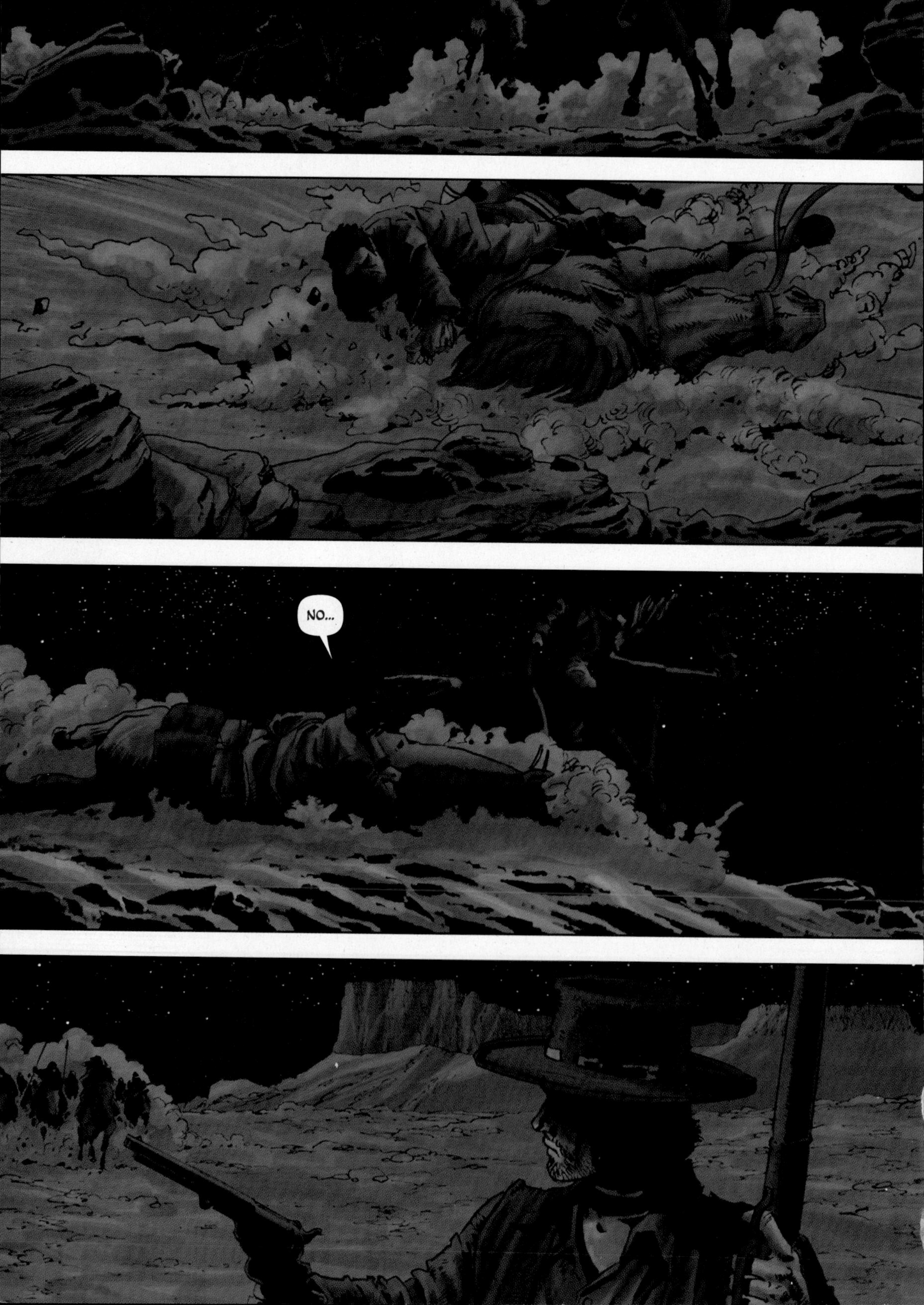
NO...

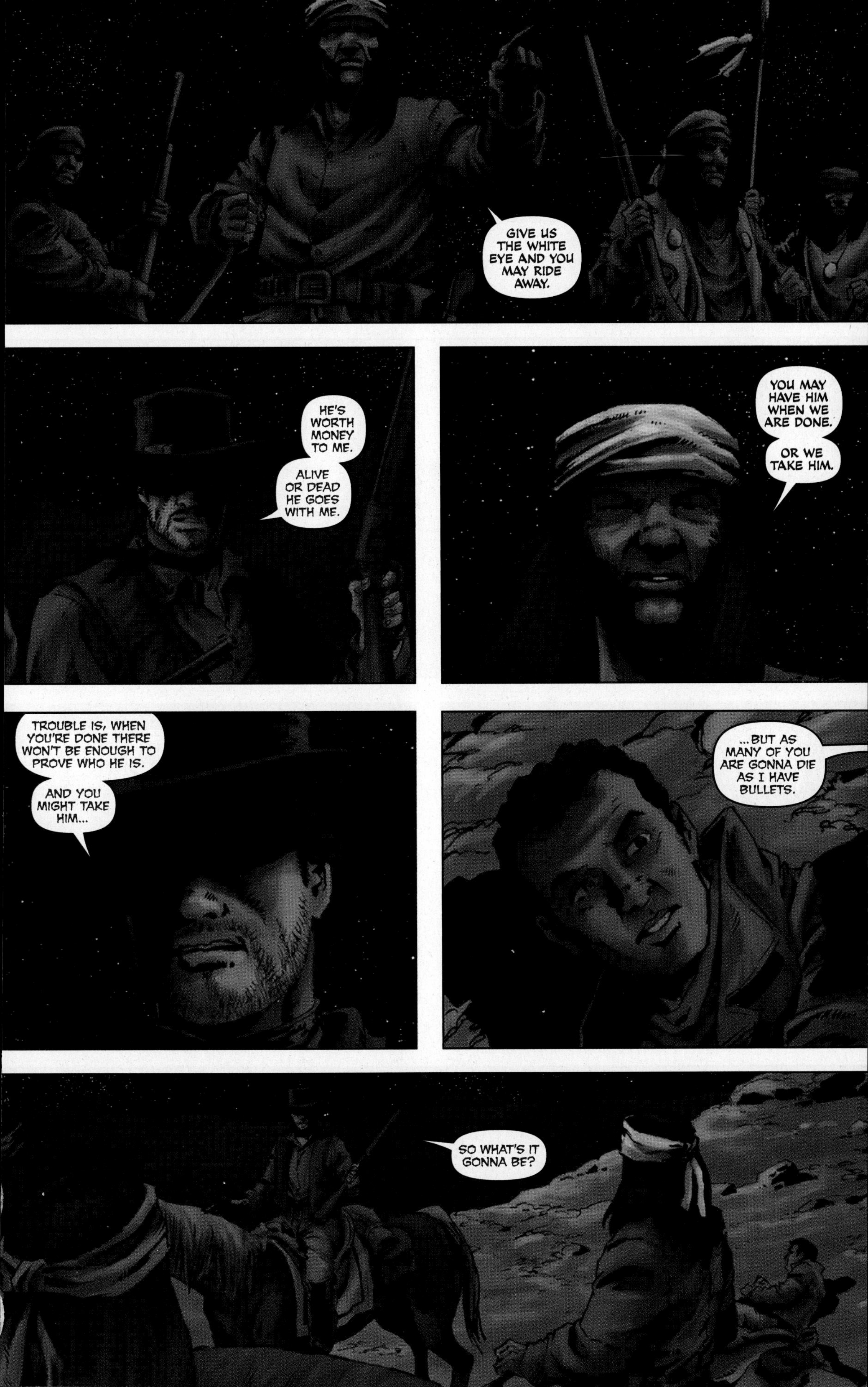
GIVE US THE WHITE EYE AND YOU MAY RIDE AWAY.
HE'S WORTH MONEY TO ME.
ALIVE OR DEAD HE GOES WITH ME.
YOU MAY HAVE HIM WHEN WE ARE DONE.
OR WE TAKE HIM.
TROUBLE IS, WHEN YOU'RE DONE THERE WON'T BE ENOUGH TO PROVE WHO HE IS.
AND YOU MIGHT TAKE HIM...
...BUT AS MANY OF YOU ARE GONNA DIE AS I HAVE BULLETS.
SO WHAT'S IT GONNA BE?

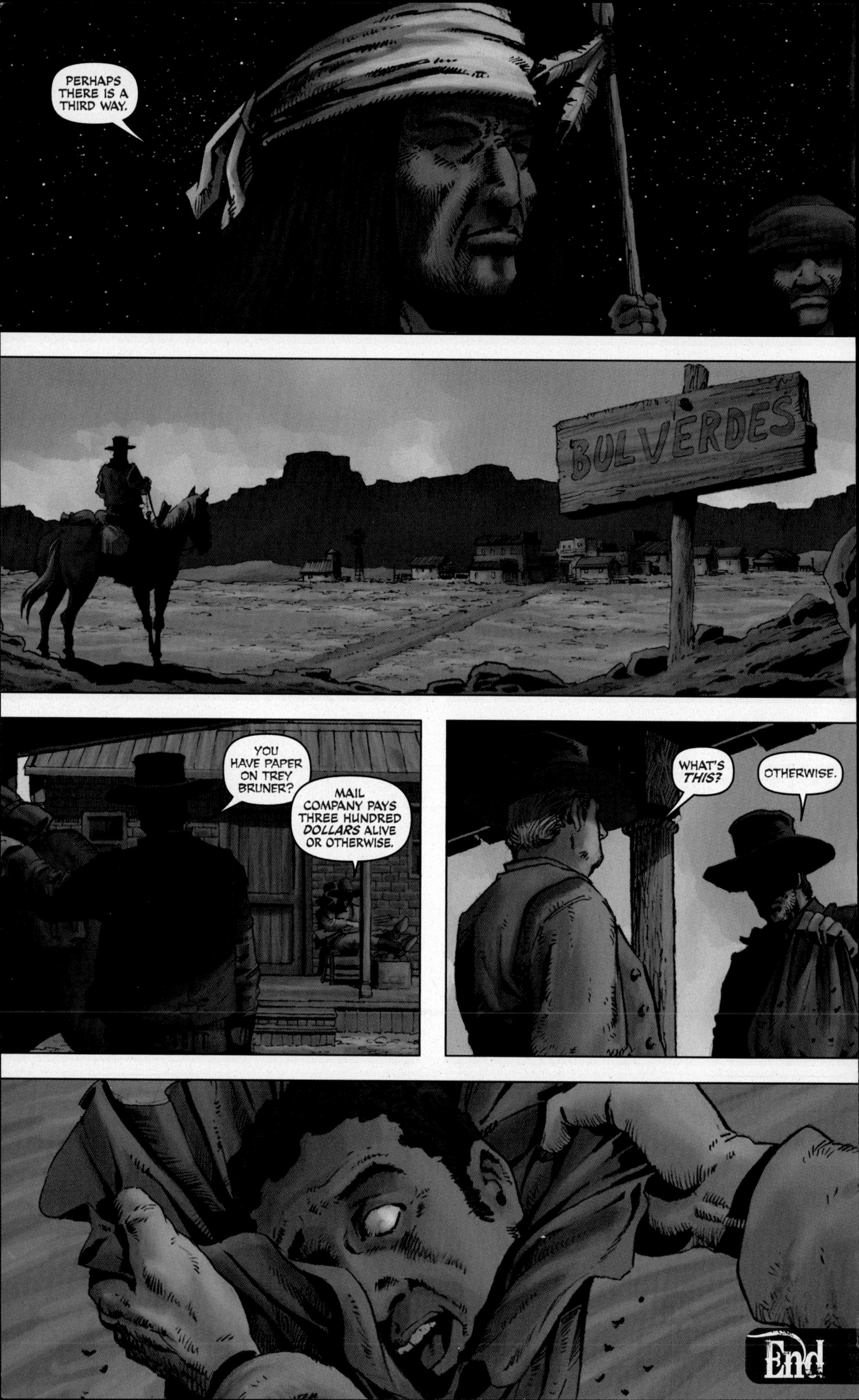
PERHAPS THERE IS A THIRD WAY.
BULVERDES
YOU HAVE PAPER ON TREY BRUNER?
MAIL COMPANY PAYS THREE HUNDRED *DOLLARS* ALIVE OR OTHERWISE.
WHAT'S *THIS*?
OTHERWISE.
End

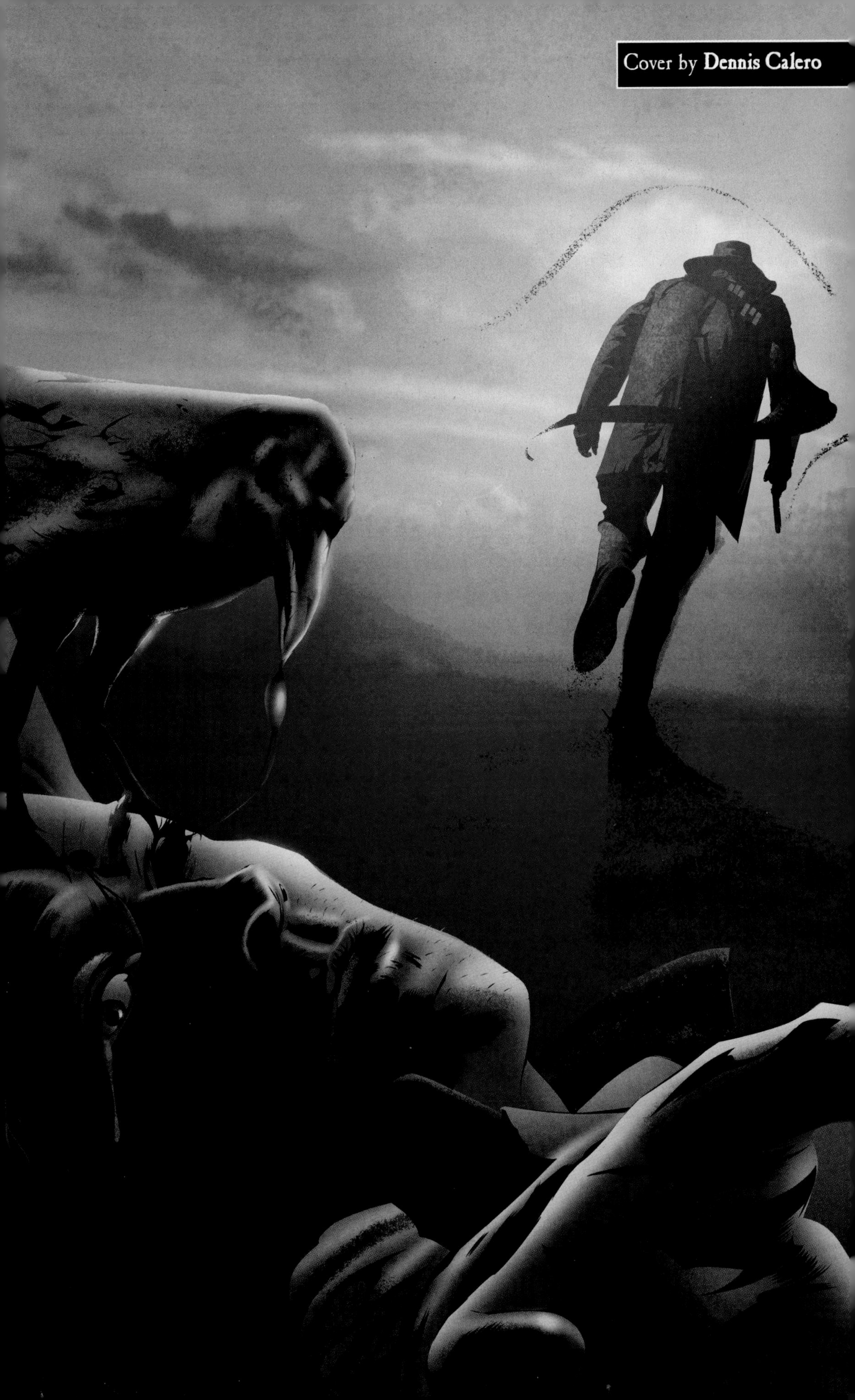
Cover by **Dennis Calero**

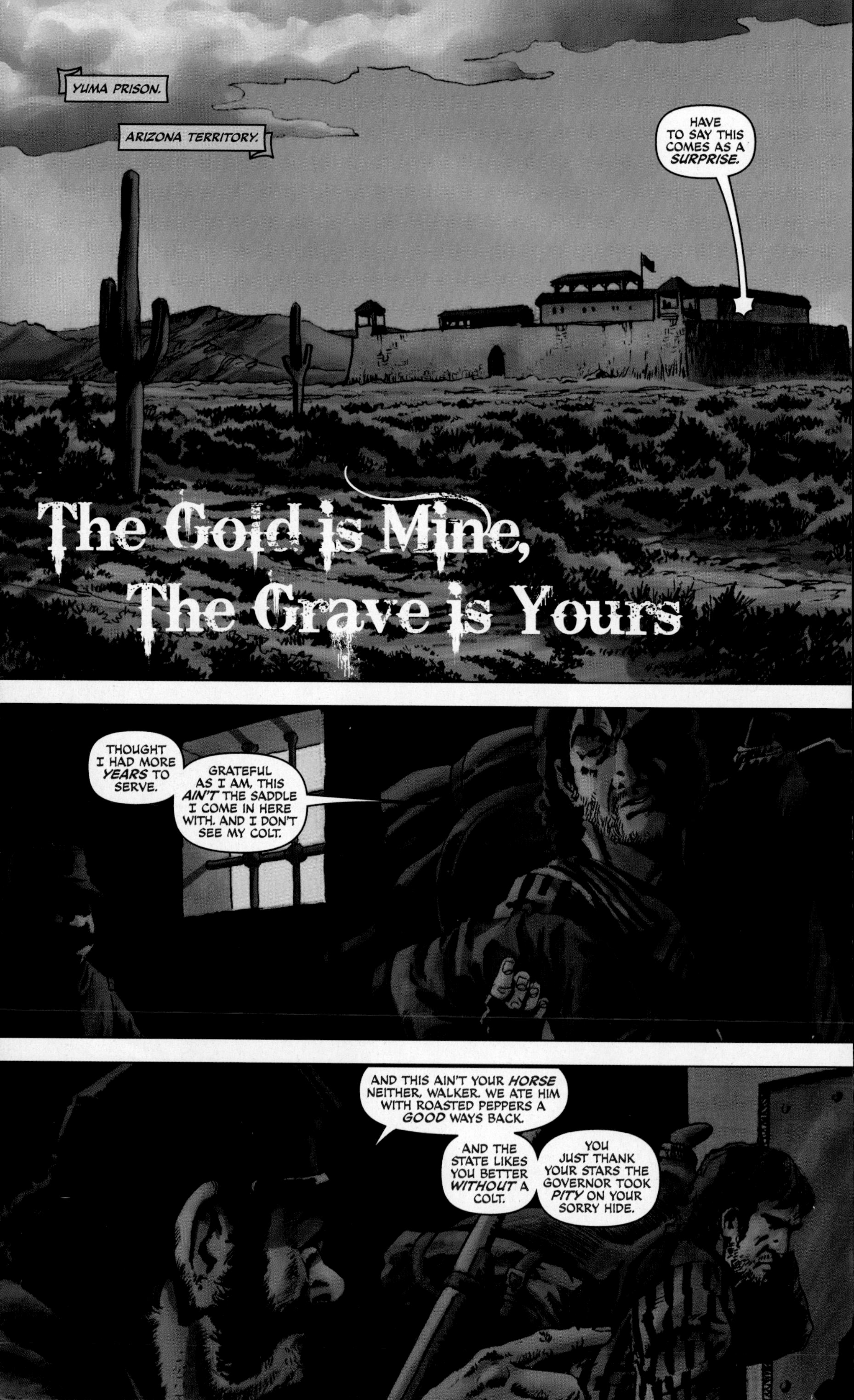
YUMA PRISON.
ARIZONA TERRITORY.
HAVE TO SAY THIS COMES AS A SURPRISE.
The Gold is Mine, The Grave is Yours
THOUGHT I HAD MORE YEARS TO SERVE.
GRATEFUL AS I AM, THIS AIN'T THE SADDLE I COME IN HERE WITH. AND I DON'T SEE MY COLT.
AND THIS AIN'T YOUR HORSE NEITHER, WALKER. WE ATE HIM WITH ROASTED PEPPERS A GOOD WAYS BACK.
AND THE STATE LIKES YOU BETTER WITHOUT A COLT.
YOU JUST THANK YOUR STARS THE GOVERNOR TOOK PITY ON YOUR SORRY HIDE.

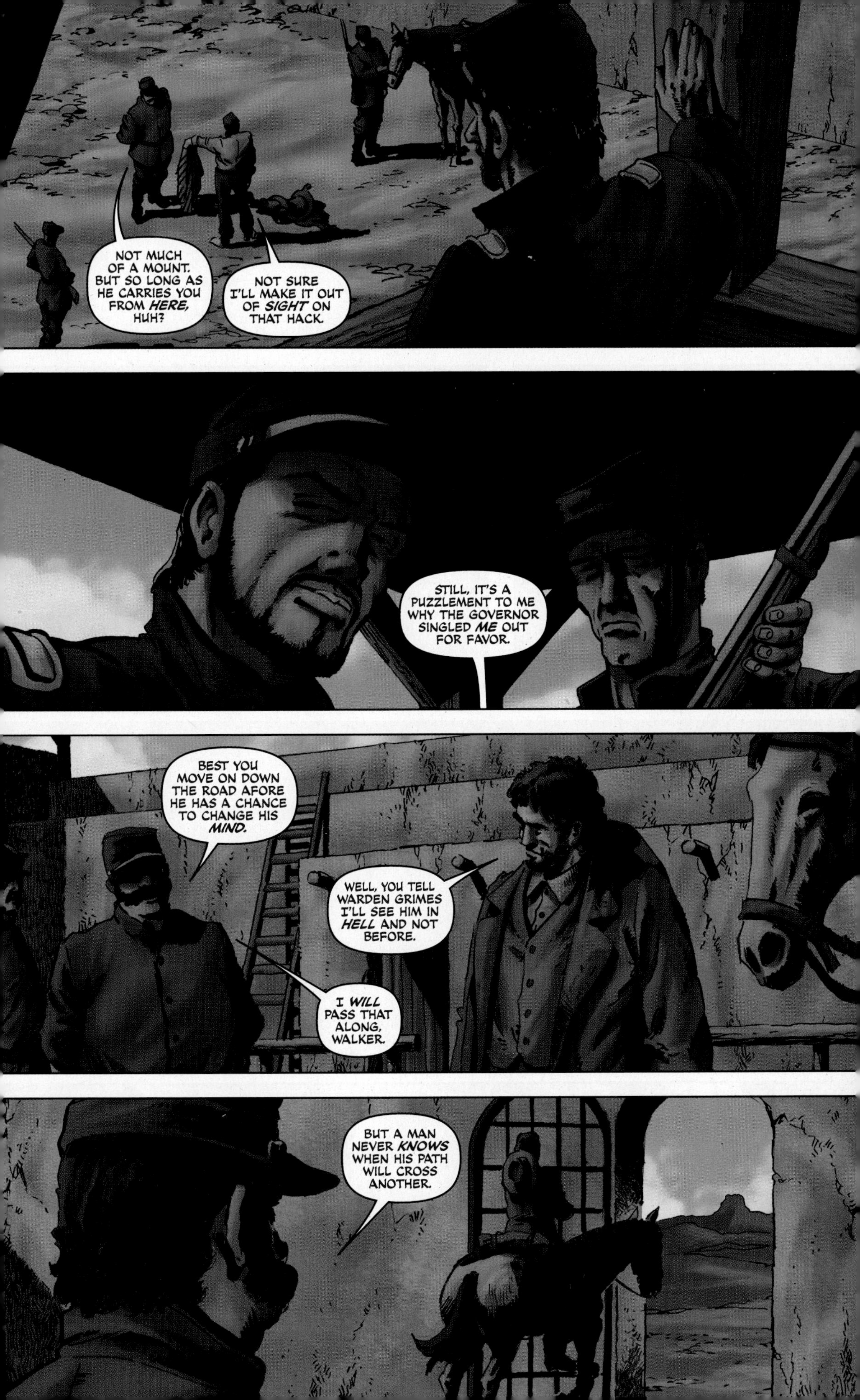
NOT MUCH OF A MOUNT. BUT SO LONG AS HE CARRIES YOU FROM HERE, HUH?
NOT SURE I'LL MAKE IT OUT OF SIGHT ON THAT HACK.
STILL, IT'S A PUZZLEMENT TO ME WHY THE GOVERNOR SINGLED ME OUT FOR FAVOR.
BEST YOU MOVE ON DOWN THE ROAD AFORE HE HAS A CHANCE TO CHANGE HIS MIND.
WELL, YOU TELL WARDEN GRIMES I'LL SEE HIM IN HELL AND NOT BEFORE.
I WILL PASS THAT ALONG, WALKER.
BUT A MAN NEVER KNOWS WHEN HIS PATH WILL CROSS ANOTHER.

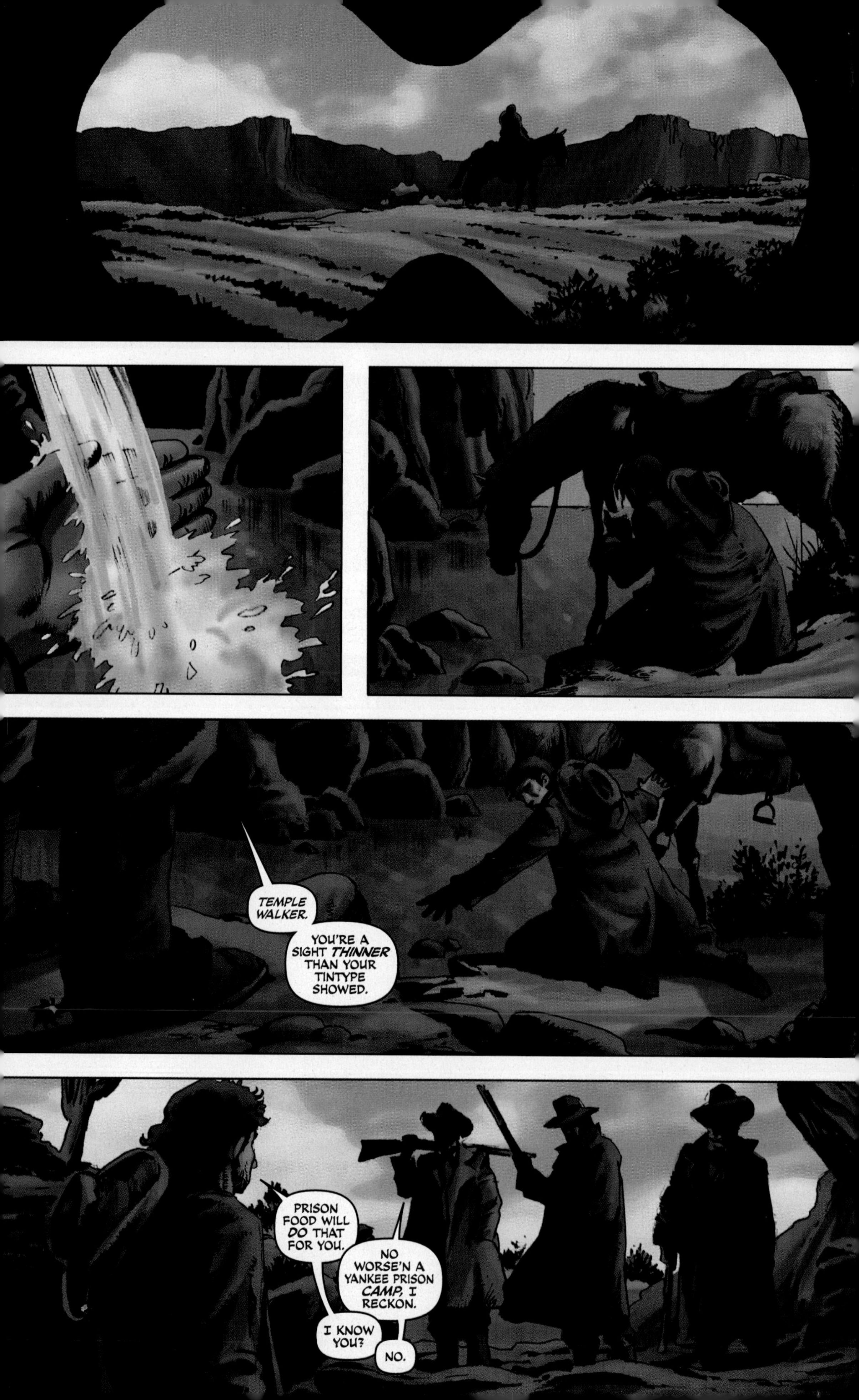
TEMPLE WALKER.
YOU'RE A SIGHT THINNER THAN YOUR TINTYPE SHOWED.
PRISON FOOD WILL DO THAT FOR YOU.
NO WORSE'N A YANKEE PRISON CAMP, I RECKON.
I KNOW YOU?
NO.

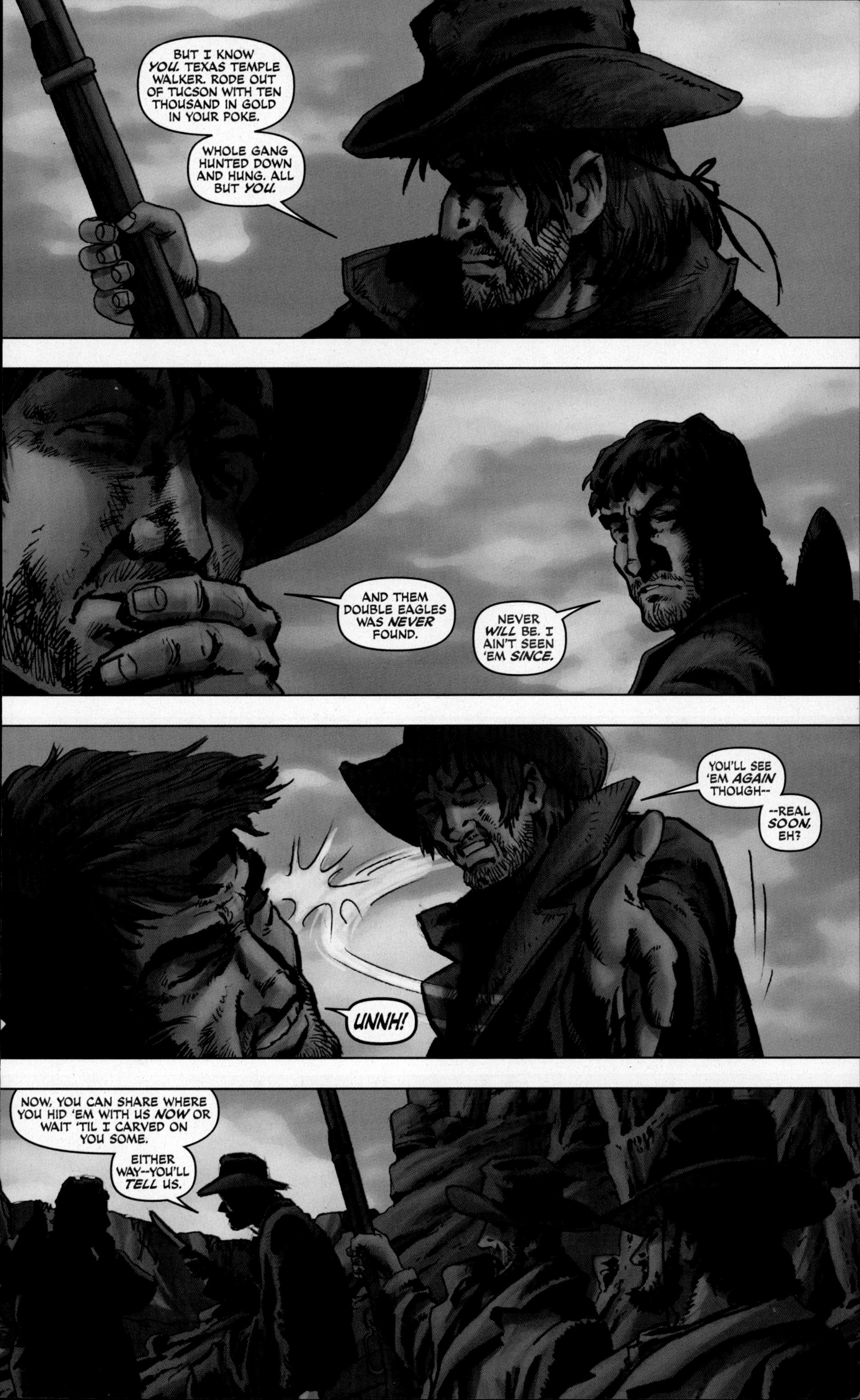
BUT I KNOW YOU. TEXAS TEMPLE WALKER. RODE OUT OF TUCSON WITH TEN THOUSAND IN GOLD IN YOUR POKE.
WHOLE GANG HUNTED DOWN AND HUNG. ALL BUT YOU.
AND THEM DOUBLE EAGLES WAS NEVER FOUND.
NEVER WILL BE. I AIN'T SEEN 'EM SINCE.
YOU'LL SEE 'EM AGAIN THOUGH--
--REAL SOON, EH?
UNNH!
NOW, YOU CAN SHARE WHERE YOU HID 'EM WITH US NOW OR WAIT 'TIL I CARVED ON YOU SOME.
EITHER WAY--YOU'LL TELL US.

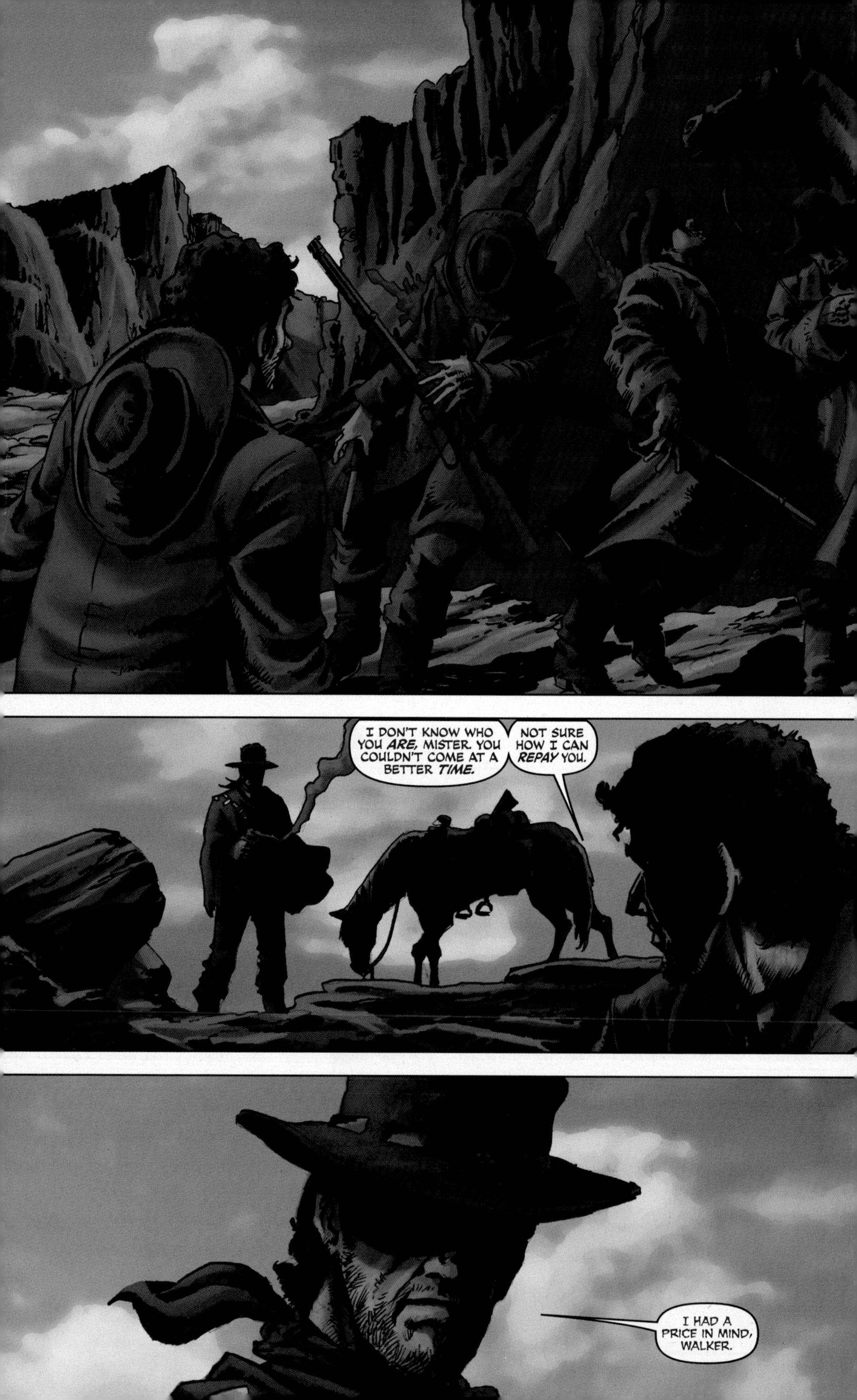
I DON'T KNOW WHO YOU *ARE*, MISTER. YOU COULDN'T COME AT A BETTER *TIME.*
NOT SURE HOW I CAN *REPAY* YOU.
I HAD A PRICE IN MIND, WALKER.

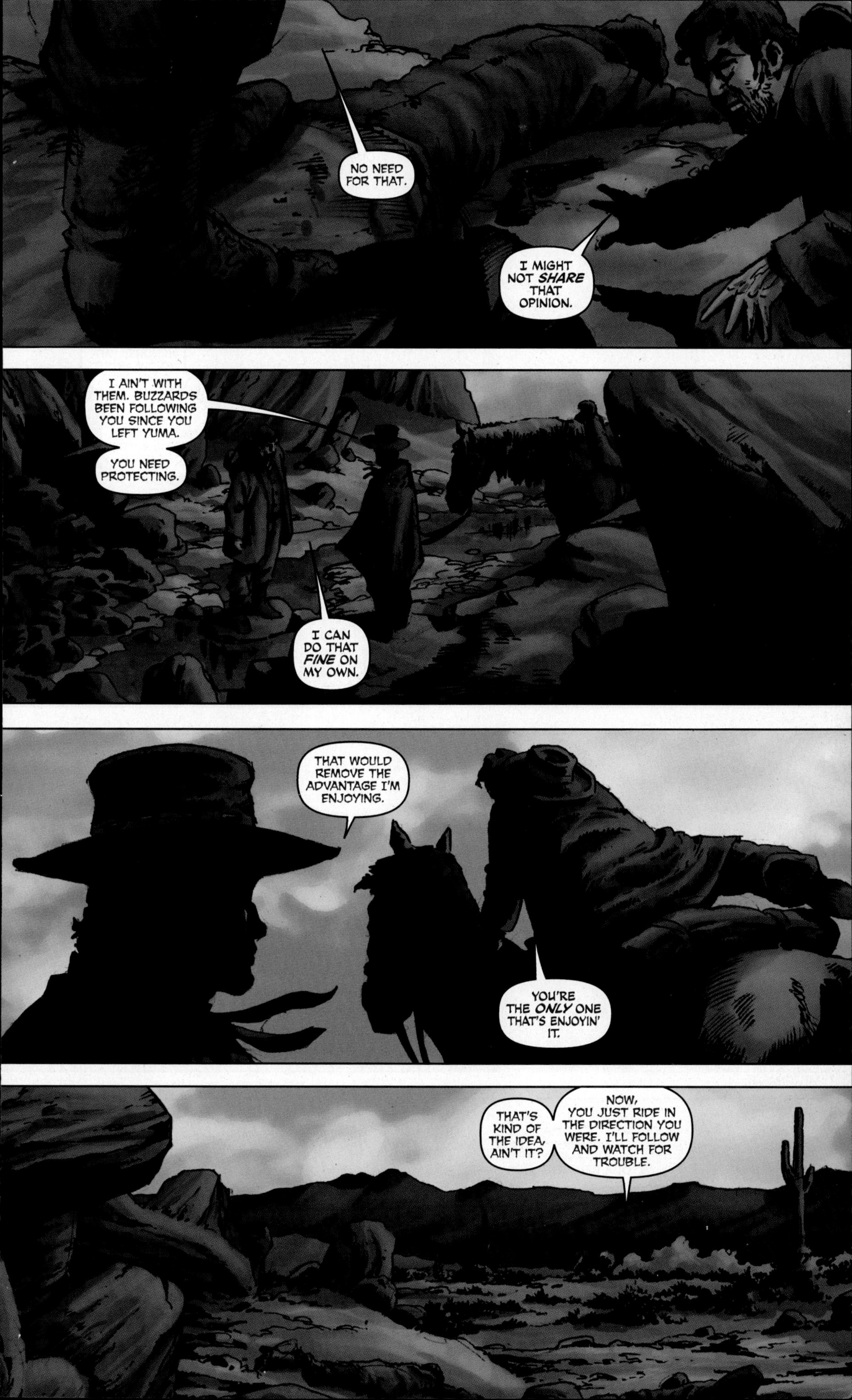
NO NEED FOR THAT.
I MIGHT NOT SHARE THAT OPINION.
I AIN'T WITH THEM. BUZZARDS BEEN FOLLOWING YOU SINCE YOU LEFT YUMA.
YOU NEED PROTECTING.
I CAN DO THAT FINE ON MY OWN.
THAT WOULD REMOVE THE ADVANTAGE I'M ENJOYING.
YOU'RE THE ONLY ONE THAT'S ENJOYIN' IT.
NOW, YOU JUST RIDE IN THE DIRECTION YOU WERE. I'LL FOLLOW AND WATCH FOR TROUBLE.
THAT'S KIND OF THE IDEA, AIN'T IT?

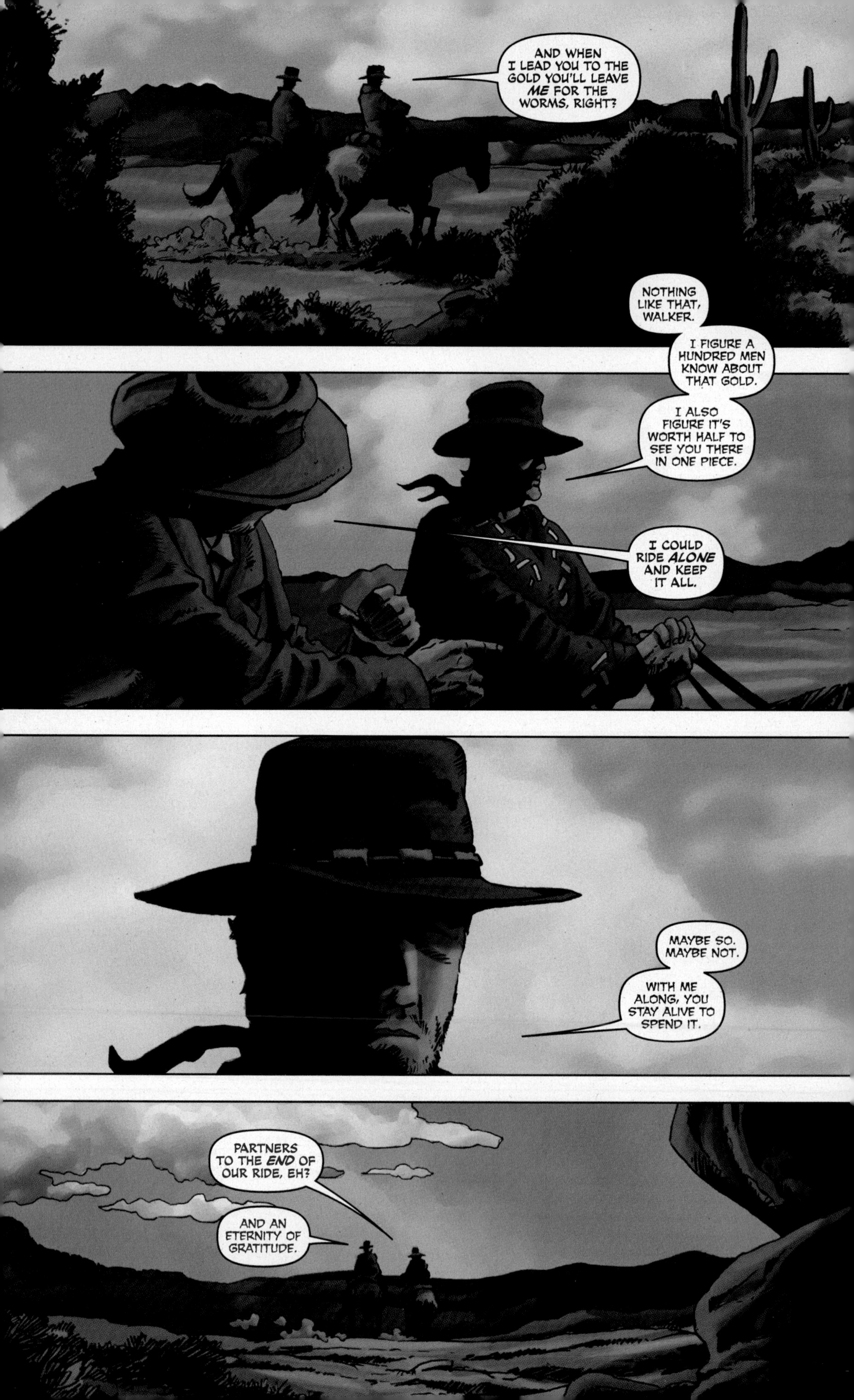
AND WHEN I LEAD YOU TO THE GOLD YOU'LL LEAVE *ME* FOR THE WORMS, RIGHT?
NOTHING LIKE THAT, WALKER.
I FIGURE A HUNDRED MEN KNOW ABOUT THAT GOLD.
I ALSO FIGURE IT'S WORTH HALF TO SEE YOU THERE IN ONE PIECE.
I COULD RIDE *ALONE* AND KEEP IT ALL.
MAYBE SO. MAYBE NOT.
WITH ME ALONG, YOU STAY ALIVE TO SPEND IT.
PARTNERS TO THE *END* OF OUR RIDE, EH?
AND AN ETERNITY OF GRATITUDE.

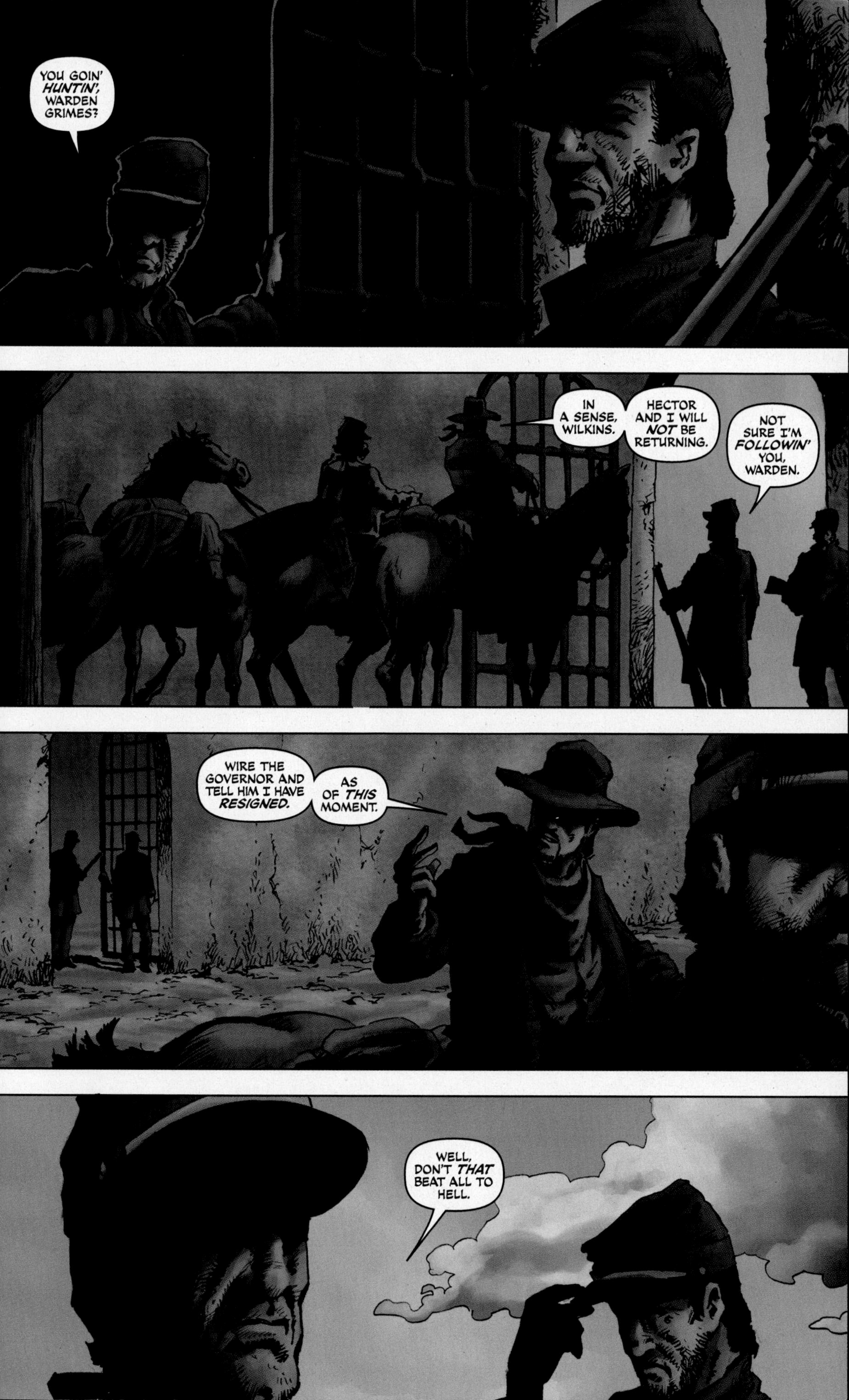
YOU GOIN' HUNTIN', WARDEN GRIMES?
IN A SENSE, WILKINS.
HECTOR AND I WILL NOT BE RETURNING.
NOT SURE I'M FOLLOWIN' YOU, WARDEN.
WIRE THE GOVERNOR AND TELL HIM I HAVE RESIGNED.
AS OF THIS MOMENT.
WELL, DON'T THAT BEAT ALL TO HELL.

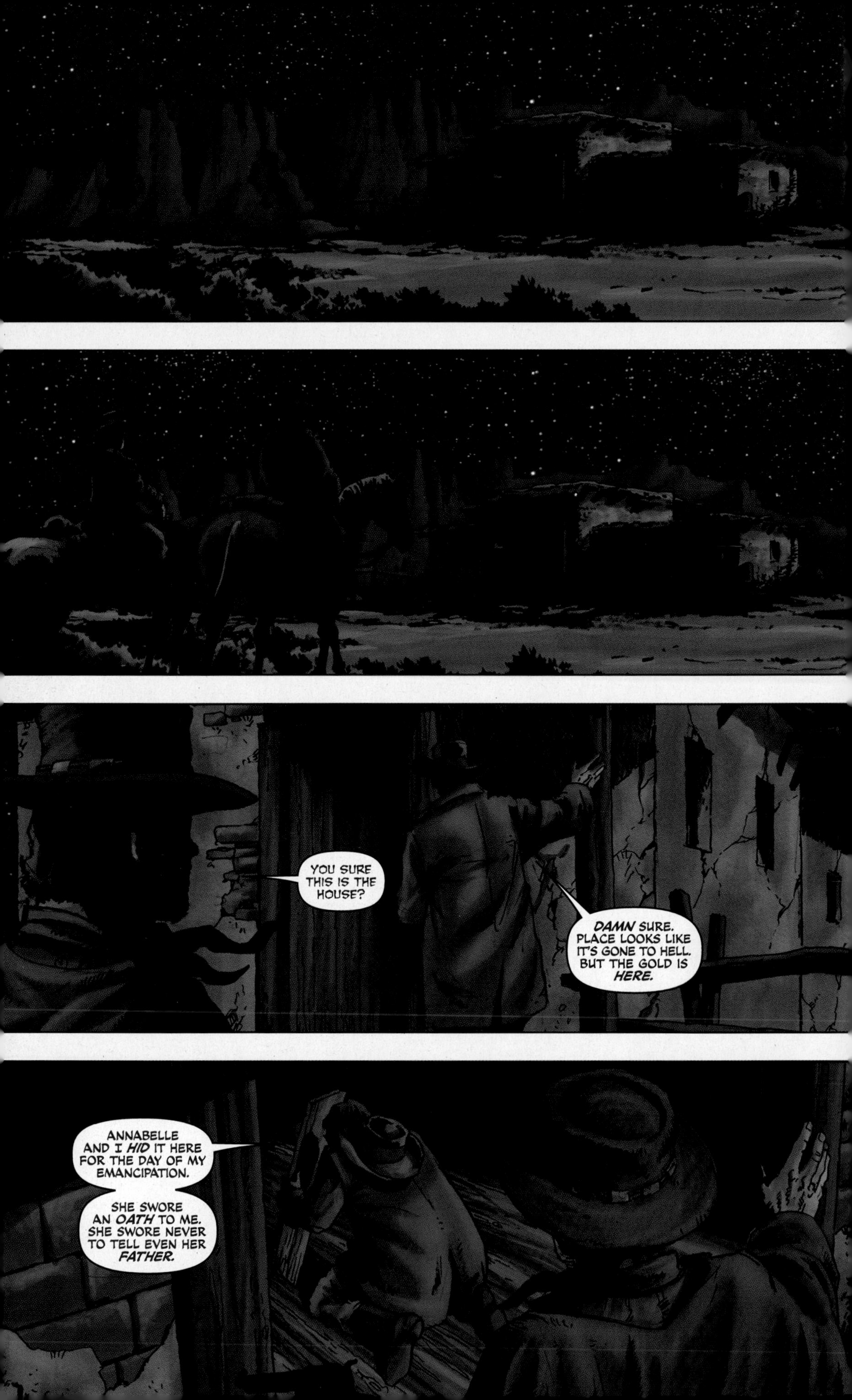
YOU SURE THIS IS THE HOUSE?
DAMN SURE. PLACE LOOKS LIKE IT'S GONE TO HELL. BUT THE GOLD IS HERE.
ANNABELLE AND I HID IT HERE FOR THE DAY OF MY EMANCIPATION.
SHE SWORE AN OATH TO ME. SHE SWORE NEVER TO TELL EVEN HER FATHER.

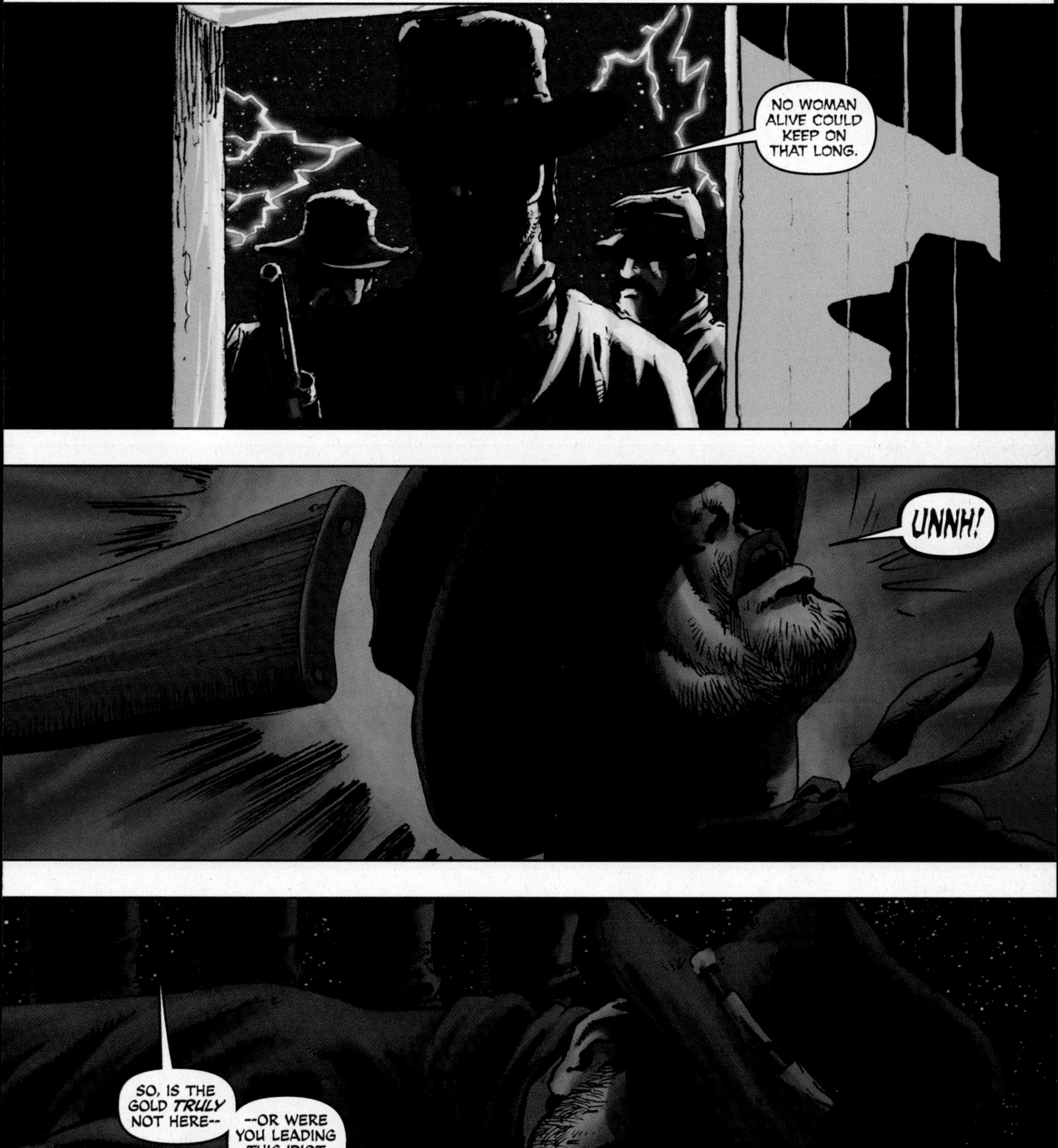
NO WOMAN ALIVE COULD KEEP ON THAT LONG.
UNNH!
SO, IS THE GOLD *TRULY* NOT HERE--
--OR WERE YOU LEADING

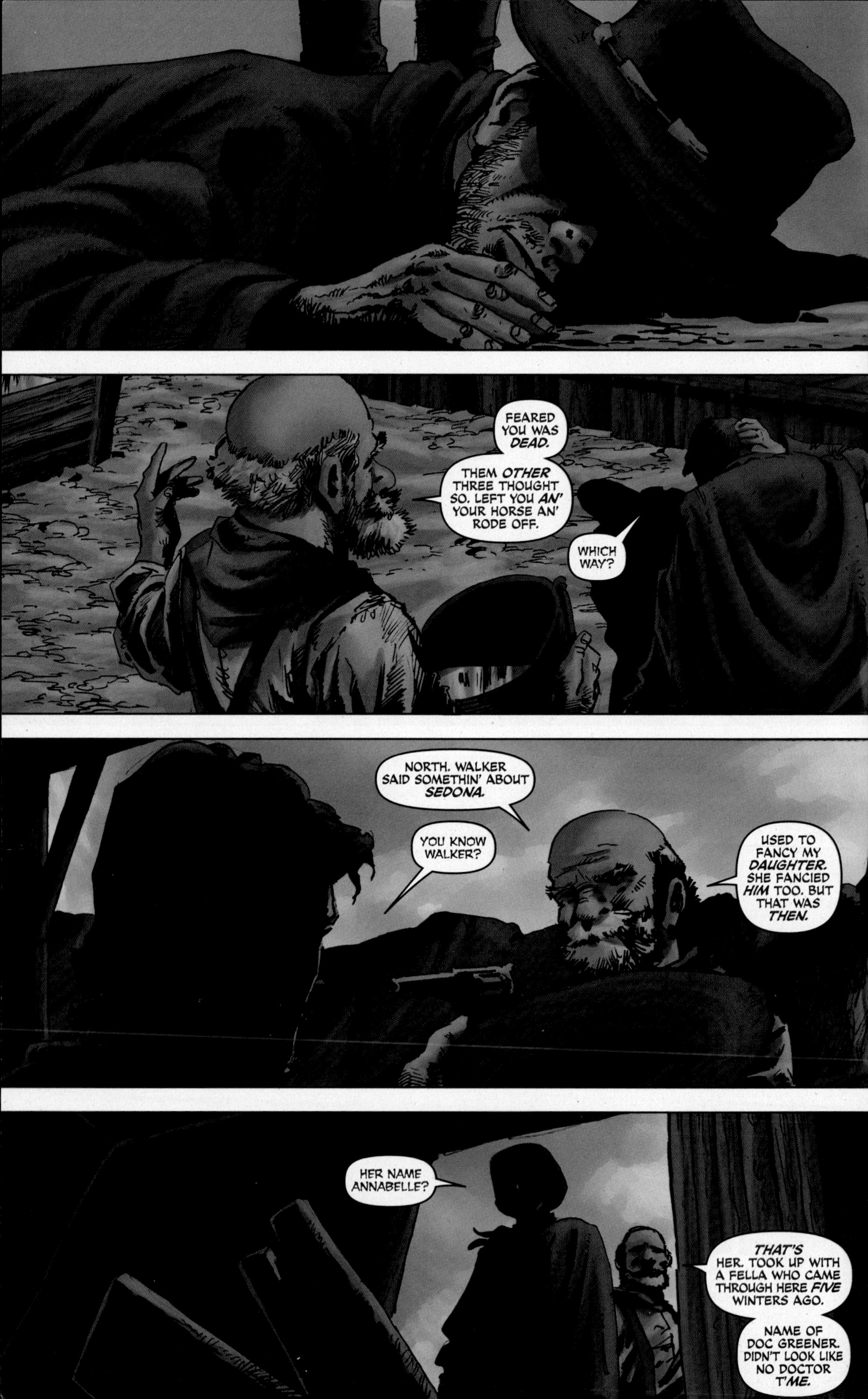
FEARED YOU WAS DEAD.
THEM OTHER THREE THOUGHT SO. LEFT YOU AN' YOUR HORSE AN' RODE OFF.
WHICH WAY?
NORTH. WALKER SAID SOMETHIN' ABOUT SEDONA.
YOU KNOW WALKER?
USED TO FANCY MY DAUGHTER. SHE FANCIED HIM TOO. BUT THAT WAS THEN.
HER NAME ANNABELLE?
THAT'S HER. TOOK UP WITH A FELLA WHO CAME THROUGH HERE FIVE WINTERS AGO.
NAME OF DOC GREENER. DIDN'T LOOK LIKE NO DOCTOR T'ME.

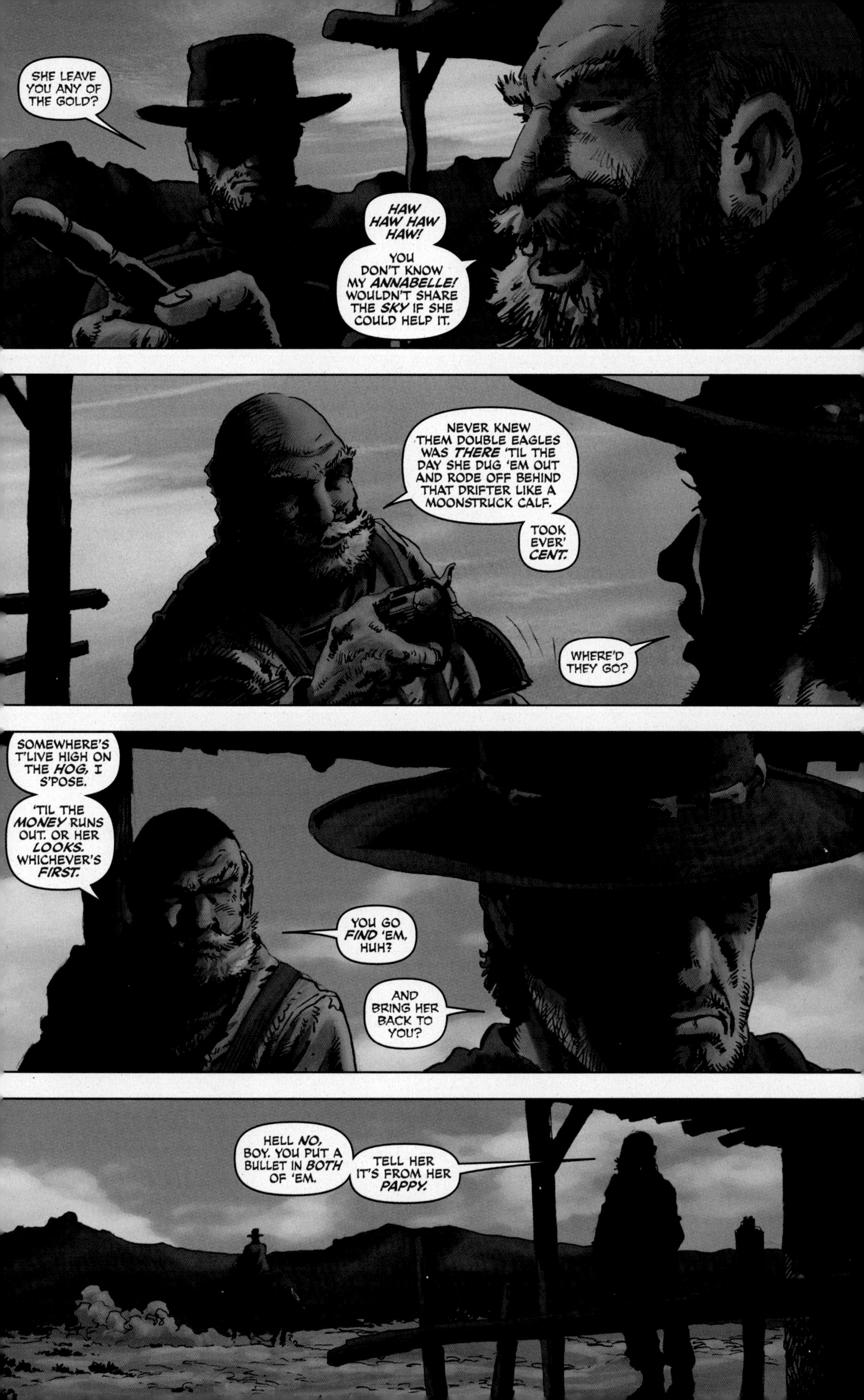
SHE LEAVE YOU ANY OF THE GOLD?
HAW HAW HAW HAW!
YOU DON'T KNOW MY ANNABELLE! WOULDN'T SHARE THE SKY IF SHE COULD HELP IT.
NEVER KNEW THEM DOUBLE EAGLES WAS THERE 'TIL THE DAY SHE DUG 'EM OUT AND RODE OFF BEHIND THAT DRIFTER LIKE A MOONSTRUCK CALF.
TOOK EVER' CENT.
WHERE'D THEY GO?
SOMEWHERE'S T'LIVE HIGH ON THE HOG, I S'POSE.
'TIL THE MONEY RUNS OUT. OR HER LOOKS. WHICHEVER'S FIRST.
YOU GO FIND 'EM, HUH?
AND BRING HER BACK TO YOU?
HELL NO, BOY. YOU PUT A BULLET IN BOTH OF 'EM.
TELL HER IT'S FROM HER PAPPY.

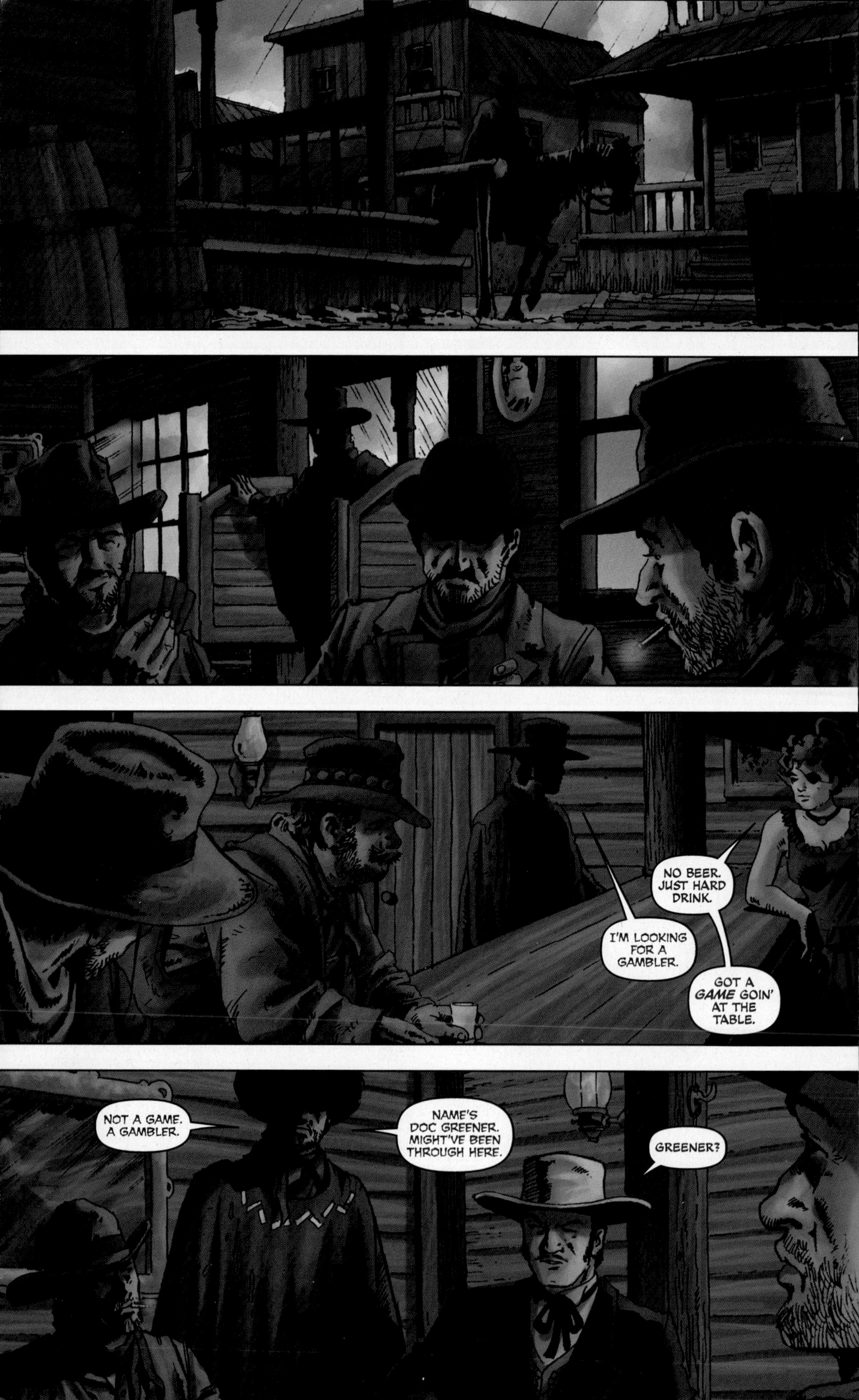
NO BEER. JUST HARD DRINK.
I'M LOOKING FOR A GAMBLER.
GOT A *GAME* GOIN' AT THE TABLE.
NOT A GAME. A GAMBLER.
NAME'S DOC GREENER. MIGHT'VE BEEN THROUGH HERE.
GREENER?

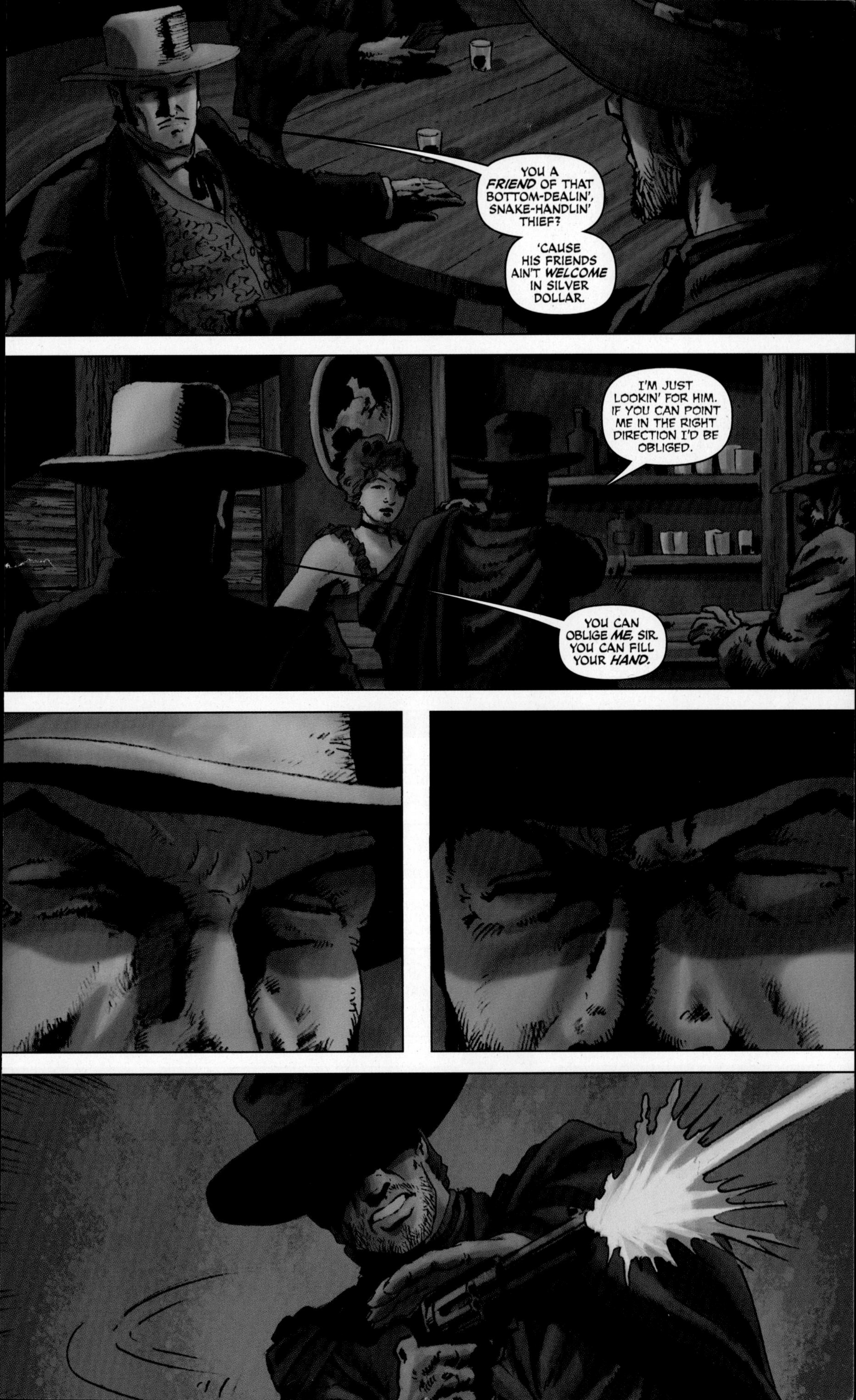
YOU A FRIEND OF THAT BOTTOM-DEALIN', SNAKE-HANDLIN' THIEF?
'CAUSE HIS FRIENDS AIN'T WELCOME IN SILVER DOLLAR.
I'M JUST LOOKIN' FOR HIM. IF YOU CAN POINT ME IN THE RIGHT DIRECTION I'D BE OBLIGED.
YOU CAN OBLIGE ME, SIR. YOU CAN FILL YOUR HAND.

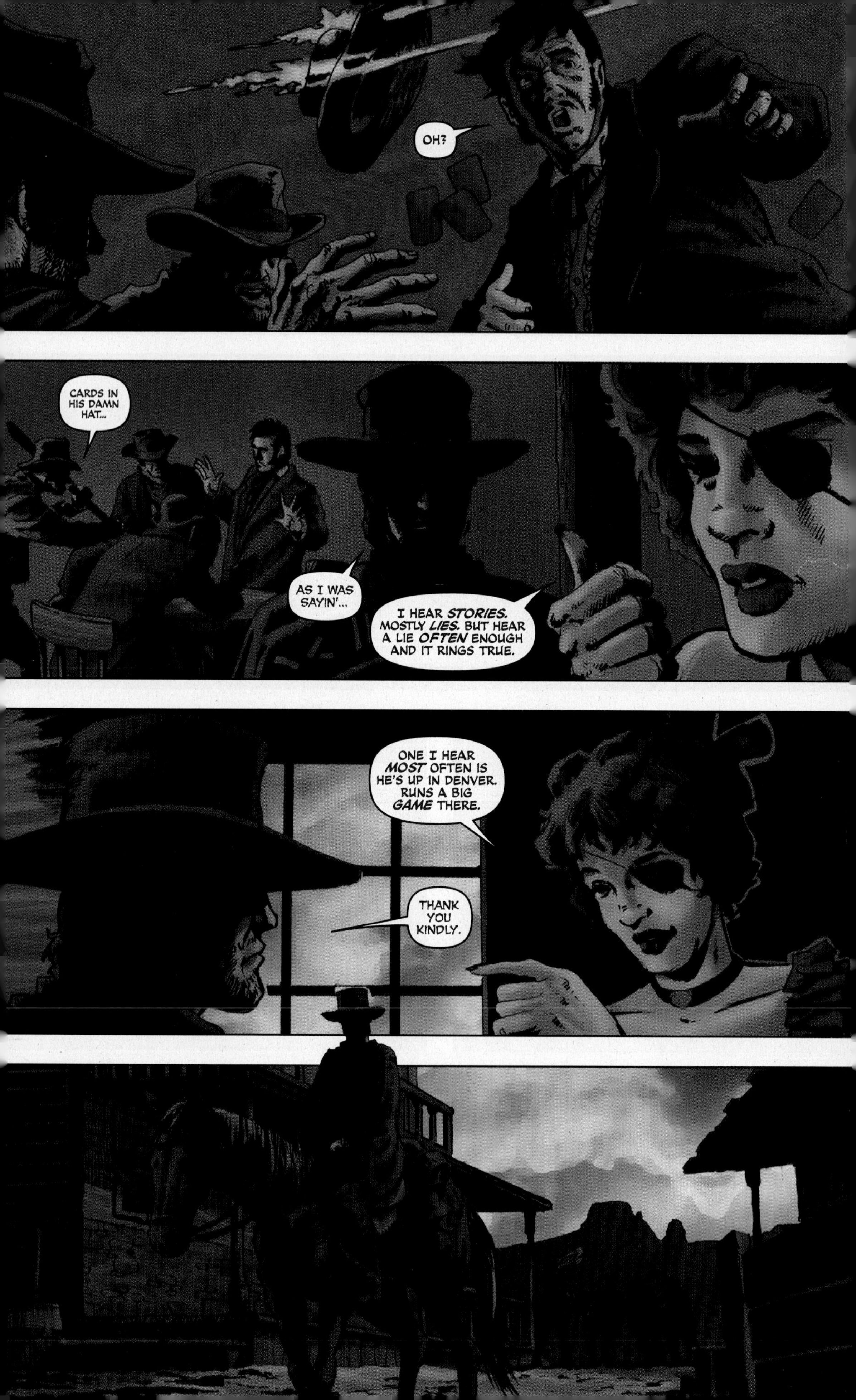
OH?
CARDS IN HIS DAMN HAT...
AS I WAS SAYIN'...
I HEAR STORIES. MOSTLY LIES. BUT HEAR A LIE OFTEN ENOUGH AND IT RINGS TRUE.
ONE I HEAR MOST OFTEN IS HE'S UP IN DENVER. RUNS A BIG GAME THERE.
THANK YOU KINDLY.

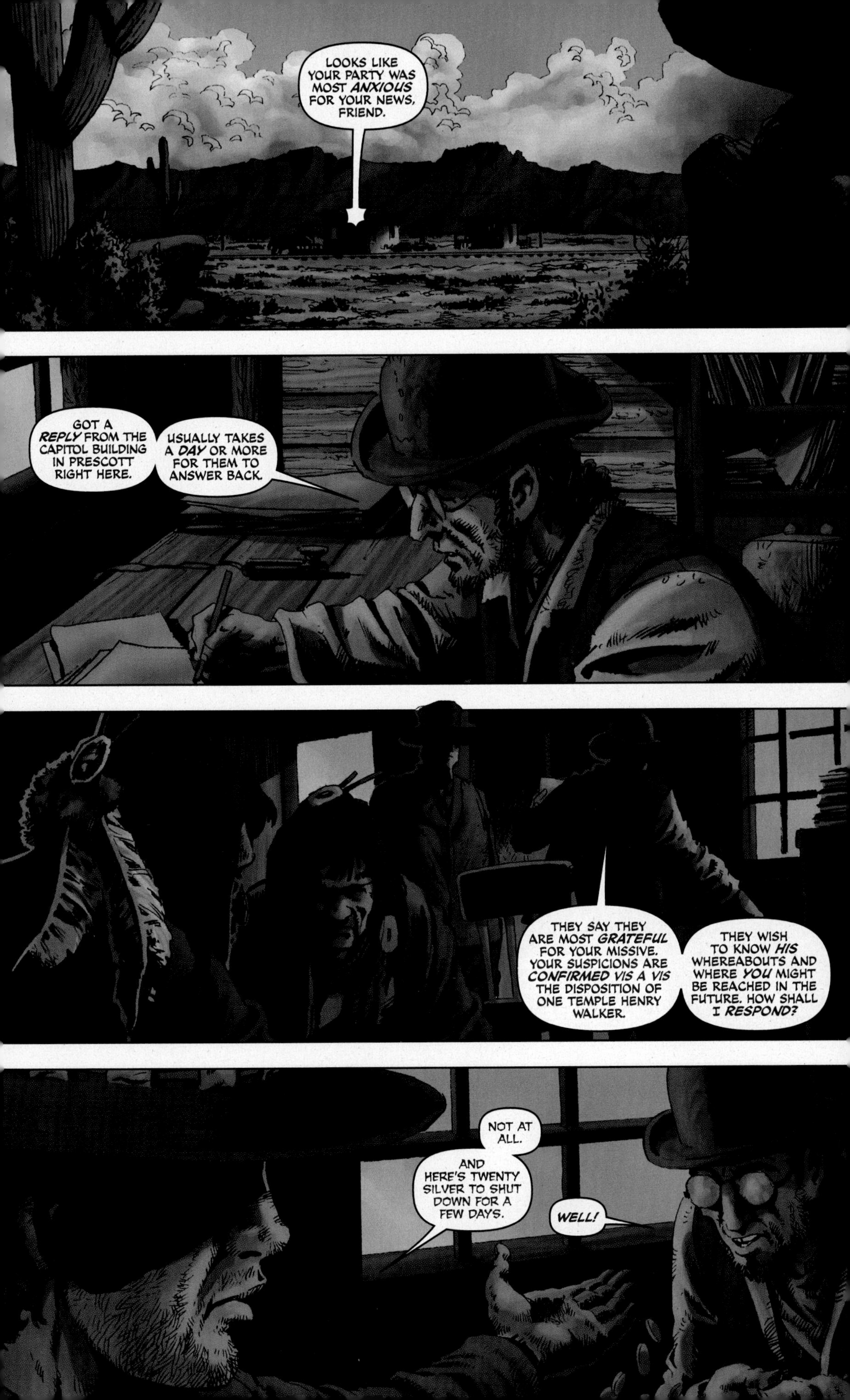
LOOKS LIKE YOUR PARTY WAS MOST *ANXIOUS* FOR YOUR NEWS, FRIEND.
GOT A *REPLY* FROM THE CAPITOL BUILDING IN PRESCOTT RIGHT HERE.
USUALLY TAKES A *DAY* OR MORE FOR THEM TO ANSWER BACK.
THEY SAY THEY ARE MOST *GRATEFUL* FOR YOUR MISSIVE. YOUR SUSPICIONS ARE *CONFIRMED VIS A VIS* THE DISPOSITION OF ONE TEMPLE HENRY WALKER.
THEY WISH TO KNOW *HIS* WHEREABOUTS AND WHERE *YOU* MIGHT BE REACHED IN THE FUTURE. HOW SHALL I *RESPOND?*
NOT AT ALL.
AND HERE'S TWENTY SILVER TO SHUT DOWN FOR A FEW DAYS.
WELL!

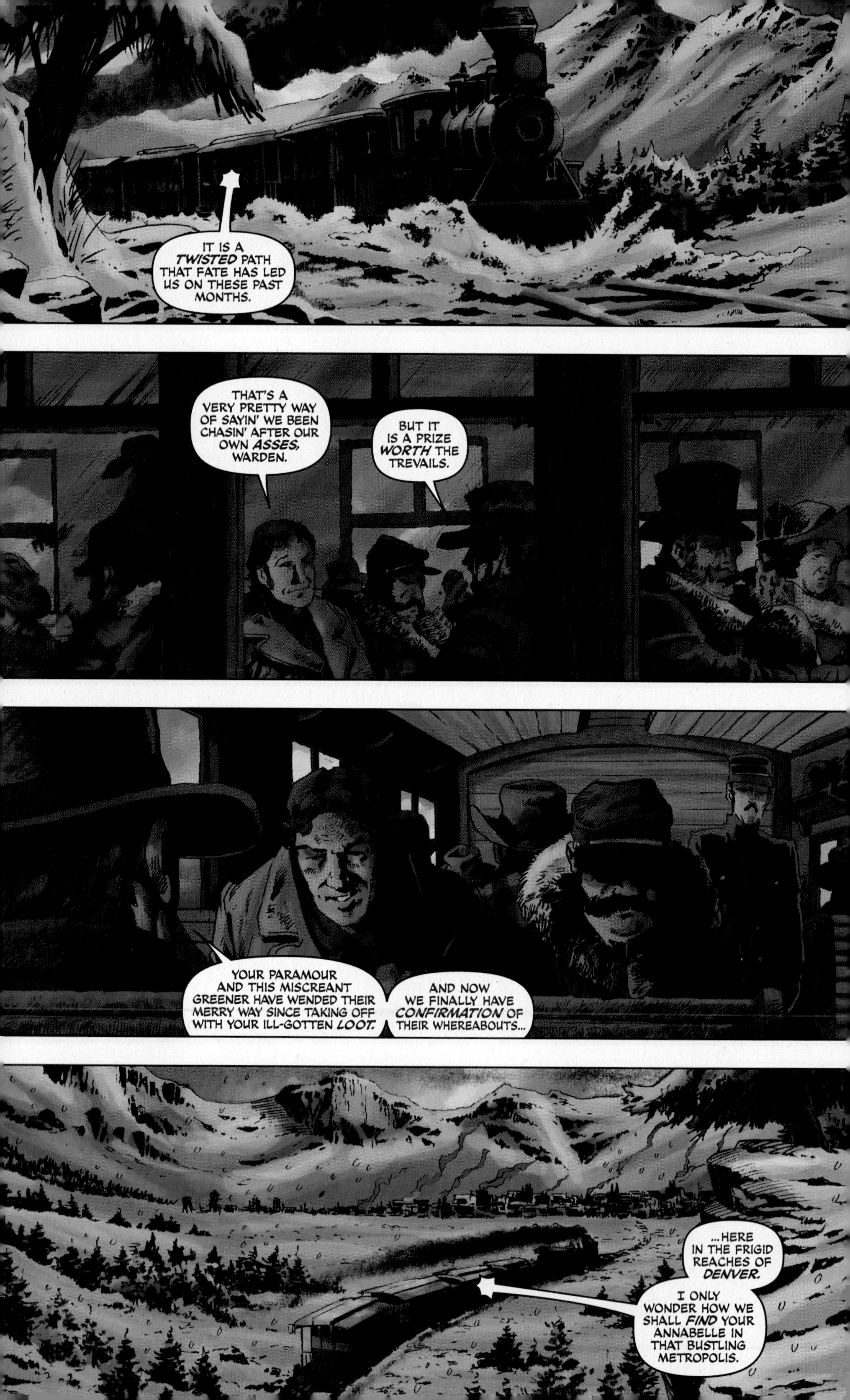

IT IS A *TWISTED* PATH THAT FATE HAS LED US ON THESE PAST MONTHS.
THAT'S A VERY PRETTY WAY OF SAYIN' WE BEEN CHASIN' AFTER OUR OWN *ASSES,* WARDEN.
BUT IT IS A PRIZE *WORTH* THE TREVAILS.
YOUR PARAMOUR AND THIS MISCREANT GREENER HAVE WENDED THEIR MERRY WAY SINCE TAKING OFF WITH YOUR ILL-GOTTEN *LOOT.*
AND NOW WE FINALLY HAVE *CONFIRMATION* OF THEIR WHEREABOUTS...
...HERE IN THE FRIGID REACHES OF *DENVER.*
I ONLY WONDER HOW WE SHALL *FIND* YOUR ANNABELLE IN THAT BUSTLING METROPOLIS.

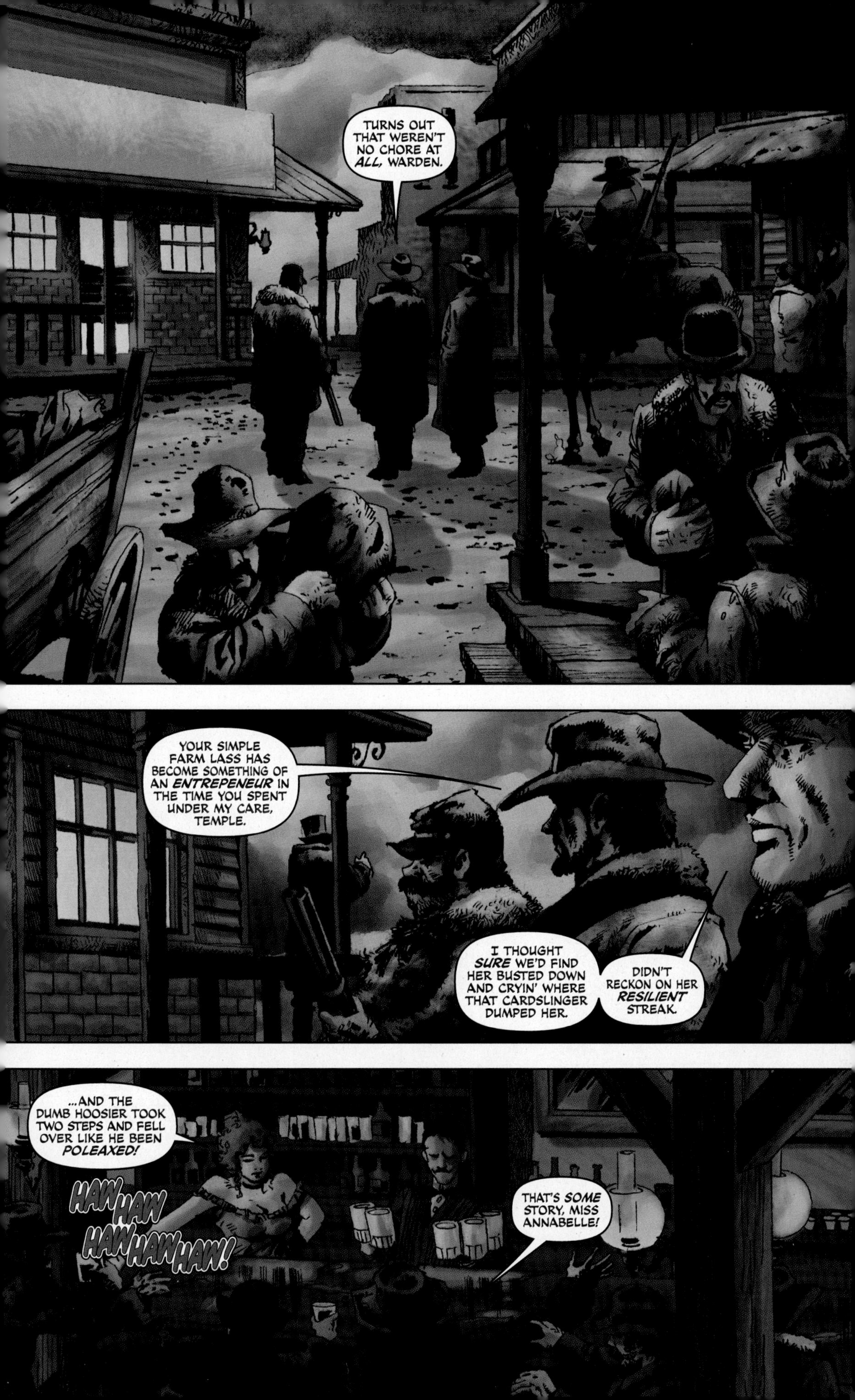
TURNS OUT THAT WEREN'T NO CHORE AT ALL, WARDEN.
YOUR SIMPLE FARM LASS HAS BECOME SOMETHING OF AN ENTREPENEUR IN THE TIME YOU SPENT UNDER MY CARE, TEMPLE.
I THOUGHT SURE WE'D FIND HER BUSTED DOWN AND CRYIN' WHERE THAT CARDSLINGER DUMPED HER.
DIDN'T RECKON ON HER RESILIENT STREAK.
...AND THE DUMB HOOSIER TOOK TWO STEPS AND FELL OVER LIKE HE BEEN POLEAXED!
HAW HAW HAW HAW HAW!
THAT'S SOME STORY, MISS ANNABELLE!

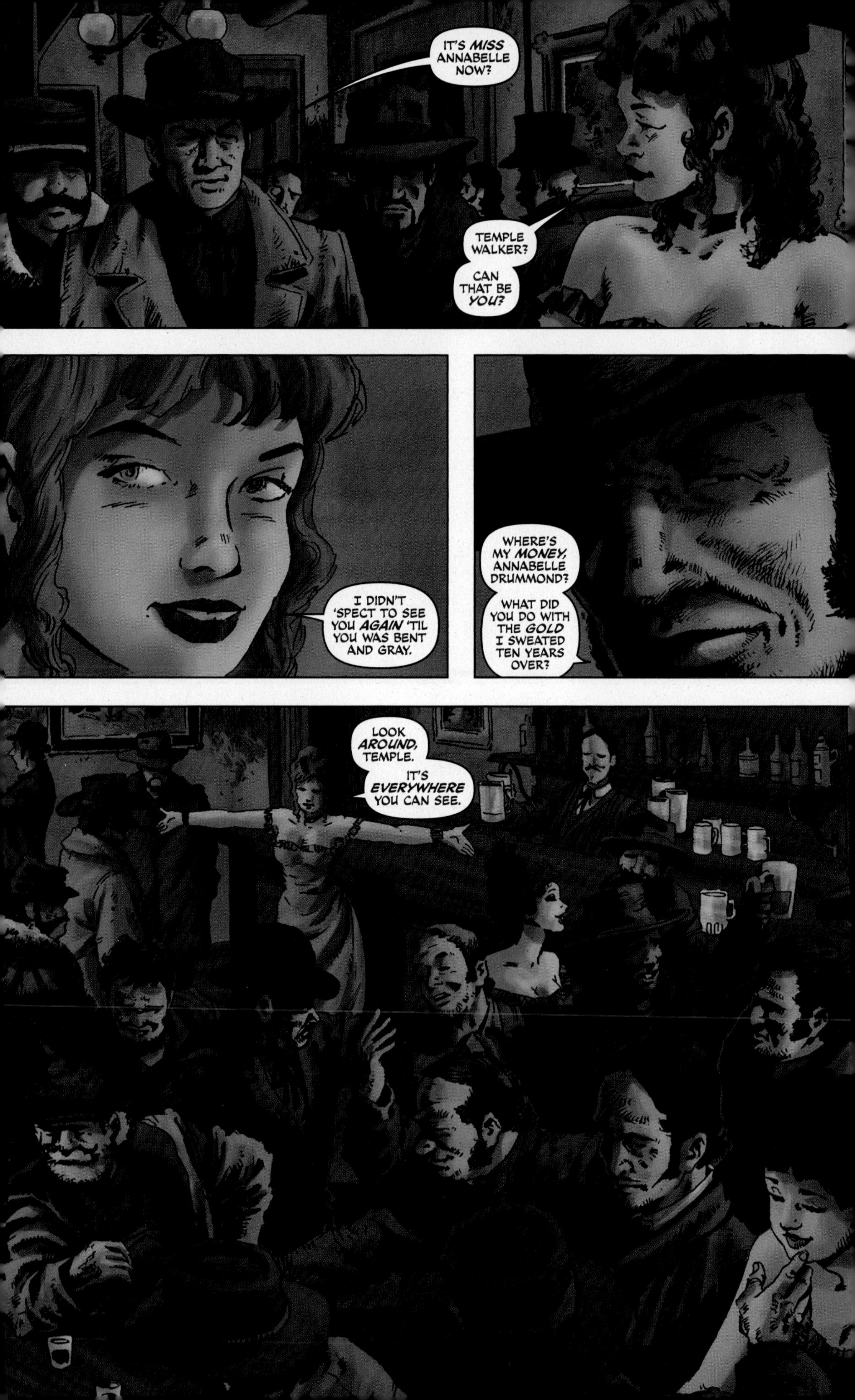

IT'S MISS ANNABELLE NOW?
TEMPLE WALKER?
CAN THAT BE YOU?
I DIDN'T 'SPECT TO SEE YOU AGAIN 'TIL YOU WAS BENT AND GRAY.
WHERE'S MY MONEY, ANNABELLE DRUMMOND?
WHAT DID YOU DO WITH THE GOLD I SWEATED TEN YEARS OVER?
LOOK AROUND, TEMPLE.
IT'S EVERYWHERE YOU CAN SEE.

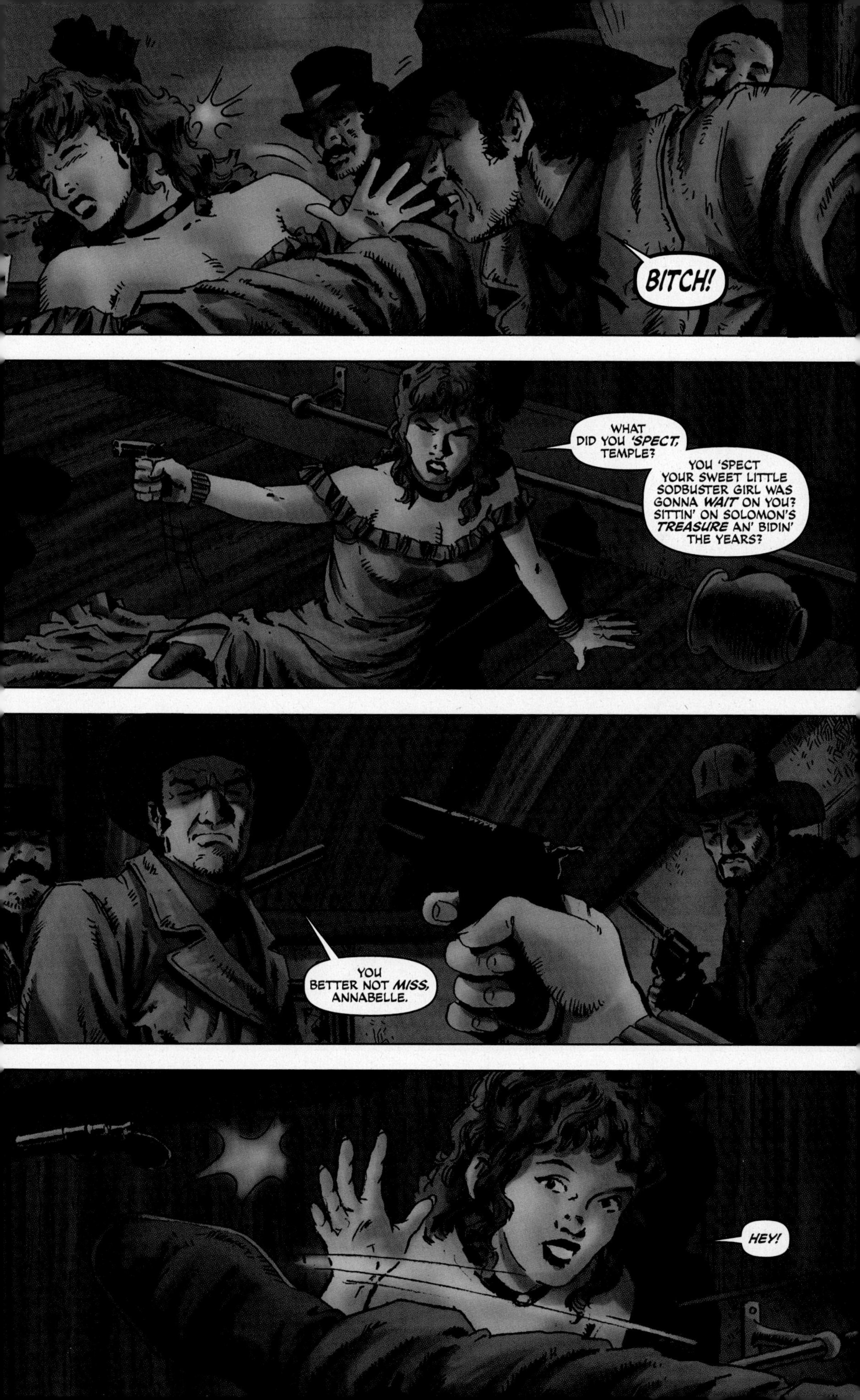
BITCH!
WHAT DID YOU 'SPECT, TEMPLE?
YOU 'SPECT YOUR SWEET LITTLE SODBUSTER GIRL WAS GONNA WAIT ON YOU? SITTIN' ON SOLOMON'S TREASURE AN' BIDIN' THE YEARS?
YOU BETTER NOT MISS, ANNABELLE.
HEY!

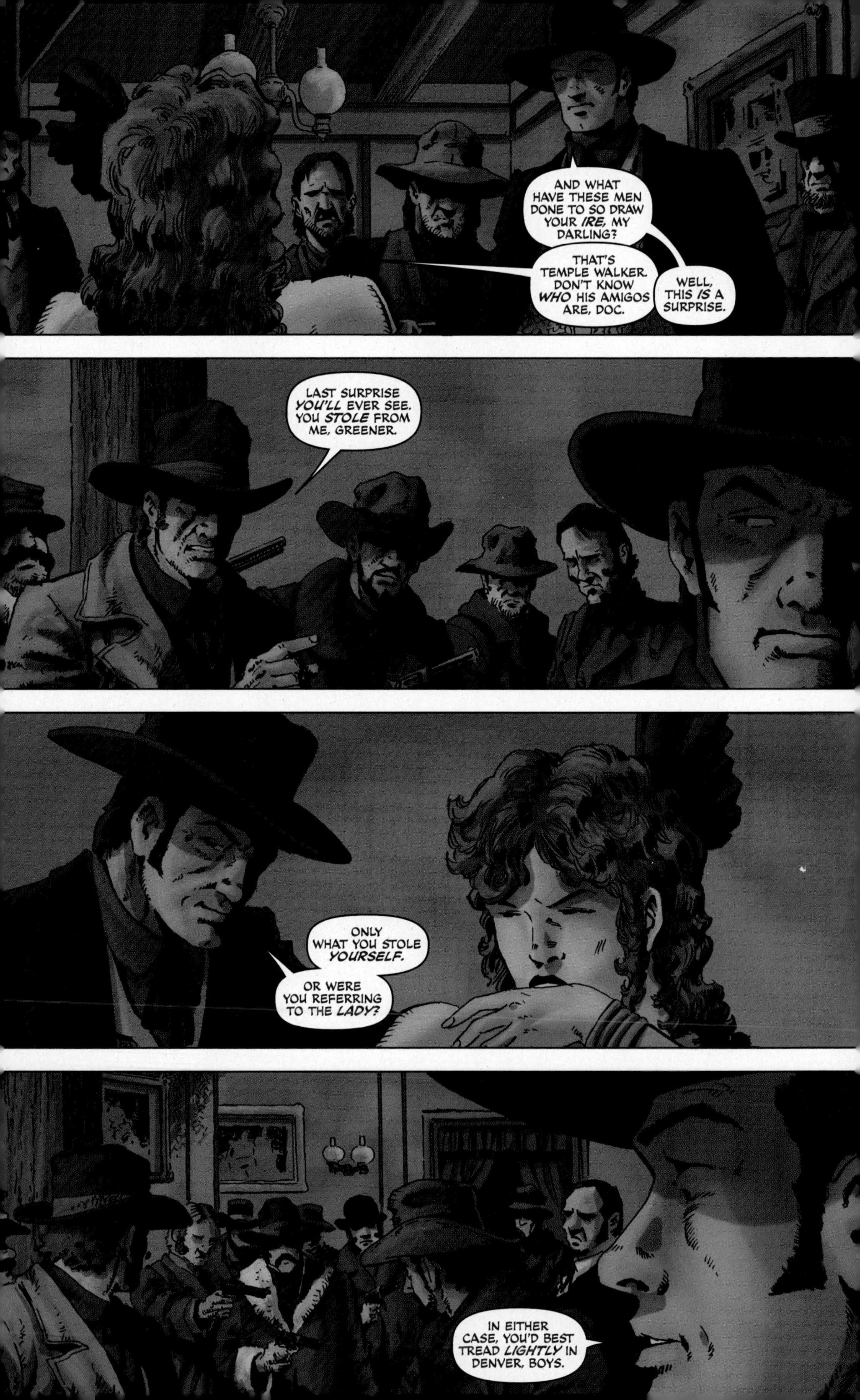
AND WHAT HAVE THESE MEN DONE TO SO DRAW YOUR *IRE,* MY DARLING?
THAT'S TEMPLE WALKER. DON'T KNOW *WHO* HIS AMIGOS ARE, DOC.
WELL, THIS *IS* A SURPRISE.
LAST SURPRISE *YOU'LL* EVER SEE. YOU *STOLE* FROM ME, GREENER.
ONLY WHAT YOU STOLE *YOURSELF.*
OR WERE YOU REFERRING TO THE *LADY?*
IN EITHER CASE, YOU'D BEST TREAD *LIGHTLY* IN DENVER, BOYS.

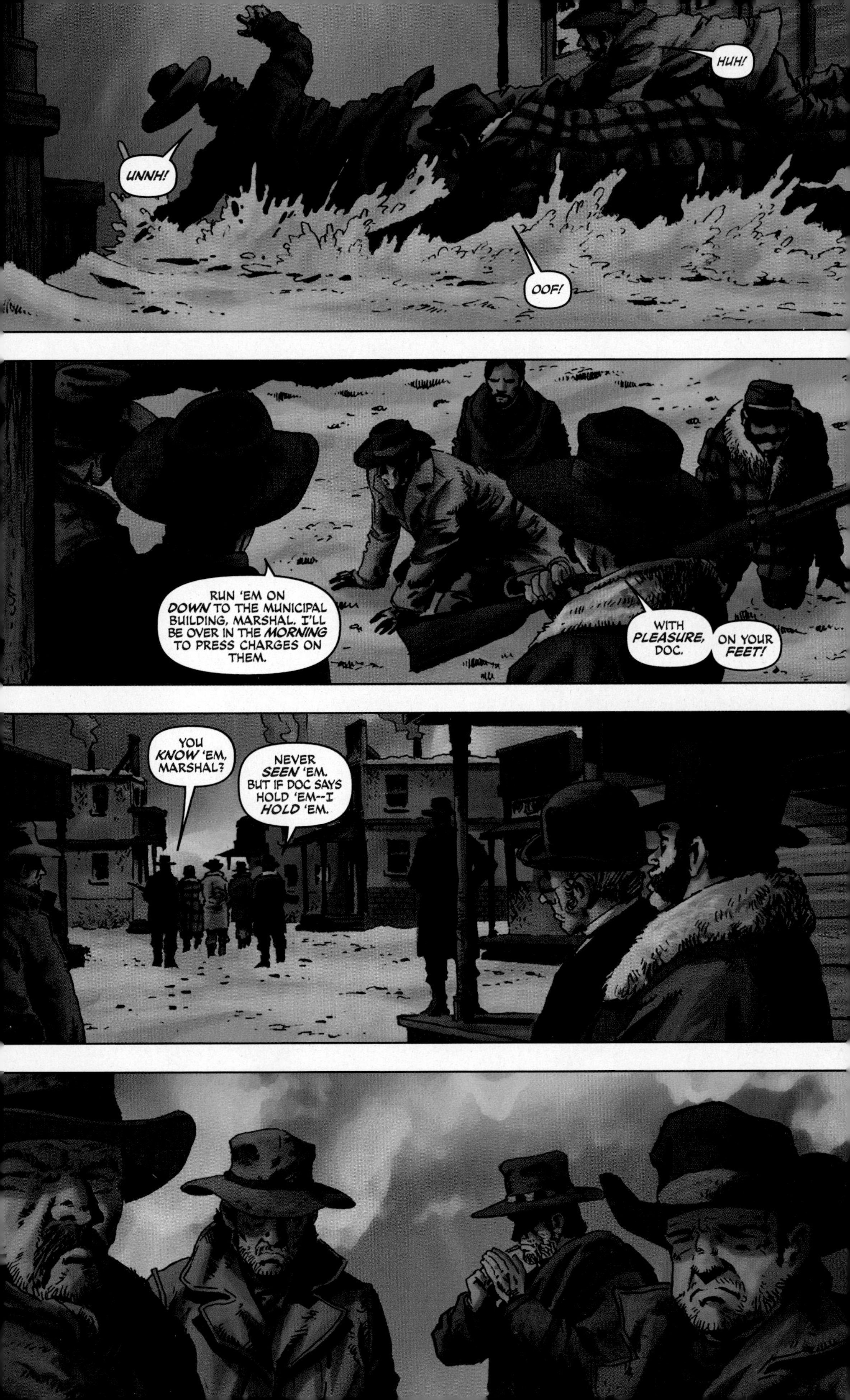
HUH!
UNNH!
OOF!
RUN 'EM ON DOWN TO THE MUNICIPAL BUILDING, MARSHAL. I'LL BE OVER IN THE MORNING TO PRESS CHARGES ON THEM.
WITH PLEASURE, DOC.
ON YOUR FEET!
YOU KNOW 'EM, MARSHAL?
NEVER SEEN 'EM. BUT IF DOC SAYS HOLD 'EM--I HOLD 'EM.

Cover by **Dennis Calero**

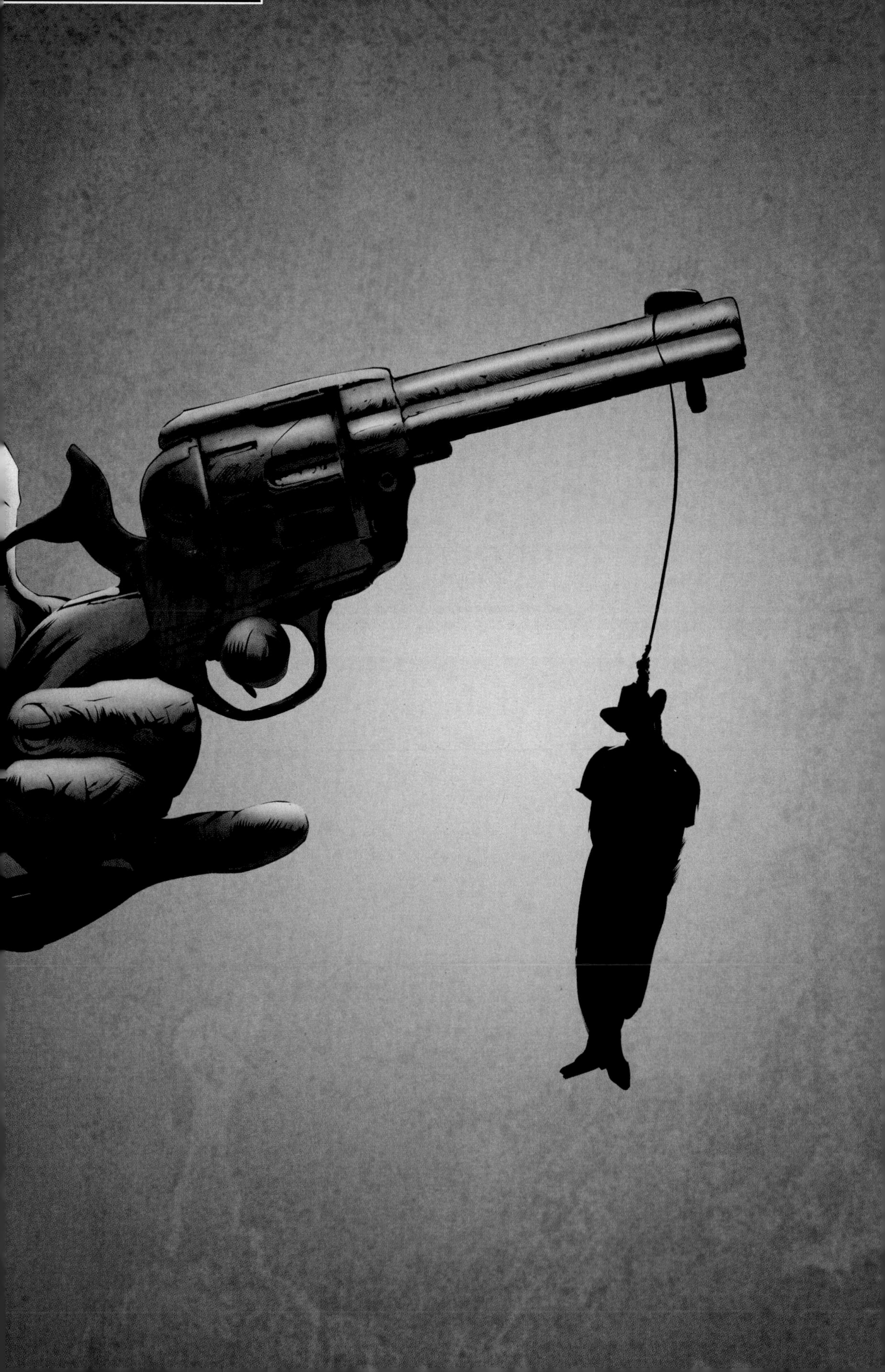

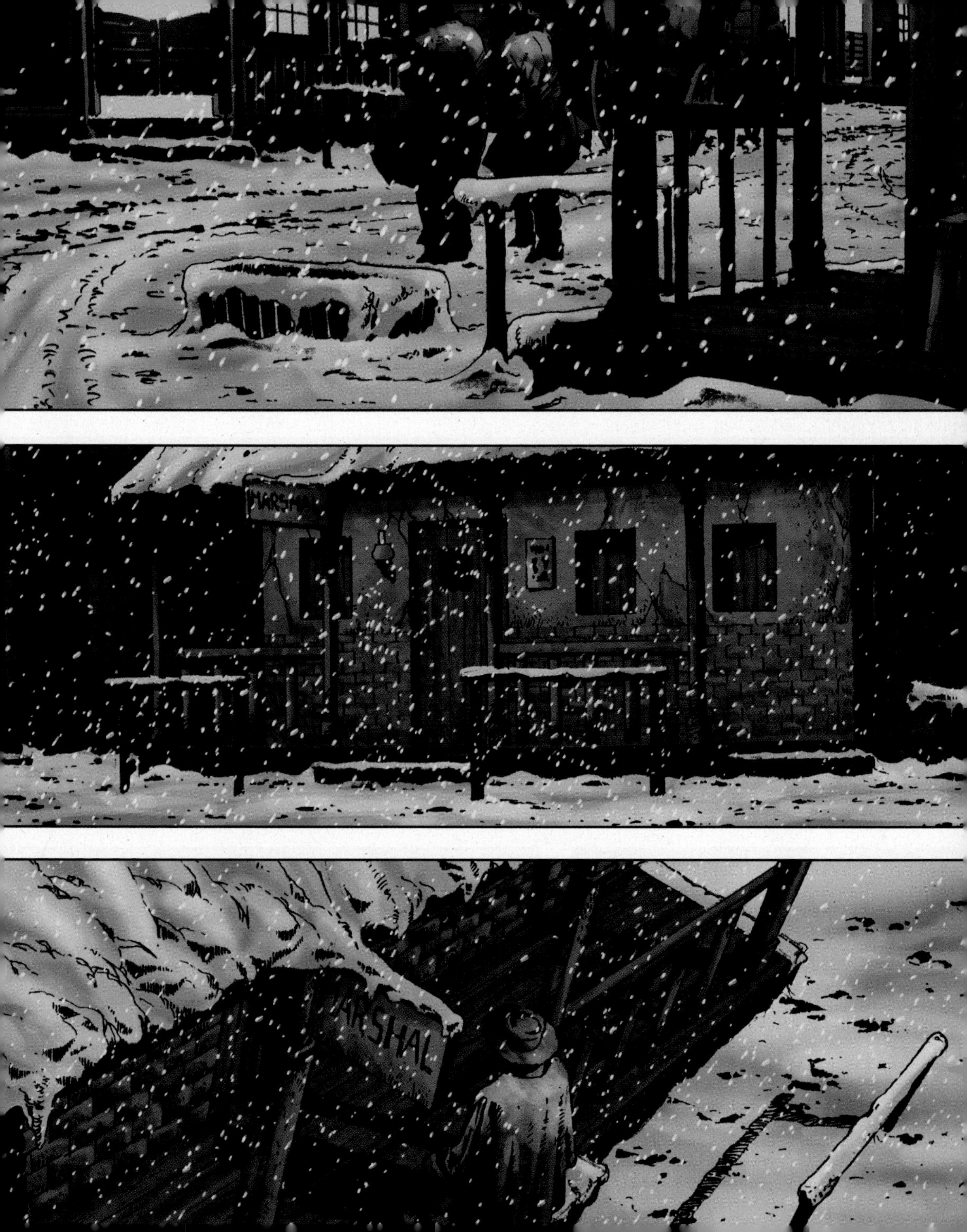
ARSHAL

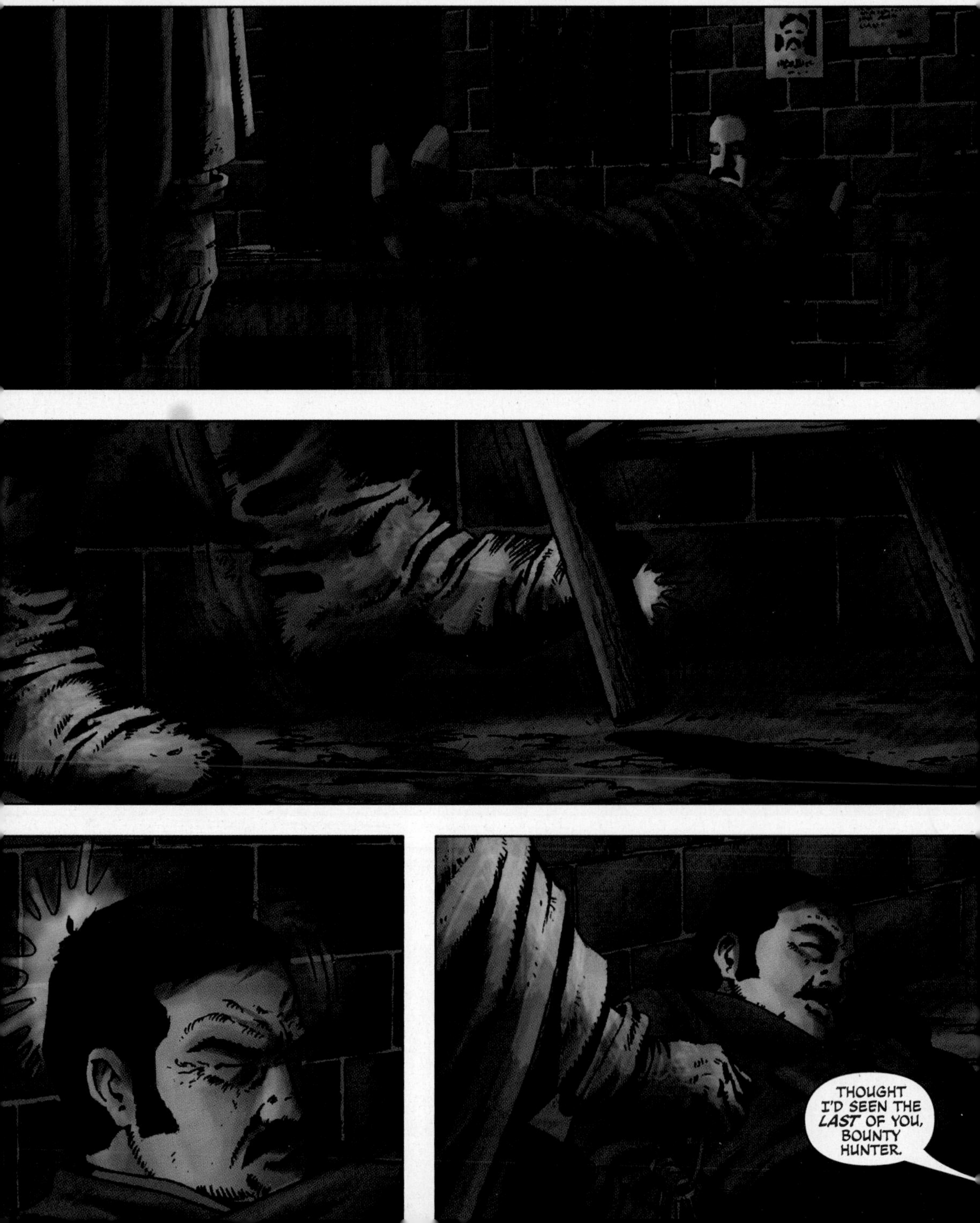
THOUGHT I'D SEEN THE LAST OF YOU, BOUNTY HUNTER.

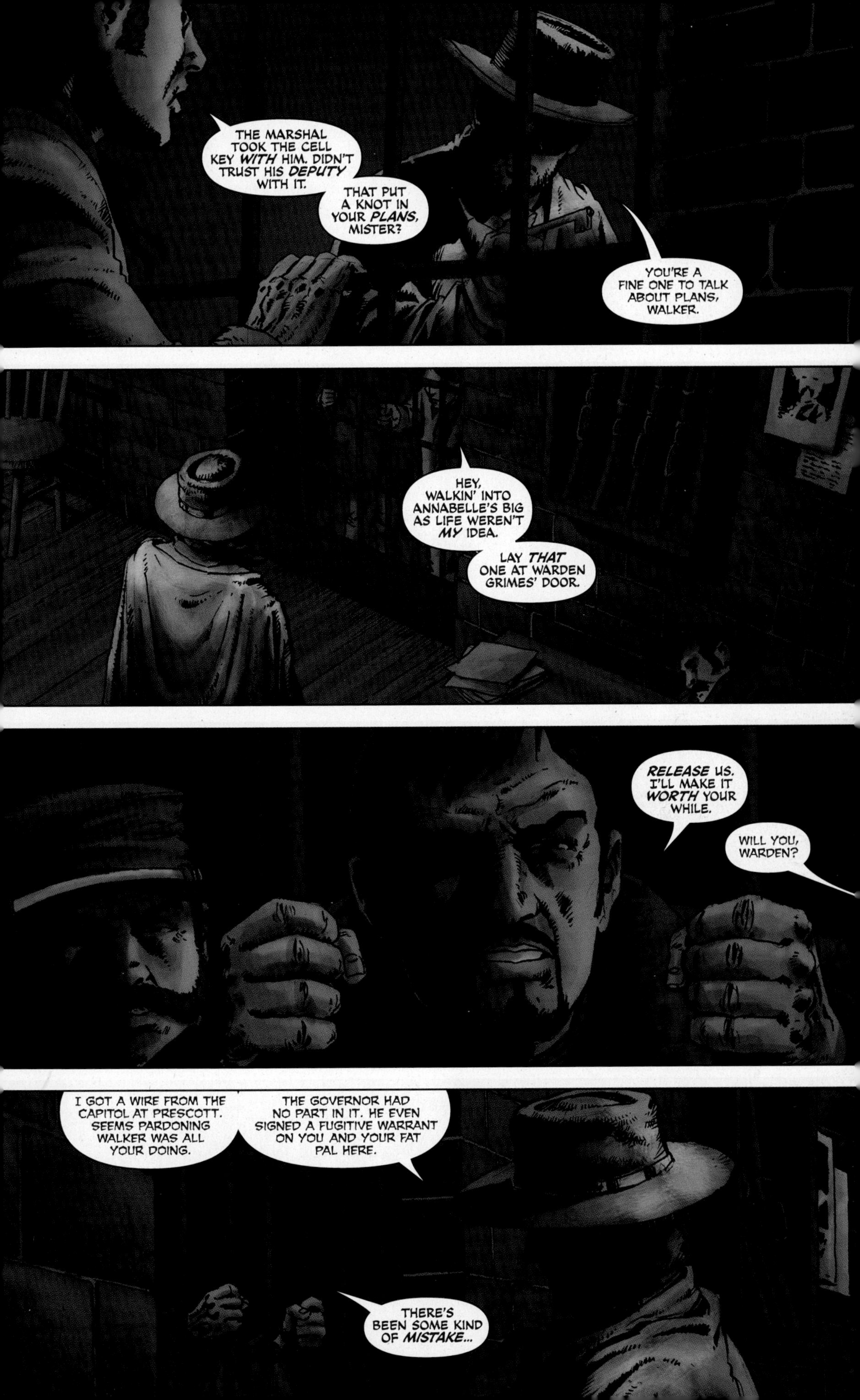
THE MARSHAL TOOK THE CELL KEY WITH HIM. DIDN'T TRUST HIS DEPUTY WITH IT.
THAT PUT A KNOT IN YOUR PLANS, MISTER?
YOU'RE A FINE ONE TO TALK ABOUT PLANS, WALKER.
HEY, WALKIN' INTO ANNABELLE'S BIG AS LIFE WEREN'T MY IDEA.
LAY THAT ONE AT WARDEN GRIMES' DOOR.
RELEASE US. I'LL MAKE IT WORTH YOUR WHILE.
WILL YOU, WARDEN?
I GOT A WIRE FROM THE CAPITOL AT PRESCOTT. SEEMS PARDONING WALKER WAS ALL YOUR DOING.
THE GOVERNOR HAD NO PART IN IT. HE EVEN SIGNED A FUGITIVE WARRANT ON YOU AND YOUR FAT PAL HERE.
THERE'S BEEN SOME KIND OF MISTAKE...

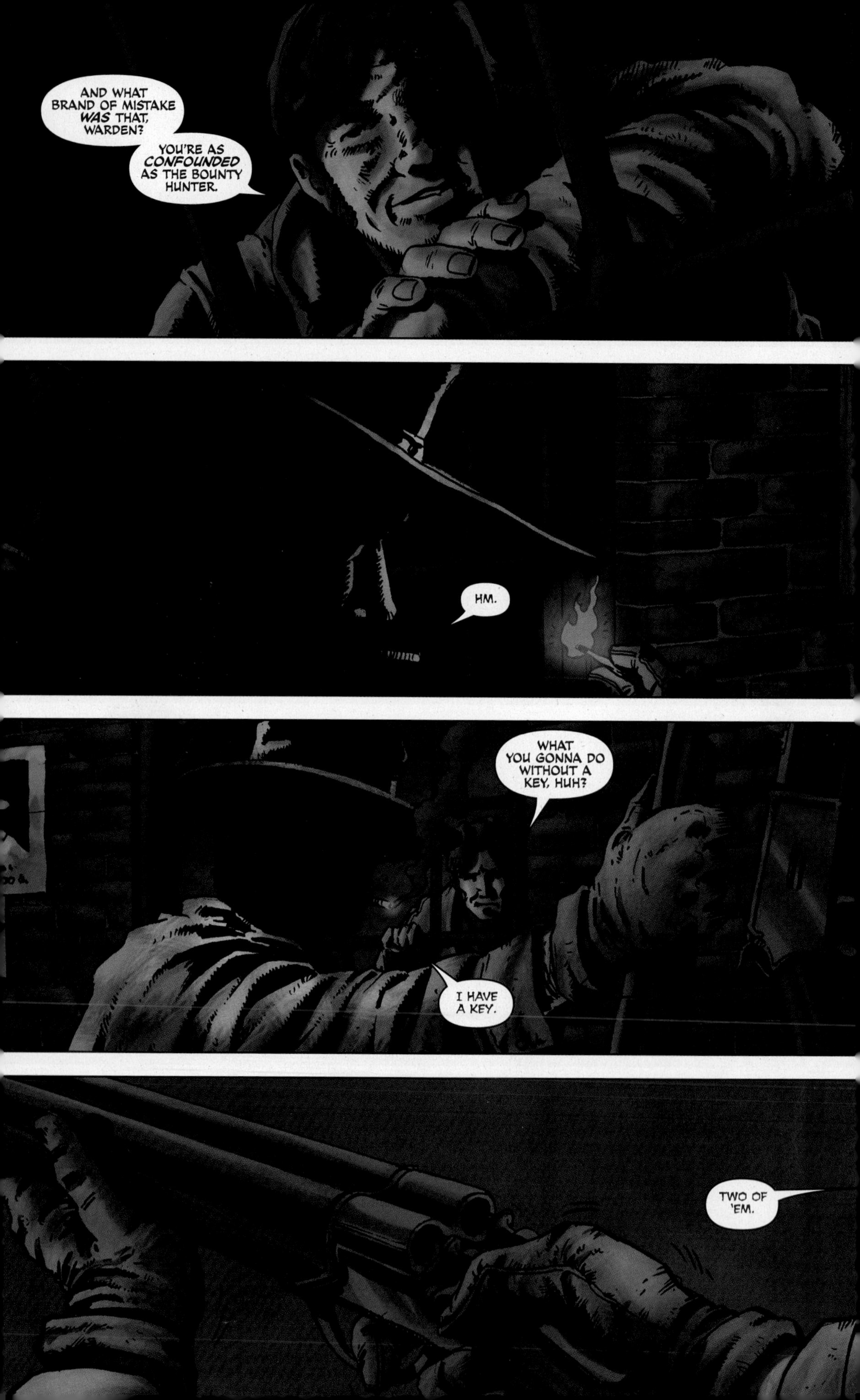
AND WHAT BRAND OF MISTAKE *WAS* THAT, WARDEN?
YOU'RE AS *CONFOUNDED* AS THE BOUNTY HUNTER.
HM.
WHAT YOU GONNA DO WITHOUT A KEY, HUH?
I HAVE A KEY.
TWO OF 'EM.

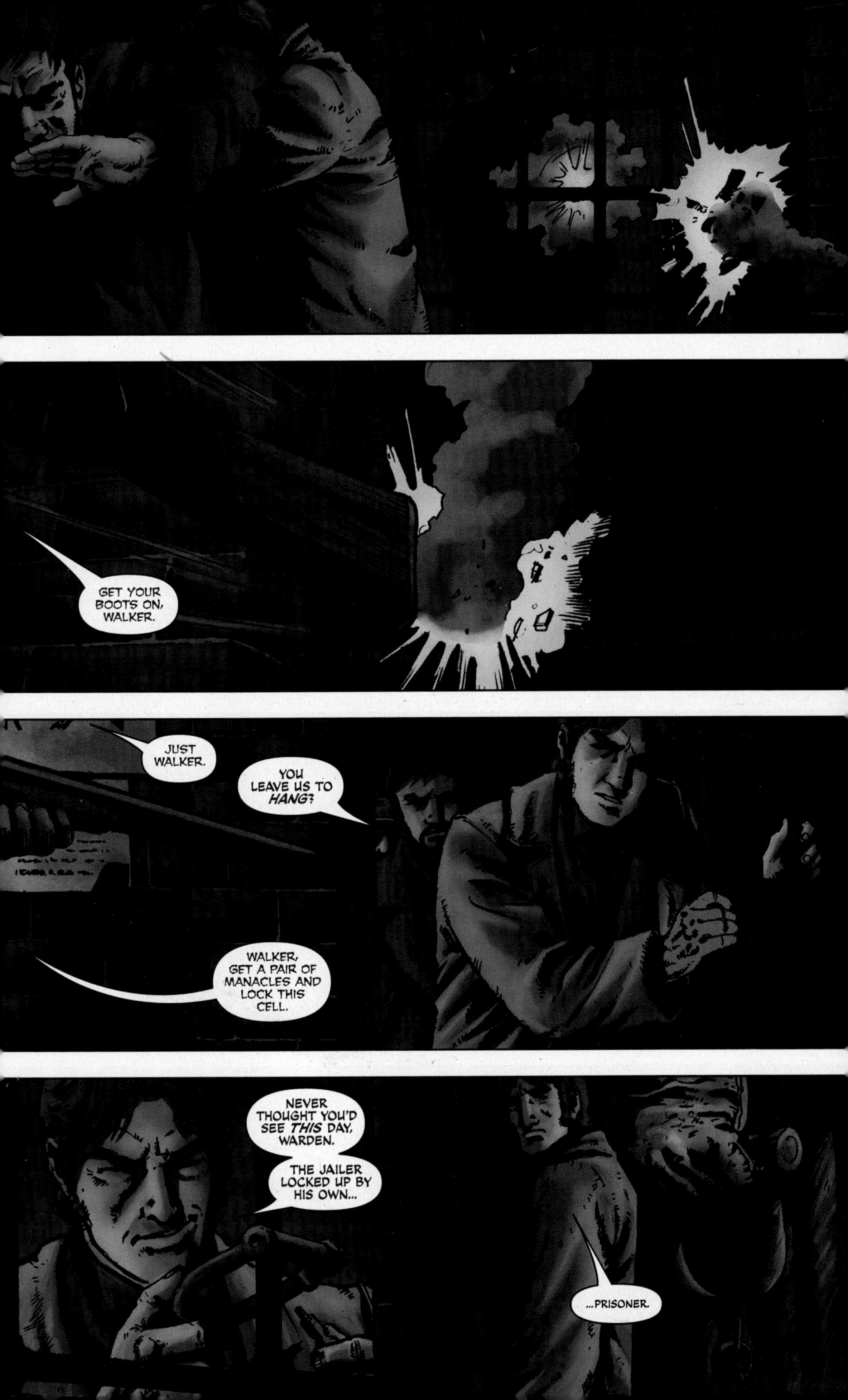
GET YOUR BOOTS ON, WALKER.
JUST WALKER.
YOU LEAVE US TO *HANG*?
WALKER, GET A PAIR OF MANACLES AND LOCK THIS CELL.
NEVER THOUGHT YOU'D SEE *THIS* DAY, WARDEN.
THE JAILER LOCKED UP BY HIS OWN...
...PRISONER.

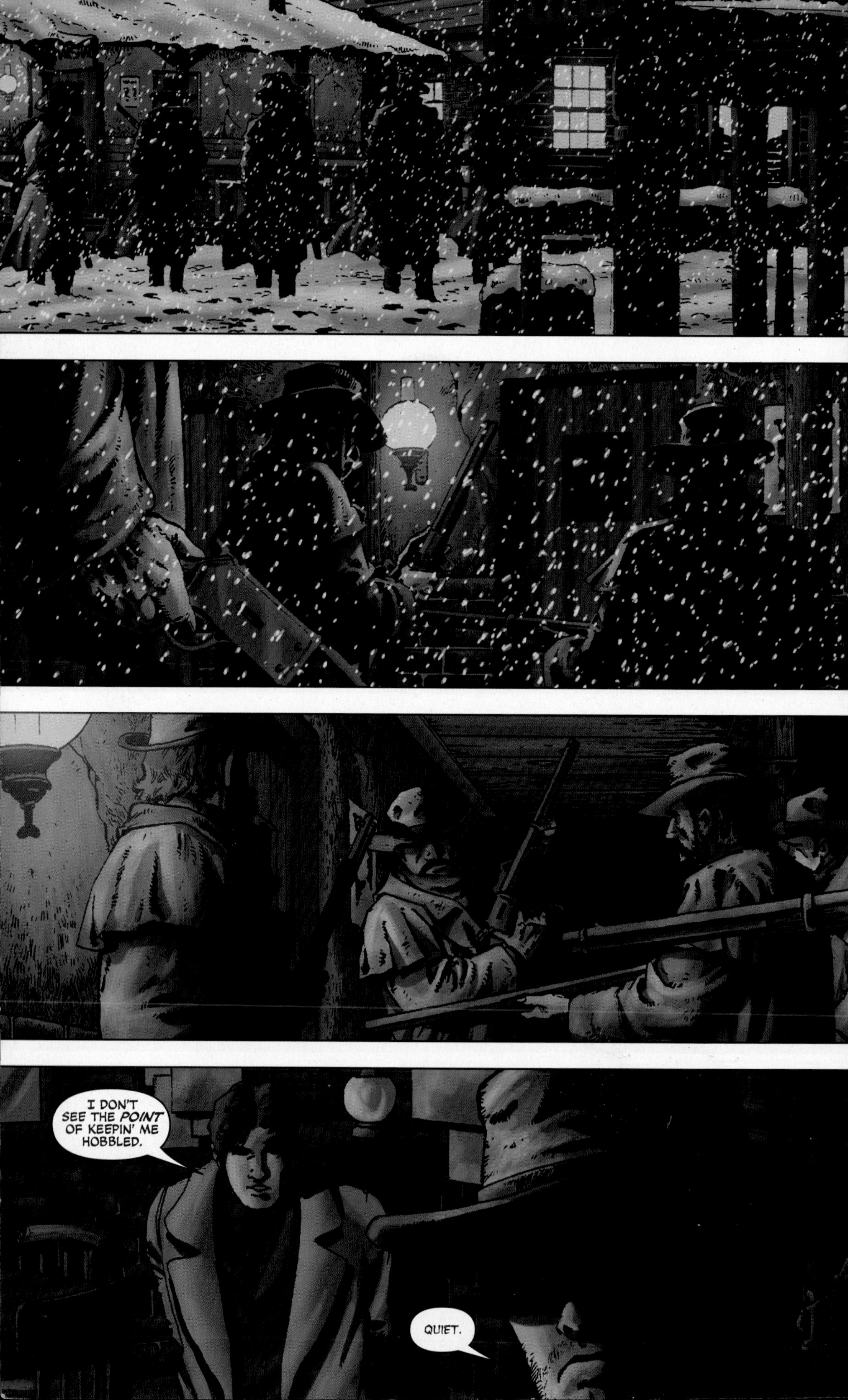
I DON'T SEE THE *POINT* OF KEEPIN' ME HOBBLED.
QUIET.

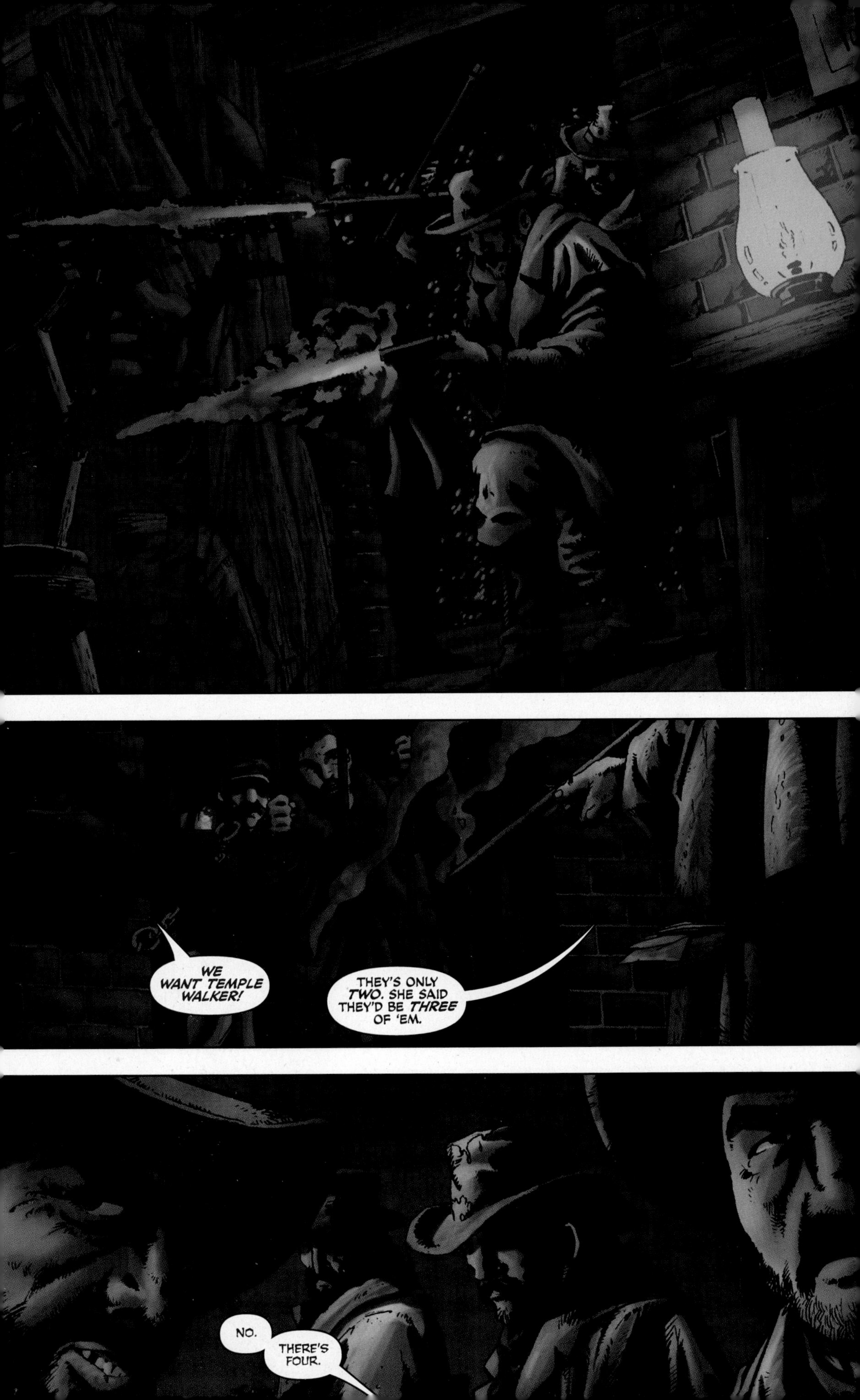
WE WANT TEMPLE WALKER!
THEY'S ONLY TWO. SHE SAID THEY'D BE THREE OF 'EM.
NO.
THERE'S FOUR.

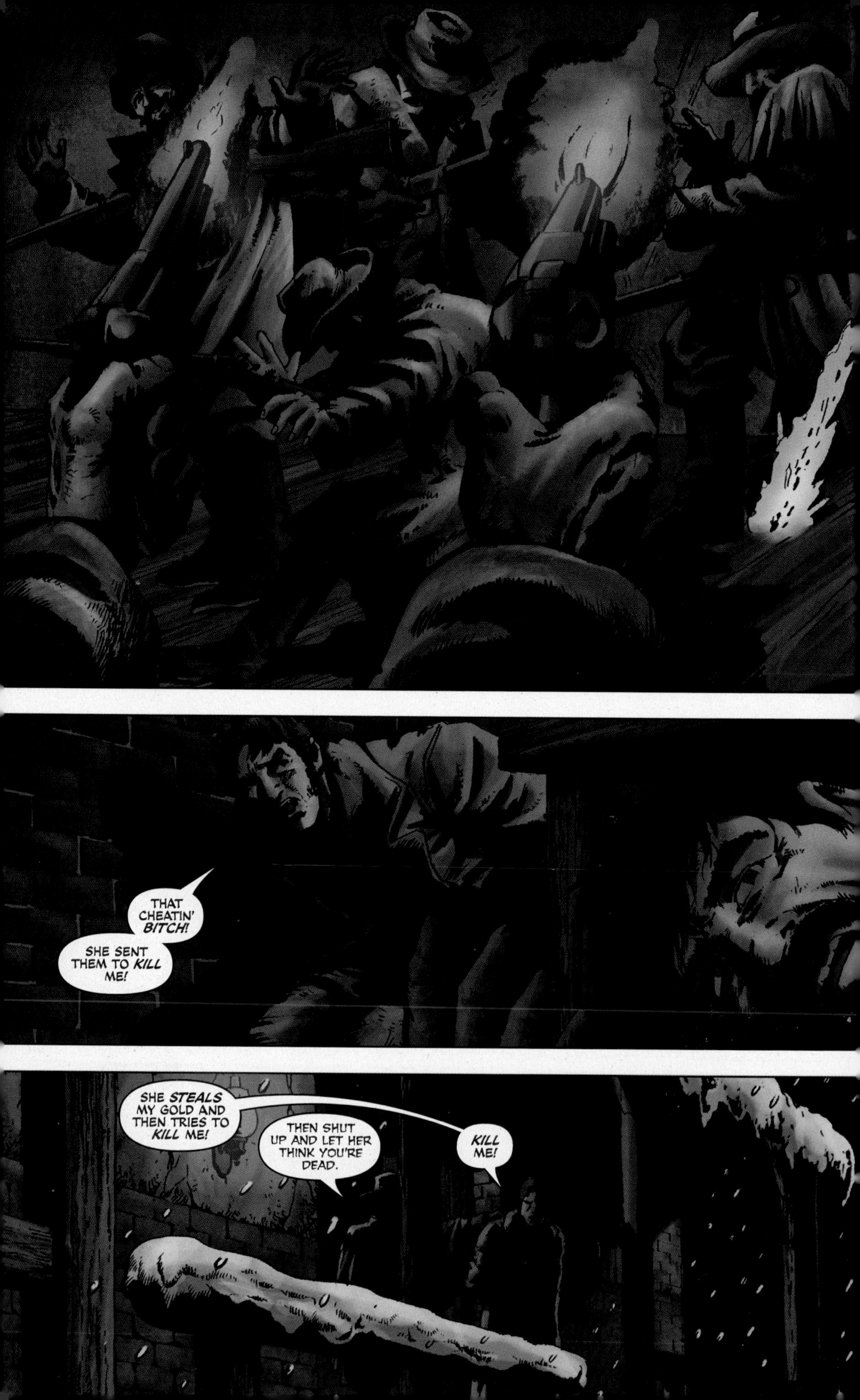
THAT CHEATIN' BITCH!
SHE SENT THEM TO KILL ME!
SHE STEALS MY GOLD AND THEN TRIES TO KILL ME!
THEN SHUT UP AND LET HER THINK YOU'RE DEAD.
KILL ME!

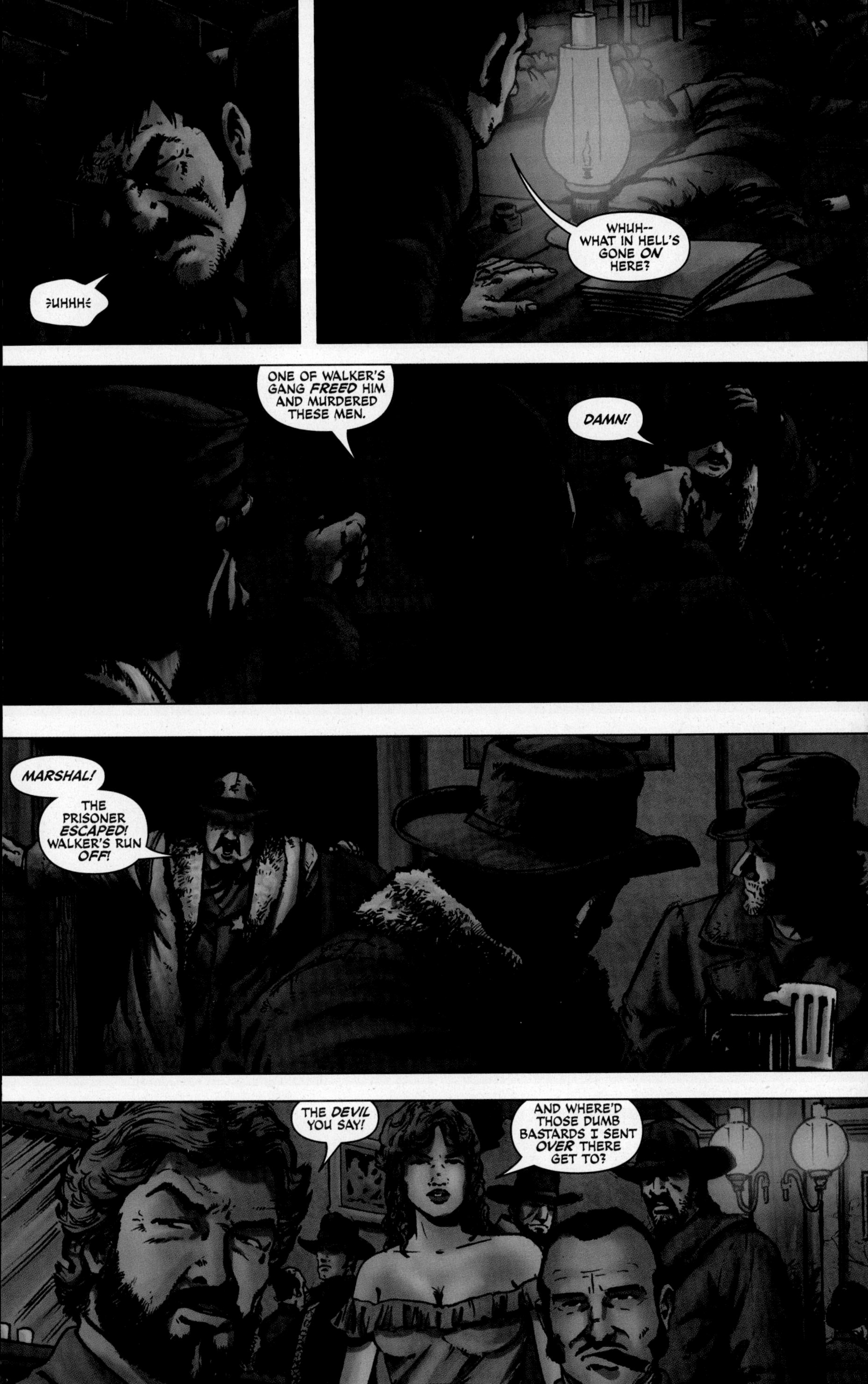

UHHHH
WHUH-- WHAT IN HELL'S GONE ON HERE?
ONE OF WALKER'S GANG FREED HIM AND MURDERED THESE MEN.
DAMN!
MARSHAL!
THE PRISONER ESCAPED! WALKER'S RUN OFF!
THE DEVIL YOU SAY!
AND WHERE'D THOSE DUMB BASTARDS I SENT OVER THERE GET TO?

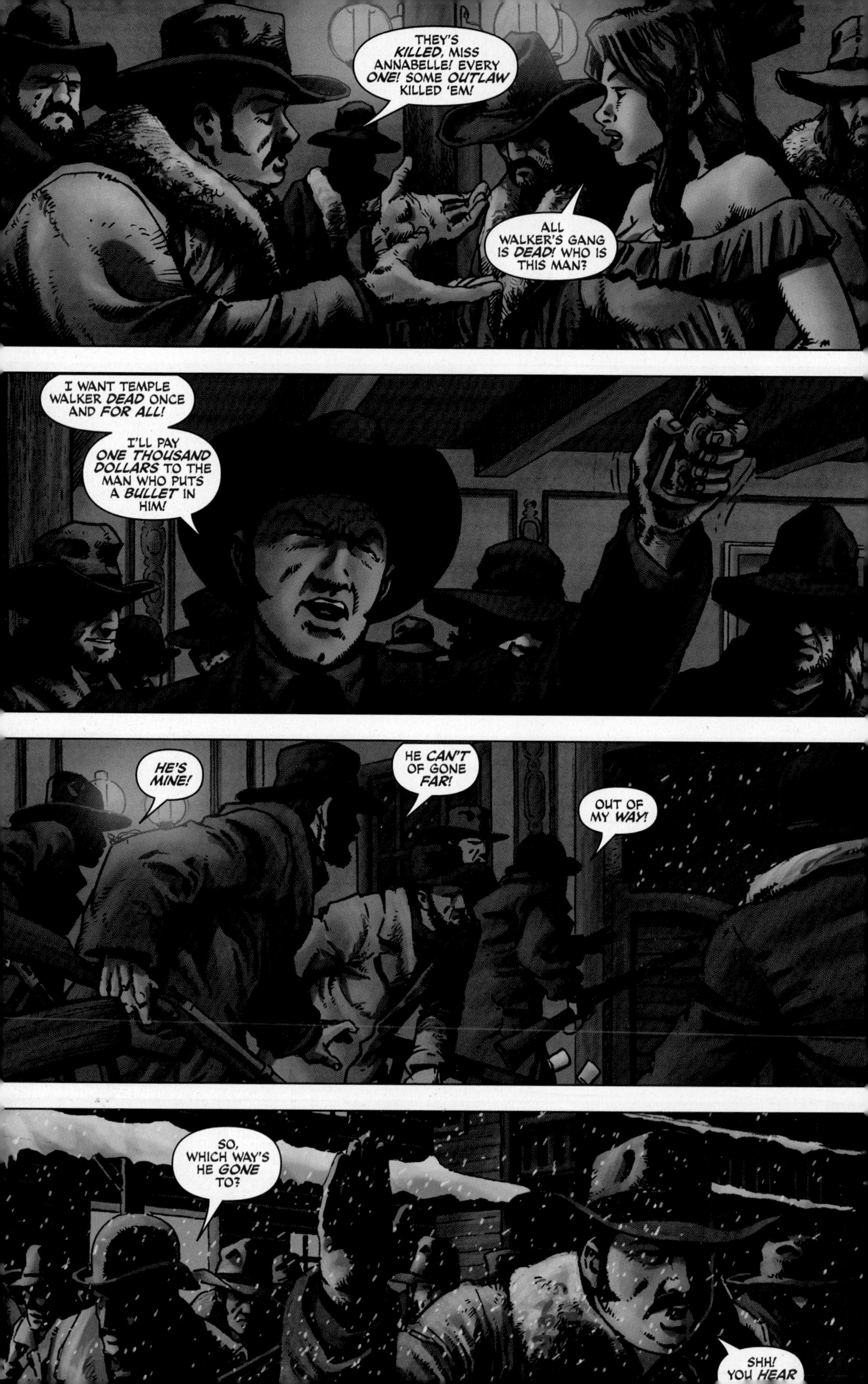
THEY'S KILLED, MISS ANNABELLE! EVERY ONE! SOME OUTLAW KILLED 'EM!
ALL WALKER'S GANG IS DEAD! WHO IS THIS MAN?
I WANT TEMPLE WALKER DEAD ONCE AND FOR ALL!
I'LL PAY ONE THOUSAND DOLLARS TO THE MAN WHO PUTS A BULLET IN HIM!
HE'S MINE!
HE CAN'T OF GONE FAR!
OUT OF MY WAY!
SO, WHICH WAY'S HE GONE TO?
SHH! YOU HEAR

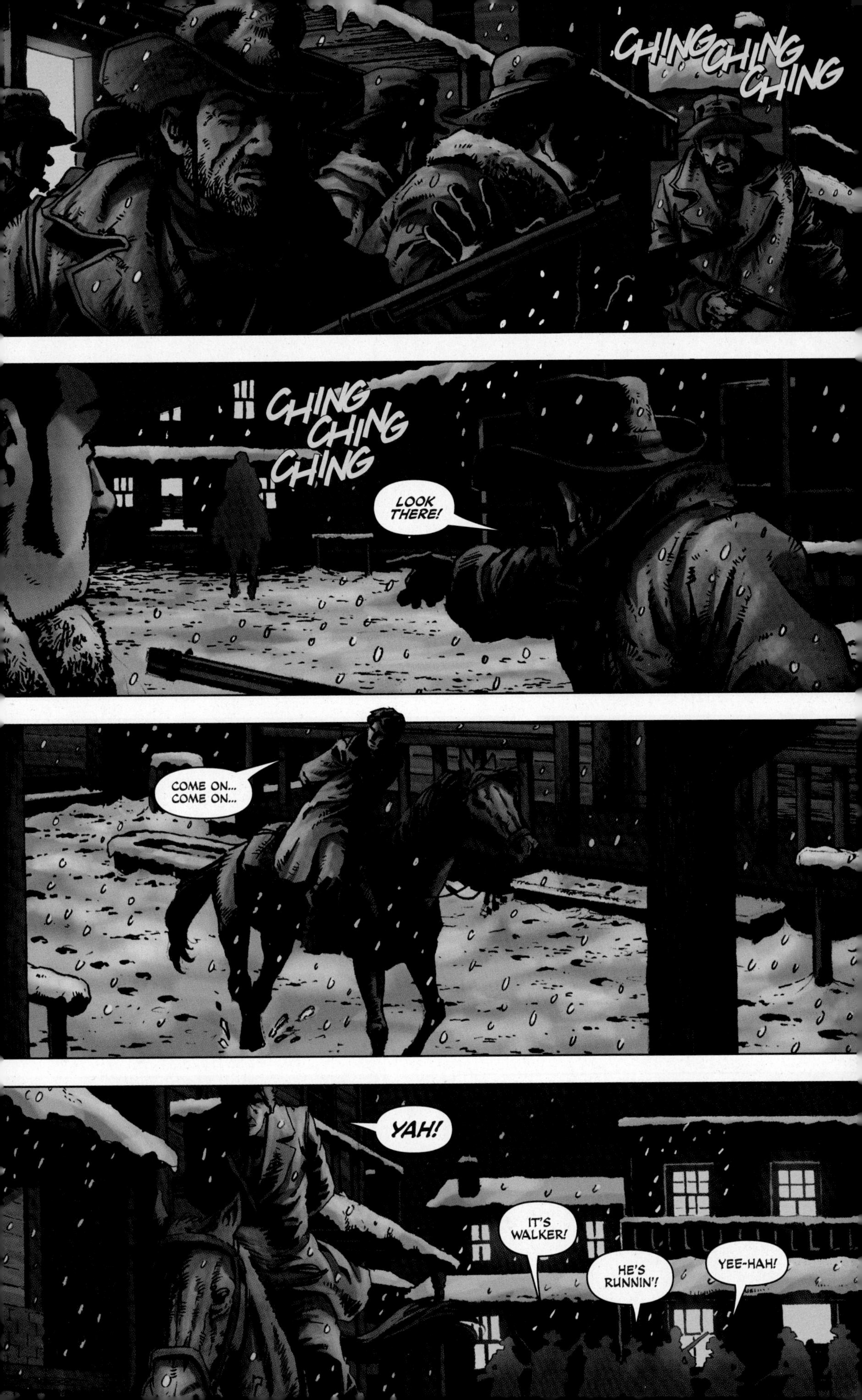
CHING CHING CHING
CHING CHING CHING
LOOK THERE!
COME ON... COME ON...
YAH!
IT'S WALKER!
HE'S RUNNIN'!
YEE-HAH!

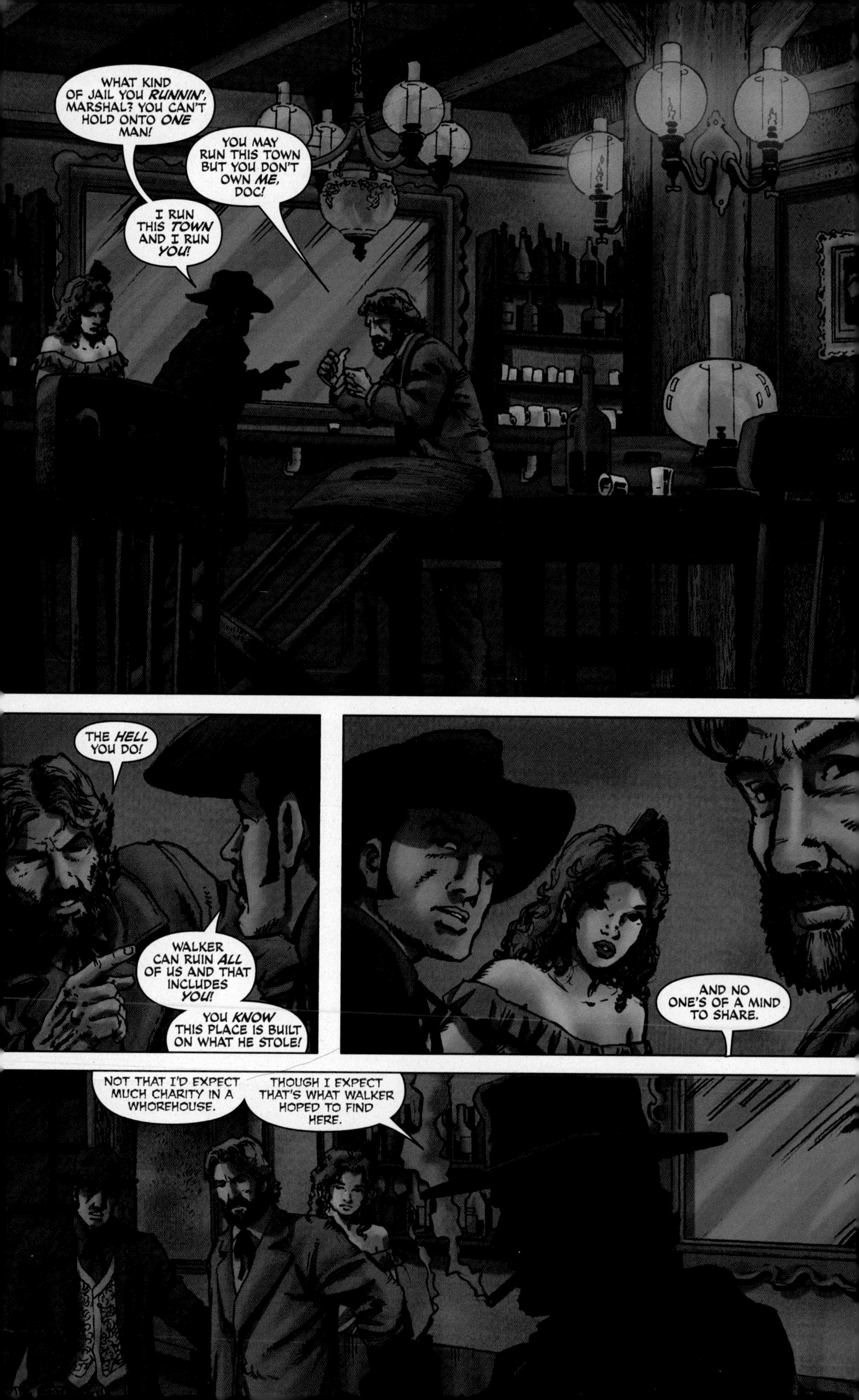
WHAT KIND OF JAIL YOU RUNNIN', MARSHAL? YOU CAN'T HOLD ONTO ONE MAN!
I RUN THIS TOWN AND I RUN YOU!
YOU MAY RUN THIS TOWN BUT YOU DON'T OWN ME, DOC!
THE HELL YOU DO!
WALKER CAN RUIN ALL OF US AND THAT INCLUDES YOU!
YOU KNOW THIS PLACE IS BUILT ON WHAT HE STOLE!
AND NO ONE'S OF A MIND TO SHARE.
NOT THAT I'D EXPECT MUCH CHARITY IN A WHOREHOUSE.
THOUGH I EXPECT THAT'S WHAT WALKER HOPED TO FIND HERE.

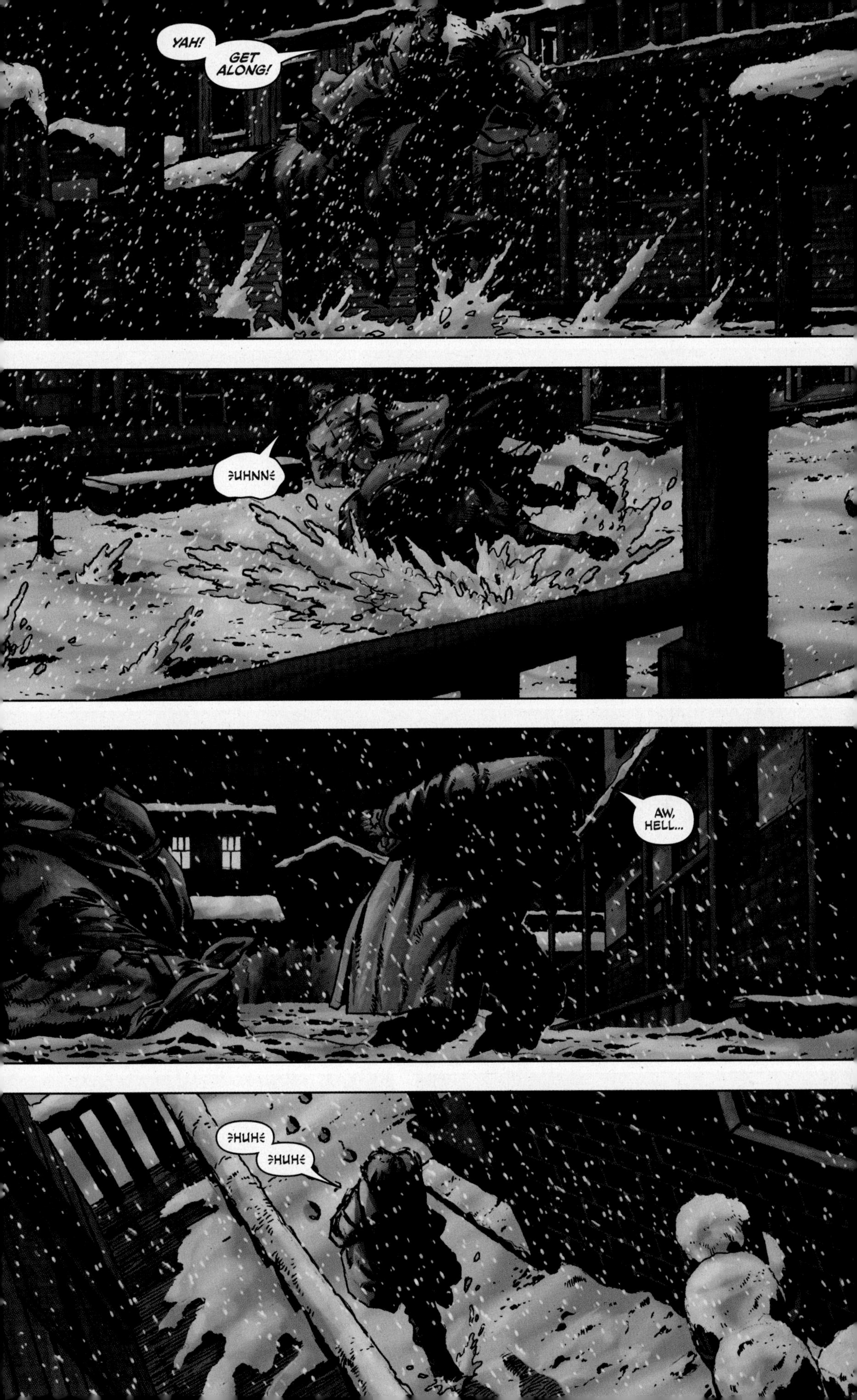

YAH!
GET ALONG!
UHNN
AW, HELL...
HUH
HUH

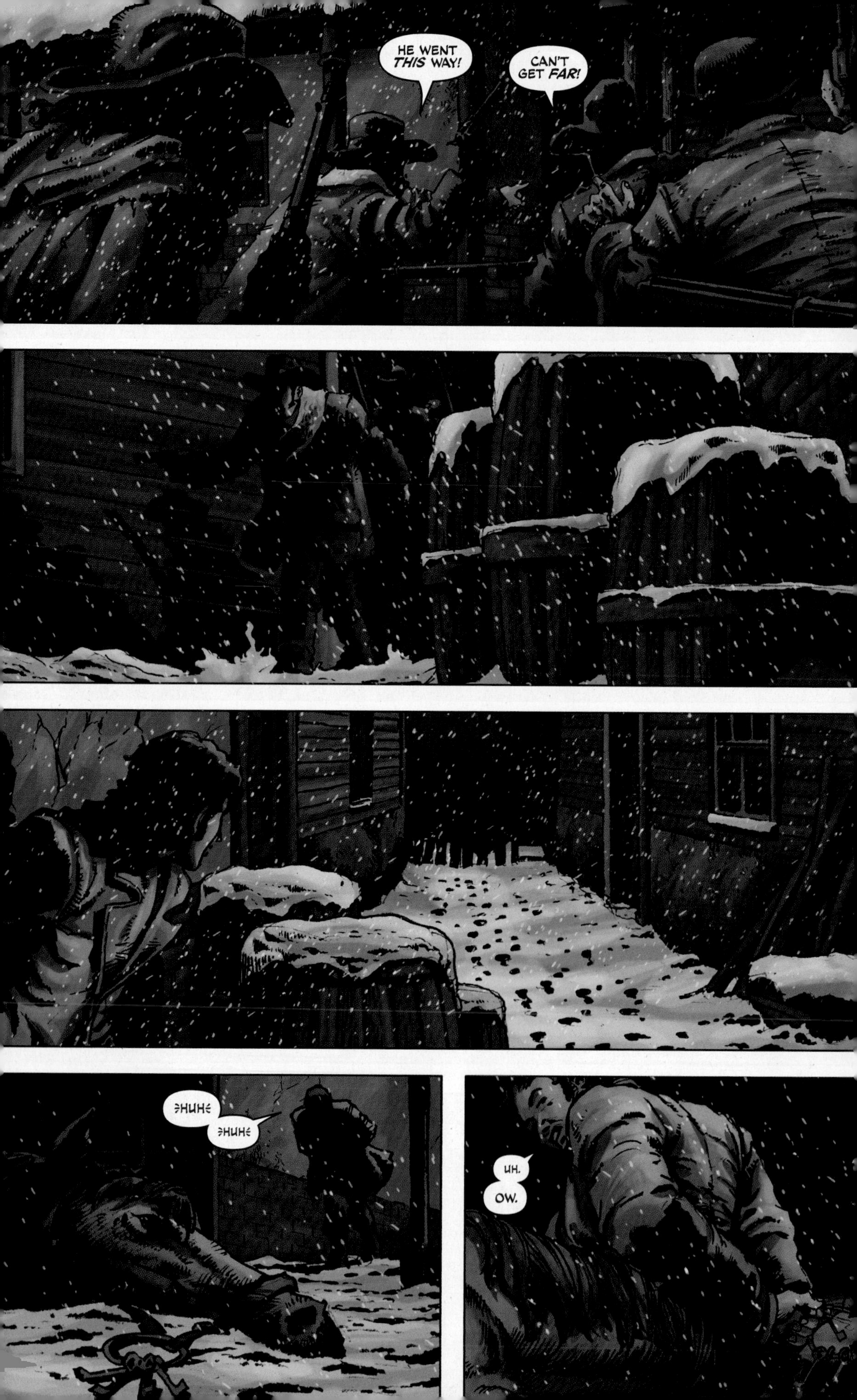
HE WENT THIS WAY!
CAN'T GET FAR!
HUH
HUH
UH.
OW.

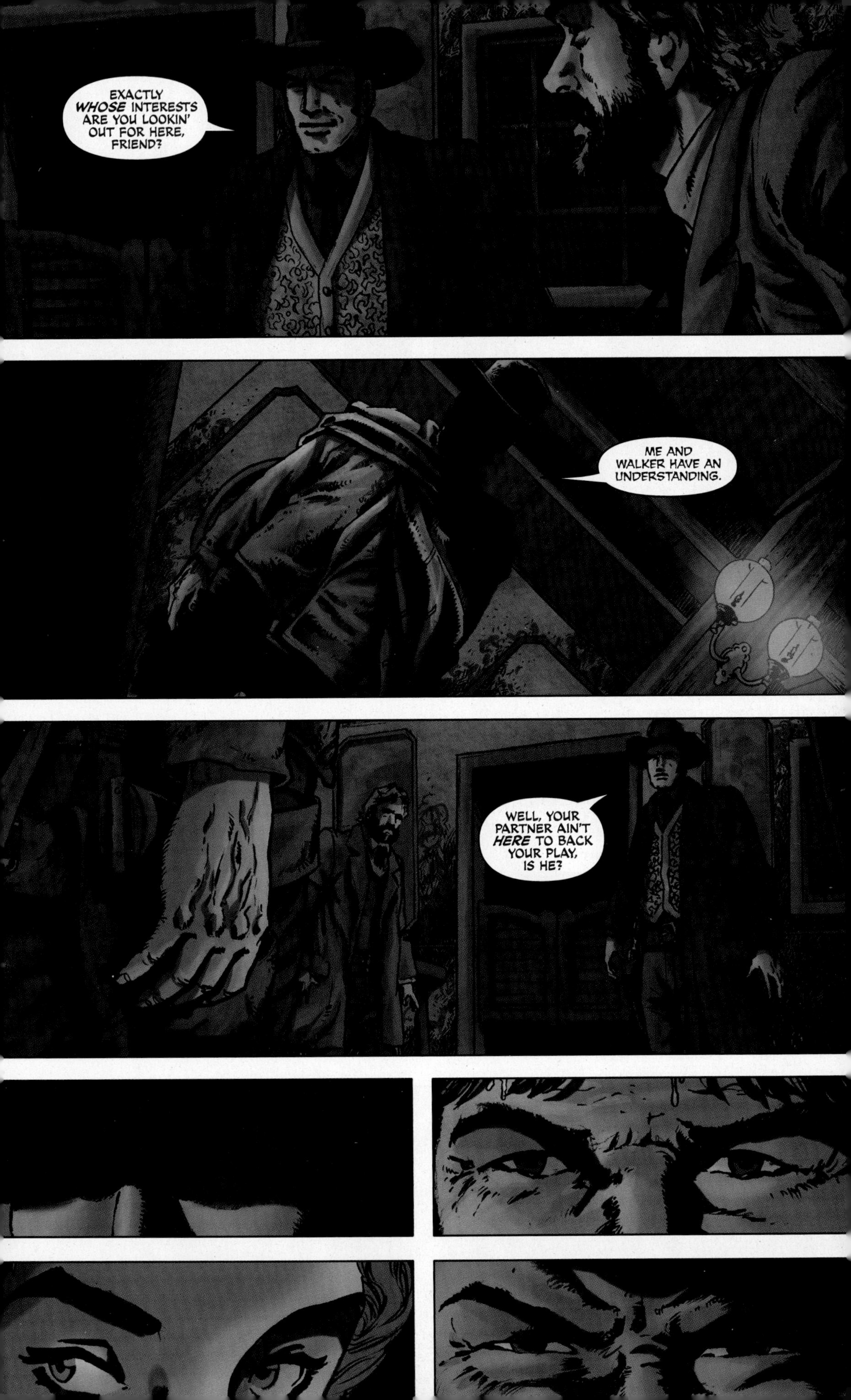
EXACTLY *WHOSE* INTERESTS ARE YOU LOOKIN' OUT FOR HERE, FRIEND?
ME AND WALKER HAVE AN UNDERSTANDING.
WELL, YOUR PARTNER AIN'T *HERE* TO BACK YOUR PLAY, IS HE?

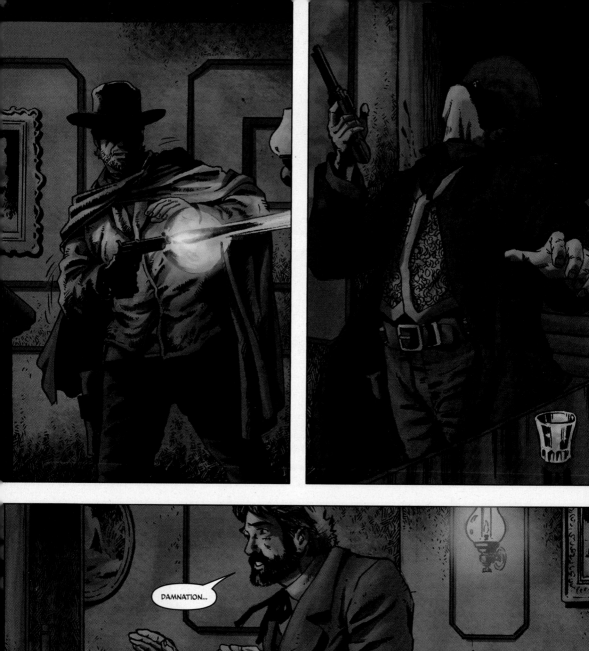

DAMNATION...

LORD HELP ME!

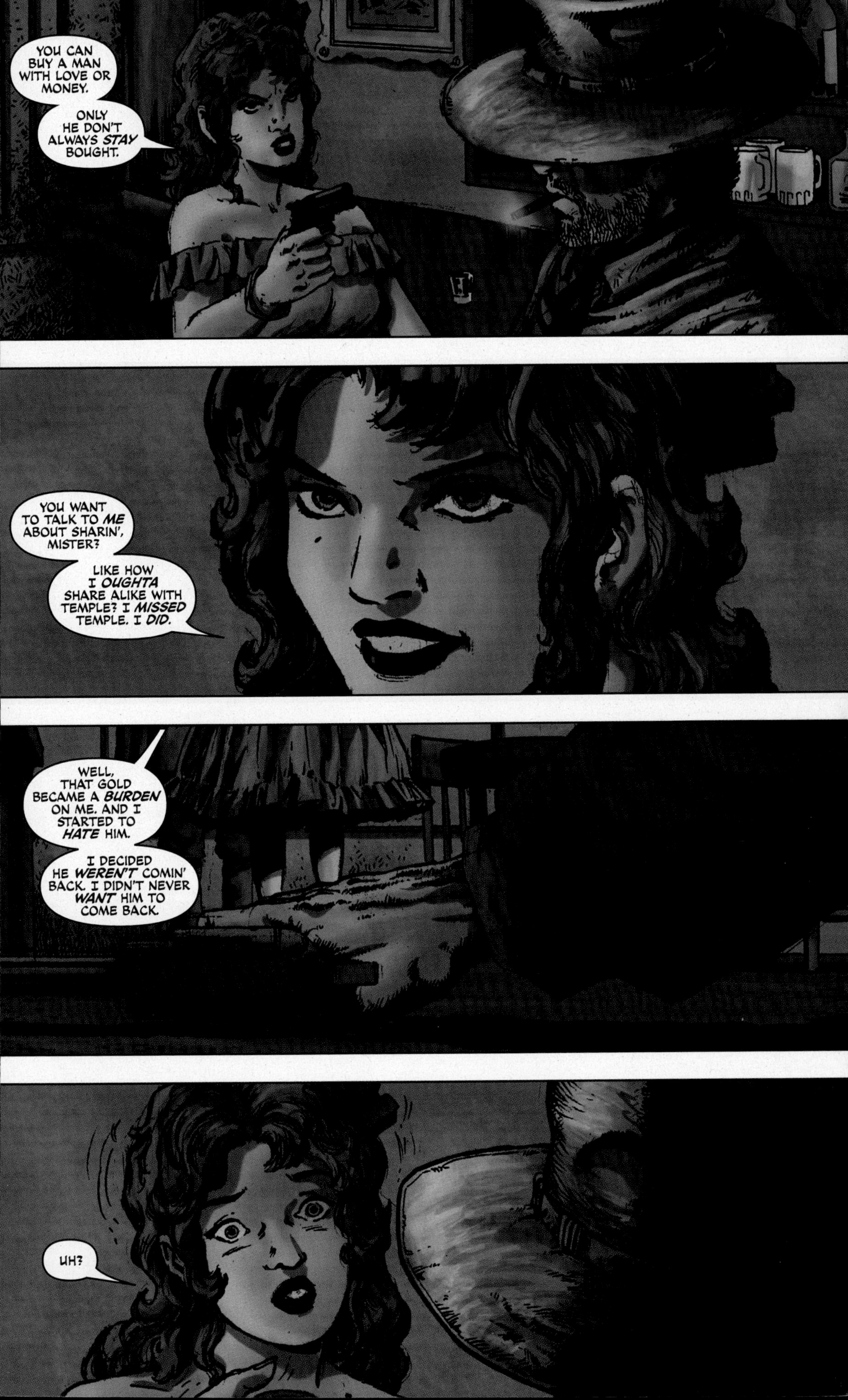
YOU CAN BUY A MAN WITH LOVE OR MONEY.
ONLY HE DON'T ALWAYS STAY BOUGHT.
YOU WANT TO TALK TO ME ABOUT SHARIN', MISTER?
LIKE HOW I OUGHTA SHARE ALIKE WITH TEMPLE? I MISSED TEMPLE. I DID.
WELL, THAT GOLD BECAME A BURDEN ON ME. AND I STARTED TO HATE HIM.
I DECIDED HE WEREN'T COMIN' BACK. I DIDN'T NEVER WANT HIM TO COME BACK.
UH?

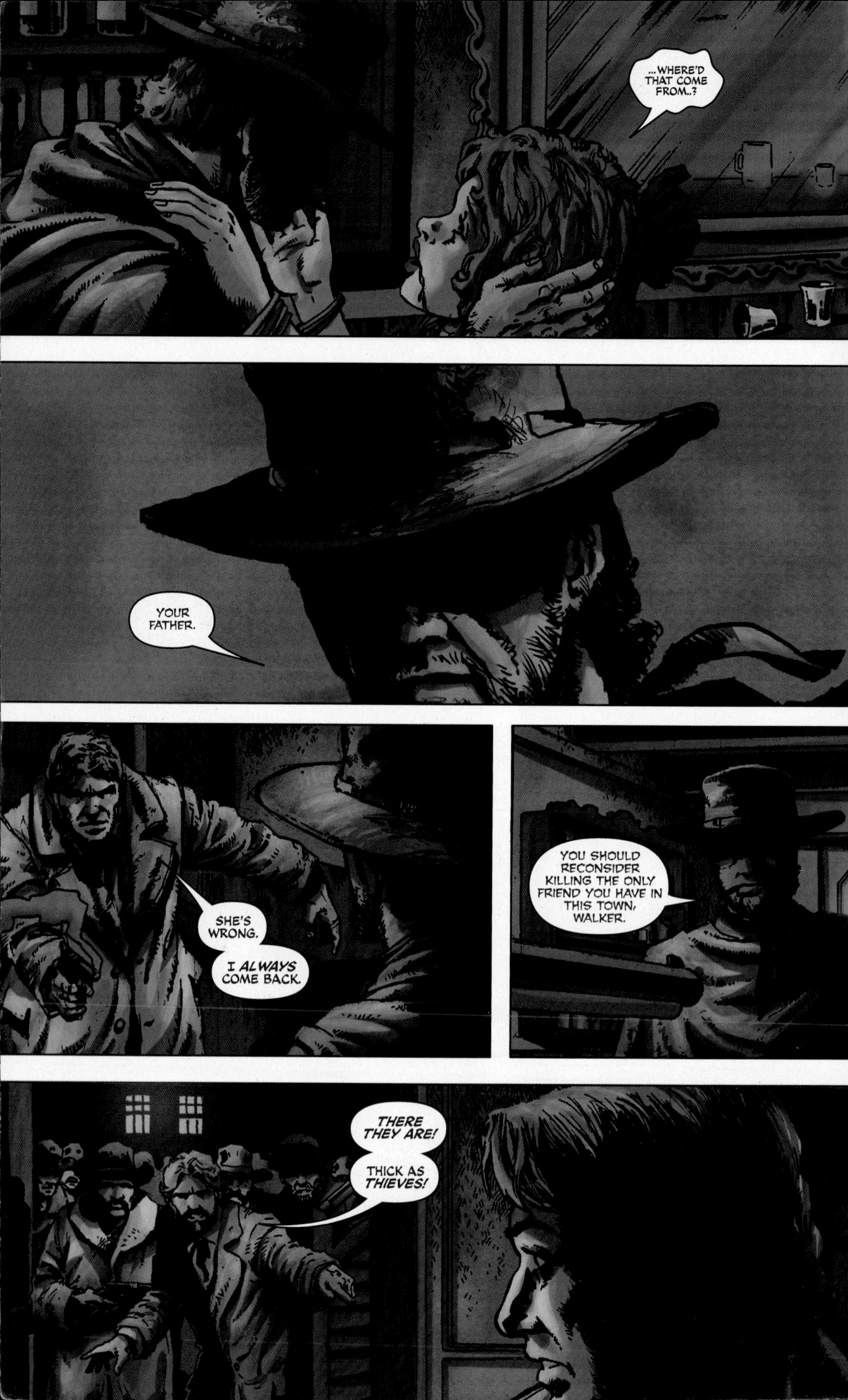
...WHERE'D THAT COME FROM..?
YOUR FATHER.
SHE'S WRONG.
I ALWAYS COME BACK.
YOU SHOULD RECONSIDER KILLING THE ONLY FRIEND YOU HAVE IN THIS TOWN, WALKER.
THERE THEY ARE!
THICK AS THIEVES!

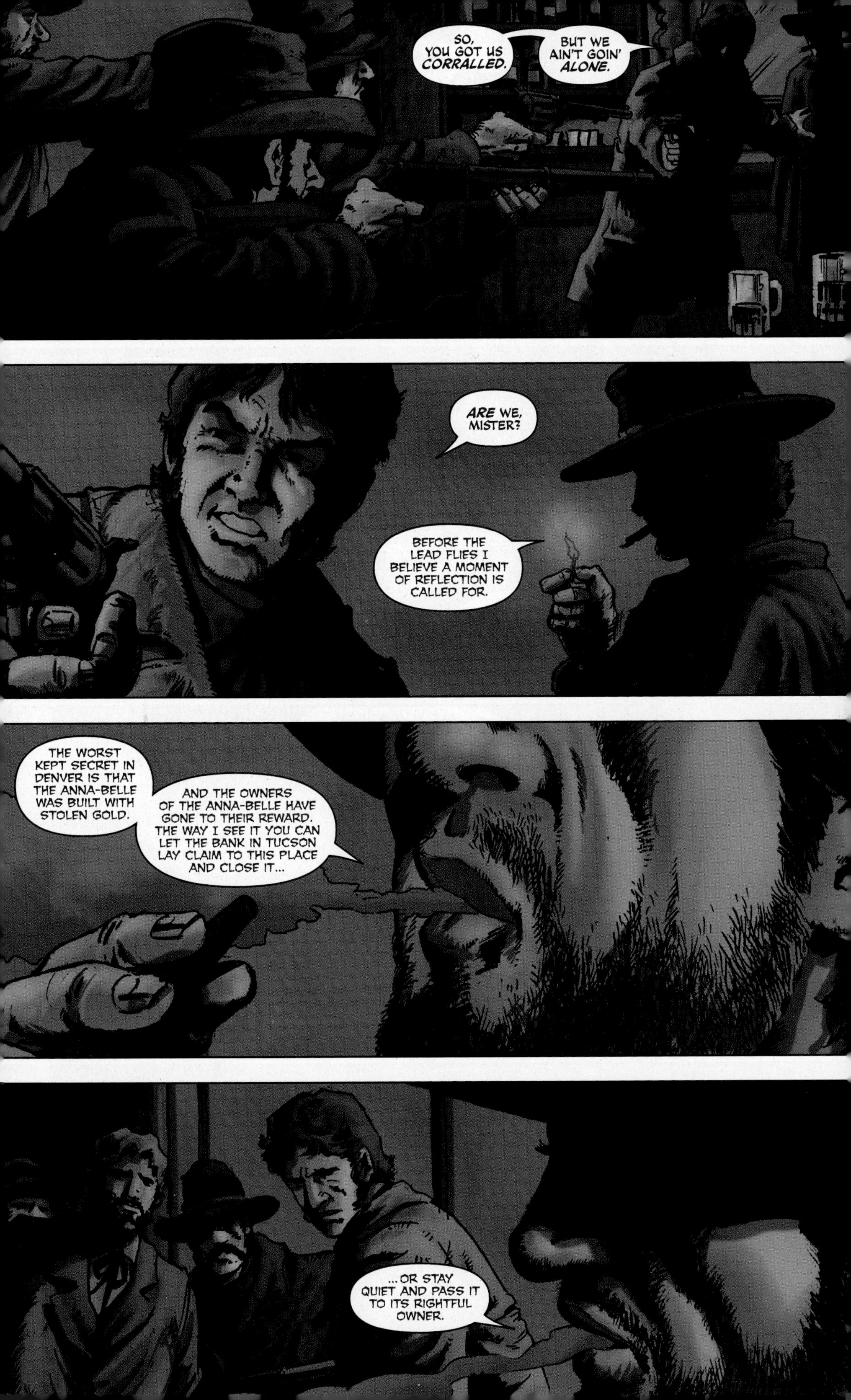
SO, YOU GOT US CORRALLED.
BUT WE AIN'T GOIN' ALONE.
ARE WE, MISTER?
BEFORE THE LEAD FLIES I BELIEVE A MOMENT OF REFLECTION IS CALLED FOR.
THE WORST KEPT SECRET IN DENVER IS THAT THE ANNA-BELLE WAS BUILT WITH STOLEN GOLD.
AND THE OWNERS OF THE ANNA-BELLE HAVE GONE TO THEIR REWARD. THE WAY I SEE IT YOU CAN LET THE BANK IN TUCSON LAY CLAIM TO THIS PLACE AND CLOSE IT...
...OR STAY QUIET AND PASS IT TO ITS RIGHTFUL OWNER.

WELL THEN... DRINKS ON THE HOUSE!

GONNA RE-NAME THE PLACE, WALKER?

THE LEAST I CAN DO IS PROVIDE ANNABELLE A PRETTY TOMBSTONE, MARSHAL.

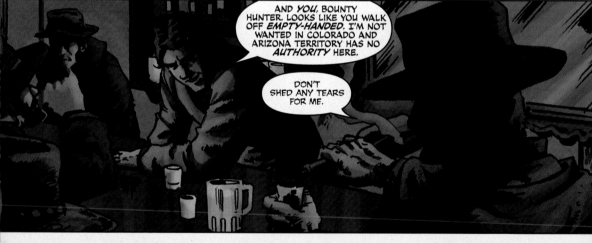

AND YOU, BOUNTY HUNTER. LOOKS LIKE YOU WALK OFF EMPTY-HANDED. I'M NOT WANTED IN COLORADO AND ARIZONA TERRITORY HAS NO AUTHORITY HERE.

DON'T SHED ANY TEARS FOR ME.

I HAVE MY COMPENSATION.

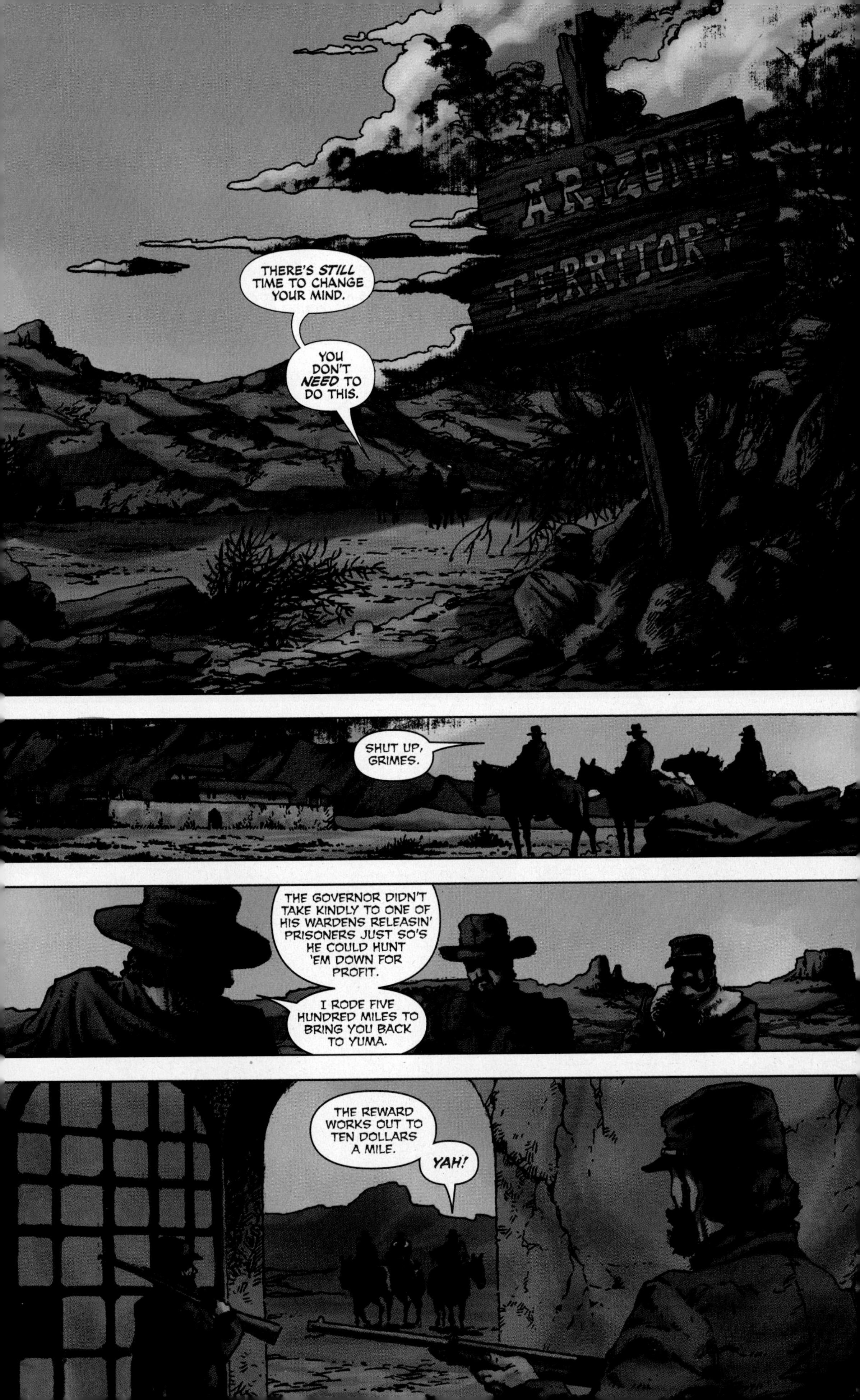
ARIZONA TERRITORY
THERE'S STILL TIME TO CHANGE YOUR MIND.
YOU DON'T NEED TO DO THIS.
SHUT UP, GRIMES.
THE GOVERNOR DIDN'T TAKE KINDLY TO ONE OF HIS WARDENS RELEASIN' PRISONERS JUST SO'S HE COULD HUNT 'EM DOWN FOR PROFIT.
I RODE FIVE HUNDRED MILES TO BRING YOU BACK TO YUMA.
THE REWARD WORKS OUT TO TEN DOLLARS A MILE.
YAH!

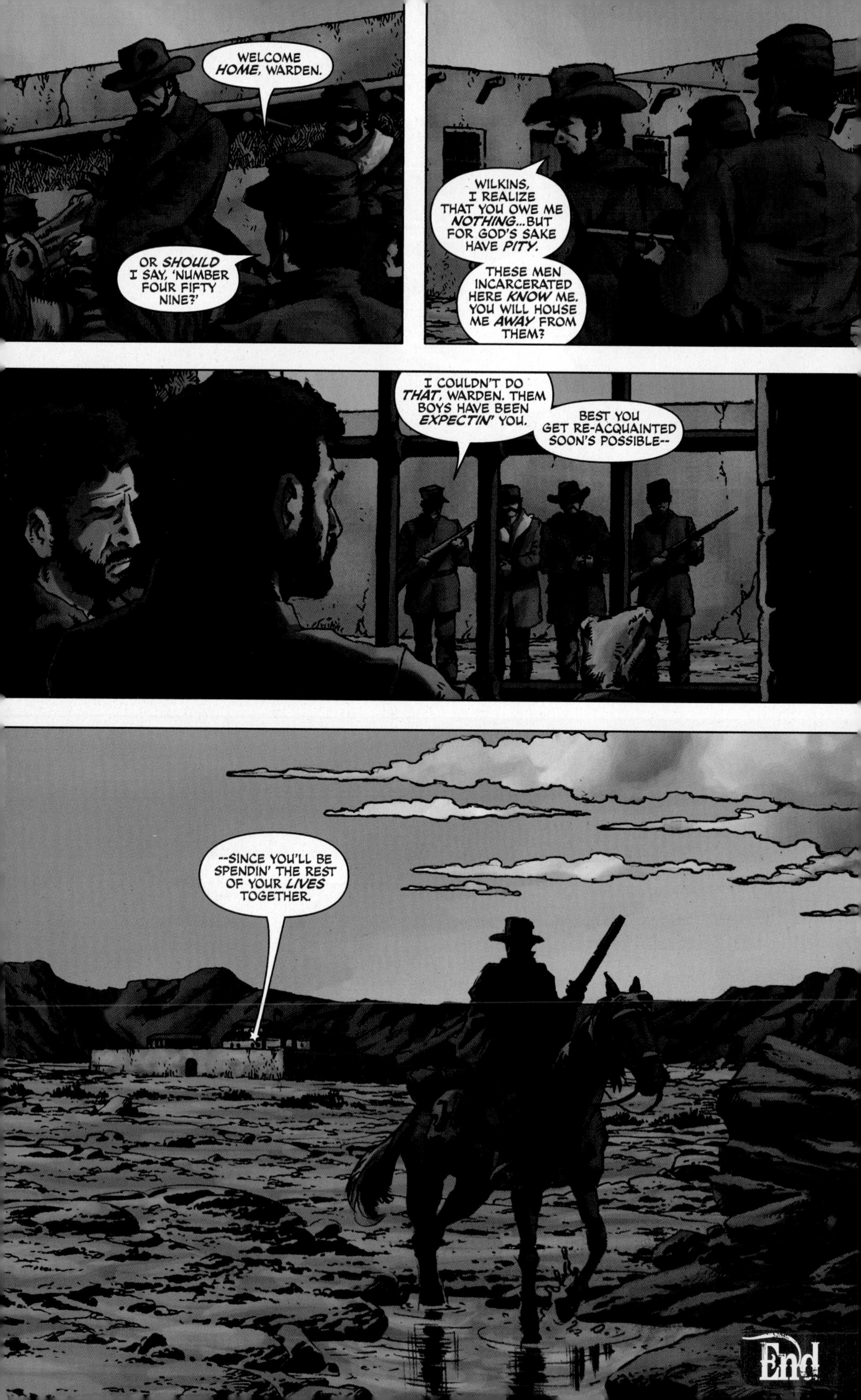
WELCOME HOME, WARDEN.
OR SHOULD I SAY, 'NUMBER FOUR FIFTY NINE?'
WILKINS, I REALIZE THAT YOU OWE ME NOTHING...BUT FOR GOD'S SAKE HAVE PITY.
THESE MEN INCARCERATED HERE KNOW ME. YOU WILL HOUSE ME AWAY FROM THEM?
I COULDN'T DO THAT, WARDEN. THEM BOYS HAVE BEEN EXPECTIN' YOU.
BEST YOU GET RE-ACQUAINTED SOON'S POSSIBLE--
--SINCE YOU'LL BE SPENDIN' THE REST OF YOUR LIVES TOGETHER.
End

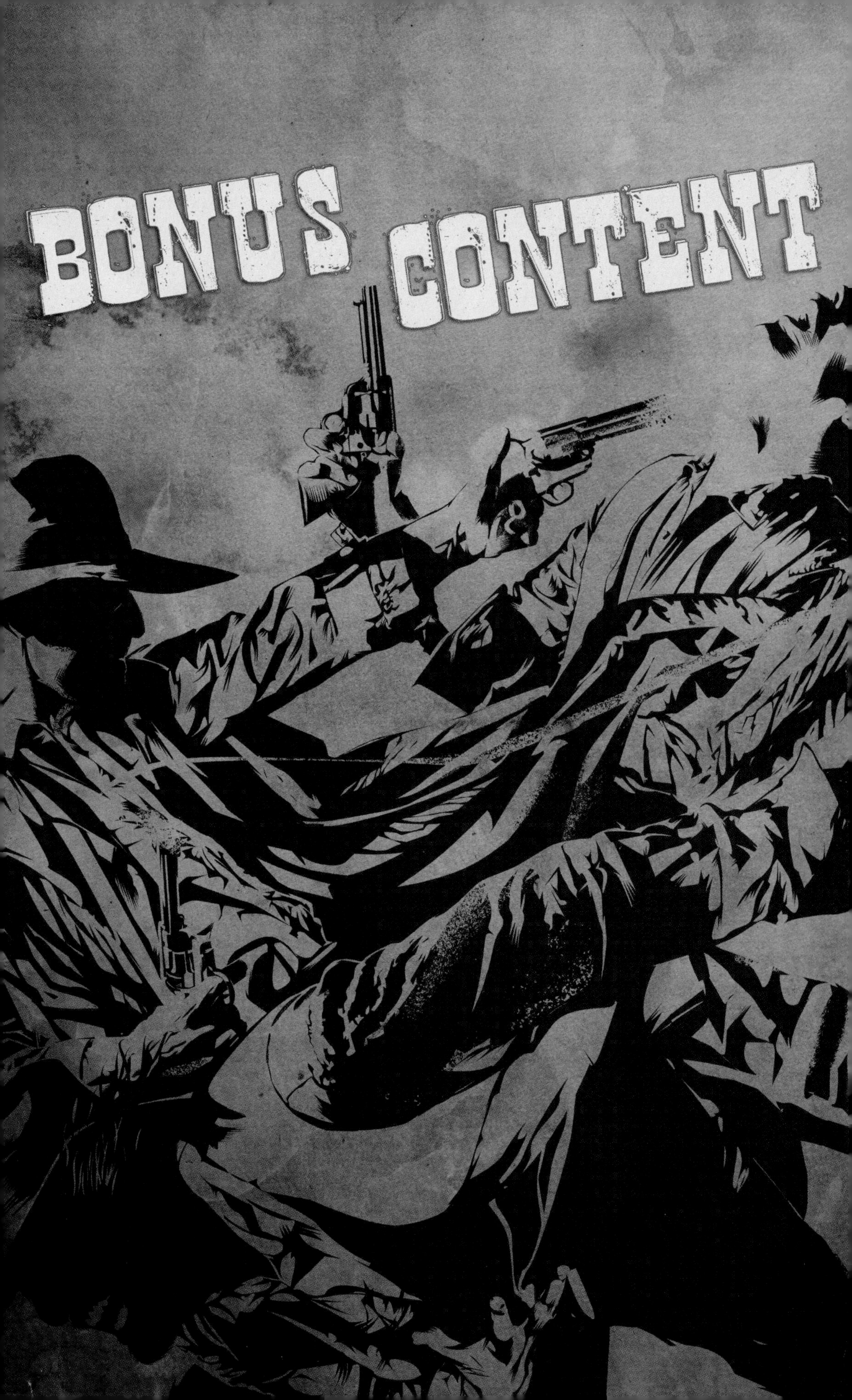
BONUS CONTENT

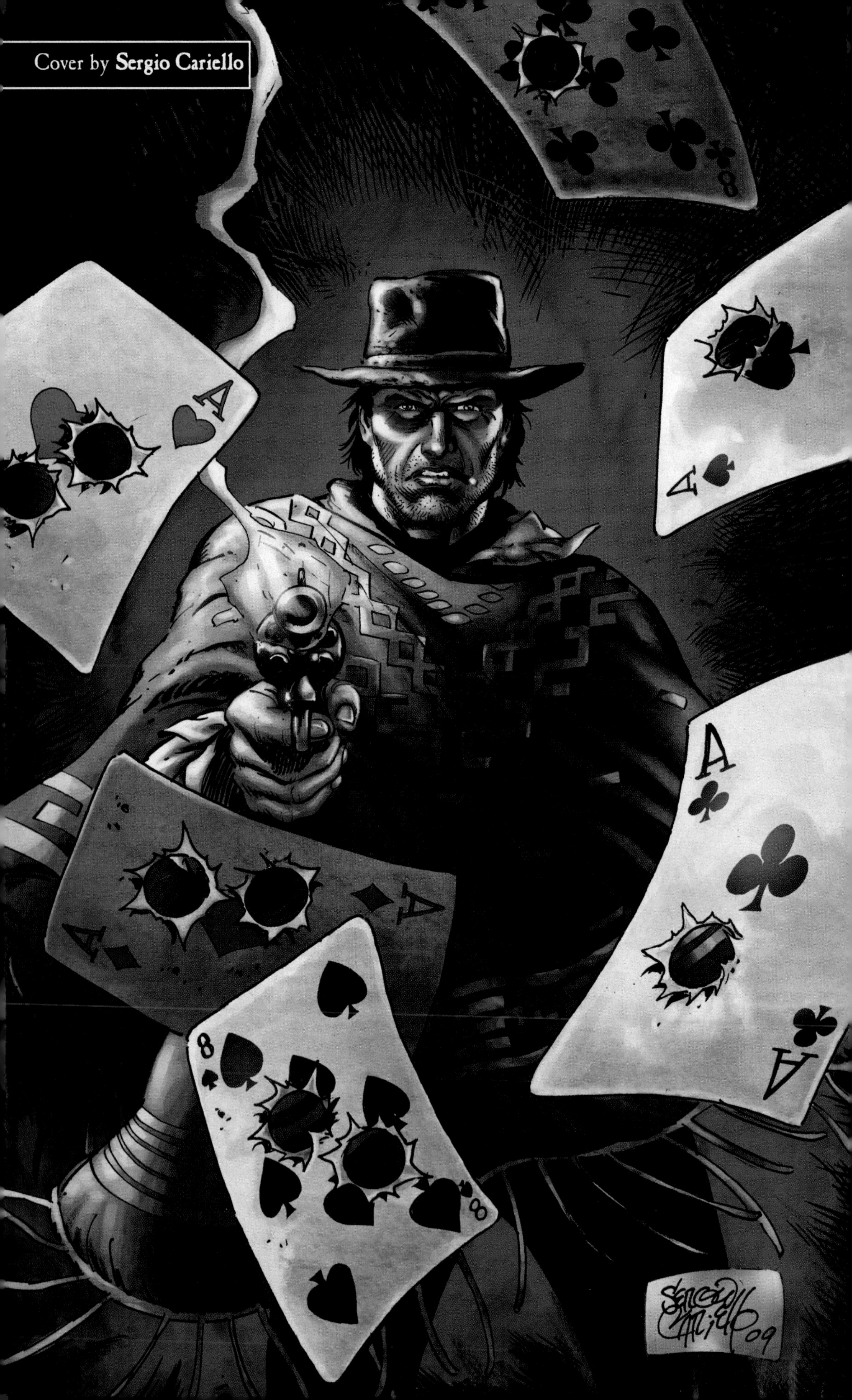
Cover by **Sergio Cariello**

Cover by **Francesco Francavilla**

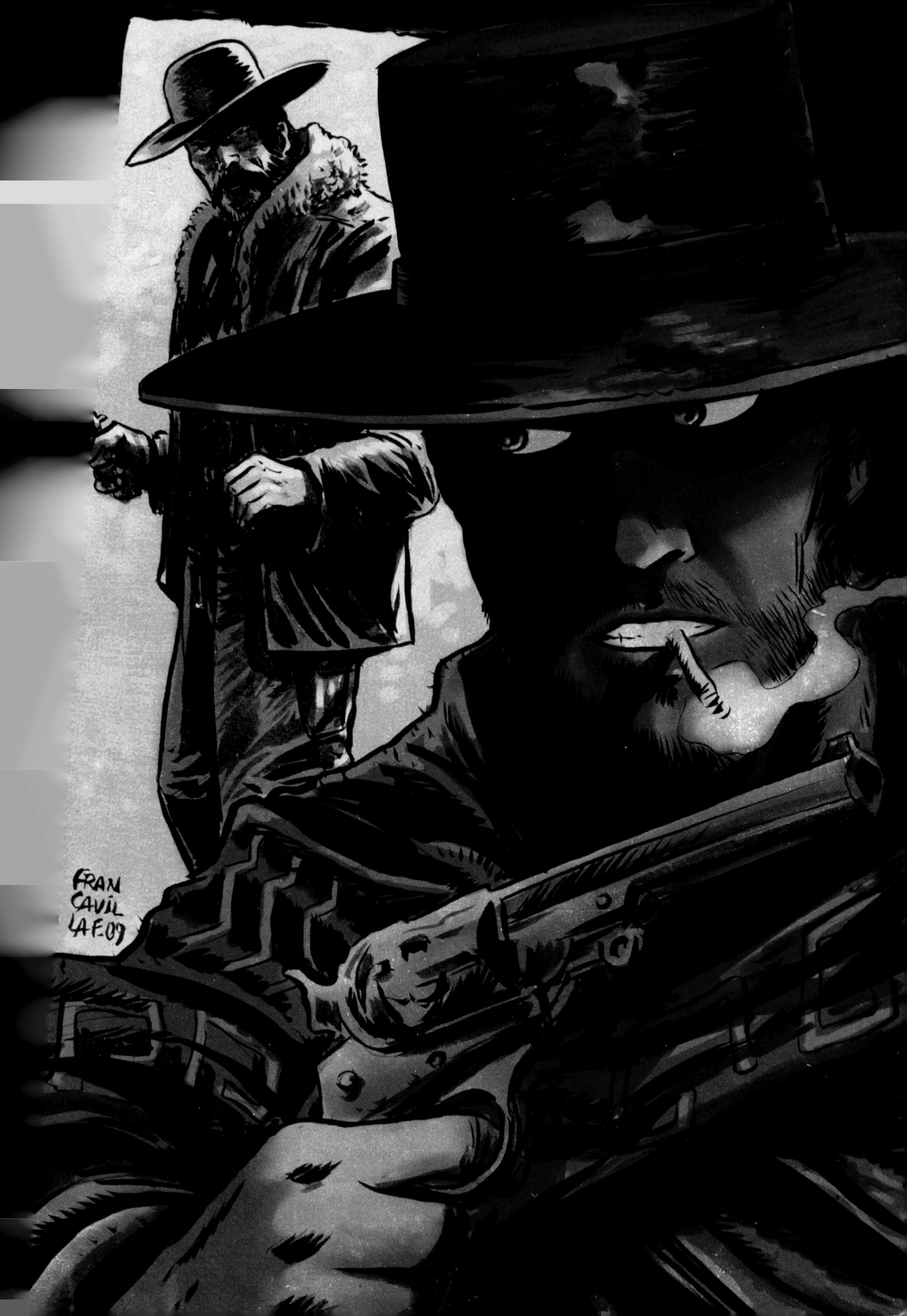
FRAN
CAVIL
LA F.09

WHAT EXACTLY IS A SPAGHETTI WESTERN?

Euro-western 101

By Chuck Dixon

"Spaghetti western" was first applied to the Italian western sub-genre by critics who dismissed them as junk cinema back in the 1960s. But the term has long been embraced by fans to describe the stark, moody and violent gunfighter epics that were turned out by European studios in the hundreds over a period lasting less than a decade.

Beginning in the 1950's Italian studios had long been turning out epic period action films in the "sword and sandal" genre. Countless variations of Hercules, Samson, Maciste and dozens of other mythological strongmen were cranked out on soundstages in Rome and in the deserts and mountains of Spain. But the popularity of these period flicks began to wane at about the same time that Hollywood slowed its own production of that other movie staple; the western.

Westerns are, without question, the most enduring American contribution to the world's cinema. The very first feature film was about an old time train robbery. Shoot-em-up stories dominated American movies through the silents and the era of the singing cowboy and right up through Gary Cooper and John Wayne to the arrival of television where, at one time, 40% of network programming was guys in cowboy hats. But the sun sets on everything eventually and even the rustlers and cowpokes and sheriffs knew when to pack it in.

As they fell from favor here on both the TV and big screen, they remained popular around the world and particularly in Italy. Randolph Scott retired from movies. John Wayne, Jimmy Stewart and Glenn Ford were getting older and no young guns were rising to replace them. Less and less westerns were being produced for audiences in the USA. To fill the void left behind by this, Italian studios experimented with westerns to some degree of success. The Johnny Ringo series did solid box office but these were basically standard American westerns with European casts and ersatz plotlines about lost gold mines and greedy ranchers.

It wasn't until Sergio Leone imported a young TV actor named Clint Eastwood to star in a low budget western originally titled *The Magnificent*

Gunman that the genre really took hold in Europe. The classic that would eventually be known as *A Fistful of Dollars* was a whole new brand of western action movie never seen before. Its hero was a quiet-talking gunfighter with no interest in saving the rancher's daughter of cleaning up the town. Cleaning *out* the town was more his style. The character who became known for having no name also had utterly no morals and was only the hero of the film in contrast to the vile and sadistic bad guys he was up against.

The action was swift and brutal and set against stark landscapes with a driving and haunting soundtrack by the ingenious Ennio Morricone. The whole package was something new and exciting. The western was reborn with a new, more aggressive style; pared down to its violent essence and no pretense to nobility or honor. Much like James Bond had re-vitalized the spy movie, the cigarillo chomping dude in the serape had put some giddy-yap in the old horse opera.

The movie caused a sensation in Europe years before it reached the birthplace of the western. Always eager for a quick buck, Italian studios would crank out more than 700 imitators in less than an eight year period. Suddenly, American TV and film stars were flocking to Rome to be cast in westerns. James Garner, James Coburn, Charles Bronson, Ernest Borgnine, Eli Wallach and many, many lesser lights traveled to ride and shoot and win the hearts of Euro-western fans. These movies range from wretched to quite good. While none of them approach the artistry of Leone's seminal Man With No Name movies, there were some excellent entries by "the other Sergios." Signors Corbucci and Sollima would produce some worthy spaghettis.

Sergio Corbucci introduced *Django*, a character who made Clint's nameless gunhand seem more like Roy Rogers. Django (who appeared in countless un-authorized sequels) was the Man With No Horse. He would travel by foot from one remote prairie town to another dragging a coffin behind him on a length of rope. Inside the coffin was a Gatling gun that Django would only bring out when he had to. And he had to *a lot*.

Corbucci also dealt in what could only be called political westerns. A committed communist, he would set his stories against the backdrop of the bloody Mexican revolution to vilify the ruling class and make heroes out of amoral bandits who killed in the name of the peasantry. This prolific director also dabbled in dark allegory such as his masterpiece, *The Grand Silence* and in quite silly action romps such as *Navajo Joe* starring Burt Reynolds (who mistakenly thought he was working under the direction of the same Italian who turned Clint Eastwood's career around).

Sergio Sollima is another director worth noting even though he directed only three westerns. *The Big Gundown*, with spaghetti western icon Lee Van Cleef, is seen by many fans of the genre as second only to Leone's work. The unofficial sequel, *Run Man Run*, in which Tomas Milian reprises his role as Cuchillo, is also highly regarded and an excellent example of the genre.

Another enormously successful director was Enzo Barboni (AKA E. B. Clucher) who helmed several comedy westerns in the spaghetti vein starring Terence Hill as Trinity; the laziest saddletramp ever to appear on screen. Trinity was so unmotivated that, rather than actually ride his horse, he would be pulled along on a travois behind it and doze between destinations. Bud Spencer was always cast as his perpetually grouchy brother and together they were the Right and Left Hands of the Devil; the fastest gunfighters alive. The movies are violent, low-brow slapstick fests much like a Three Stooges effort if one of the Stooges was devastatingly handsome.

Other heroes populated the screen as well; Sabata, Sartana, The Stranger, Manaja and a stampede of other bounty hunters, gringos and amoral bandits. Each had their own gimmick and way of doing business and each of their films ratcheted the body counts higher and higher.

The hallmarks of the genre are desolate locations, pounding scores, enigmatic heroes and not a whole lot of dialogue. The protagonist (one hesitates to call them "heroes") usually has a profit motive and doesn't mind killing the wrong kind of folks to fill his saddle bags with gold. Normally, he rides into a situation already rife with violence and ripe with corruption. In most cases, every single other character on the screen deserves to die for one reason or another and often *does*. There are few innocents in this world and they are saved only as a second, or third, priority by the lead character. The violence escalates along with the threat to the hero until a final confrontation on some godforsaken wasteland is inevitable. A stirring soundtrack utilizing pan pipes, drums, trumpets or, in one unforgettable climax, a harmonica, rises in the background. The final scene usually takes the form of the lone gunman facing impossible odds and coming out the sole survivor thanks to his near supernatural ability with a Colt revolver. Knives, dynamite and cannons can also play part. But it is the six-gun that takes precedence in this kind of flick. In the end, everyone is dead and our hero is left alone once more to ride away to, presumably, more mayhem in some unfortunate town beset by sin.

Though violent, these movies are seldom actually bloody and never gory. There's a tendency toward sadism in a number of them as there is in a lot of Italian entertainment such as the period epics and their slasher films (the genre that, along with kung fu movies, would eventually supplant the Italian westerns). Also, being Italian in origin, they can be very operatic with grand storylines and lots of life and death situations. Mostly *death*, actually.

Spaghettis are also remarkably sexless for what is basically an exploitative sub-genre. Sure there's the town whores and the occasional bad girl in search of some action in the sagebrush, but very little of that and not much screen time in total for naughtiness of that nature across the entire output of the various studios cranking these out by the wagonload. Women play a very small role in these movies as either victim or love interest. It's truly a man's world. In fact, Claudia Cardinale was the only actress ever to be billed above the title in an Italian-produced western; Leone's magnum opus *Once Upon a Time in the West*.

By the early '70s the Italian westerns had pretty much run their course with the exception of the marvelous *My Name is Nobody* (1973) which serves as a eulogy to the genre with its allegory of a young gunfighter (Terence Hill) arranging a final, glorious one-against-all showdown for the outlaw he idolizes (Henry Fonda).

Now the genre is recalled endlessly in commercials and cartoons and comedies. That moment of confrontation played out by a series of tight, intense close-ups against the strumming of a guitar and a jangle of spurs are the iconic tropes of the spaghetti that everyone instantly recognizes even if they have only the faintest awareness of Italian westerns.

The spaghetti western endures.

THE MAN WITH NO NAME
Trade Paperback Collections

THE MAN WITH NO NAME VOL. 1: SINNERS & SAINTS

Blondie enters into a deadly alliance of hate to steal a fortune in dead man's gold in this direct continuation from the classic western film "The Good, The Bad and The Ugly" from Dynamite Entertainment! Collecting issues 1-6 of The Man With No Name.

Written by **CHRISTOS GAGE**
Illustrated by **WELLINGTON DIAS** Cover by **RICHARD ISANOVE**

THE MAN WITH NO NAME VOL. 2: HOLLIDAY IN THE SUN

The sins of Tuco and Blondie's past come back to haunt them in the present as they take an unwelcome "Holliday in the Sun!" Collecting issues 7-11 of The Man With No Name!

Written by **LUKE LIEBERMAN & MATT WOLPERT**
Illustrated by **DIEGO BERNARD** Cover by **RICHARD ISANOVE**